Public Purchasing and Materials Management

Public Purchasing and Materials Management

Harry Robert Page
The George Washington
University

LexingtonBooks
D.C. Heath and Company
Lexington, Massachusetts
Toronto

Library of Congress Cataloging in Publication Data

Page, Harry Robert.
  Public purchasing and materials management.

  Bibliography: p.
  Includes index.
  1. Government purchasing—United States. 2. Materials management—
United States. I. Title.
JK1673.P33   353.0071'2   79-2039
ISBN 0-669-03059-7

Copyright © 1980 by D.C. Heath and Company

Second printing, December 1982

Published simultaneously in Canada

Printed in the United States of America

International Standard Book Number: 0-669-03059-7

Library of Congress Catalog Card Number: 79-2039

Contents

Contents

List of Figures
and Tables

Preface

This book has as its objective increased efficiency, economy, and effectiveness in public purchasing and supply activities. These activities are treated here as components of a system. Each activity, or component, interacts with others in the accomplishment of the total function of public purchasing and materials management. The overall system is composed of five subsystems, each consisting of a sequence of procedures: requirements determination; inventory management and control; purchasing: preaward activities; purchasing: postaward activities; and physical distribution.

Public-sector purchasing of materials, supplies, services, and construction represents upwards of 40 percent of the annual budgets of many governmental jurisdictions. Such purchasing in the United States aggregates to approximately $500 billion per year, over 20 percent of the country's gross national product. Of this, about $300 billion is state- and local-level purchasing, and $200 billion is on the federal level.

Public purchasing covers a range of value and complexity all the way from the acquisition of a multibillion-dollar major weapon system by a military service to the relatively casual cash purchase of a two-dollar office-supply item by a town clerk. Public materials management also ranges all the way from the control of spare components for a space vehicle to the supervision of a tool room in a police-department garage.

This book provides an overview of the purchasing and materials-management systems employed at the several levels of government. Each activity or component is introduced in sequence and is treated in the depth possible in a single volume. Notes refer readers to more comprehensive treatment of specific topics. Much of the material included here is in the form of law and government issuances of all kinds: regulations, directives, manuals, and training material. Very little of it has been available in the general literature previously. I have drawn extensively on three significant reports: the *Report of the Commission on Government Procurement*, the Council of State Governments' *State and Local Government Purchasing*, and the American Bar Association's *A Model Procurement Code for State and Local Governments*.

Federal agencies and state and local jurisdictions across the country have responded to my requests for material. The number is too large to acknowledge and thank each individually here. I do acknowledge here the contributions of the professional organizations—the National Association of Purchasing Management (NAPM), the National Contract Management Association (NCMA), the National Institute of Governmental Purchasing (NIGP), and the National Association of State Purchasing Officials—as well as the assistance of the Institute of Purchasing and Supply of Great Britain.

All have sponsored studies and publications in the field. Finally, I thank the Section of Local Government Law and the Section of Public Contract Law of the American Bar Association for their assistance.

1   Overview

The subject of this book is management, in particular the management of materials. The book thus takes its place with other literature dealing with management of resources, for example the literature of financial management and of personnel management. Such literature emphasizes the fact that management is basically a matter of the organized use of resources; human resources, financial resources, and material resources. Purchasing is separately identified in the title because it is the most complex of the elements of materials management. The inclusion in the title of the word "public" commits the book to an emphasis on management in the public sector, rather than in the private or industrial sector.

The principles and many of the techniques of purchasing and materials management employed in the public and private sectors are basically the same. Both are concerned with making available the right goods or services, at the right price, at the right time. Some considerations, however, are present in the public but not the private sector.

1. The funds being expended are public funds, not those of a business proprietor or a corporation, and thus they may be expended only as prescribed by law. Rigid budgetary restrictions and public auditing procedures apply.

2. The objects being acquired and distributed are for the use of the several requisitioning bureaus or departments. They are generally not for resale or for use in manufacturing.

3. The personnel performing and managing the function are merit-system employees. They are not motivated by the need to show a profit, as are employees in the private sector.

4. The process is, or should be, conducted in full public view. Everything done is a matter of public record; there are no secrets. In the private sector, management is not required to divulge requirements, specifications, sources, bid provisions, or prices paid.

5. The process is much more closely prescribed. With few exceptions, public-purchasing and materials managers must operate within rigid legal and administrative restraints. They have relatively little flexibility compared to that of their peers in the private sector. As a result, innovations in the public sector take place rather slowly.

6. As public officials, managers are subject to censure by the public and the press. Instances of malfeasance, misfeasance, and nonfeasance are

1

news. In private business only the most flagrant instances of incompetence or fraud are reported by the press; the rest are settled internally.

7. Government, particularly federal government, can and does act in a sovereign capacity. Also government can dominate a market. These conditions place a public-purchasing official in a position of considerable leverage, which can be unfairly used. Few businesses hold such leverage.

Scope and Magnitude of the Function

In fiscal year 1979 the civil and military agencies of the federal government purchased $200 billion worth of supplies and services. During the same period, state and local governments purchased an estimated $300 billion worth of supplies and services, for a total of $500 billion in public purchases in the United States during the fiscal year.

As of fiscal year 1979, the bureaus, agencies, commissions, commands, and installations of the federal government employed an estimated 139,000 managerial, technical, and administrative persons in the purchasing and materials function. The fifty state governments and the 81,300 counties, municipalities, townships, districts, and special authorities employed an estimated 417,000 in the same function. Thus the total purchasing and materials-management work force approaches 560,000. The magnitude of the function in terms of both national product and the utilization of human resources is clearly significant.

Historical and Legislative Background

Historically public purchasing at the municipal level predates purchasing by other levels of government. Much of the early concern in the settlements and colonies was over printing, one of the few services actually contracted out by government. Most public materials needs were met by the appointment of commissioners or commissaries who received a percentage, a commission on what they supplied to the militia or for other public uses. By the late 1800s state legislatures were beginning to appoint boards and/or to form bureaus responsible for supplying penal and public-welfare institutions. In 1910 the state of Oklahoma formed a board authorized to purchase centrally for all state departments and agencies. Central purchasing was not widely or readily accepted, however; school boards, highway commissions, police departments, and hospital boards were reluctant to give up this important activity. Exemptions and exclusions from statewide central purchasing were common and still are. Today the advantages of central purchasing at the state and municipal level are quite generally recognized. The late 1970s saw a concentrated effort in this regard, leading to development and publication of the *Model Procurement Code for State and Local Governments*, discussed in chapter 5.

At the federal level, purchasing authority appears to be derived under the Constitution as incident to the general powers of government. The Constitution does provide in article I, section 8, that the Congress shall "raise and support Armies" and "provide and maintain a Navy." The founding fathers seem to have overlooked the possibility that the government would have to support activities other than armies and navies. In fact it was not until 1831 that the courts found that there had been no specific authority granted by the Constitution for the government to enter into contracts. On the other hand, the Supreme Court recognized that the sovereign could seek contractual arrangements and enforce them even though that authority was not expressly granted by the Constitution or statutes: "The United States, being a body politic may within the sphere of the constitutional powers confided to it, and through the instrumentality of the proper department to which those powers are confided, enter into contracts not prohibited by law and appropriate to the just exercise of those powers."[1] This decision laid the foundation of express authority for the executive branch to enter into contracts within the broader authorities of the Constitution. The legislative branch shares this authority; it is vested with the power to appropriate or withhold public monies to pay for the contractual arrangements.

The first purchasing action of the new nation, as a nation, was taken in 1778 when the Continental Congress approved the appointment of purchasing commissaries, who were paid 2 percent of the value of their disbursements in support of the Continental army. By the end of the year, the excessive costs and possibilities of fraud under this arrangement became apparent, and the purchasing officers were put on salary: $100 a month plus rations for themselves and their assistants.

The U.S. Congress passed the first act dealing with purchasing by the federal government in 1792. The Departments of War and Treasury were authorized to make purchases in the name of the United States. The first significant acquisition was to be a group of six large frigates designed to form the nucleus of the new U.S. Navy. The Department of War was directed on 27 March 1794 to begin construction. Under political pressure, contracts were let to six separate shipyards in six states. It was the end of the year before the six keels were laid. The six yards proceeded independently, purchasing much of the needed material and components in Europe. Delays and cost overruns caused the Congress to cancel three of the contracts. The other three were completed by 1797. One of them was the U.S.S. *Constellation* built in Baltimore, Maryland, and still berthed in Baltimore harbor, and another was the U.S.S. *Constitution* ("Old Ironsides") on display in Boston harbor.

The first comprehensive legislation dealing with procurement was the Purveyor of Public Supplies Act (1795), which became the basis for procuring supplies and equipment needed to support the military establishment of that day, which had fewer than a thousand officers and men.[2] Early difficulties under the law were allegedly traceable to misconduct of congressmen attempting to use their positions to secure favors for private associates and enterprises. These abuses led to the Procurement Act (1809), which established the general requirement for the use of formal advertising in government procurement. The act also offered options to the contracting officer, who could employ an open-purchase method or an advertising-for-proposals method. The open purchase was simply buying whatever was needed on the open market. The first statutory preference for formal advertising came in the Civil Sundry Appropriations Act (1861). This act made formal advertising mandatory with two exceptions: for purchases of personal services and for procurements to meet public exigencies. A third exception was later added: "impracticability of competition."

Purchasing in support of military operations in World War I was conducted under existing law. The president established by executive order the War Industries Board (WIB), which dealt with problems as they arose. For example, the WIB required contractors to sign a covenant against contingent fees, dealing with the problem of finder's fees, kickbacks, and payoffs of many kinds. Procurement was characterized by the use of cost plus a percentage of cost contracts, now specifically outlawed.

During the Great Depression, the president, by executive order, consolidated practically all procurement in the Procurement Division of the Department of the Treasury. Only the Army Corps of Engineers retained some independent procurement authority. (Interestingly, Andrew Hamilton had proposed such a consolidated, totally centralized procurement division in the 1790s.)

The procurement and production problems of World War II were met by an executive order establishing the War Production Board (WPB). The order signed on 14 January 1942, thirty-eight days after the attack on Pearl Harbor, granted the WPB extraordinary powers over governmental procurement. The board established rules for negotiated contracts, for the allowance of costs, for the government financing of war-production plants, for price revisions, for renegotiations and terminations under many circumstances, and for the expeditious use of simple letter contracts.

Until the Armed Services Procurement Act (1947) was passed, the 1861 statute was the guiding authority. Formal advertising as a primary philosophy of procurement has guided contracting officers from 1861 through the present, a system that worked reasonably well until World War II. But the rapid growth of technology and burgeoning costs in the postwar period caused increased use of negotiated procurements. Resort to negotiated procurements by the federal government in relation to formally advertised procurements had reached a ratio of about 85 percent to 15 percent. Contracting officers therefore had to cope with a philosophy of procurement that emphasized the minority activity (formal advertising) and treated the primary activity (negotiated procurement) as an exception. The *Report of the Commission on Government Procurement* (1972), discussed in chapter 7 includes a recommendation that may alter the preference. The language of the report retains the requirement for use of formal advertising when conditions justify its use, but competitive negotiation methods are recognized as an acceptable and efficient alternative to formal advertising.

According to the Constitution, the Congress determines the extent of procurement that can be exercised by the executive branch. The executive departments, in turn, derive their procurement authorities from the president (by delegation) and from Congress (by laws that specify functions, powers, and responsibilities).

Pending passage of the Federal Acquisition Reform Act (see Appendix B) or similar legislation, there are two basic laws controlling the federal government's procurement of supplies and services. The first is the Armed Services Procurement Act (1947). It applies to the departments of the army, navy, air force, the Defense Logistics Agency and the National Aeronautics and Space Administration in the procurement of all property, except land, and all services for which payment is made from appropriated funds. The second is the Federal Property and Administrative Services Act (1949), which applies to the procurement of property or services by the General Services Administration (GSA) and any other executive agency, in conformity with the authority to apply such law as delegated by the general services administrator. *The Federal Acquisition Reform Act* is discussed at length in chapter 5. *The Federal Acquisition Reform Act*, currently in committee, is intended to replace and repeal the two acts discussed above.

Many other laws set forth rules that must be followed in federal government procurement. Most of them were enacted as responses to social and economic conditions of the times. The Tucker Act (1887) overturned the Middle Ages and common-law doctrine that said that a citizen could not sue the sovereign. One result of the Civil War had been a flood of private bills introduced to compensate Americans for all sorts of damages at the hands of government. To avoid more private bills, Congress established that citizens could sue the United States in the court of claims (for damages of $10,000 or more) or in federal district courts (for less than $10,000). Under the Tucker Act, the court decides if there are damages and certifies a claim. The U.S. Treasury pays the claim, but Congress first must appropriate funds for the payments.

The Davis-Bacon Act (1931) requires that firms receiving contracts for the construction of federal government buildings pay their construction workers at least the minimum wage rates established by the secretary of labor.

The Buy American Act (1933) generally prohibits the purchase of supplies or materials that have not been produced or manufactured in the United States unless the price differential is deemed "unreasonable."

The Copeland Act (1934) and the Anti-Kickback Act (1946) prohibit subcontractors from making payments to a prime contractor or a higher-tier subcontractor in order to secure a subcontract under certain specified cost-type contracts. It also stipulates that employees are not required to return to their employers any portion of the minimum wages received under the Davis-Bacon Act.

The Walsh-Healey Public Contracts Act (1936) requires that contractors pay covered workers time and one-half for all hours worked in excess of eight hours a day or forty hours a week. The act also prohibits the employment in contract work of boys under sixteen and girls under eighteen years of age and convict labor. Other provisions apply to minimum-wage rates and safety and health. Failure of the contractor to comply with the provisions of the act can result in the contract's being terminated for default. The purpose of the act was to increase the purchasing power of employees and to decrease the hours of work in order to spread employment among potential workers.

The Assignment of Claims Act (1940) provides that claims against the government, including claims for payment under a contract, may be assigned to a financing institution. The act is designed to facilitate the financing of contractors by private financial institutions.

The Small Business Act (1953), among other things, authorizes the Small Business Administration (SBA) to make loans to small business and to act in the capacity of a prime contractor for the purpose of securing government contracts in behalf of small businesses. The SBA has various other powers designed to facilitate government procurement from small business. The act states that a fair proportion of federal purchases will be awarded to small business firms. This has been implemented by providing that on procurements where there are a sufficient number of small-business firms interested, that the procurement be awarded to a small business firm only. Where there is no sufficient interest, a portion of the procurement may be set aside for small business. Similar partial set asides may also be made for labor surplus area concerns. However, no premium in price can be paid to effect an award to a small business or labor surplus area firm.

The Contract Work Standards Act (1962) provides maximum working hours and time and one-half for overtime in excess of the maximum for various types of contracts, basically public works and supply contracts.

The Contract Services Act (1965) extends minimum wage standards to government contracts for performing services.

All of these laws and many others—more specific in application—contain policies, procedures, limitations, prohibitions, and requirements that must be observed.

Managerial Challenges

Public purchasing and materials management has been referred to as a business activity conducted in a political environment. Part of the post-Watergate reaction has been the establishment of oversight groups charged with checking very closely on what agencies of government are doing. At the federal level, the General Accounting Office (GAO), an arm of the congress, has become much more active. Following suit, state legislatures are establishing oversight groups concerned with contract awards and supply operations.

Public managers report either directly or indirectly to elected officials. Their perceptions might or might not include business-type objectives for a public function. Managers in industry, for example, attempt to achieve efficiency, economy, and effectiveness with the objective of rendering a profit. Managers in the public sector, among other things, attempt to achieve efficiency, economy, and effectiveness with the objective of maintaining or gaining a favorable image for the incumbent administration. Managers who are not successful in their work may earn press and public criticism.

The public purchasing and materials manager's job involves a continuing battle against waste and fraud. Sometimes they are not successful. Recent examples include a newspaper article describing tons of unused metal office furniture bought by the GSA lying crushed, damaged, run over, rained on, and forgotten in a warehouse the size of several airplane hangars. A similar item reported that a newly elected city administration discovered warehouses filled with critically short building repair and maintenance supplies. Another allegation, later proven in court, was that supply officials signed delivery documents for millions of dollars worth of nonexistent supplies. The vendors maintained special accounts to cover these phony transactions and funneled a share of the proceeds to public officials. At the time, forty-one public officials had been indicted in the case and thirty-three had entered guilty pleas. Similarly public-building supervisors were reported as certifying that painting had been done, which had not, or that repairs had been made, which had not. The kickbacks to the supervisors were substantial; they were far greater than their government salaries. Also supplies, furnishings, and other equipment were reported as taken from government storerooms for personal use or resale. Wholesale quantities of school-supply-type items disappear in August as public employees supply their own children for the return to school. Large quantities of desk sets, briefcases, and other items suitable as gifts disappear just before Christmas. Also reported were examples of agencies that got into emergency purchasing situations and thus had to pay premium prices. Incorrect decisions led to instances in which contracts were canceled, with sizable dollar penalties and other losses. In another item, a public buyer was reported as locking himself in with a preferred supplier, who continued to hold the account year after year. Another newspaper article described a case in which the supplier to a large government agency was discounting the government 6 percent while at the same time dicounting other customers as much as 50 percent, and the items involved were generally available in retail stores for 17 percent off the list price. Finally an FBI investigation of a state's purchasing operation reported improprieties in placing orders. Discussion of the report in the general assembly oversight committee revolved around liquor, prostitutes, and the other favors bestowed on the purchasing staff by vendors. In reviewing this situation before a gathering of state and local officials, in 1978, President Jimmy Carter said:

> When a program is poorly managed—when it is riddled with waste and fraud—the victims are not abstractions, but flesh and blood human beings. They are the unemployed teenager shut out of a job; they are the senior citizen deprived of needed medical service; they are the school child who goes without a nutritious meal, or they are taxpayers whose hard-earned dollar goes down the drain.[3]

The challenges to public-purchasing managers are these:

1. Maintaining the integrity of the operation by making every effort to forestall waste and fraud and thus protect the public interest and treasury.
2. Maintaining the responsiveness of the operation, within the resources provided by making every effort to respond to the needs of the jurisdiction; to provide the needed item, of proper quality, at the right price, at the right time.
3. Operating efficiently by using the resources provided as productively as possible, promoting efficient methods and procedures, and maintaining a high benefits-to-costs ratio.

4. Operating economically by generating all possible savings, reducing costs through money-saving innovations, and encouraging innovation among vendors.
5. Operating effectively by increasing and improving the support provided to using agencies, reducing errors and delays, and reducing investment in inventory and facilities without reducing the level of service provided.
6. Maintaining accountability through a system of checks incorporated in the system, stringent accounting controls, and periodic reports to supervising officials and to the public.
7. Maintaining flexibility by responding readily to changing requirements and changing market situations and being able to deviate from standard practices in emergencies.

Careers in Public Purchasing and Materials Management

A wide range of occupations engage workers employed in public purchasing and materials management. A career could begin in warehousing and distribution, in supply record keeping, in cataloging, or in inventory taking. On the purchasing side, a career could begin as an assistant buyer of some commodity, as a price and market analyst, or as an expediter. Closely related are opportunities for specialists in working with the various supplying industries. Entry-level jobs are also found in inspection activities, quality control, and quality assurance. Careers are found in the management of transportation and traffic by working with the carriers (rail, truck, air, water) on routes and rates. Another opportunity would be work in a resale store or a service outlet. Finally there are jobs in property disposal: identifying, assembling, and marketing the material no longer needed.

The U.S. Office of Personnel Management publishes a series of job classification standards describing the many occupations.[4] Each is assigned a general schedule (GS) number. Some examples follow.

1. Supply program management (GS 2003). This series includes positions that require the management, direction, or administration of a supply program that involves two or more technical-supply functions at the departmental, intermediate echelon, or installation level. It also includes work in a staff capacity—managerial or administrative work primarily concerned with analyzing, developing, evaluating, or promoting improvements in the policies, plans, methods, procedures, systems, or techniques of such a supply program. Some positions are also concerned with the management of activities related to supply (such as procurement, property utilization

and disposal, production, maintenance, quality assurance, transportation, funds control, or automated data processing) that are classifiable in other occupational groups, provided that knowledge of supply management is the paramount qualification requirement. Positions in this series deal with supply management in terms of broad, overall program responsibilities. Thus incumbents must have a broad understanding of the process of supply; they must see it not as an assortment of individual and separate functions but as an interrelated chain of activities, typically but not necessarily extending from the conception or acquisition of a new item through storage, distribution, consumption, or disposal.

2. Inventory management (GS 2010). This series includes all positions that involve technical work in managing, regulating, coordinating, or otherwise exercising control over supplies, equipment, or other material. Control relates to any one or more phases of materials management from initial planning, including provisioning and requirements determination, through acquisition and distribution, up to ultimate issue for consumption, retention, or disposal. Such work requires the application of a knowledge of systems, techniques, and underlying management concepts for determining, regulating, or controlling the level and flow of supplies. In addition, some work of this series requires knowledge of the support needs peculiar to assigned major items of equipment, weapon systems, or special programs (such as construction, maintenance, or modification)

3. Contract and procurement (GS 1102). This series includes positions involving work concerned with obtaining contractual agreements through negotiation with private concerns, educational institutions, and nonprofit organizations to furnish services, supplies, equipment, or other materials to the government; ensuring compliance with the terms of contracts and resolving problems concerning the obligations of either the government or private concerns; analyzing negotiations and settling contractor claims and proposals in contract-termination actions; examining and evaluating contract price proposals; purchasing supplies, services, equipment, or other materials by formally advertised bid and negotiated procurement procedures; planning, establishing, or reviewing procurement programs, policies, or procedures; formulating policies, establishing procedures, and performing services for small business in contracting and procurement; or providing staff advisory service in one or more of the specializations in this occupation. The work requires a knowledge of business and industrial practices, market trends and conditions, relationships among costs of production, marketing, and distribution, and procurement and contracting policies and methods.

Various job titles are used in this series. Procurement officers have responsibility for managing a procurement program of an agency or activity. Procurement analysts perform staff advisory work in establishing, analyzing, planning, or reviewing procurement programs. Procurement agents buy supplies, services, equipment, or material using formally advertised bid and negotiated procurement methods. Contract negotiators meet with representatives of commercial firms, manufacturers, and educational institutions to develop contracts and contract revisions for goods or services through discussion and agreement. Contractor administrators oversee or ensure compliance with terms of contracts and negotiate with contractors to resolve problems concerning obligations of either the government or private concerns. Contract termination specialists advise contractors on procedures required in terminating government contracts, determine reasonableness of claims and settlement proposals, and meet with contractors to negotiate settlements equitable to them and to the government.

4. Purchasing (GS 1105). This series includes positions that involve purchasing, rental, or lease of supplies, services, and equipment through informal open-market methods and formal, competitive, bid procedures, when the primary objective of the work is to ensure rapid delivery of goods and services in direct support of operational requirements. The work requires knowledge of commercial-supply sources and of common business practices with respect to sales, prices, discounts, deliveries, stocks, and shipments.

5. Quality inspection (GS 1960). This series includes positions involving work concerned primarily with inspection of material, facilities, services, or processes; planning, development, and administration of inspection programs; or alteration or improvement of inspection processes, methods and techniques, test methods, and performance measurements. Positions in this occupation require knowledge, and application of quality-inspection methods, practices, and techniques.

6. Traffic management (GS 2130). This occupation includes positions that involve developing policies and plans for the management of traffic programs; planning and directing traffic operations; or performing technical work in one of several traffic-management areas to obtain economical and efficient transportation of freight, personal property, and passengers (or all three), by common, or common and other, transportation carrier services. Positions in this occupation require knowledge of traffic-management principles; knowledge of operations and technical capabilities of carriers and of the technological developments in equipment, facilities, safety, and other features of transportation; knowledge of the special requirements of freight and other kinds of traffic; knowledge of the relationships between traffic management and other agency programs; ability to evaluate traffic-program operations, to analyze operating conditions, to recommend improvements; and, in some instances, to plan, direct, and coordinate traffic programs and operations.

7. Distribution facilities and storage management (GS 2030). This series

covers positions that involve technical or managerial work concerned with receiving, handling, storing, maintaining while in storage, issuing, or physically controlling items within a distribution system. Included is management responsibility for distribution and storage programs. Positions covered by this series require as their primary qualification a knowledge of the principles, practices, and techniques of managing the physical receipt, custody, care, and distribution of material, including the selection of appropriate storage sites and facilities.

8. Property disposal (GS 1104). This series includes positions involving administrative, managerial, or technical work concerned with the utilization, redistribution, donation, sale, or other disposition of excess or surplus personal property in government activities. Work covered by this series primarily requires a knowledge of characteristics of property items and their proper identification and uses; merchandising and marketing methods and techniques; and the policies, programs, regulations, and procedures for the disposition, including redistribution, of excess or surplus property.

9. Logistics management (GS 346). This series covers the higher-level positions concerned with directing, developing, or performing logistics-management operations that involve planning, coordinating, or evaluating the logistical actions required to support a specified activity or program. The work involves identifying the specific requirements with program plans to ensure that the needed support is provided at the right time and place. Logistics work requires knowledge of agency program planning, funding, and management-information systems, broad knowledge of the organization and functions of activities involved in providing logistical support, and ability to coordinate and evaluate the efforts of functional specialists to identify specific requirements and to develop and adjust plans and schedules for the actions needed to meet each requirement on time. The paramount qualification requirement is the ability to integrate the separate functions in planning or implementing a logistics-management program.

Professional Organization of Purchasing Managers

A major endeavor in recent years has been to raise the standards of performance of purchasing personnel by means of professionalization. By definition, a profession is characterized by possession of specialized knowledge of principles and skills, acquired through formal education and a period of preparation. A professional person must also demonstrate competence to practice, usually proven by examination or by combination of examination and actual performance. There is a commitment to standards of performance and ethics. Usually an oath or other formal promise is extracted from the aspirant. Finally there is a commitment of services to the profession and to the public.

Several organizations have been formed for the purpose of advancing the professionalization of the purchasing field. The oldest, largest, and broadest in interest is the National Association of Purchasing Management (NAPM), formed in 1915.[5] Membership is open to persons employed in purchasing and materials management in both the private and public sectors. Memberships are individual. To qualify for membership an applicant must be:

1. A director, manager, or purchasing agent or any person in charge of a purchasing department or a related department essentially concerned with purchasing or procurement in all of their phases.
2. An assistant, supervisor, or buyer in such a department or organization.
3. A member of a department or organization having responsibility for purchasing research, value analysis, inventory control, materials management, or other activity or function (other than a routine clerical or record-keeping function), which is directly related to purchasing.
4. An editor, secretary, or business manager employed by an affiliated association.
5. A teacher, research specialist, department head, or director or dean of a college, university, or other academic institution, who is concerned with purchasing, procurement, purchasing management, or related fields or subjects as part of a regular assignment but who is not regularly employed as a consultant.

These eligibility qualifications are designed to exclude any person engaged in selling or soliciting orders. Interested and qualified people apply for membership in one of the 132 local associations (for example, the Purchasing Management Association of Baltimore). When accepted into membership, the individual automatically becomes a member of the National Association of Purchasing Management (NAPM) and of the International Federation of Purchasing and Materials Management. The purpose of the association is to serve the professional interests and meet the learning needs of purchasing managers. This is done through an extensive series of local, regional, national, and international programs, conferences, and seminars. A certification program leads to the designation of certified purchasing manager (C.P.M.). Interest groups are organized in the several functional and industrial areas (for example, a health-industries group, an electronics-industries group, or a governmental and institutional buyers' group).

Four publications provide information on business trends, the outlook for critical materials, purchasing methods and techniques, and significant developments and research in procurement and materials management. The *Report on Business* is an up-to-the-minute analysis of business conditions, with particular reference to production, new orders, inventories, buying policy, employment, and prices. It is compiled from information supplied by purchasing managers in representative industries who comprise the NAPM Business Survey Committee. The *National Purchasing Review* is a bimonthly magazine distributed to all members. It reports on educational and professional development activities, carries a variety of general news of interest to purchasing managers, and features practical articles on purchasing and materials management. The quarterly *Journal of Purchasing and Materials Management* carries research reports, scholarly studies, and comprehensive articles on important developments and trends in the procurement field. NAPM is also responsible for editing the *Purchasing Handbook*, the standard reference work on purchasing policies, methods, procedures, contracts, and forms.[6]

The National Institute of Governmental Purchasing (NIGP) was formed in 1944.[7] It is a private, nonprofit educational and technical society of governmental-buying agencies in the United States and Canada, established to raise the standards of public purchasing through the interchange of technical and professional information and ideas and to professionalize the field by offering training, qualification, and certification. The basic membership structure consists of agencies; national-level bureaus or departments, commissions, boards, authorities, or institutions; states or provinces, state authorities, or commissions; cities and counties; and local authorities. There are also classes of limited membership for individual persons. Agency members are assessed annual fees based upon their dollar volumes of purchasing. The stated purposes of the institute are to:

1. Do all things necessary for the purpose of raising and maintaining the standards and ethics of the governmental purchasing department, agencies, and organizations.
2. Study, discuss, and recommend improvements in governmental purchasing.
3. Share ideas and experiences and obtain expert advice on local, state, and national governmental purchasing problems.
4. Collect and distribute to governmental purchasing officials information on the organization and administration of governmental buying.
5. Develop and promote simplified standards and specifications for governmental buying.
6. Promote effective purchasing structures and uniform purchasing laws and procedures.
7. Promote and foster the professional competence and stature of all persons engaged in governmental buying.
8. Set an academic and professional standard for all such persons and award diplomas, certificates, and distinctions to any such persons after examination or otherwise.

9. Achieve recognition of the place of public purchasing in the governmental structure with emphasis on cabinet or top management status for public-purchasing officials.
10. Work for or against proposals affecting the welfare of governmental buying agencies.
11. Give to taxpayers information on governmental buying problems in order to foster interest in public affairs and cooperation between governmental buyers and those they serve.

Services provided by the institute include a quarterly magazine, the *Public Purchaser*, which reports on legislation pending before Congress of interest to purchasing officials, latest developments in purchasing and related fields at all levels of government, news of colleagues, training opportunities in public purchasing, and other matters of interest to government executives and public-purchasing officials. A monthly newsletter handles requests from purchasing officials concerning problems and needs, notices of employment opportunities, and items for sale. It also lists new specifications that may be of interest to members. The institute maintains a reference library of purchasing publications, reports, and specifications. It holds an annual conference and products exposition that features seminars, assemblies, informal discussions, and speakers. The products exposition, held concurrently with the conference, provides an opportunity for purchasing executives and industry representatives to meet in a professional atmosphere for discussion of product development and of technological innovations and advances. Technical assistance is provided in the development of specifications, contract formats and methods, bid evaluation, award criteria, and related matters. Consulting services, management reviews and surveys of purchasing organization, policy, operation, and reporting are available. Educational and professional development programs, seminars, and workshops in public purchasing are offered. A certification program jointly operated with the National Association of State Purchasing Officials provides a comprehensive program guiding public purchasers to certification as a certified public purchasing officer (CPPO).

The National Association of State Purchasing Officials (NASPO) was formed in 1947 to promote cooperation toward the more efficient conduct of state purchasing.[8] The association is composed of the senior purchasing officials and their assistants and deputies of all of the states, commonwealths, and territories of the United States. The *Newsletter* is published quarterly. Association officials meet regularly, and summaries of meeting topics and special reports are published. A secretariat to the association is provided by the Council of State Governments.

The National Contract Management Association (NCMA) was formed in 1959 to increase the effectiveness of contract management by assisting members in improving their contract-management skills through educational programs and contact with knowledgeable persons in the field, establishing a uniform code of ethics for those engaged in contract management, encouraging an increasingly professional attitude toward contract management and procurement, and enabling members to share in the wide range of experience and knowledge represented by the membership as a whole.[9] Membership is open to individuals engaged in or interested in contract management, broadly defined as professional experience in any form of contracting with federal, state, county, city, and other forms of government, including procurement, production, quality control, engineering, negotiation, contract administration, termination, auditing, program management, logistics, accounting, legal, pricing, general management, and management systems. Members are affiliated with the seventy-five chapters located across the United States. Services provided by the association include a monthly magazine, *Contract Management*, containing articles on governmental contracting, news of meetings and conferences, and special features. A quarterly journal contains in-depth articles and technical and academic papers on procurement-management problems, developments, and trends. Workshops, educational conferences, technical meetings, and industrial field trips are held regularly. The association sponsors educational programs leading to college credit and certification. A program of citations and awards recognizes outstanding men and women in the field. A certification program leads to the certificate of professional contracts manager (CPCM).

The American Purchasing Society (APS) was formed in 1969.[10] It publishes a monthly magazine, *Purchasing Update*, containing purchasing news and an abstract of purchasing articles from the major business publications. An annual seminar program is arranged. Employment and compensation surveys and an employment clearinghouse service are provided to members. A purchasing and purchasing personnel news-release service is provided. The society conducts a professional-certification program and an annual program of awards for outstanding contribution to the profession.

The National Purchasing Institute (NPI) was founded in 1968.[11] Its objectives include study, discussion, and action to improve purchasing; development and promotion of simplified standards of specifications; the exchange of ideas and job-proven methods and techniques; the collection and distribution of useful information; promotion of uniform purchasing laws relating to the field of public purchasing; and direct assistance to members. Services provided by the institute include a comprehensive library of specifications, purchasing manuals, and forms available to the members. An annual conference on purchasing subjects is arranged, including discussions of problem areas. A monthly newsletter, the *NPI Purchasing News*, covers association activities, business trends, purchasing news, specifications, current legislation, job opportunities, appointments, and promotions. An educational program is conducted in conjunction with colleges, institutions, and other educational entities. A correspondence course on the fundamentals of purchasing is offered by Louisiana State University in cooperation with the institute. A certification program, designated certified purchasing officer (CPO), recognizes public-purchasing officials who by study, research, and experience have attained professional status. This program is also conducted in cooperation with Lousiana State University. Membership in the association is open to state, county, municipal and township activities, public-school systems, publicly owned and operated hospitals and utilities, colleges, universities and other public and nonprofit institutions, provided they are located in the United States or its territories. Membership rests in the member agency or in the individual representing the member agency. Associate membership is open to purchasing agents, assistant purchasing agents, or employees of a member agency who spend the majority of their time performing the customary duties of the purchasing function. Honorary memberships recognize individuals who have made distinguished contributions to the purchasing professional or this association.

The National Assistance Management Association (NAMA) is the newest of this group of professional organizations; it was founded in 1978.[12] Its concern is with those involved in the administration of grants and cooperative agreements, discussed in chapter 14. The objectives of NAMA are:

1. To improve the management and administration of assistance programs by uniting all persons directly or indirectly involved.
2. To contribute to the improvement of training and education in the fields of assistance management and administration.
3. To promote and enhance the professionalism of assistance-program managers in both the public and private sectors.
4. To foster improvement in the management of assistance programs by promoting the advancement of appropriate management principles and techniques, which provide control and accountability consonant with the assistance relationship.
5. To conduct or sponsor surveys and other studies relating to the management and administration of assistance programs.
6. To encourage and foster the free exchange of ideas among assistance managers in both the public and private sectors.

Services and benefits provided to members include courses, seminars, and workshops in grants and assistance-management subjects. The association publishes a newsletter containing reports of current developments, new legislation, programs, and employment information; a journal containing reports, surveys, abstracts, and book reviews; and a membership directory. Placement assistance is available, and a program of professional meetings is scheduled.

There is considerable evidence that the certification programs sponsored by these organizations will eventually merge into a uniform system of certification. NIGP and NASPO have taken a large step in that direction with the formation of the Universal Public Purchasing Certification Council. Certification programs are discussed in chapter 4.

Several other professional organizations are active in more-specialized areas: the National Association of Educational Buyers, the Hospital Purchasing Institute, the National Council of Physical Distribution Management, and the American Production and Inventory Control Society. Others include the Purchasing Management Association of Canada and those of other nations, the Florida Association of Governmental Purchasing Officers, and the California Association of Public Purchasing Officers. The worldwide professional organization is the International Federation of Purchasing and Materials Management, an association of associations.

Terminology

A glossary of terms in use in public purchasing and materials management is found at the end of this book, but certain of the more general terms are defined here.

Materials management refers to the total concept and organizational structure unifying the systematic flow and control of materials and services from need identification to user delivery. Included are the material functions of planning, scheduling, purchasing, storing, moving, and distributing.

Purchasing is an integral part of materials management. It is the acquiring of title for a price, the specific buyer-seller exchange.

Procurement refers to a concept broader than purchasing. It is the act of obtaining property or services in any of several ways: by purchase, lease, exchange, barter, gift, or theft. At the federal level, the term *procurement* is in disfavor; it has been succeeded by *acquisition.*

Acquisition refers to any relationship entered into to obtain property or services through purchase, lease, or barter to meet a public need. It includes such related functions as determination of the particular public need, solicitation, selection of sources, award of contracts, contract financing, and contract performance.

Contracting refers to the bargaining that leads to formation of a contract, thus arriving at the legal agreement to perform and to compensate.

Contracting officer refers to the person specifically authorized to obligate the government. This person signs contracts on behalf of the government. In larger agencies and activities, contracting officers may specialize. A procuring contracting officer (PCO) develops and awards the contract. An administrative contracting officer (ACO) administers the contract during performance. The terminations contracting officer (TCO) becomes involved in any termination settlement.

Grant agreements and *cooperative agreements* refer to the legal instruments transferring money, property, services, or anything else of value between governments to accomplish a public purpose. They are used primarily as devices for extending federal assistance to state and local governments.

Notes

1. Quoted from *United States* v. *Tingey*, 39 U.S. (5 Pet.) 114 (1831).

2. The immediately following paragraphs draw from research by Richard T. Mankin, while a student at The George Washington University.

3. Speaking to a U.S. Department of Health, Education and Welfare meeting of state and local officials, Washington, D.C., December 13, 1978.

4. U.S. Office of Personnel Management, *Qualification Standards for White Collar Positions Under the General Schedule*, handbook X-118, rev. (1975). Available from the Superintendent of Documents, U.S. Government Printing Office, Washington, D.C. 20402. Catalog CS 1.45:X-118/975.

5. Membership, program, and certification information can be obtained by writing to: National Association of Purchasing Management, 11 Park Place, New York, New York 10007.

6. George W. Aljian, ed., *Purchasing Handbook*, 3d ed. (New York: McGraw-Hill, 1973).

7. Membership, program and certification information can be obtained by writing to: National Institute of Governmental Purchasing, Suite 101, Crystal Square 3, 1735 Jefferson Davis Highway, Arlington, Virginia 22202.

8. Program and certification information can be obtained by writing to: National Association of State Purchasing Officials, P.O. Box 11910, Lexington, Kentucky 40578.

9. Membership, program, and certification information can be obtained by writing to: National Contract Management Association, 6728 Old McLean Village Drive, McLean, Virginia 22101.

10. Membership, program, and certification information can be obtained by writing to: American Purchasing Society, 6055 East Washington Boulevard, Los Angeles, California 90040.

11. Membership and program information can be obtained by writing to: National Purchasing Institute, P. O. Box 20549, Houston, Texas 77025.

12. Membership and program information can be obtained by writing to: National Assistance Management Association, P.O. Box 57051, Washington, D.C. 20037.

2 Materials Management as an Operating System

Materials management, defined as the total concept and organizational structure unifying the systematic flow and control of materials and services from need identification to user delivery, is an all-encompassing concept that is a fairly recent development. In industry, materials management is now recognized as the sixth key member of the management team, along with finance, personnel, marketing, engineering, and production. The emerging attitude appears to be that materials should be managed by an executive whose performance is evaluated entirely on how well this job is done. The adoption of the materials-management concept can provide several benefits. The several subactivities and subfunctions become united in a single purpose (to get the materials job done as effectively as possible). The activities and functions are more directly coordinated so there is less likelihood of interdepartmental conflict and of communication failures. In problem situations, decisions are more readily reached because there is a single decision maker who is also a member of top management. There is a single point of contact on all materials matters; agency officials, vendors, and clients thus know whom to go to with complaints and problems. There are more latitude and freedom for the personnel involved; inspection personnel, for example, feel more freedom to work with storekeepers and inventory clerks. Thus more problems are solved at the working level. Better coordination and communication result in effective performance at lower inventory levels so expensive shortages and delays can be minimized. Lower inventory levels mean lessened warehousing and storekeeping needs. Better coordination and communication also result in greater efficiency, leading to reduced operating costs. Finally, using agencies—the customers—are better served, lead times are reduced, and stock-outs and back orders are minimized.

The objective in materials management is to take traditionally separate and often widely scattered activities and organize them into a meaningful whole.[1] The several activities are identified below, discussed in the sequence in which they are accomplished.

Materials Planning and Policy Making

1. Basic policy development and coordination. This includes working with other elements and levels of agency management (particularly using activity

management), resolving policy issues, and determining what will be the material support philosophy, what will be provided by using in-house resources and what will be contracted out, and what goods and services will be centrally provided.

2. Materials planning and procedural development. This includes determining the range and volume of goods and services to be supplied, developing identification and cataloging techniques, establishing authorization and allowance policies and procedures, establishing the system of standards and specification to be used, establishing the system for requirements identification and the requisitioning cycle, determining levels of operating effort, developing manpower needs and budgets for the operation of the materials activity, and establishing follow-up and evaluation procedures.

3. Inventory planning. This includes establishing an inventory (stock) control system, setting inventory levels, determining order and reorder policies and procedures, setting safety-stock levels, determining requisitioning periods and procurement lead times, and designing inventory-taking procedures.

4. Materials and purchasing research. This includes establishing procedures for cost, price, and value analysis; for the analysis of vendor performance; and for the evaluation of effectiveness of supply to the customer accounts.

Sourcing and Obtaining Materials

5. Assembling and programming requirements. This includes obtaining using activity statements of needs, reviewing and challenging stated requirements as appropriate, checking requirements against items on hand, identifying funds to be committed, programming timely and orderly acquisition and expenditure, and preparing the specific procurement requests.

6. Identifying sources. This includes issuing public notice of goods and services to be acquired, inviting statements of interest, establishing bidders' lists, studying catalog and business directories, and conducting briefings of interested vendors.

7. Solicitation and selection of sources. This includes issuing specific invitations for bid or requests for proposal, resolving inquiries and difficulties, analyzing bids and proposals, selecting sources, and issuing purchase orders or other forms of contract.

8. Contract administration. This includes coordinating and communicating with the vendor as necessary, resolving of problems, negotiating changes and adjustments as required, assuring performance and quality, and evaluating performance for future reference.

Receiving, Storing, and Distributing

9. Incoming traffic. This includes determining the type of transportation to be used, selecting specific carriers, choosing the appropriate commodity classification, negotiating transportation rates, tracing and expediting incoming shipments, auditing freight bills, and filing claims for damage in transit.

10. Receiving. This includes taking legal possession of items acquired from vendors and/or carriers, verifying items and quantities received, recording apparent damage or poor condition, completing traffic and transportation paperwork, notifying other materials-management activities (purchasing, traffic, inventory control, inspection) of arrival, notifying accounts payable, dispatching items to point of inspection, storage, or use, and preparing insurance claims as necessary.

11. Incoming quality control. This includes measuring the physical and chemical characteristics of the item, usually by sampling; comparing measurements against the standards and specifications; accepting or rejecting the goods as indicated by the inspection; reporting defective goods; and maintaining data on levels of the quality of vendors.

12. Warehousing. This includes providing a systematic arrangement for identifying and recording storage location, providing physical safeguards and security, rotating stock as necessary to prevent deterioration or obsolescence, and packaging and preserving as necessary.

13. Distribution. This includes physically moving material from point of receipt to point of inspection, storage, or use; issuing material to using departments; positioning material; and recording the transfer of accountability for the material.

Disposition of Excess, Surplus, and Salvage

14. Collecting and segregating. This includes identifying and assembling items no longer needed—material excess to the activity, surplus to the total jurisdiction, recoverable scrap, and waste—and segregating such items for view by potential users or buyers.

15. Redistribution and reuse. This includes internally advertising items available, determining possible reuse with the jurisdiction, and transferring to new users.

16. Disposition. This includes publicly advertising items available, inviting bids on surplus and salvage, making the final sale, and crediting the proper accounts with the amounts realized.

This long sequence of activities cannot be simply treated serially. An error in inventory planning, for example, creates a problem in property disposition, or a mistaken classification in receiving of an incoming shipment triggers a location mix-up in warehousing. Because of the many such interfaces among activities, purchasing and materials management is best dealt with as a system.

The Systems Viewpoint

From the systems viewpoint, management is a matter of understanding that the whole is different from the sum of its parts.[2] Managers must analyze the links between the parts and their effects upon the whole and clearly understand how the parts relate to each other. The modeling of the system will reveal the relevant relationships and any decisions that need to be made. The model might be a verbal description or a schematic diagram. Materials management is an open system; that is, it interacts with its environment. It exchanges information and material with other systems, and it reacts to what happens in those other systems. For example, the school authority's materials-management system reacts to a breakdown in the textbook-publisher's production system.

The system has boundaries, perhaps not too rigidly defined. The materials-management system reacts with the agency's personnel-management system, but it does not intrude very far into personnel matters. The materials-management system fully encompasses its functional area.

It survives because it produces. Inputs in the form of human energy, funds, and materials are converted into elements of service to the business or governmental unit of which it is a part. It remains in equilibrium when the levels of inputs and outputs are generally equal.

It provides for informational feedback, reporting on the state of the system and warning of breakdowns and imbalance.

It is itself a subsystem of something larger, and it is made up of subsystems. For example, inventory management is a subsystem of the materials-management system. Its subsystems consist of groups of procedures by which the several activities are accomplished—for example, the procedure for periodic replenishment of an item of supply. Its procedures are accomplished by methods that prescribe how each job will be done (for example, requiring that automotive spare parts be ordered by using DF Form 41A in triplicate).

The system will change as demands upon it increase, decrease, or are otherwise modified. New procedures and methods will emerge, displacing others, reacting to changes in the social, political, economic, legal and technical environments.

Modeling the materials-management system begins with identifying the parts making up the whole. These parts consist of the several subsystems, and the body of procedures within each.

Subsystems	*Procedures*
Requirements determination	1. Developing engineering standards that govern the design and specifications of items entering the system.
	2. Identifying the specifications that will apply in an acquisition.
	3. Qualification of products.
	4. Classifying and coding items of material.
	5. Identifying and cataloging items.
	6. Standardizing items in the system.
	7. Establishing authorizations and allowances.
	8. Computing quantitative requirements.
Inventory management and control	1. Selecting ordering strategy.
	2. Setting stock levels.
	3. Selectively controlling inventory.
	4. Determining shelf life.
	5. Determining order quantity.
	6. Determining when to order.
	7. Physically counting (taking) inventory.
	8. Identifying items for disposition.
Purchasing Preaward	1. Receiving the purchase request describing items needed and citing the funds to be obligated.
	2. Identifying potential sources.
	3. Issuing invitations to bid.
	4. Communicating with potential vendors and establishing working relationships.
	5. Evaluating the bids or proposals and analyzing price, cost, and value.
	6. Conducting negotiations.
	7. Awarding the order or contract.
Purchasing Postaward	1. Modifying the order or contract.
	2. Adjusting prices.
	3. Conducting inspections and assuring quality.
	4. Following up and expediting.
	5. Handling discrepancies or deficiencies.
	6. Dealing with default and terminating.
	7. Handling claims, disputes, and appeals.
	8. Administering payment provisions.
	9. Auditing the purchase.
Physical distribution	1. Transporting and receiving incoming shipments.
	2. Warehousing and location control.

Subsystems   *Procedures*

3. Packaging and preserving.
4. Order filling from stock.
5. Disposing of excess and surplus.

Computer Applications in Materials Management

Most management systems today are computer oriented, and materials management is no exception.[3] Each of the procedures listed above can make use of computer capabilities. The performance of the function at all depends upon a flow of information from within and without the organization. From within the agency, purchasing must learn what materials and services are required and when they are needed. In addition, purchasing must provide information, such as what has been ordered and when it will be received and who must be paid when it is received. From without the organization, purchasing must gather information about market trends and new sources of supply. In turn, it must make known what it desires to purchase and on what terms. Traditionally this information has been in the form of a mass of paperwork: requisitions, requests for quotations, purchase orders, change orders, inspection reports, receiving reports, invoices, and so forth. The characteristic emphasis on paperwork has given purchasing and materials management the image of being a clerical function. Most efforts to reduce the cost of the purchasing process itself concentrate on reducing the paperwork involved by using one form to serve a number of purposes, thereby eliminating other forms. In some instances, handwritten requisitions are actually preferred to typewritten forms because they are faster and less costly.

The purchasing function also relies upon a great deal of information kept on file, and forms are important also in this regard. Many purchasing and supply actions are predicated upon past transactions, and records of a vendor's past performance help determine the wisdom of reordering from the same source again. Information about new products may be stored for retrieval when circumstances dictate a possible application. Price lists and catalogs are common tools of the trade.

A function such as purchasing that is characterized by so many clerical tasks is an obvious candidate for automation. Historically inventory control has been the first subsystem to make use of the computer. All inventory records are filed in the computer's memory, including part number, name, required descriptive data, historical-use data, and the current balance. Organizations that can accurately predict use rates utilize a predetermined reorder-point figure. Each time the machine posts a withdrawal from inventory, it compares the remaining balance against such a point figure, and when the balance falls below it, a purchase requisition is automatically printed out. Once the machine is programmed to keep track of what is on hand, it can initiate a reorder.

The quantity the machine orders may be a predetermined quantity or it might be the most economical quantity, based on current inventory carrying costs, acquisition costs, usage, and price. The economic-order quantity calculation depends upon the computer's holding all of the pertinent and current data in its memory. At the same time the computer prints the purchase requisition, it can also punch a corresponding purchase-order card, which is sent to buyers for additional information, such as follow-up dates or a change of vendors. When these data are fed back into the computer, it can prepare the purchase order for mailing to the vendor. Either the same form can be used for a number of purposes or other forms can be printed automatically for use as vendor acknowledgment, follow-up or expediting memoranda, receiving slips, and even invoices and payment checks.

In addition to performing a number of the clerical tasks, the computer can provide buyers with valuable information to aid them in the performance of their duties. For example, it can maintain a list of all open purchase orders and can highlight those that are behind schedule or require special attention for some other reason. Many purchasing departments use the computer to help rate suppliers. With the information already in the computer, the buyer can get a vendor rating on delivery performance, reject rates, or quantity discrepancies. And the computer can aid buyers in evaluating competitive bids by printing out comparative analyses.

In addition to these operational applications, computers can be used in managerial reporting and decision making. Managers find it useful to review the agency's supplier base periodically to discover how many sources are being used, how the suppliers are distributed against the range of goods and services being purchased, and whether the agency is becoming too dependent upon a shallow supplier base. A managerial report answering these questions would be an inexpensive by-product of the operational outputs. Similar possibilities exist for managerial analysis of costs and prices, lead times, and buyer or vendor performance.

The ultimate computer application is the development of a total materials-management-information system. A management-information system (MIS) is an integrated man-machine system for providing information to support the operational, managerial, and decision-making functions of the organization. The MIS utilizes computer hardware and software, manual procedures, management and decision models, and a data base. It systematically collects and stores the necessary data. The design of the MIS begins with careful analysis of the data inputs and outputs of each of the subsystems and procedures. As these data needs are identified, the working relationships of the subsystems and procedures are established and charted using standard systems-notation techniques.[4]

A representative and highly successful computer-assisted purchasing and inventory-management system is the International Business Machines Corporation (IBM) INVEN/3, a program package for the IBM System/3.[5] It consists of a number of programs designed to help purchasing and materials managers analyze an inventory in many different ways and to assist buyers by interpreting ordering policies into specific ordering suggestions by item and item groups or vendor lines. The program analyzes past-demand history, forecasts future demand based on the history combined with the buyer's estimates, calculates safety stocks and economic order quantities, and attempts to build orders rendering the best achievable discounts. It is intended to be used on inventories where the items are supplied repetitively rather than infrequently. Given sufficient data input, the program package can:

1. Project or estimate forecasting values for each item. Once the forecasting values have been analyzed and accepted by the buyer, they will be used in subsequent reports to project future demand.
2. Estimate the yearly costs of various ordering frequencies for each vendor line, from which the buyer can select an optimum ordering strategy.
3. Show the level of inventory investment required to operate at specified service levels while indicating the actual inventory performance.
4. List usage volumes and inventory levels for items and vendors, ranked from high to low. There are twenty-two different ranking reports: They highlight items with extraordinarily high or low stock levels and help isolate problems. These reports assist buyers in determining which items or vendor lines should be monitored closely.
5. Suggest items that should be reordered and estimate complete vendor-line order suggestions for the buyer's decision.
6. Provide data-base status reports. These reports become, in effect, the data base for use when reviewing orders, making changes, evaluating performance, and managing the inventory in general. These reports are based upon data input to the system by the user.
7. Notify the purchasing and materials manager of exceptional conditions, outside of parameters set by the buyer, that may require corrective action or review.

The program package also allows users to simulate conditions that managers may want to experiment with. Users can put the system in a "what if" mode, update the data base in any valid way, and produce the necessary reports. Buyers can simulate the impact of proposed changes such as varying discount structures, ordering frequencies, vendor lead times, or other conditions and observe the results of these conditions in the system reports.

INVEN/3 consists of three major subsystems: a transaction-preparation subsystem, a transaction-processing subsystem, and a reporting subsystem. The transaction-preparation subsystem consists of programs and procedures that users employ to create the input work files for the transaction-processing subsystem. The transaction processing subsystem consists of programs and procedures that read the user-prepared input files, update the system data-base files, and report data-entry errors and other exceptional conditions for the user's attention. Users may have to repeat the execution of the first two subsystems until all conditions causing errors have been corrected. Uncorrected errors can be logged in an error log file. The reporting subsystem consists of a series of programs that read the data base and generate the various reports. All headings and message texts are contained in a set of files. They can be altered without recompiling the programs. The formats of all reports are, however, fixed.

The system also provides stand-alone programs to allocate disk space for the system files, list the contents of the error log file, reorganize the data base, delete or retain "what if" records, and modify headings and messages.

The system does not affect any of the user's current files; it establishes and maintains its own data base from which all reports are obtained. The data base is kept updated through a process in which data are extracted from the user's files and the transaction records are written into a work file. Data can also be key entered to create transaction work files.

The transaction-processing subsystem prints error message when invalid transactions are detected. An option provided by the system is the posting of all errors in an error log file, which enables users to request a listing of all uncorrected errors at any time. The error postings are deleted by the system when corrections to the errors are processed.

The programs have been assigned to run on an IBM System/3 model 8, 10 or 12, with at least 24k main storage available or an IBM System/3 model 15 with at least 30k main storage available for user programs.

The program package is designed to assist materials managers in decision making in the inventory-control and purchasing subsystems; it is not designed or intended to be an automatic inventory-control and/or purchase-order-writing system. Organizations planning to install such a computer-assisted system must be in a position to write the data-entry programs; classify vendors according to the number of products they provide; create, update, and verify the data base; verify or estimate the management-control factors (such as carrying cost, order cost, and service level); set up procedures for communication between the users (purchasing and materials management) and the data-processing department; and modify source code statements to correspond to the configuration being used. The result will be improved service to the using activities at reduced purchasing and materials-management operational cost, and lower inventory investment.

Managers who have installed computerized materials-management information systems report that the technical problems of planning and organizing the flow of data, and the information outputs, are overshadowed by the human problems. Managerial and operational employees alike may be confused over organizational objectives in introducing a computer system. Is the objective to reduce payroll costs, perhaps displacing current employees? If so, what plans are there to utilize the individual workers who might be eliminated in the function? Will other jobs in the agency open up for them? If no internal jobs are available, will management assist in outside referral and placement? Or is the objective to meet an increasing work load without adding new employees? No matter what the objective is, management must present the situation to the affected employees as best it can. Perhaps management can make the case that the function has developed to the point where it can no longer be efficiently performed without the use of computers and that the true objective is to maintain the desired level and quality of material support.

Even when objectives have been thought out and fairly well communicated to employees, resistance to the change may still be encountered. Key personnel may feel that they were left out of the planning and preparation and thus had no chance to make contributions based on their knowledge and experience. They may be quick to fault the plans that others have made. Another reaction that is not uncommon is the withholding of data or the deliberate submission of late or inaccurate data, behavior that borders on sabotage. Other employees might openly cooperate in the operation of the computerized materials-management information system but continue to maintain the manual system because they fear that the new system might not be trustworthy. In some instances, they have been right. A more important reaction is a general lowering of employee morale, a state of indifference, reflecting what some refer to as the dehumanizing of the work place. Human relations are replaced by man-machine relations, which are not very satisfying. Also more-senior employees may demonstrate loss of self-confidence. The computer hardware and software are strange to them, and they may feel that they cannot acquire the new skills needed. Even if they do develop the newer skills, younger employees might view them as vestiges of an older system, so their ego suffers.

The challenge to management is clear. All managerial and operational employees must be involved and informed about changes. Sensitive issues—objectives, job impact, retraining, possible hardships—must be discussed openly. As many employees as practical should be asked to participate in systems planning and design. A sense of involvement must be deliberately and honestly pursued. Timing of the many steps in the changeover from a manual to a computer system must be carefully worked out with balanced concern for the technical and the human aspects.

Notes

1. A widely referenced discussion of the scope of industrial-materials management is Harold E. Fearon, "Materials Management: A Synthesis and Current View," *Journal of Purchasing* 9 (February 1973):28.

2. A standard text and reference on use of the systems approach in management is Fremont E. Kast and James E. Rosenzweig, *Organization and Management Theory: A Systems Approach* (New York: McGraw-Hill, 1970).

3. A widely used text and reference on use of computers in management is Gordon B. Davis, *Introduction to Computers*, 3d ed. (New York: McGraw-Hill, 1977).

4. For a comprehensive explanation of MIS design, see Gordon B. Davis, *Management Information Systems: Conceptual Foundations, Structure, and Development* (New York: McGraw-Hill, 1974). For assistance in analyzing information systems and dealing the several organizational and behavioral aspects, see Philip Ein-Dor, and Eli Segev, *Managing Management Information Systems* (Lexington, Mass.: Lexington Books, D.C. Heath and Company, 1978).

5. IBM Field Developed Program Number 5798-NCX, GB30-0688-0, February 8, 1977, International Business Machines Corporation, General Systems Division, P.O. Box 2150, Atlanta, Georgia 30301.

3 Establishing Objectives and Performance Criteria

The primary objective of public purchasing and materials management is to acquire needed goods and services of suitable quality economically and to provide them to the requisitioning unit when needed. This is referred to here as the materials-support objective. Increasingly at the federal level and in larger state and local programs, a secondary objective is recognized: the socioeconomic objective. This refers to the use of government contracts to achieve goals generally irrelevant to the materials support being procured. Examples are in the use of government contracts to aid minority businesses, to increase veterans' employment opportunities, or to reduce the use of child labor.

Materials-Support Objectives

There are many conflicting points of view regarding materials-support objectives. The requisitioning, or using, unit is looking for effectiveness. Its management wants needed goods and services to be readily available. Generally this means a wide range of items in the supply system, with sufficient quantities of each on hand. Also it means a well-developed base of quick-response vendors. Other members of management are looking for economy. They prefer that the investment in inventory be held to a minimum and that the rate of inventory turnover be as high as possible. They also prefer that the expense of holding inventory be held down by using fewer square feet of warehousing, lower storeroom staffing, and lower security costs. They look for the purchasing and materials-management system to be cost effective and prefer that the users accept some trade-offs of reduced effectiveness where costs might be high. Others, among them the materials manager, stress efficiency. The objective here is to get the most out of the purchasing and materials-management system. They attempt to consolidate orders to minimize the number of contracts awarded, try to streamline requisitioning, and issue procedures to reduce paperwork.

Effectiveness thus deals with the degree to which the system causes the needed goods and services to be delivered when required and at a suitable level of quality. Effectiveness involves close coordination between using departments and materials management with a constant awareness of demand; establishment of inventory levels, stock-turnover rates, order quantities, and purchasing-frequency rates that respond to the demand frequency and volume; and minimizing the incidence of stock-outs, emergency orders, late deliveries, and product rejections.

Economy deals with savings and cost-saving improvements within the system. It involves a continuing analysis of price, cost, and value and searching for price reduction through consolidation, standardization, and competition; minimizing investment in inventory through constant monitoring of levels and usage rates and minimizing the cost of holding and caring for that inventory; and maximizing in-house capability to perform materials-support functions.

Efficiency deals with the effort devoted to performing the function. It involves developing an organization that operates smoothly and with the minimum incidence of error; minimizing the ratio of persons performing the purchasing and materials function to persons and activities supported; minimizing the effort per purchasing and service transactions; and constantly increasing the skill and performance level of system employees through training, sound supervision, and incentives.

Material-support objectives can and should be articulated by every jurisdiction. Many do. For example, the states of California and Kentucky include statements of objectives in their purchasing procedures manuals.[1] The aims and objectives of the Office of Procurement, Department of General Services, of the state of California are:

1. To buy the right material of the right quality in the proper quantity at the right time from the proper source.
2. To conserve public funds through reduction in cost and improvement in the quality of materials purchased.
3. To reduce the overhead cost of buying.
4. To reduce the volume and streamline the flow of paperwork.
5. To promote a system of material simplification and standardization throughout the state in order that better materials at minimum cost may be secured for all agencies.
6. To improve the speed of delivery to agencies by predetermining through contracts or other appropriate means the sources of supply before an actual need for the material in question becomes known.
7. To bring the sources of supply as geographically close to the point of use of materials as is consistent with economical purchasing through contracts or other means—in short, to decentralize the sources of supply if decentralization does not command a price premium.

In a somewhat different vein, the Division of Purchases of the commonwealth of Kentucky states that in adopting the regulations on purchasing transactions, the division sought to establish practicable and efficient purchasing procedures based on statutory provisions so as to obtain:

1. The most value for each dollar spent by the state.
2. Prompt deliveries to the state.
3. Uniform enforcement of contractual obligation for all persons or firms having state contracts.
4. Interest in bidding by all responsible vendors who can furnish property and services meeting state specifications.
5. Fair and open competition among bidders.
6. Full opportunity for all bidders to compete for state business on an equal basis.
7. An understanding by state officials of state government's procurement policies and procedures.
8. An understanding by all bidders of state government's procurement policies and procedures.
9. An understanding by all interested persons of the basis for awarding any particular type of state contract.

At the federal level, the Federal Acquisition Reform Act declares it to be the policy of the United States that the acquisition of property and services by the federal government shall be performed so as to meet public needs at the lowest total cost, maintain the independent character of private enterprise by substituting for regulatory controls the incentives and constraints of effective competition, and encourage innovation and the application of new technology by stating public needs so that prospective suppliers will have maximum latitude to exercise independent business and technical judgments in offering a wide range of competing alternatives. It should also promote both new and small business by permitting all qualified and interested sources to compete for and grow through government contracts; provide private contractors with the opportunity to earn a profit on government contracts commensurate with the contribution made to meeting public needs and with comparable profit opportunities available in other markets requiring investments, risks, and skills similar to the technical and financial risks undertaken, and safeguard the public interest through individual accountability of public officials and maximum use of effective competition. To achieve these goals, it is the policy of the United States to rely on and promote effective competition. Sellers are encouraged to respond to a public need by creating, developing, demonstrating, or offering products or services that best meet that need, whether that need is an agency mission need, a desired function to be performed, performance or physical requirements to be met, or some combination of these. Effective competition is present when there is timely availability to prospective sellers of information required to respond to the public needs, independence of action by buyer and seller, availability to the government of alternative offers that provide a range of concept, design, performance, price, lifetime ownership costs, service and/or delivery; absence of bias or favoritism in the solicitation, evaluation, and award of contracts; and ease of competitive entry for new and small sellers.

The pursuit of these objectives is greatly affected by the existence of a secondary set of socioeconomic objectives.

Socioeconomic Objectives

At the federal level, and in many states, government contracting officers must take into account in their placing of orders such factors as unemployment rate, racial discrimination, and wage differential. As reported by the Commission on Government Procurement,

> Government contracts have been used to serve many interests and beneficiaries other than the contractor, to wit, big business, small business, materialmen, laborers, consumers, every race, color, creed, origin, sex, the old, the young, apprentices, prisoners, the blind, animals, safety, health, distressed areas, hardcore areas, disadvantaged enterprises, gold flow, the environment, the technological base, the production base, and geographical distribution.[2]

Early attempts to use the government procurement process to implement socioeconomic policies are found in the Naval Service Appropriation Act (1865) and the Army Appropriation Act (1876), which mandated the purchase of only American-made bunting and the preference for American labor and material for public-improvement contracts.[3] Another early example was an 1887 act that prohibited the use of convict labor on government projects. An 1892 act established the eight-hour workday for employees of contractors to the government. A related concern was the possible effect of labor disputes upon the performance of government contracts. An early illustration was the creation of the Cantonment Adjustment Commission in 1917. In that year the army released plans, under the pressures of World War I, for sixteen army cantonments, the largest building program the nation had ever undertaken. The secretary of war felt he could not tolerate any loss of time occasioned by possible labor disputes. Consequently an informal agreement, dated 19 June 1917, signed by the secretary of war and the president of the American Federation of Labor, Samuel Gompers, turned the matter of wages, hours, and conditions over to the Cantonment Adjustment Commission. The agreement provided that the commission use the union scales of wages, hours, and conditions in force on 1 June 1917 in the locality where each cantonment was situated. A similar technique was also used in the procurement of army clothing. To help ensure the prompt production and delivery of uniforms by contractors, the Board of Control for Labor Standards in Army Clothing was created. It conducted source inspections and certified as qualified only those contractors who maintained satisfactory working conditions, complied with state labor laws, and provided proper protection against fire.

The Great Depression of the 1930s provided another setting for attempts to achieve socioeconomic objectives through the government-procurement process. The depression years saw record unemployment, greatly reduced earnings, and widespread business failure. Responding to this situation, the Davis-Bacon Act (1931) was enacted, which required federal contractors to pay wage rates not less than the prevailing rate for work of a similar nature in the civil subdivision of the state in which the construction took place. Then the National Industrial Recovery Act (1933) provided codes for both prices and wages. The act was declared unconstitutional by the Supreme Court on the grounds that regulation of labor standards and the use of the commerce powers of the Constitution for this purpose were beyond the reach of congressional legislation. However, as a result of the success of Davis-Bacon, it did appear within the reach of Congress to require that the purchasing power of the government be used to prevent contractors to the government from profiting by depressing wages and working conditions. Accordingly the Congress passed the Walsh-Healey Act (1936), establishing the eight-hour workday and the forty-hour workweek, which required time and one-half for overtime, prohibited child labor, set safety standards, and authorized the secretary of labor to determine prevailing minimum wages for performance on federal government supply contracts. Other depression-era socioeconomic legislation required performance bonds to protect subcontractors, employees, and material men on construction contracts; prohibited the payment of kickbacks by employees on construction work; directed the procurement of products and services from workshops for the blind and from prison industries; and provided preference for domestic over foreign supplies.

World War II mobilization gave further impetus to the use of the government contract for accomplishing other than procurement objectives. In 1941 President Roosevelt issued executive order 8802, which provided for mandatory inclusion of a nondiscrimination clause in government contracts. The Korean War brought the issuance in 1952 of Defense Manpower Policy 4, designed to target contracts to geographical areas of persistent or substantial labor surplus. The Congress also provided another goal; the Defense Production Act (1951) authorized the Small Defense Plants Administration and the procuring agencies to set aside certain agreed-upon contracts for exclusive participation by small business. Subsequently the Congress passed the Small Business Act (1953), which provided:

> It is the declared policy of the Congress that the Government should aid, counsel, assist, and protect, insofar as is possible, the interests of small-business concerns in order to preserve free competitive enterprise, to insure that a fair proportion of the total purchases and contracts or subcontracts for property and services for the government . . . be placed with small-business enterprises, to insure that a fair proportion of the total sales of government property be made to such enterprises.[4]

The 1960s saw continuation of the trend. A 1964 amendment to the Davis-Bacon Act expanded the prevailing wage concept to include fringe benefits as well as actual wages. Further, the wage- and labor-standard policies established by Davis-Bacon and Walsh-Healey for construction and manufacturing contractors, respectively, were expanded to cover service employees by the Service Contract Act (1965). Executive orders extended and amplified equal-employment-opportunity policy, requiring that contractors take positive steps (affirmative action) to ensure that applicants and employees were treated without regard to race, color, religion, or national origin. In 1969, the decision was made to employ section 8(a) of the Small Business Act to reinforce existing minority-controlled firms and to create and advance new ones. This section of the act allowed the Small Business Administration to enter into contracts with departments or agencies of the government and to sublet such contracts to small-business concerns.

The 1970s brought other initiatives. The Clean Air Act (1970) prohibits the government from contracting with firms found in violation of air-pollution standards. The Economic Stabilization Act (1970) requires vendors to the government to be in compliance with price, rent, wage, salary, dividend, and interest controls. Later efforts in this area turned to encouraging voluntary compliance with wage and price guidelines. The Vietnam Veterans Readjustment Act (1974) requires vendors to the government to give employment preference to disabled and other veterans of military service during the Vietnam era.

The extensive and increasing use of the procurement process to achieve socioeconomic objectives is of deep concern in materials management. The Commission on Government Procurement has concluded that the "cumulative effect of programs [socioeconomic] already imposed on the procurement process and the addition of those contemplated could overburden it to the point of threatening breakdown." The commission also stated, "These requirements add administrative costs by necessitating additional time for making awards, increased requirements for contract provisions, and more personnel for their implementation."[5]

Ethics, Morals, and Social Responsibility

Every person in a position of trust is expected to act within a framework of values that includes four aspects of personal behavior: legal, ethical, moral, and social responsibility.

Part of the effort now underway to professionalize purchasing and materials management concerns this topic because every profession has a code or codes of ethics. Every profession concerns itself with living up to its stated ideals. A point of departure for discussion of the ethics of management in the public sector is found in President Lyndon B. Johnson's executive order 11222 (8 May 1965). The order states that employees of the government should avoid any action that might result in or create the appearance of:

1. Using public office for private gain.
2. Giving preferential treatment to any organization or person.
3. Impeding government efficiency or economy.
4. Losing complete independence or impartiality of action.
5. Making a government decision outside official channels.
6. Affecting adversely the confidence of the public in the integrity of the government.

Instances of fraud and waste obviously fly in the face of this order. Those involved show no sense of calling and no feeling of responsibility either to their employers or their peers.

Codes of ethics, sometimes referred to as standards of professional practice, are common to all professional organizations. The principles and standards of purchasing practice of the National Association of Purchasing Management (NAPM) were the first to be published. The language reflects the private-sector orientation of the association. Three principles are laid down: loyalty to one's company, justice to those with whom one deals, and faith in one's profession. From these three principles are derived the NAPM standards of purchasing practice:

1. To consider, first, the interests of his company in all transactions and to carry out and believe in its established policies.
2. To be receptive to competent counsel from his colleagues and to be guided by such counsel without impairing the dignity and responsibility of his office.
3. To buy without prejudice, seeking to obtain the maximum ultimate value for each dollar of expenditure.
4. To strive consistently for knowledge of the materials and processes of manufacture, and to establish practical methods for the conduct of his office.
5. To subscribe to and work for honesty and truth in buying and selling, and to denounce all forms and manifestations of commercial bribery.
6. To accord a prompt and courteous reception, so far as conditions will permit, to all who call on a legitimate business mission.
7. To respect his obligations and to require that obligations to him and to his concern be respected, consistent with good business practice.
8. To avoid sharp practice.
9. To counsel and assist fellow purchasing agents in the performance of their duties, whenever occasion permits.
10. To cooperate with all organizations and individuals engaged in activities designed to enhance the development and standing of purchasing.

The code of ethics of the National Institute of Governmental Purchasing reflects the public-sector orientation of that organization. The institute believes that the following ethical principles should govern the conduct of every person employed by a governmental buying agency:

1. He does not seek or accept a position as head or employee of a governmental purchasing agency unless fully in accord with the professional principles of governmental purchasing and unless he is confident that he is qualified to serve under these principles to the advantage of the governmental jurisdiction which employs him.
2. He believes in the dignity and worth of the service rendered by government and his own social responsibility as a trusted public servant.
3. He is governed by the highest ideals of honor and integrity in all public and personal relationships in order that he may merit the respect and inspire the confidence of the agency and the public which he serves.
4. He believes that personal aggrandizement or personal profit obtained through misuse of public or personal relationships is dishonest.
5. He believes that members of the Institute and its staff should at no time, or under any circumstances, accept, directly or indirectly, gifts or other things of value from vendors.
6. He keeps the governmental jurisdiction which employs him informed, through appropriate channels, on problems and progress of the agency which he serves, but keeps himself in the background by emphasizing the importance of the facts.
7. He resists encroachment on his control of personnel in order to preserve his integrity as a professional administrator. He handles all personnel matters on a merit basis. Political, religious and racial considerations carry no weight in personnel administration in the agency which he directs or serves.
8. He does not seek nor dispense personal favors. He handles each administrative problem objectively without discrimination on the basis of principle and justice.

A ninth principle requires that the employee subscribe to and support the professional objectives of the institute.

The code of ethics and professional responsibility of the National Contract Management Association reflects its combined industry and government membership. It holds that a professional contracts manager shall:

1. Be mindful, and consider the interest, of the public in the performance of contract management functions.
2. Observe and uphold the standards, and assist in developing and maintaining the competence and integrity of the contract management profession.
3. Continually seek to increase his or her professional knowledge and skills and, therewith, continually seek to better serve employers, colleagues, and others associated with contract management.

4. Conduct himself or herself in a manner that will promote cooperation and constructive relations among contract managers and in a manner that will enhance the public stature of the contract management profession.
5. Serve an employer to the best of his or her ability, consistent with his or her responsibilities to the public and to the profession of contract management.
6. Maintain his or her integrity and objectivity at all times so as to exercise competent and independent professional judgment on behalf of an employer.
7. Recognize that government contracts are matters of public interest and public record and, therefore, shall conduct his or her management activities so that they can be fully substantiated and properly supported.
8. Avoid engagement in acts or association with activities which are contrary to the public interest.
9. Avoid conflicts of interest and all appearances of professional impropriety.
10. Avoid conduct of personal affairs which discredit personal reputation or which impair the reputation of contract management as a profession.

The National Purchasing Institute requires its members to subscribe to the following:

1. A member shall be loyal to his organization and will not secretly represent conflicting interests, but will devote himself exclusively to the welfare of his principal.
2. A member believes in the importance and dignity of the service rendered by government and is aware of his own social responsibilities as a trusted employee and public servant.
3. A member is governed by the highest ideals of honor and integrity with regard to all business and personal relationships in order that he may be deserving and inspire the confidence of those he serves.
4. A member believes the misuse of public or personal relationships to achieve selfish ambitions is dishonest.
5. A member should never, under any circumstances, accept gifts or other things of value from vendors.
6. A member has the obligation to keep his employer informed of the activities of NPI and to promote a better understanding of the ethics and functions of purchasing.
7. A member handles all personal matters on a merit basis. Political, religious and/or racial considerations carry no weight in personnel administration of the organization represented.
8. A member resists interference of control of personnel in order to preserve his integrity as a professional administrator. He handles each administrative problem objectively, without discrimination of the basis of principle and justice.
9. A member cooperates with all organizations engaged in activities which develop and further enhance purchasing as a profession.
10. A member subscribes to and supports the professional objectives of the National Purchasing Institute.

A common theme of honesty, justice, and loyalty is recognizable in all four examples.

Failure to behave ethically leads to the legislation of ethics. Much of our law, particularly that dealing with unfair business practices, came about in reaction to unacceptable managerial behavior. As long ago as 1809 the Congress enacted legislation barring members of Congress from sharing in government contracts. Since then many other measures have been adopted that evoke criminal penalties, forfeiture, debarment, and/or damages and apply to government contractors and employees, among others. Offenses dealt with include the offering and acceptance of gratuities, bribes, kickbacks, and contingent fees. At the state level also, ethics have been legislated. For example, in Minnesota violation of the statement of purchasing practices is a felony. The statement reads:

> No employee of the Division of Procurement shall be financially interested, or have any personal beneficial interest, directly or indirectly in any contract or purchase order for supplies, materials, equipment, or utility services used by or furnished to any department or agency of the state government; nor shall any employee accept or receive directly or indirectly from any person, firm or corporation to whom any contract or purchase order may be awarded, by rebate, gift or otherwise, any money or anything of value, or any promise, obligation or contract for future reward or compensation. A violation of this policy is a felony according to law. Inexpensive advertising items, bearing the name of the firm, such as pens, pencils, paper weights, calendars, etc., are not considered articles of value or gifts in relation to this policy.

> The following practices are also specifically forbidden:
> 1.   Using information available to an employee solely because of his state position for personal profit, gain or advantage.
> 2.   Directly or indirectly furnishing estimating services, or any other services or information not available to all prospective bidders, to any person bidding on, or who may reasonably be expected to bid on, a contract with the department.
> 3.   Providing confidential information to persons to whom issuance of such information has not been authorized.
> 4.   Providing, or using, the names of persons from records of the department for a mailing list that has not been authorized.
> 5.   Accepting, taking or converting to one's own use products of any kind in the course of or as the result of inspections of such products or the facilities of the owner or possessor.
> 6.   Using a position or status in the department to solicit, directly or indirectly, business of any kind or to purchase supplies or equipment at special discounts or upon special concessions for private use from any person who sells or solicits sales to the state.
> 7.   Serving, either as an officer, employee, member of the board of directors, or in any capacity for consideration, the interests of any organization which transacts or attempts to transact business with the state for profit when such employee holds a state position of review or control—even though remote—over such business transactions.[6]

Maintaining ethical standards is especially difficult in the purchasing function. In 1978 a survey of the members of the NAPM was conducted by the Center for the Study of Ethics in the Professions, an activity of the Illinois Institute of Technology.[7] It was reported that the sales departments of more than 80 percent of the companies surveyed gave gifts to buyers. The buyers in turn reported on the frequency of offers of favors and gifts: 98 percent had received offers of lunches, 96 percent had received offers of advertising souvenirs, 90 percent had received offers of dinners, 86 percent had received offers of theater and sports tickets, 85 percent had received offers of Christmas gifts, 83 percent had received offers of trips to vendor plants, 74 percent had received offers of golf outings, 65 percent had received offers of food and liquor, 46 percent had received offers of discounts on personal purchases, 33 percent had received offers of small appliances, 26 percent had received offers of vacation trips, 15 percent had received offers of articles of clothing, 13 percent had received offers of major appliances, 3 percent had received offers of loans, and 2 percent had received offers of automobiles. The reported acceptances of the offers ranged from 87 percent for the lunches to zero percent for the major appliances, loans, and automobiles.

Ethics is a matter of behaving in accord with the stated standards of the group to which one belongs. Morals go beyond ethics to the total character of the person. Each of us must state our own code of morals, our own standard of integrity. Harland Cleveland, a widely respected public executive, says that he routinely asks himself a question to help him make responsible moral choices: If this action is held up to public scrutiny, will I still feel it is what I should have done and how I should have done it?

Social responsibility, by contrast, is a matter of acting in the public interest. A member of public-sector management has a special responsibility to insure that the health and welfare of the public are protected, the public is not victimized by unfair or fraudulent practices, the economic environment is protected, the natural environment is protected and natural resources are not wasted, and the aesthetic environment is protected so that the quality of life in our society is sustained.

Against this considerable body of materials-support objectives, socioeconomic objectives, ethical standards, and social responsibilities there must be established a procedure for evaluating performance.

Evaluating Performance

As an aid to state and local governments the General Accounting Office (GAO) has developed a checklist for evaluation of performance of the purchasing and materials-management function. Although it is addressed specifically to the state and local level, much of the checklist is equally applicable to activities at the federal level. The format calls for yes or no answers and is designed to generate explanations and comments on negative answers. Nine topics are covered.

Authority and responsibility:

1. Is there statutory or ordinance authority for placing purchasing authority with one official or department? (a) Does the authorization extend to federally funded programs? (b) Does the authorization prohibit delegation of portions of the authority to other units in the government? (c) If not, what delegations of authority are currently in effect?
2. Is there a written procurement statute, ordinance, or policy statement: (a) Locating purchasing responsibility in a special position within the government independent of major using activities? (b) Describing the overall purchasing goals and objectives? (c) Specifying the authority of the purchasing department in all aspects of acquisition, contract administration, quality assurance, and surplus property transfer and disposal? (d) Specifically setting out all aspects of purchasing delegated to other departments and the manner in which such activities are to be monitored and controlled by purchasing? (e) Providing that purchasing may promulgate implementing regulations? (f) Covering a code or standard of conduct governing the performance of purchasing officials and personnel, as well as contractors or their agents?
3. Do the statutes, ordinances, or regulations prescribe dollar limits for each of the varying degrees of formality used in soliciting bids?
4. Does purchasing have written policies and guidelines defining what factors are to be considered in determining the responsiveness of a bid, as well as the contractor's capacity to perform? Are these factors included in the invitation for bids so that the potential bidder knows what is required?
5. Does purchasing have written policies and guidelines governing the use in the bid specification of such clauses as: (a) Option for additional units above the specific quantity, (b) Alternate prices, with and without trade-ins, (c) Conditions under which all bids may be rejected in a whole or in part?

Planning and scheduling acquisitions:

1. Is the purchasing department included in top-level planning affecting future procurement practices or needs?
2. Does purchasing have written instructions governing itself or using departments and agencies (a) To forecast future item needs and (b) To provide past-usage data?
3. Is the government's financial management-information system structured to accumulate such data as quantities purchased, ordering frequencies, vendor performance, and unit prices per transaction?

4. Does the purchasing department use market research to secure economic information that may affect purchasing, such as: (a) Current market conditions of items bought on long-term contracts? (b) Changes in local program needs? (c) Technical progress affecting supply or equipment production? (d) Seasonal requirements or fluctuating markets? (d) Transportation costs?
5. Are value-analysis appraisals made annually for a stipulated percentage of items being procured? If so, which of the following considerations are covered by the appraisals: (a) New sources of supply? (b) Standardization of items? (c) Identification of new and better products? (d) Identification of alternative products, including aspects of price and quality? (e) Storing, handling, and vendor stocking costs?
6. Does purchasing review at least annually past usage and requirement forecasts to assess the potential for consolidating and/or reducing purchase requirements?
7. Does purchasing have an ongoing program to assess the appropriateness of the manner used to satisfy requirements? Does the program involve the use of questionnaires or discussions with other government units, as well as prospective suppliers?
8. Does purchasing use for satisfying requirements contracting methods such as: (a) Definite quantity, definite period? (b) Minimum (guarantee) quantity, definite period? (c) Estimated (indefinite) quantity, definite period? (d) Estimated (indefinite) quantity, indefinite period (until canceled by either party)? (e) Has the decision to use a particular form of contracting for satisfying specific requirements been reassessed during the last year?
9. Does purchasing make lease-versus-purchase comparisons in acquiring equipment, such as vehicles?
10. Does purchasing evaluate whether it is more economical to make the item or perform the service in-house versus contracting out?
11. Does purchasing: (a) Monitor frequency and volume of purchases of the same or similar items to see whether a term contract might be cheaper? (b) Monitor different departments' purchase requests for the same or similar items to see whether consolidation may achieve economies? (c) Have written procedures to govern how such potential is to be identified? (d) Require that requisitions or purchase requests be signed by responsible department officials?

Competition:

1. Does a statute, ordinance, or regulation require purchasing to use competitive procedures for acquiring supplies, materials, equipment, and services other than professional? Does purchasing: (a) Participate in contracting for professional services? (b) Prescribe procedures followed in such contracting? (c) Review the procurements made for compliance with such procedures?

2. In securing formal bids for contract purchases, does purchasing: (a) Prepare or have the authority for review and approval of bid invitations? (b) Maintain and update a list of prospective bidders? (c) Have written criteria governing the addition, deletion, and reinstatement of bidders and vendors, and the potential of bidders to perform under the terms and conditions of the proposed procurement? (d) Have written procedures governing the receipt, control, opening, and evaluation of bids? (e) Have authority to determine which bids have the terms and conditions of the invitation? (f) Maintain a record (such as a bid-history record) to help purchasing identify collusive bidding practices?

3. Is there a provision governing procurement when formal bidding is not required? (a) Are written records required for all informal negotiations except imprest fund purchases? (b) Is the number of vendors required to be contacted under various conditions specified?

4. Is there a policy stipulating the conditions under which blanket-purchase orders may be used?

5. Is there a provision defining the special procedures to be followed when competitive procedures are not used: (a) In emergencies? (b) Where there is no responsible competition or one source; where patents or proprietary rights exist; or where standardization/interchangeability is advantageous? (c) When items are to be acquired solely for testing?

6. Are there statutes, regulations, or policies affecting open competition, such as local-purchase requirements?

7. Is there a formal program for identifying suppliers not previously solicited? Is there a requirement to document the results of the program periodically?

Standardization and specifications:

1. Does purchasing standardize items commonly used by two or more departments or agencies? (a) Is there a central stockroom from which all departments and agencies are required to draw supplies and equipment? (b) Is there a catalog of items available from the stockroom?

2. Does purchasing require written justification for item acquisition outside the stockroom standard?

3. Where specifications are prepared for special items or services by departments and agencies, does purchasing have the power to review, modify, and approve them? (a) Are brand names avoided or expressly stated to be only descriptive (identifying salient features) and not restrictive? (b) Are performance specifications rather than prescriptive specifications used?

4. Does purchasing consider using commercial standards or specifications developed by the federal, state, or other local government units and found acceptable, in lieu of developing its own specifications?

5. Does purchasing use qualified-product lists or lists of acceptable brands as an alternative to developing its own specifications? Are there written criteria covering procedures for placing and removing products and brands from these lists?

Inspection and testing:

1. Does purchasing have the authority to establish and oversee a program of inspection of deliveries to ensure that items delivered meet specifications?
2. Are there written instructions governing receipt and inspection of deliveries?
3. Does purchasing routinely monitor the inspection program?
4. Has there been a determination as to: (a) The items to be tested to determine compliance with specifications? (b) The frequency of the testing? (c) Those who should do the testing?
5. Are there written procedures covering the handling of user and/or contractor complaints?

Property management:

1. Does purchasing participate in the inventory procedures to ensure that: (a) Expendable property is properly controlled? (b) Nonexpendable property is identified or assigned for accountability to specific units of government? (c) Periodic inventories of expendable and nonexpendable property are taken?
2. Does purchasing secure a copy of the inventory documents for all units of government so that it may identify equipment that may be available to reduce or eliminate purchase of additional items?
3. Is purchasing assigned the authority to supervise the surplus and scrap programs? Are spot checks made and records kept of supplies and equipment utilization?
4. Does purchasing have written procedures for: (a) Timely identification and reporting of surplus and scrap items? (b) Notifying other departments and agencies of available usable surplus? (c) Disposing of unneeded or unusable items?

Professional development:

1. Does the government encourage the purchasing officials and technical staffs: (a) To keep current with procurement trends (for example, by affiliating with professional purchasing associations)? (b) To secure formal training and education as a supplement to their job-acquired knowledge?

2. Does the government provide support for such development by providing funding?

Cooperative purchasing:

1. If there are not statutory prohibitions, does purchasing: (a) Enter into joint or cooperative purchasing agreements with other local government? (b) Purchase from centrally placed state contracts? (c) Have a program for continually searching for ways to increase potential savings through increased use of cooperative purchasing arrangements?
2. Where cooperative purchasing is used, does purchasing have a program for evaluating any additional costs involved to determine whether the total costs may be higher than costs of buying separately?

Audit and evaluation:

1. Is there an internal or external audit of the procurement system to evaluate the effectiveness or economy with which it is making purchases?
2. Are annual performance goals, both quantitative and qualitative, established for the purchasing unit? (a) Does purchasing report periodically on its performance? (b) Is management required to measure the purchasing organization's performance? If so, is this periodically accomplished and documented? (c) Are indexes such as the following maintained or otherwise available to monitor purchasing activities: Purchasing cost (includes cost of central stores operation) per $1,000 of procurement, purchasing cost per purchase order issued, cost of warehousing per $1,000 of procurement, user complaints, out-of-stock condition, dollar value of inventory, and emergency purchases.

Comprehensive evaluation of the overall effectiveness, economy, and efficiency of purchasing and materials management is covered in chapter 16.

Notes

1. The statements are cited and quoted in Council of State Governments, *State and Local Government Purchasing,* (Lexington, Ky., 1975), pp. 17.9-17.10.
2. U.S. Commission on Government Procurement, *Report of the Commission on Government Procurement* (Washington, D.C.: Government Printing Office, 1972), 4:223.
3. The immediately following paragraphs draw from research done by Richard J. Hampton while a student at The George Washington University.

4. Small Business Act of 1953, 67 Stat. 384, sec. 1; 15 U.S.C. 631 et seq.

5. Commission on Government Procurement, *Report on Government Procurement*, 1:111, 121.

6. Council of State Governments, *State and Local Government Purchasing*, p. 12.12.

7. Ernest D'Anjou, "IIT Center Completes Ethics Survey for N.A.P.M.," *National Purchasing Review* 4 (January-February 1979):2.

4 Organizing and Staffing for Governmental Purchasing and Materials Management

Organizational arrangements must facilitate the attainment of the stated objectives with the lowest possible incidence of unwanted events, diversions, distractions, and unsought consequences. Each agency, department, bureau, division, branch, or section must contribute an identifiable element to the accomplishment of this overall function. Each must be limited in size to the scope of operations, range of facilities, and number of employees that an individual can effectively manage. The lines of authority and responsibility must be direct and clear. The responsibility of subordinates to their superiors must be absolute and inescapable.[1]

For practical reasons, organizations must be balanced. Work and responsibility must be divided and distributed as equitably as possible, given the resources and talent available. In organizing to accomplish purchasing and materials management, four issues arise: (1) At what organizational level should executive responsibility for the function be placed? (2) What should be the extent of centralization of the function? (3) What should be the internal organization of the department? (4) What will be the pattern of external organizational relationships, and how will this influence the organizational structure?

Organizational Placement of Purchasing and Materials Management

Governments are hierarchical organizations that have multiple levels of responsibility. At which level does the purchasing and materials-management function belong? Should it be established as a cabinet- or executive-level department, a bureau, a division of a bureau? In industry, materials management is increasingly being reorganized as a vice-presidential function, thus placing the manager at the same organizational level at which are located the top executives for finance, research and engineering, manufacturing, and marketing.

In the federal government, there is no single identifiable organizational unit responsible for purchasing and materials management. The highest located office is the Office of Federal Procurement Policy (OFPP), charged with establishing a system of uniform procurement policies and regulations applicable throughout the executive branch of the government. As to materials management, the commissioners of the Federal Supply Service (FSS), part of the General Services Administration (GSA) refer to their activity as the, "national supply system." It is really not that at all. The FSS supply system is responsible for only $4 billion of the $200 billion expended each year by the federal government for goods, services, and construction.

The National Supply System

The FSS, cooperating with purchasing and supply activities of the many other federal agencies, is the closest there is to a national supply system. It procures and distributes such items as office furniture and supplies, firefighting equipment and related items, paints, hardware, paper products, and a large number of essential military-support items. FSS operates a supply-distribution-facilities system consisting of twenty wholesale depots and seventy-three self-service stores. The self-service retail stores provide a readily available source of standard office supplies for the convenience of federal agencies. The depot system provides wholesale distribution of approximately thirty thousand commonly used items held in inventory for issue to federal agencies. These agencies request and receive from FSS the material they need promptly and at the low prices FSS allegedly obtains by large quantity procurements.

Direct delivery of desired supplies from contractors is made available to federal agencies through the use of federal supply schedules, the largest procurement program in FSS. Agencies can order directly from these schedules for delivery to their immediate location. Items such as office, communications, photographic, and laboratory equipment are available from the schedules.

Ordering agencies can also submit their requisitions directly to GSA-FSS regional offices for direct delivery of nonstock items, such as vehicles, locomotives, appliances, helicopters, and patrol boats.

To provide centralized management of certain commodities, FSS has established three commodity centers: the National Furniture Center, the National Automotive Center, and the National Tools Center. These centers consolidate in one location contracting, specifications, and standards development and inventory management for each product group.

FSS records and manages a great amount of logistics data in mechanized files and interchanges the data with civil agencies and military services to facilitate the total supply support process. It also provides advice and guidance to federal agencies through promulgation of policies, techniques, and informational publications in the field of supply, on-site assistance to agencies in improving their internal supply systems, and in interagency training in supply activities.

A regulatory role is performed by publishing policies and procedures in the Federal Property Management Regulations (FPMR) applicable to supply and personal-property management; transportation, public utilities, and motor-equipment management; and the personal-property utilization and disposal program.

FSS maintains a staff of experts versed in transportation and procurement regulations for the use of government agencies, represents the government in negotiations of rates or contracts with the transportation industry, represents the government's interest as a consumer before transportation regulatory boards, and prescribes regulations covering transportation of personnel and personal effects. In addition, it provides consultative services in the transportation field to federal departments. FSS operates government-wide excess-utilization and surplus-donation programs, designed to minimize expenditures and ensure maximum utilization of personal property already owned by the federal government. It makes known throughout the government the availability of property excess to the needs of any one federal agency and arranges for its transfer to such agencies for their further use or, in some cases, for use by their grantees and contractors.

FSS also operates a program for the maintenance, repair, rehabilitation, and reclamation of in-use and excess personal property. Federal departments and agencies provide GSA with their maintenance and repair requirements, and GSA awards competitively advertised contracts to small-business firms, including minority-owned firms, for maintenance and repair services. The primary purpose of the program is to extend the useful life of the property, thereby reducing new procurement costs. Additionally policy and procedures are established for recycling and resource recovery and for the reclamation of such precious metals as platinum and silver. The metal-reclamation program is coordinated with reclamation activities of the Department of Defense. GSA also administers the interagency Committee on Resource Recovery.

FSS regulates and exercises general supervision over the sale of surplus property of all government agencies. Through the use of various competitive merchandising and marketing techniques, FSS attempts to ensure the government of the highest possible return on its initial investment.

Beyond the FSS there exist some sixteen hundred executive branch entities engaged in purchasing and supply. As an aid to vendors, the Small Business Administration publishes a list of these activities, cross-referenced to lists of the goods and services purchased by each.[2] The following examples illustrate the broad organizational decentralization of federal purchasing and supply activity.

In the Department of the Army, the Army Materiel Development and Readiness Command handles materials procurement and supply for the army. It accomplishes all army procurement except for items procured and furnished to the army under Department of Defense single-department programs and by the Defense Logistics Agency or authorized for procurement from FSS or local sources. The command operates through subordinate commands, such as the Army Munitions Command and the Army Electronics Command. Posts, camps, and installations under the Continental Army Command are authorized to buy from local sources of supply. Army construction services are contracted for by the Corps of Engineers.

Procurement for the U.S. Navy is handled by each of the functional commands of the navy under the supervision and guidance of the assistant secretary of the navy for manpower, reserve affairs, and logistics. The majority of navy procurement is accomplished by the Naval Materiel Command through supporting functional commands, such as the Naval Air System Command. Each of the functional commands designs, procures, and maintains the equipment pertinent to its own function. Secondary-supply items, such as repair parts and expendable items, are procured and managed by the Naval Supply Systems Command through its Naval Supply Centers and Depots.

There are three main programs of U.S. Air Force procurement. The systems-procurement program involves the purchase of aircraft and missile systems, space systems, and communication systems. It begins with initial development and continues until the systems are accepted into air force inventory. The Air Force Systems Command at Andrews Air Force Base in Maryland bears this responsibility. The support-procurement program involves procurement of supplies and services that are necessary to support weapons and communications systems after they have been accepted into the air force inventory. Support procurement is the responsibility of the Air Force Logistics Command at Wright Patterson Air Force Base in Ohio. The base-procurement program involves the procurement of the hundreds of thousands of items needed in the daily operation of bases. It is performed by the numerous individual air force bases in the United States. Most of the items required in base procurement are secured from local businesses or from FSS regional offices.

The Defense Logistics Agency (DLA) is separately organized within the Department of Defense, but it is outside the military departments. It is under the direction, authority, and control of the secretary of defense and provides information to and receives guidance from the Office of the Assistant Secretary of Defense (Manpower, Reserve Affairs and Logistics). DLA operates through various centers. The Defense Personnel Support Center is responsible for the procurement of food, clothing, and medical supplies; the Defense Fuel Supply Center procures petroleum products and provides for their storage and handling; the Defense Electronics Supply Center supplies electronic components and parts; the Defense Industrial Supply Center acquires supplies for industrial-type items; the Defense Construction Supply Center procures and supplies common commercial items used in construction and maintenance, including repair parts for equipment; and the Defense General Supply Center procures and supplies materials-handling equipment, services and trade equipment and cleaning, plastic, and electrical supplies.

The Army Corps of Engineers is responsible for: planning, directing, and supervising an engineering, construction, and real-estate service for the army and the air force and the provisioning and servicing of engineer material required by the army, and as assigned, for the navy and the air force. It also handles all matters relating to construction, maintenance, and real estate for the control and improvement of rivers and harbors. Construction programs of the Corps of Engineers are handled through a decentralized organization of division engineers and subordinate district engineers. District engineers are usually the contracting officers and have jurisdiction over the execution of contracts.

The Federal Aviation Administration, located within the Department of Transportation, purchases a wide variety of equipment, supplies, and supporting spare parts in the aircraft, communications, air-navigation, and air-traffic-control fields. Procurements are made at various locations throughout the country, depending on the type of requirement to be satisfied. The Washington, D.C., procurement office is primarily concerned with research and development and with the acquisitions of major air-navigational and air-traffic-control systems for world-wide installations.

Each of the National Aeronautics and Space Administration's field installations makes its own contracts for support of its operations, for equipment, for construction, and for research and development projects assigned to the installation.

These few examples illustrate the broad organizational decentralization of purchasing and supply activity in the federal government.

Recognizing the problems of such wide decentralization, in August 1979 President Jimmy Carter directed the establishment of what could become a true national supply system (NSS). His directive visualizes a uniform, integrated, federal system for the acquisition, supply, and distribution of personal property and related services, with authority to establish, enforce, and monitor policies and procedures, worldwide in scope and application. The NSS would encompass the following:

1. A unified body of supply policies, program directives, and related central-management activity.
2. A cataloging system for the identification, specification, and standardization of items.
3. A standard system for the acquisition of material.

4. An item-management system for designating managers for individual items and/or classes of items in order to optimize the one item-one manager concept.
5. A standardized requisitioning and issue procedure with automated and manual capabilities and an order-status tracking capability.
6. A standardized logistics-communications system.
7. A system of contract administration to include quality assurance.
8. An integrated distribution system to accommodate the receipt, inspection, storage, issue, and movement of material in which the depot facilities would be used on a common-use basis.
9. An integrated system for the reutilization and disposal of excess and surplus property.
10. A system for collecting, developing, communicating, and disseminating acquisition and property-management data, which takes into account the needs of the Congress, the executive branch, and the private sector.
11. A supply-management system to include requirements computation, initial provisioning, and inventory management.
12. Continuous close cooperation with central personnel management authority to promote programs for improved qualification and position classification standards and similar activities toward improving the recruitment, training, career development, motivation, and performance evaluation of acquisition and supply personnel.

The OFPP has been directed to design and describe the system, with phased implementation, to begin 1 March 1981.

State and Local Organization

Central responsibility for purchasing and materials management is much more clearly established at the state and local levels. State-level approaches to the organizational issue resemble somewhat the pre-World War II federal approach in which, for a time, all federal purchasing was centralized in the treasury department. For example, as in many other states, the Division of Purchases of the commonwealth of Kentucky is part of the Executive Department for Finance and Administration.

Purchasing officials must deal fairly with vendors, coordinate with other government departments, provide timely service of good quality, and protect the public interest.[3] To accomplish these responsibilities, the central purchasing authority must be able to exercise independent professional judgment. It must also be able to deal with vendors and with all department heads from a position of authority commensurate with its responsibilities. Purchasing's independence and effectiveness can be either positively or negatively affected by its placement within the government hierarchy. Factors such as organizational and management philosophy, tradition, the size of the purchasing program, and resources available to it have a major impact on this issue. There is no one best arrangement; what may work well in one state or local government may not work well in another.

In the 1960s, there was a strong movement to include purchasing in a department of finance or administration as a means of integrating fiscally related functions. This is currently the case in many governments. In the approach receiving the most attention today, however, the purchasing function is part of an overall general-services responsibility. Recent governmental reorganizations in several jurisdictions have taken this direction. In many governmental structures, however, a department of administration actually serves the same purpose as a general-services department, so it provides an equally suitable location for the purchasing function.

In one state, purchasing still functions as a separate department, which is not consistent with prevailing reorganization efforts to reduce the numbers of departments. In two other states, a separate board appointed by the governor oversees purchasing activities and the activities of various other central services. In two other cases, purchasing is housed in a department of administration with a commission including legislative members serving as the policy body. Although unusual, the last two arrangements can afford certain strong advantages.

Fundamentally, however, the need is to place the central purchasing authority in the governmental hierarchy so that the number of levels between the chief purchasing official and the chief executive is lessened. The majority of state and local governments have one person between the chief purchasing official and the chief executive. In these governments, public purchasing operates as one bureau or division among several within a department. The chief purchasing official is the person charged with the legal responsibility for purchasing activities. He might not oversee all of the day-to-day operations, but he retains responsibility for them.

A major recommendation of the Commission on Government Procurement was the establishment of an office of federal procurement policy. Several states have already established boards or commissions that serve a similar purpose. In states where this development has been successful, the purchasing function operates under an independent board or commission, which allows the goals and objectives to be pursued relatively free from governmental and outside pressures. The board or commission, which serves as the governing body of the purchasing program, may be composed of government officials and/or private citizens. Members may or may not serve for a specified term, and the terms may or may not overlap. The board may appoint a full-time director who serves as the chief purchasing official.

The board is concerned with rules and regulations and with the overall direction of the purchasing department. Under this type of organization, purchasing is partially protected from direct, external pressures. The board serves as an advocate of purchasing and lends its credibility to the improvement of the purchasing operations. To the extent that government officials serve on the board, a healthy mixture of viewpoints is provided. Overall such a board can provide a check on purchasing activities, but to be effective it must meet regularly and be actively interested. It functions best as a small body, and care must be taken that its members avoid any conflicts of interest.

For cities and counties where the size and volume of the purchasing activity call for a central office, its goals and objectives are more likely to be met if it is established as a separate unit on equal footing with other major departments. For local governments where the central purchasing authority rests with a single individual, that person needs sufficient power and responsibility to achieve the purposes of purchasing.

No single organizational arrangement is best for all state or local governments, but a strong recommendation can be made for a policy board. Beyond that, whatever the organization, the central purchasing authority should occupy a position that provides the stature necessary to coordinate and deal with other departments and agencies effectively and is designed to prevent decisions that are based on partisan political pressures or favoritism.

Internal Organization

Internal organization of purchasing and materials-management departments can be expected to vary tremendously, reflecting differences in the volume and variety of items managed, the size of the budget and personnel authorization, the qualifications of its employees, and the managerial style and capacity of the department head. Also the organization should be capable of overall materials management, not just purchasing. At each level, materials should be managed by an executive whose success or failure hangs upon how well the total materials-management job is done.

The internal organization accommodates three broad activities: acquisition, standards and quality assurance, and disposition (see figure 4-1). Acquisition encompasses the activities of planning and scheduling; designing invitations for bids and soliciting bids; receiving, opening, and evaluating the bids and making awards; expediting; and contract administration.[4] Planning and scheduling is an aspect that needs greater emphasis than it has

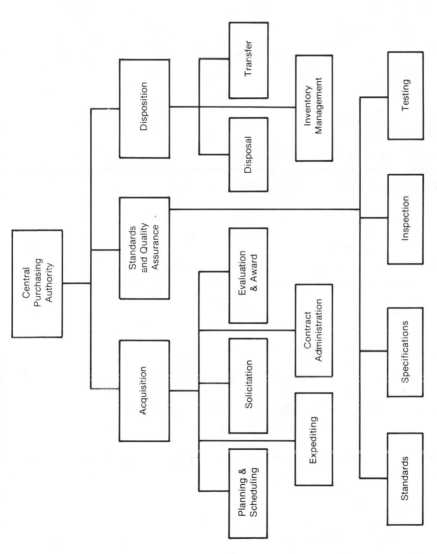

Source: *State and Local Government Purchasing* (Lexington, Ky.: Council of State Governments, 1975).

Figure 4-1. Internal Functional Organization of a Central Purchasing Authority

been given traditionally. This activity should play an important role in budgeting, reducing unit costs through volume buying, consolidating and validating agency needs, and determining how these needs can best be met. Greater attention must also be given to contract-administration activities; these need to be defined and centrally administered to ensure that suppliers meet contractual terms and conditions.

The design of the invitation for bids is critical to every procurement. Basic considerations are the terms and conditions that must be prepared to ensure and protect the interest of the government; openness of specifications; requirements for transportation and delivery; and instructions as to how the bidder is to submit the proposal. Solicitation also includes the organization and maintenance of bidders' lists, the option of prequalification of suppliers, the need for public notice, and the need, if any, for bid security. Bid solicitation should seek maximum competition for all purchases and fair and equal opportunity for all qualified persons or firms. Bid evaluation and award involve establishing criteria for award and rejection of bids, a determination of the lowest and best or lowest responsible bidder whose proposal is most advantageous to the government, and public awareness of the prices and products obtained.

To the extent that a cooperative purchasing program exists between or among government units, the management responsibility for such a program should lie with the central purchasing authority. The leasing or renting of equipment and the accompanying lease-versus-buy decisions are also a responsibility of the central purchasing authority, as are contracts for repairs and maintenance of equipment and contractual needs such as janitorial and laundry services. Whether central purchasing actually handles solicitation and awards of such contracts or delegates aspects of them to operating agencies is determined by geographical factors, local conditions, staff size, and work load. When they are delegated, it is good practice for central purchasing to design and require the use of a uniform bid solicitation document for each particular type of requirement, including the contract terms and conditions.

Questions sometimes arise about whether purchasing must have all of the technical expertise necessary to buy certain items, such as insurance or printing. Some purchasing programs have separate sections, including risk managers, that are responsible for purchasing insurance. In other cases, program appropriateness and decisions to self-insure or purchase are made by risk managers outside of purchasing or by insurance boards. In the case of printing, the laws governing public purchasing apply, and there are often special statutes that provide added coverage. As with insurance, some purchasing programs have separate sections that handle the purchase of printing. Items such as these are not too different from many other commodities assigned to purchasing specialists. Sometimes it is difficult to hire the proper technical personnel to do the job. If purchasing is unsuccessful in hiring appropriate personnel, it must obtain expert advice from individuals outside its own organization. In any case, the actual purchases should be made by central purchasing.

Similar considerations relate to the purchase of professional services, among them, management consulting, architect and engineering, and medical and legal services. User agencies must necessarily play an important role in drafting statements of work and in evaluating technical proposals (where such proposals are called for and received). In some state and local governments, the personnel department must determine that the hourly or other rates proposed are within the upper and lower limits of the current rates for such services. In some states, the attorney general must approve the contract before it is signed. Given the need for these types of technical assistance and administrative controls, however, the central purchasing authority should be responsible for the procurement of professional services.

If a state or local government makes a purchase under a total-cost concept, which takes into consideration initial costs plus maintenance and operating costs, data from using agencies often are needed to make necessary cost comparisons and evaluations. Purchases of high-technology items such as x-ray equipment, telecommunications equipment, and computer hardware and software usually require the combined expertise of several agencies working together with central purchasing. For example, when computer equipment is being procured, experts in automatic data processing would provide certain technical information for preparing and evaluating bids, and the using agency would supply information on the intended use of the equipment. Purchasing, however, would manage the acquisition process. It would be the focal point for preparing the invitation for bids, soliciting bids, and evaluating responses. After the award, purchasing would be responsible for the administration and management of all phases of the contract throughout its duration, with reliance on the using agency for information as needed.

Two additional areas are worthy of special note. The first concerns the operation of government motor pools. Although the acquisition and disposal of government vehicles should be the responsibility of purchasing, the maintenance and operation of the motor pool should not. This distinction is made because acquisition and disposal are integral functions of a materials-management program, but operation and maintenance are not. The same reasoning applies to the operation of a central data-processing activity or a copying and duplicating center.

The second area relates to the purchase of real estate and buildings, including the leasing of space. The acquisition of real estate is usually governed by a separate set of rather complex laws. It can be argued that real estate is not a biddable item, but this in itself should not be a reason for excluding it from the responsibility of purchasing. While real estate is traditionally excluded from central purchasing responsibility, there is no reason to believe that with the assistance of outside expertise, purchasing should not have a responsibility in the purchase and leasing of lands and buildings, with the exclusion of condemnations, rights of way, and lands for recreation.

In discussing the acquisition program as it relates to internal organization, the concepts of team buying and rotation are important. Team buying—more than one person is responsible for purchasing in the same commodity area—is a highly recommended practice. It improves commodity specialization by providing several persons who are knowledgeable in the same areas, ensures backup, and allows for group decision making, with overall responsibility resting with the team leader. Although some governments rotate buyers as a means for providing backup, this practice is not recommended because many commodities have become so highly specialized that rotation is not feasible. It is often necessary for more than one person to be aware of current developments in any given commodity area, but all purchasing agents need not try to be specialists in all commodities.

The standards and quality-assurance program embodies the activities of standardization, specification writing, inspection, and testing. Vendor performance and commodity usage are important factors. The activities of developing standards and specifications address the subject of commodity usage, while inspection and testing measure vendor performance. Vendor performance refers not only to whether specifications are met but also to whether deliveries are timely and complete and whether there are any unauthorized substitutions or other failures in performance. Many government units do not have strong standards and quality assurance programs. In some governments, the writing of specifications is completely outside the central purchasing authority, and in others it is relegated to a status of minor importance within central purchasing. Wherever possible, the four major activities of a complete program should be an integral part of the central purchasing authority.

Although the basic duty of the standards and quality-assurance effort is to serve as the major technical resource to the overall procurement effort and to provide it technical support, it should be a distinctive organizational entity with its own job descriptions and with well-defined assignments and responsibilities. Too often among both state and local governments this is not the case.

The value of an effective standards and inspection program can be substantial, and in any complex purchasing organization it is essential. For states, cities, and counties without the resources for a separate staff, the individual responsible for quality assurance can look to the federal government and to other state and local governments for assistance. Also a highly effective arrangement can be developed whereby much of the everyday specification work is handled by the specialist purchasing official, with a single individual or small technical staff concentrating on standard specifications, inspection, and testing. No matter how limited a government's resources, quality assurance remains a responsibility of the central purchasing authority. In a broad-based purchasing program, traveling field inspectors can play important roles, especially for large governmental units that serve agencies over a wide geographic area.

The two primary activities associated with the disposition program are the transfer of surplus property from one agency to another and its disposal through sealed bids, auction, posted prices, site sales, or direct negotiation. (The last two methods are usually reserved for scrap or garbage.) Although some governments trade in used equipment for new equipment, most of them find that they receive more return by outright sale.

At the state level, two separate surplus programs—state and federal—exist. Consequently the organizational implications are more complex than at the local levels. Consideration needs to be given to the advantages and disadvantages of combining the state and federal surplus programs. Sharing warehouse and distribution facilities can work to the benefit of both programs by attracting more visits from and providing more exposure for screeners and users from using agencies. The potential for reducing manpower needs is also a factor. A disadvantage, however, lies in the fact that there is considerable difference between the two programs both as to the nature and volume of activities. The federal program is more complicated in operation by virtue of its strict federal guidelines, rules, and regulations, which limit eligibility requirements for participation and include detailed utilization and compliance requirements on the part of recipients together with special record keeping. But because the disposal of surplus property is very much part of the total materials-management concept, the advantages of combining the state and federal surplus programs into one entity can outweigh the disadvantages. The disposal of all surplus property and scrap, whether federal or state, should therefore be the responsibility of the central purchasing authority. Figures 4-2, 4-3, and 4-4 illustrate the actual organizational structures in three jurisdictions.

The internal organization of the federal government, however, cannot easily be depicted. The OFPP, located in the Office of Management and Budget, the highest management echelon of the executive branch, provides a central point of policy formulation and related guidance. It maintains a close working relationship with the many heads of procurement-purchasing-acquisition throughout government. Departments and agencies are free to organize internally pretty much as they wish.

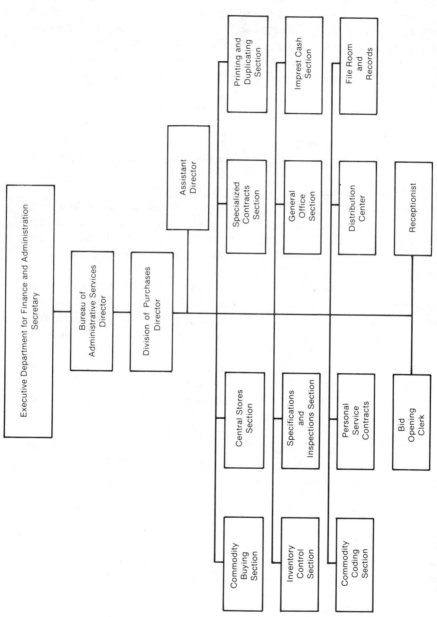

Figure 4-2. Organization of the Office of the Division of Purchases, Commonwealth of Kentucky

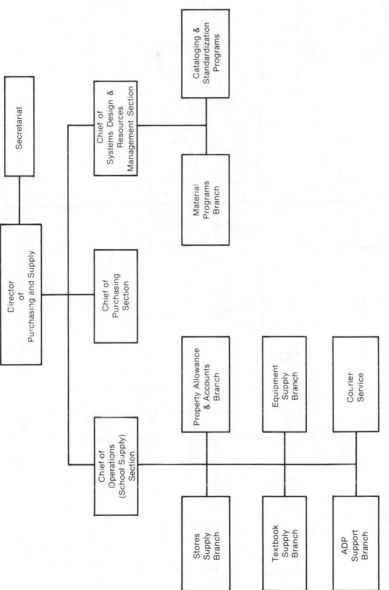

Figure 4-3. Organization of the Office of the Director of Purchasing and Supply, Fairfax County, Virginia

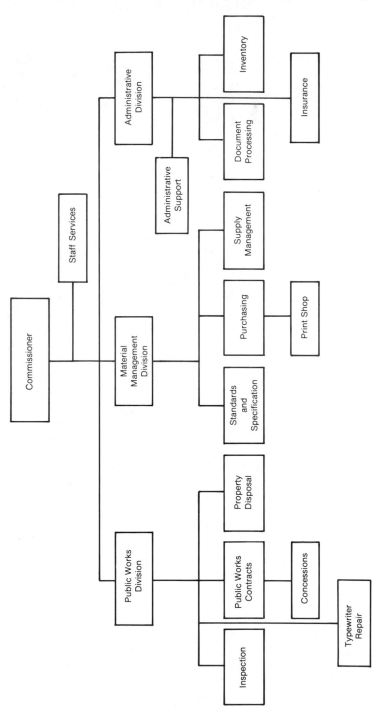

Figure 4-4. Organization of the Procurement Department, City of Philadelphia

Project Management and Major Systems Acquisition

The generally most-workable organizational structure, and thus the customary one, is functional and common to all of the organizations just described and illustrated. In the acquisition of large and complex systems, such as weapon, space, and transportation systems, it has been found that the traditional functional form of organization needs to be supplanted by a form variously referred to as project management, program management, and/or matrix management.

Project management should be viewed as temporary, even fragile. A team is organized to accomplish a specific undertaking. Members are drawn from the various functional units. When the project is completed or terminated, the project team is disbanded and the personnel returned to their parent organizations or otherwise reassigned. A multidisciplinary team is necessary because of the wide range of actions and contacts involved. The challenge to the team is to research, design, develop, test, produce, and deliver the system on schedule.

The design, development, production, and operation of a system involve several functions normally managed by separate elements of an organization. For example, funding is a comptroller function; procurement is accomplished by purchasing offices; storage, distribution, and maintenance as well as training of personnel are separate functions. The project manager is given the responsibility for coordinating and directing all of the efforts required to place the system in operation.

There is no single method or formula for the program manager that fits all systems. The particular management arrangement selected depends on such factors as the nature of the item, the state of the art, the degree of urgency, and in-house and industrial capability. As an indication of the scope of the problem, the Nike-Hercules weapon-system program had ten thousand subcontractors and suppliers whose efforts had to be controlled and time phased. Effective planning and programming are required with respect to management of all the equipment and facilities that compose such a system. It not only must be done initially; it must be revised again and again.

Systems acquisition is usually broken down into phases. It begins with the conceptual phase; when the concept of the system is thoroughly reviewed and analyzed. This usually precedes the determination to acquire the system. The considerations that support the determination of the need for a program, together with a plan for that program, are carefully documented. Once the decision is made to go ahead with a program, the procurement normally takes place in three phases. The first phase involves contracts for design and development work and construction of mock-ups. Contracts under the second phase call for the completion of engineering, production of prototype units, and testing of prototypes. The third phase is quantity production. The length of time and the number of contracts in each phase vary among programs, depending on the nature and complexity of the system being procured.

External Organizational Relationships

Purchasing and materials-management activities work with various using agencies and with other activities having an interest in the materials-support function. The using agencies establish the demand and state the requirements. The other interfaces are technical and legal. The situation at the federal level illustrates the range and nature of such relationships. The external organizational relationships of a federal agency purchasing activity would include but not be limited to:

1. The agency comptroller and budget officer, who controls the availability of operating and acquisition funds and who monitors in detail the spending out of the program.
2. The agency inspector general, who conducts audits and investigations relating to the programs and operations of the agency and recommends actions to promote economy and efficiency and to prevent and detect fraud.
3. Authorizing, appropriating, and oversight committees of the Congress, who expect to be kept informed of problems and who reserve the right to approve reprogramming.
4. The General Accounting Office, an arm of the Congress, which conducts external audits, prepares cost-effectiveness studies, critiques procedures, and monitors cost overruns.
5. The Defense Contract Audit Agency, which conducts internal audits of purchasing, enforces the truth-in-negotiations concept, and adjudicates price reduction, among other things. (This applies only to activities in the Department of Defense.)
6. The OMB, which approves the budget, controls the apportionment of funds for acquisition, monitors obligation rates, and examines purchase requirements.
7. The OFPP, part of the OMB, the clearinghouse for procurement policies and regulations.
8. The SBA, which may actually contract, and then subcontract, work it sees suited to small business. It will refer firms and arrange set-asides of contracting opportunities.
9. The Cost Accounting Standards Board, which promulgates accounting standards to be followed by contractors and subcontractors and requires disclosure of accounting practices.
10. The Board of Contract Appeals, which resolves contract disputes and breaches of contract.

11. The U.S. Court of Claims and the district courts, which render judgment upon claims against the United States founded upon any express or implied contract with the government.

Staffing

Staffing fills the organizational roles with personnel who are able and willing to perform in those roles. This involves careful definition of the role (positions) and effective recruiting, selection, and training of those who occupy the positions. The performance of the occupants should be continually appraised and their contributions appropriately recognized. There should be a program of both formal and informal training and development.

Purchasing and materials management has often been cited as one of the less attractive career fields, a field into which individuals might drift from positions in engineering, production, finance, or marketing. But there is considerable evidence in both industry and government that the situation is changing. Economic developments—upward spiraling material costs, critical shortages, and disruption of supply—have focused increased attention on those who plan for, acquire, and control the flow of materials and services.

Some 560,000 managerial, technical, and administrative personnel are currently employed in the public-purchasing and materials-management function in the United States. Of these, close to 110,000 are federal civilian employees. In 1971 the Commission on Government Procurement de-

Table 4-1
Ages of Federal Public-Purchasing and Materials-Management Employees

Age	Number	Percentage
20 and under	12	—
21-25	1,206	2.3
26-30	3,093	5.8
31-35	4,324	8.1
36-40	5,934	11.1
41-45	7,215	13.5
46-50	11,235	21.1
51-55	10,845	20.4
56-60	6,176	11.6
61-65	2,674	5.0
66-70	579	1.1
Total	53,293[a]	100.0

[a]Some respondents did not indicate age.

veloped a profile of these employees through a survey questionnaire to which 53,568 persons responded. Their ages are reported in table 4-1, their experience in table 4-2, and their level of education in table 4-3. The modal age of this work force is between forty-six and fifty, over half have somewhat less than ten years of experience in the field, and the average educational level is high school plus three months of college. The work force was characterized at that time by one commission member as "over aged and under educated." Responding to this situation and the similar conditions at other levels of government, agencies, professional organizations, and the academic community are developing a broad-based educational, training, and professional certification program.

Education and Training

The competence of the work force is the most important factor in achieving organizational goals. Personnel must be able to perform the tasks assigned. And yet the Commission on Government Procurement reported that more than half of the civilian agencies of the federal government were using as contracting officers personnel whose training, education, experience, and expertise did not qualify them; personnel who did not have knowledge of applicable laws and regulations essential to the contracting function; and who were exercising the contracting officer authority that resided in the position occupied although no determination had been made of their qualifications to do so. No comparable study has been made of the qualifications of personnel at the state and local levels. Even so the commis-

Table 4-2
Experience of Federal Public-Purchasing and Materials-Management Employees

Government Procurement Experience	Number	Percentage
None or less than one year	4,303	8.0
1-5 years	13,809	25.8
6-10 years	13,078	24.5
11-15 years	8,593	16.0
16-20 years	7,609	14.2
21-25 years	3,739	7.0
26-30 years	2,041	3.8
31 years and over	396	0.7
Total	53,568	100.0

Table 4-3
Level of Education of Federal Public-Purchasing and Materials-Management Employees

Level of Education	Number	Percentage
Less than high school	2,073	3.9
High school	20,864	38.9
Post-high school	1,513	2.8
At least 30 semester hours of college credit	4,228	7.9
At least 60 semester hours of college credit and/or a junior-college certificate	3,812	7.1
At least 90 to 120 semester hours of college credit	2,787	5.2
Bachelor's degree	14,529	27.1
Master's degree	2,183	4.1
Law degree	1,104	2.1
Doctor's degree	475	0.9
Total	53,568	100.0

sion report, written in 1972, provides one appraisal of the level of education and training of the purchasing work force at that time.

The education and training that a professional employee in purchasing and materials management should have can be examined by four skill areas.[5] The first is business knowledge and skills. Employees should have knowledge in accounting, business and economic statistics, data processing, economics, and purchasing. Within purchasing they should understand legal, regulatory, and policy matters; pricing, sourcing, and negotiation; administrative policy and practices; and planning and control. And they should have knowledge of some special procurement practices. Their related business knowledge should encompass financial, manufacturing, marketing, and engineering practices.

The second area is communication skills. This includes knowledge of human relations, conference leadership, oral and graphic presentation, and professional writing.

General managerial skills, the third area, refers to planning, programming, controlling, and decision making.

The final area, conceptual skills, encompasses creative and causative thinking and analytical ability.

The similarity of these areas to a standard college curriculum in business administration is striking, except for the purchasing and materials-management content.

Purchasing and materials management is a truly interdisciplinary field of study and endeavor. It presents a business-management challenge with public-policy overtones. It demands that its decision makers have the ability to review critically and assess the implications of proposed undertakings involving diverse technical and/or engineering efforts. At the same time, it requires an ability to cope with a multitude of socioeconomic and political objectives. Nevertheless its daily activities are those of business management. For example, the purchasing manager must attract and organize industrial and innovative resources in a manner that maximizes the probability of success of programs that frequently are not fully defined. In this arena, the behavior and motivation of organizations and personnel is extremely complex.

Historically most of the training in this field has been on the job or through short courses and seminars. Recently, and particularly since the work of the Commission on Government Procurement, there has been considerable activity at both the undergraduate and graduate levels. The Federal Acquisition Institute (FAI) is encouraging and promoting the establishment of additional college-level courses and programs. Working with the academic community, FAI has developed model educational programs at the associate, baccalaureate, and master's levels. The University of the State of New York, for example, offers a sixty-semester-hour Associate in Science with concentration in purchasing and contracting. Courses include basic procurement, contract administration, cost and pricing, small purchases, acquisition practices and procedures, and government contract law. A representative program leading to the degree of Bachelor of Business Administration is offered by the University of the District of Columbia. It includes all of the usual courses found in such a degree, plus courses in principles of purchasing, government programs and the procurement process, public contracts, contract management, government property management, cost and price analysis, cost accounting, contract negotiation, procurement law, and materials management. A model program at the American University, also located in the District of Columbia, has a broader focus. Its courses include a series similar to those provided by the University of the District of Columbia, plus courses in grants and assistance management. Another pioneer in undergraduate education has been Bowling Green State University, Ohio.

The model program at the master's level is based upon the offering of The George Washington University. The degree objective is the Master of Business Administration. Students aspiring to the degree must meet several requirements. All must present prerequisite course work in economic theory, statistics, accounting, business law, business finance, production, and marketing. All must undertake a group of courses in administrative theory and practice, executive decision making, and problem analysis. All are required to undertake courses in quantitative concepts and techniques, the behavioral sciences, and human behavior in organizations. The purchasing and materials-management concentration is covered in five courses:

1. Purchasing and Materials Management. Industrial purchasing and materials-management principles and practices. Organization and functions in materials management. Determination of requirements, source selection, buying practices, policies, and ethics.
2. Procurement and Contracting. Principles and concepts essential to effecting large procurement programs. Planning, sourcing, and contractual design for diverse acquisitions. Emphasis on federal government policy with comparison of buying at other governmental levels and the private sector.
3. Government Contract Administration. Surveillance and management of contract performance. Measurement of progress; specification interpretation; quality assurance; changes, negotiation, and adjustment; financial considerations; property; terminations; regulatory and policy concerns.
4. Pricing and Negotiation. Scope and objectives of negotiated procurement; preparation, conduct, and recording of negotiations; analysis of cost, price, profit, investment, and risk; cost principles; incentives; relationship of contract type to work requirements; techniques of negotiation.
5. Systems Procurement and Project Management. Major systems acquisition: needs, objectives, and organizational relationships. Design, establishment, and execution of project management plans and procurement processes. Developing adequate intercontractual business relationships within the environment of public procurement. Management of projects under contract.

In addition to their specialized work in purchasing and materials management, MBA students are encouraged to elect courses in managerial accounting, management planning and control, unionism and collective bargaining, and distribution logistics, among others.

The U.S. Air Force and the U.S. Navy offer graduate instruction primarily for commissioned officers. At the Air Force Institute of Technology in Ohio, a program leads to the degree of Master of Science in logistics management with a contracting major. At the Naval Postgraduate School in Monterey, California, a program leads to the degree of Master of Science in management with specialization in acquisition and contract management.

A survey by the National Association of Purchasing Management

(NAPM) indicates that some two hundred four-year colleges offer at least one course in purchasing and materials management. Perhaps a dozen offer enough instruction to constitute a field of specialization.[6] The number and quality of offerings is steadily improving.

Short courses and seminars abound, varying in length from a single day to two weeks. They are offered in-house by units of government, by the professional organizations, by private for-profit and nonprofit firms, and by colleges and universities. The courses are taught by both practitioners and academics, many of whom have made careers in this work.

The U.S. Office of Personnel Management provides training for federal, state, and local government employees through a nationwide system made up of training centers in Washington, D.C., and in each of the ten regions, four executive seminar centers, and the Federal Executive Institute (FEI). Specific information about the training available at each is provided by the Office of Personnel Management.[7] The courses run from two to ten days in length. Examples include:

1. Federal procurement process (two days): an overview of how procurement laws and regulations came to be developed; its hope is that understanding will make compliance easier. The course covers the contract presolicitation and solicitation phases, contract pricing, types of contracts, the contract award phase, the contract administration phase, contract completion and closeout, contractual rights and remedies, and special sources of supply.

2. Basic contracting (five days): an orientation to the Federal Procurement Regulations and an overview of the basic statutes and authorities which underlie the procurement process. The content of the course includes: basics of government procurement, authority and responsibilities of the contracting officer, the procurement cycle, types of contracts, procurement by formal advertising, two-step formal advertising, procurement by negotiation, development of determinations and findings, requests for proposals, proposal evaluation, negotiation techniques, contract awards, and government-furnished property.

3. Contracting with small business enterprises (two days): an orientation to federal policies designed to ensure that small businesses and minority enterprises receive a fair proportion of government contracts. The course explains government policies on aiding these businesses, points out appropriate procurement procedures and discusses the role of the Small Business Administration. Problems affecting relationships with small business and minority enterprises are also discussed.

4. Federal grant process (two days): intended for employees who need to be familiar with the interfaces and interrelationships among those activities involved in the grant process. The course covers the following topics: history of the growth of the grant, types of grants, grant proposal preparation, accounting for and managing the grant, cost ac-

counting for the grantee, cost accounting procedures for matching funds, program monitoring and reporting, and grant closeout procedures.
5. Research-and-development contracting (five days): a course developing an awareness of the application of the basic principles of government contracting to the specialized requirements of research and development. The course covers the entire cycle of research and development procurement from initiation of the requirement to completion or termination of the project. Problem areas unique to research-and-development projects are emphasized.

The National Institute of Governmental Purchasing conducts the most extensive of the professional-association training programs in public purchasing and materials management.[8] Its three-phased seminar program includes a three-day basic seminar, a three-day intermediate seminar, and a three-day advanced seminar. They are offered several times each year at locations nationwide. The basic course coverage includes:

1. General Objectives and Polices
   Development of centralized purchasing
   Objectives and benefits of centralized purchasing
   Basic purchasing policies
       Intragovernmental and intergovernmental relations
       Supplier relations
       Public relations
2. Standards and Specifications
   Standardization, standards, and simplification
   Types of specifications
   Standards committees
   Value analysis
   Product evaluation
3. Purchase Methods
   Open-market purchases
   Term contracts
   Small purchases
   Sole-source items
   Professional services
   Nonprofessional services
   Emergency purchases
4. Competitive Bidding
   Requisitioning
   Sources of supply
       Source search
       Prequalification of bidders
       Bidders' lists

    Buying history

    Bid solicitations

      Informal

      Formal

      Bid advertising

      Bid sureties

      Amendments to solicitations

    Bid processing

      Receipt and tabulation

      Late bids

      Withdrawal of bids

      Modification of bids

    Bid evaluation and awards

      Evaluation of competitive bids

      Evaluation of special cases: sole source, only bid, alternate bids, tie bids, bid errors or omissions, "lump sum" bids, "all or none" bids, low total bids, disqualified bids, waiving defects, technicalities, informalities

      Preference for local suppliers

5. Administration of Purchase Orders and Contracts

    Delivery and performance

      Follow-up and expediting

      Receiving reports and records

      Delinquent deliveries

      Partial deliveries

      Substitution

      Nonperformance

    Inspection and testing

      Receiving inspection and rejections, and reports

      Damage in shipment

      Latent defects

      Return authorization

    Payment

      Full payment

      Progress payments

      Assignment of payment

6. Surplus, Salvage, and Scrap Disposal

    Types: scrap, worn, obsolete, surplus

    Sources of salvageable materials

    Value analysis of salvage

    Recycling materials

    Methods of disposal

      Sealed bids

      Spot bids

      Public auction

Trade-ins
Negotiated sales to other public utilities.

The intermediate course coverage includes:

1. Law and Enabling Authority
   Public authority to contract
      Express requirements
      Transactions outside of authority
      Ratified transactions
      Unauthorized purchases: control, liability, remedies
   Uniform Commercial Code
   Law of Sales and Agency
   Formation of a contract
      Requisites of a valid contract
      Legal time length of public contracts
   Robinson-Putnam Act; Sherman Anti-Trust Act; Federal and State
   Fair Trade Acts; Walsh-Healy and Davis-Bacon acts
   Foreign trade and exchange
   Notary certification and attestation
   Transfer of property and title
2. Organization and Personnel
   Materials-management organization within a level or unit
   of government
   Materials-management within operating agencies and departments
   Personnel
      Qualifications
      Training of employees and supervisors
   Organization charts, tables and assignments, job descriptions,
   and personnel appraisal
3. Purchase Methods
   Request for proposals
   Competitive negotiation
   Total cost purchasing
   Cooperative purchasing
   Price-adjustment contracts
4. Purchase Requirements and Requisitioning
   Price forecasting
   Determining economic order quantity and delivery schedules
   Fiscal procedure and control
5. Materials-Inventory Control
   Stock numbering, inventory categories, and classifications
   Usage forecasting
   Inventory-control techniques
   Materials accounting-charge back to using departments

6. Stores Management
   Stores policy and organization
      To store or not to store
      Selection of materials for storage
      Stores planning, design, and location; centralization versus decentralization
   Materials handling
      Receiving techniques
      Storage methods and stock issuance and control
      Distribution techniques
      Storage and materials-handling techniques and equipment
7. Transportation and Traffic
   Traffic-purchasing relationship
   Types of transportation
   Title and control of goods
   Packaging requirements and effect on transportation costs and material handling
   Commerce commissions' requirements and authority
   Tariffs, rates, and freight equalization
8. Quality Control
      Laboratory facilities
      Technical testing and inspection instruments
      Statistical quality control
      Testing and inspection reporting
      Personnel qualifications

The advanced course coverage includes:

1. Management Concepts
   Purchasing and materials-management organization types, forms, and place in overall organization
   Relations with other departments; techniques, problems, risks, and benefits
   Employee motivation
   Management by objectives
2. Communicating with Management
   Personal communication
   Monthly activity report
   Annual report
   Budget preparation
3. Electronic Data Processing in Purchasing and Materials Management
   EDP equipment functions and capabilities
   Applications
   Systems development

4. Human Relations
   Buyer-seller relations
   Intradepartmental relations and coordination
   Common understanding of policy, purposes, and problems
   Human problems in supervision
5. Ethics and Conflict of Interest
   Code of ethics
   Proper business conduct
   Avoidance of personal profit and gifts
   Ways and means of meriting public confidence
   Acts of destroying public confidence
   Cause and effect of violating public trust—penalties
6. Model Laws and Ordinances
7. Review of NIGP Certification Requirements for CPPO

Most of the other professional organizations also offer short courses and seminars. There is a great deal of interassociation cooperation in the presentation and promotion of such programs.

Representative of private enterprises offering training in purchasing and materials management is Procurement Associates.[9] At locations nationwide it presents courses of three or more days' duration on such topics as contract administration and management, contracting in an inflationary economy, government contract audits, improvement curves, and subcontract management.

Numerous variations exist in training programs offered by colleges and universities outside the usual credit-hour structure. UCLA Extension has a well-established block of courses leading to the professional designation in government contract management, the advanced professional designation in government contract management, and the professional designation in purchasing and materials management.[10] The professional courses include fundamentals of purchasing and materials management, inventory management systems, elements of government contract administration, negotiation principles and techniques, and financial management of government contracts. These courses are offered in cooperation with the National Contract Management Association, NAPM, and the Hospital Purchasing Agents Association of Southern California.

Another long-standing program is the twelve-day purchasing and materials-management seminar offered by Michigan State University.[11] This program is also sponsored by NAPM. The courses are presented by a team of university faculty and outstanding practitioners in the field. Each year's program presents a varied and balanced selection of professional topics.

Still another variation is the certificate program in procurement and grants management offered by the University of Virginia School of Continuing Education.[12] Although part of a certificate program, each course earns three semester hours of college credit. Twelve courses are offered. They include work in purchasing and materials management, contract law and administration, and grants management. This represents only a small part of the range of education and training available. Local chapters of the professional associations can suggest locally available programs.

Many of the programs carry designated numbers of semester hours of college credit. Most that do not earn continuing education units under a system developed and conducted by the Council on the Continuing Education Unit.[13]

Professional Certification

The most significant development in the staffing area has been certification, long required in the fields of medicine, pharmacy, law, and engineering. The accounting profession also long ago provided for the certification of public accountants (the CPA), and later the management accountant (CMA). In these and other cases, certification attests that the individual has attained a prescribed level of knowledge through formal course work or examination, has completed a prescribed minimum term of work experience in the field, and has made a commitment to a standard of behavior and performance. Holders of a professional certificate can present themselves to the community as possessing greater values and potential than the uncertified.

The need for a certification system for the purchasing occupation has long been recognized by both government and industry. The National Institute of Governmental Purchasing (NIGP), organized in 1944, had as one of its objectives the academic training of public-purchasing agents. The NAPM as early as 1953 worked out a professional-development plan with the Illinois Institute of Technology for training industrial purchasing agents. In 1960 the California Association of Public Purchasing Officers prepared a format for certification of public purchasing agents. As early as 1931 the Purchasing Officers Association of Great Britain introduced formalized training for buyers and purchasing agents in industrial buying, and in 1949 the British Institute of Public Supplies was founded to support a similar service for governmental buyers. Most recently the National Contract Management Association (NCMA) has developed a certification plan. Canada has adopted a training and certification plan for its national purchasing personnel based upon the NIGP plan.

NIGP has developed a comprehensive professional development program that guides the public purchaser to certification as a certified public purchasing officer (CPPO). The CPPO has been officially recognized by the National Association of State Purchasing Officials (NASPO) as a criterion for selecting and promoting individuals involved in the purchasing activities of the state governments. The Department of Defense has coded the CPPO designation into its automated career management system. And several local jurisdictions formally recognize the CPPO as a meaningful standard for employment and advancement of public-purchasing personnel.

The certified professional contracts manager program (CPCM) was established by NCMA in 1974 and is available to both members and nonmembers. Applicants must possess a bachelor's degree and have completed certain specialized courses to qualify to take a written examination. This certification has also been officially accepted and recognized by the Department of Defense and other government agencies and by numerous companies.

The certified purchasing manager (C.P.M.) program is conducted by NAPM using the testing facilities and network of the Educational Testing Service. The C.P.M. designation has been adopted by three other professional organizations: the National Purchasing Institute (NPI), the National Association of Educational Buyers (NAEB), and the California Association of Public Purchasing Officers (CAPPO).

The most recent development has been the joining of NIGP and NASPO to create the Universal Public Purchasing Certification Council. CPPO certification is the means by which the council denotes individuals who have attained an acceptable level of professional competence in the management of supervision of purchasing in public or governmental agencies, jurisdictions, institutions, or authorities. Designation as a professional public buyer (PPB) is the means by which the council denotes those individuals who have attained a prescribed level of competence as a buyer in public or governmental purchasing. The qualification standards used in establishing these levels of competence represent the minimum knowledge and experience necessary to cover the responsibilities that are normally associated or are directly or indirectly related to the purchasing function at the management and the buyer levels, respectively.

The certification council states that it recognizes that the public-purchasing function is carried out by purchasing personnel in all levels of government and in various types of organizational arrangements. Therefore these two programs have been established to meet the requirements of all public-purchasing entities.

The basic requirement of eligibility to become a CPPO is a minimum of six years' experience in a purchasing, procurement, materials-management, contract-administration, or logistics-management position, of which at least four years of management or supervisory experience must have been acquired in a public- or governmental-purchasing position. Typical qualifying positions at which the required experience can be attained include, but are not limited to the following: the director, manager, agent, or any other person in charge of purchasing, procurement, materials management, contract administration or logistics management, or a directly related activity; an assistant, supervisor, chief buyer, buyer, purchasing analyst, or other purchasing specialist in an activity indicated above; and an executive employed by NIGP or an affiliated association or organization. The otherwise eligible candidate normally takes both a written and an oral examination, although there are provisions for exemption from the written examination. The examinations cover a broad range of material dealing with purchasing management, business and public administration, and elective subjects in fields such as economics, marketing, data processing, human behavior, and statistical quality control.

To become a PPB, an individual must have a minimum of four years' experience in a purchasing, procurement, materials-management, contract administration, or logistics-management position, of which at least two years' experience must have been acquired in a public- or other governmental-purchasing position. Typical qualifying positions at which the four years' experience may be attained are the same as those for the CPO program. Typical qualifying positions also include such related functions such as value analysis, inventory control, traffic and transportation, distribution, logistics, or any other functions such as specification writing, inspection, receiving, stores and warehousing, other than routine clerical or recordkeeping. Candidates for PPB designation must also pass or be exempted from a written examination. Further details on the CPPO and PPB can be obtained from the institute.

The NCMA requires that applicants for certification have a minimum of a bachelor's degree and two years of contracting-procurement-purchasing experience. Formal course work must include two courses in procurement and contracting; four related courses in fields such as accounting, manufacturing, and logistics; one course in the legal area; and one in finance. A written examination addresses the conceptual aspects of procurement and contracting and specific topics in legal aspects, finance, economics, accounting, production and logistics. Further details on the CPCM can be obtained from the association.[14]

It is common practice to require recertification at five-year intervals through age fifty-five. Recertification requires continuing professional activity and education. Failure to meet recertification criteria results in inactivation of the certificate. At age fifty-five, with fifteen years of professional experience, those otherwise eligible are considered for the conferral of lifetime certificates.

Certificates may also be revoked for cause, usually documented evidence of violation of the standards of behavior and performance.

Notes

1. The most widely cited text and reference on management concepts, including organizing and staffing, is Harold Koontz and Cyril O'Donnell, *Management: A Systems and Contingency Analysis of Managerial Functions*, 6th ed. (New York: McGraw-Hill, 1976).

2. U.S. Small Business Administration, *U.S. Government Purchasing and Sales Directory*, PA-6 (Washington, D.C.: Government Printing Office, 1978).

3. The immediately following paragraphs are extracted and edited from Council of State Governments, *State and Local Government Purchasing* (Lexington, Ky., 1975), pp. 3.3-3.5.

4. Ibid., pp. 3.5-3.9.

5. Based upon a listing developed by Stanley N. Sherman as part of his work with the Commission on Government Procurement. The items included represent the opinion of some five hundred respondents in a personal survey.

6. The survey, conducted by Daniel D. Roman of the George Washington University, is entitled, "Purchasing as an Academic Discipline: A Survey of Community Colleges, Four-Year Colleges and Universities Offering Courses in Purchasing and Materials Management" (New York: National Association of Purchasing Management, 1978).

7. Write to: Management Sciences Training Center, Bureau of Training (ATTN: TOS) U.S. Office of Personnel Management, 1900 E Street, NW, Washington, D.C. 20415.

8. Write to: National Institute of Governmental Purchasing, Inc., Suite 101, Crystal Square 3, 1735 Jefferson Davis Highway, Arlington, Virginia 22202.

9. Write to: Procurement Associates, Inc., 733 North Dodsworth Avenue, Covina, California 91724.

10. Write to: UCLA Extension, 10995 LeConte Avenue, Los Angeles, California 90024.

11. Write to: Director of Continuing Education, NAPM, 336 Oswego, Park Forest, Illinois 60466.

12. Write to: University of Virginia, School of Continuing Education, Charlottesville, Virginia 22906.

13. The Continuing Education Unit system is administered by Council on the CEU, 13000 Old Columbia Pike, Silver Spring, Maryland 20904.

14. Write to: National Contract Management Association, Attn: Certification Program, 6728 Old McLean Village Drive, McLean, Virginia 22101.

5 Political and Legal Considerations in Public Purchasing

Political and legal considerations in public purchasing vary considerably with the level of government at which the purchasing activity is conducted. Political considerations relate to the overall policy and general conduct of affairs of the governmental unit. Legal considerations evolve from the rules, procedures, and methods prescribed by law at the level, or higher level, of jurisdiction. The level of government could be national, state, a political subdivision, a local entity, or a local or regional public authority.

Political Considerations

The most basic political consideration is protection of the public interest and the public treasury. It is for this reason that the statutes concerning purchasing at all levels have been enacted. Closely related is the requirement that the public-purchasing process be open and visible and thus help to ensure the entity of the system. There are also more specific overall policy and political guidelines.[1]

1. The needs of the public sector will be procured from private enterprise to the maximum extent.

2. Governmental purchasing will be based upon fairness and equity and will abide by accepted business principles.

3. Governmental purchasing will rely upon and promote effective competition, to ensure the availability of alternative offers that provide a range of concept, design, performance, price, total cost, service, and delivery. The competitive entry of new vendors will be facilitated.

4. Vendors to the government will be provided the opportunity to earn a profit commensurate with the contribution made to meeting public needs and comparable to the profit made in commercial endeavors requiring similar investment, technical and financial risk, and skills.

5. Governmental purchasing will meet public needs at the lowest total cost, recognizing and accepting within the prices paid all ordinary and customary costs accepted in commercial practice.

6. Vendors to the government will be paid promptly, and interest will be paid by the government to the contractor in cases where payment is unduly delayed.

7. Government surveillance of vendor operations and performance will be held to the minimum necessary to ensure satisfactory performance.

8. Governmental purchasing will encourage innovation and the application of new technology by stating needs so that prospective suppliers will have maximum latitude to exercise independent business and technical judgment.

9. Governmental purchasing will take into account the impact of awards of contracts in counteracting unemployment and poverty.

10. To the maximum extent possible, governmental purchasing will provide opportunities to new- and small-business concerns and to minority firms.

11. Government contracts will require vendor compliance with laws and rules pertaining to equal-employment opportunity, air and water cleanliness, and occupational health and safety.

The Uniform Commercial Code and the
Model Procurement Code

The Uniform Commercial Code (UCC) was promulgated by the American Law Institute and the National Conference of Commissioners on Uniform State Laws, with the endorsement of the American Bar Association (ABA). It was completed in the Fall of 1951. The first state to enact the UCC was Pennsylvania in 1953. Revised versions of the UCC were issued in 1956, 1958, and 1962. Over the years, all states except Louisiana have adopted most provisions of the UCC.

The UCC protects the parties to a commercial transaction to the end that the aggrieved party may be put in as good a position as if the other party had fully performed. Article 2 of the UCC, referred to as UCC-Sales, covers contract for sale and the various steps of performance. It defines the terms involved and the several types of transactions.[2] These are the more significant and frequently cited provisions of the UCC. The reader should refer to the complete code for additional provisions.

According to the UCC, contracts for $500 or more are not enforceable unless in writing and unless signed by the party against whom enforcement is sought. The writing must indicate that a contract was made, but it is not insufficient merely because certain terms are omitted or incorrectly stated. Exceptions to this provision are found when the goods involved are to be specifically manufactured, are not suitable for sale to others, and/or the seller has begun work on the goods. An exception would also be found if payment had been made because this would indicate that a contract existed. Also if the aggrieved party can prove a signed confirmation to which the party charged did not object within ten days of receipt, the contract is enforceable though not signed by the party charged.

The contract may be in any form sufficient to show agreement, even though one or more terms are left open. The offer to buy or sell may be held open for a stated or reasonable time not exceeding three months. Acceptance may be in any manner, including shipment of the goods if the offer requests prompt or current shipment. Additional or different terms of acceptance become part of the contract unless the offer expressly limits acceptance to the term of the offer, they materially alter it, or written notification or objection is given within a reasonable time.

If the court as a matter of law finds the contract or any clause of the contract to have been unconscionable at the time it was made, the court may refuse to enforce the contract.

A contract implies that goods are merchantable—that is, they would pass without objection in the trade under the contract description. They are fit for the ordinary purpose for which such goods are used; they are of the quality and quantity described; they are adequately contained, packaged, and labeled; they are fit for a particular purpose; and the buyer should be able to rely upon the seller's skill or judgment to furnish suitable goods. Any exclusion or modification of the warranted merchantability of the goods must be explicit, for example, an as is where is clause.

In the event of improper delivery or performance, the buyer has the right to reject all of the goods, accept all, or accept any commercial unit(s) and reject the rest. The seller has the right to a reasonable time in which to correct the improper delivery. If goods are accepted by the buyer with knowledge of nonconformity, the acceptance cannot be revoked. If the buyer accepts goods and later finds concealed nonconformity, the acceptance may be revoked. Damage claims for accepted defective goods are not barred.

In the event of delay or failure to make delivery, the buyer has a variety of rights. He may cancel the contract. He may cover—that is, may purchase from another vendor and claim the difference in cost from the nonperforming seller. He may make a claim for damages and losses growing out of the delay or nondelivery. If the seller has become insolvent, the buyer may claim identifiable goods he has paid for. The buyer may request a decree for specific performance. On the seller's side, the seller may be excused if performance has been made impractical by the occurrence of a contingency the nonoccurrence of which was a basic assumption on which the contract was made. The seller must give the buyer reasonable notification of the occurrence. When the seller claims this excuse, the buyer has the right to terminate an unexecuted portion of the contract, modify the contract, or let it lapse.

The Model Procurement Code (MPC) was promulgated by the Section of Local Government Law and the Section of Public Contract Law of the ABA. It was completed in 1978, and that year the first state, Kentucky, enacted it. (The Kentucky Model Procurement Code is reproduced in Appendix C.)

The MPC provides the statutory guidance for the conduct of procurement of supplies, services, and construction by state and local governments; and administrative and judicial remedies for the resolution of controversies relating to public contracts. Unless specifically displaced by the provisions of the MPC, the principles of law and equity, including the UCC supplement the provision of the MPC. Managers responsible for public purchasing must therefore be familiar with both the UCC and the MPC.

The MPC provides a statutory framework consisting of twelve proposed articles.[3]

Article 1 states the general purposes of the code, specifies its applicability, provides guidance for interpretations, and contains definitions of terms used in more than one article.

Article 2 sets forth the basic organizational concepts for establishing procurement policy and for conduct of the procurement function; contains alternative language for implementation of the policy responsibilities; and provides for exemptions from central procurement and for training of procurement personnel.

Article 3 establishes competitive sealed bidding as the preferred method for contracting but also authorizes the use of other source-selection methods in appropriate, specified situations. The other source-selection methods are competitive sealed proposals, small-purchase procedures, sole-source procurement, emergency procurements, and a competitive selection procedure for designated types of services. The article contains requirements for contracting by each method. Contracts not awarded by competitive sealed bidding generally require a written justification, which is a matter of public record. The article prohibits cost-plus-a-percentage-of-cost contracts but permits the use of any other type of contract. It also requires the submission of cost or pricing data for contracts awarded without adequate price competition and for contract price adjustments.

Article 4 contains requirements for developing, monitoring, and using specifications. It requires that specifications be written in a manner to maximize competition to the extent possible.

Article 5 covers special aspects of construction procurement, including the promulgation of regulations to facilitate the use of various construction contracting and management methods; use of bid, performance, and payment bonds; and contract clauses for change orders, variations in estimated quantities, suspension of work, and termination. It also establishes criteria for making price adjustments due to changes and variations in estimated quantities. The article includes provisions governing the competitive award of contracts for architect-engineer services in lieu of competitive sealed bidding or competitive sealed proposals as provided in article 3.

Article 6 authorizes the use of clauses in contracts for supplies and services covering changes and variations in estimated quantities and sets forth the criteria for making price adjustments pursuant to such clauses. It also authorizes the inclusion of other clauses, including liquidated damages, excusable delay, and termination.

Article 7 provides for the promulgation of regulations establishing cost principles to be used to determine types of costs reimbursable under cost-type contracts.

Article 8 establishes requirements for control over the life cycle of supplies procured and criteria for management, transfer, and disposal of surplus property.

Article 9 provides disputes-resolution mechanisms for controversies relating to contract solicitations and awards, contract performance, and debarment or suspension determinations. In addition, this article provides procedures for handling contracts awarded in violation of law.

Article 10 authorizes cooperative procurement efforts among units of government. It permits standardization of specifications for use by several jurisdictions, joint use of real and personal property, and sharing of personnel among local governments and between a state and its political subdivisions. The article also holds that a state, at the request of other jurisdictions, may provide procurement information and technical services to those jurisdictions.

Article 11 provides administrative procedures for assisting small and disadvantaged businesses in learning how to do business with the enacting jurisdiction. This article could be used to incorporate state socioeconomic policies that are to be implemented through the procurement process.

Article 12 contains ethical standards with accompanying sanctions that are applicable to all participants in the public-procurement process. The proposed ethical standards cover conflicts of interest, gratuities and kickbacks, contingent fees, and misuse of confidential information. Additionally this article authorizes the establishment of an ethics commission with authority to render advisory opinions to participants in the procurement process.

Legal Aspects of Federal Procurement

The legal setting of federal-level purchasing is being dramatically altered. On 3 February 1978, the Congress passed Public law 95-224, the Federal Grant and Cooperative Agreement Act (1977).[4] It is now considering a bill referred to as the Federal Acquisition Reform Act.[5] Together they draw a sharp distinction between federal grant and cooperative-assistance relationships and federal procurement relationships, and they provide new policies, methods, and criteria for the acquisition of property and services by the federal government. (Public law 95-224 is reproduced in Appendix A; the Federal Acquisition Reform Act in Appendix B.)

Public law 95-224 requires that each executive agency shall use a type of procurement contract as the legal instrument reflecting a relationship between the federal government and a state or local government or other recipient (a) whenever the principal purpose of the instrument is the acquisition, by purchase, lease, or barter, of property or services for the direct benefit or use of the federal government, or (b) whenever an executive agency determines in a specific instance that the use of a type of procurement contract is appropriate. Second, each executive agency shall use a type of grant agreement as the legal instrument reflecting a relationship between the federal government and a state or local government or other recipient whenever: (a) the principal purpose of the relationship is the transfer of money, property, services, or anything else of value to the state or local government or other recipient in order to accomplish a public purpose of support or stimulation authorized by federal statute, rather than acquisition, by purchase, lease, or barter, of property or services for the direct benefit or use of the federal government; and (b) no substantial involvement is anticipated between the executive agency, acting for the federal government, and the state or local government or other recipient during performance of the contemplated activity. Third, each executive agency shall use a type of cooperative agreement as the legal instrument reflecting a relationship between the federal government and a state or local government or other recipient whenever: (a) the principal purpose of the relationship is the transfer of money, property, services, or anything else of value to the state or local government or other recipient to accomplish a public purpose of support or stimulation authorized by federal statute, rather than acquisiton, by purchase, lease, or barter, of property or services for the direct benefit or use of the federal government; and (b) substantial involvement is anticipated between the executive agency, acting for the federal government, and the state or local government or other recipient during performance of the contemplated activity.

The Federal Acquisition Reform Act as proposed will include several requirements. The first is that there be promulgated a single uniform procurement regulation, replacing the existing two regulations, the Armed Service Procurement Regulations and the Federal Procurement Regulation. The primary method of procurement will be by competitive sealed bids, competitive negotiation, and simplified small-purchase procedures for purchases under $10,000. Contracts may be of any type or combination of types consistent with the degree of technical and financial risk to be undertaken by the contractor, except that the cost-plus-a-percentage-of-cost contract shall not be used under any circumstances. The preferred contract type shall be fixed price. Contracts must contain a warranty that no person or agency has been employed to solicit the contract for a commission, percentage, brokerage, or contingent fee. The government may annul without liability contracts breaching the warranty.

When in the best interests of the government, a contracting officer may cancel a purchase order, cancel an invitation to bid before or after opening, and cancel a request for proposal and reject the offer. Upon request the contracting officer will inform the offerers or bidders of his reasons.

Contracts may be made for the acquisition of property or service over periods not in excess of five years where the need is reasonably firm and continuing, and such a contract will promote economies.

Agencies may make advance, progress, or partial payments under contracts, with certain safeguards and security. They may remit all or part of liquidated damages provided by the contract for delay in performing.

Any agency having reason to believe that a bid or proposal offers evidence of a violation of the antitrust laws, or of this act, shall refer the matter to the attorney general.

For firms doing business with the government for whom 75 percent of the dollar volume of revenue is from commercial or competitive government contracts, certain surveillance—such as cost-accounting standards and independent research agreements—will be waived.

The government shall pay interest to the contractor or any amount due the contractor for more than thirty days. The rate of interest shall be that established by the secretary of the treasury.

The secretary of commerce shall obtain notice of and publish announcements of all proposed acquisitions of $10,000 or more. Certain exceptions for security and urgency are allowed.

Threshold amounts, such as the $10,000 small-purchase figure, shall be reviewed every three years. Government specification shall be reviewed every five years.

Agency heads may delegate and assign purchasing responsibilities so as to facilitate the acquisition of property or service, creating joint or combined offices as appropriate.

The comptroller general shall provide for the inexpensive, informal, and expeditious resolution of protests.

Legal Aspects of State, County, and City Purchasing

Because state and local laws are so numerous, and their coverage so diverse, it is not feasible to extract specific provisions as was done with federal law. The Kentucky Model Procurement Code, Appendix C, has been cited. Appendix D is an example of a county ordinance, that of Prince George's County, Maryland.

In a pioneering effort, the Council of State Governments in 1975 published a report that included research of purchasing statutes and regulations of all the states, major counties, and cities.[6] The research led to a tabulation of essential statutory and regulatory elements. The report develops a structure of these elements recommending that the purchasing statute and/or rules and regulations adopted pursuant to the statute should:

1. Establish a central purchasing authority to manage and control all purchasing activities. Define central purchasing's authorities and responsibilities, provide for and designate the scope of its delegation authority, and exclude any blanket statutory exemptions. Require that using agencies adhere to pertinent statutory, regulatory, and central operational policies and requirements when purchase authority is delegated to them; also, direct the central purchasing authority to oversee and control all delegated purchasing activities. Require that central purchasing promulgate implementing rules and regulations, and written policies. Define the organizational placement of the central purchasing authority, ensuring that sufficient authority, independence, and safeguards are provided to foster the goals and objectives of the purchasing program. Set forth a declaration of policy for the purchasing program.

2. Charge the central purchasing authority with the responsibility for developing and managing a planning and scheduling program. Provide purchasing with the authority to review the validity and program appropriateness of purchases. Provide that purchasing establish a data information system adequate to carry out its planning and scheduling responsibilities. Require using agencies to submit usage and requirements data to central purchasing, as designated by central purchasing. Provide that purchasing maintain an ongoing program to consolidate requirements whenever practicable and to utilize term contracting and scheduled purchase techniques, as appropriate. Permit the central purchasing authority to enter into multiyear contracts (subject to the availability of funds).

3. Require that a list of qualified bidders be established and used. Set forth the policy for prequalification of bidders. Set forth the conditions under which bidders should be deleted from the bidders list and the attendant procedures to be used, i.e., reinstatement, period of suspension, notice to the bidder, and the right to an administrative review.

4. Provide that competitive procedures be used for purchase of all commodities and services. Require sealed competitive bids for all purchases expected to exceed a predetermined dollar value. Require legal notice for all purchases expected to exceed a predetermined dollar amount. Require the central purchasing authority to issue invitations for Bids to a large enough group of potential suppliers to assure adequate competition. Where formal sealed bids are required, the general rule should be that all bidders list for the item be solicited. Provision should be made for exception to this general rule if it is not feasible or necessary, under given circumstances. For all such exceptions, there should be a requirement for written documentation which supports the decision not to solicit all bidders on the bidders list. Charge the central purchasing authority with responsibility for final review and approval of Invitations for Bids. Permit central purchasing to use competitive negotiation when the conventional formal sealed bid process is determined to be inappropriate, in accordance with guidelines contained

in written rules. Designate the basic criteria permitted for evaluating bids and proposals and for awarding contracts.

5. Allow the purchasing official discretionary authority to require a bid security or bid bond adequate to protect the interest of the government and, when security is elected, require equal bid security and bid bond of all bidders. Require the purchasing official to establish procedures for maintaining accountability over bid deposits and their funds.

6. Require that the conditions and circumstances under which the requirements for obtaining competition may be waived be set forth in writing. Provide for the waiver of competition when certain designated officials determine, in accordance with written rules, that it is required to meet an emergency situation, requiring that such officials consult with the purchasing official whenever practicable before making an emergency purchase, and requiring documentation of the conditions that made the emergency purchase necessary, the method of purchase, and purchase price(s) of the commodities that were purchased. Provide for waiver of competition where the commodities or services lack responsible competition, where there are patented or proprietary rights, where standardization or interchangeability is demonstrated as advantageous to the governmental unit, and where only one source can supply the needed items, requiring that all such instances be justified in writing and approved by the central purchasing authority, in accordance with written rules.

7. Preclude the use of restrictive specifications and "most favored" customer pricing clauses. Empower the central purchasing authority, when identical bids are received, to make the award in any reasonable manner that will discourage the submission of identical bids. Define the reasons and conditions allowing "schedule contracts" and "multiple awards". Require that bidders submit statements of noncollusion with all bids. Provide criminal penalties for collusive bidding unless specifically provided elsewhere. Empower the central purchasing authority to take whatever action is appropriate to purchase needed items for which acceptable competitive bids cannot be obtained and require that these actions be justified in writing and documented in files which will be public record.

8. Permit bidders and the general public to attend bid openings. Require a tabulation of bids that is recorded and made available to the public.

9. Provide that awards under the formal sealed bid process be made to the "lowest responsible bidder who submits a responsive bid which is most advantageous to the government." Require that the central purchasing authority publish written criteria, policies, and procedures governing the evaluation-award process. Establish that any form of state or local preference is neither acceptable nor allowable. Allow for discretion on the part of purchasing officials in acting in the best interest of the government and when no bids are received or when the response to a solicitation is otherwise inadequate. Provide the authority to reject all bids, or to reject any bid in whole or in part, in accordance with written policies and guidelines, and provide authority to take alternate courses of action, as necessary.

10. Provide for public access to an openness of the procurement process by requiring the publication of all purchasing laws, rules, regulations, and procedures; public notice of all solicitations of bids, awards, and

major contract changes; documentation of all actions in the procurement process, particularly waivers of competitive bidding and public access to bid openings and all records except unopened bids, documents on which an award is pending, and vendors' proprietary data.

11. Provide for criminal penalties for attempting to influence awards through offers of reward, and for accepting such rewards; and provide that all guilty parties shall be financially liable to the government for any losses that the government incurred as a result of any contract which was so awarded. Provide that contracts are void if they result from a conflict of interest; if they were awarded to a person or firm that tried to influence the award by offering something of value to a government employee; or if a contract is awarded by a government official or employee by circumventing statutory requirements. Provide that conflict-of-interest statutes cover all government personnel who are in a position to influence contract awards, including the chief executive, legislators, cabinet-rank officials, department heads, officers, and employees, as well as their spouses. Specify the types of actions which constitute conflicts of interest. Classify as a felony all violations of the conflict-of-interest statutes. Require immediate dismissal from office for government employees convicted of a conflict-of-interest violation. Provide that, where contracts are declared void because they resulted from a conflict of interest, the public employee involved will be liable to the government for the amount of his profit plus the amount of any loss that the government suffered as a result of the contract. Set forth the conditions under which the government may be liable for a contractor's provable costs under a contract which resulted from a conflict of interest. Require that the chief purchasing official maintain surveillance to detect "back-door selling" and prescribe suitable penalties for suppliers and government employees who engage in this practice. Require a bond to protect the government against all losses caused by malfeasance or misfeasance of government officers or employees who can influence the award of public contracts, if no provision is made for such a bond elsewhere in government legislation.

12. Require that a code or standard of conduct be published to govern the performance of government employees, and especially purchasing personnel, in managing, purchasing, or otherwise expending government funds. Provide for criminal, civil, and administrative sanctions; penalties; and disciplinary actions for violation of such standards either by government officers or employees or by contractors or their agents. Establish personal liability for government personnel who authorize purchases to be made without following applicable statutes and rules.

13. Charge central purchasing with the responsibility for establishing a specification program and a standardization program, with written policies and procedures. Provide central purchasing with the authority, under defined conditions and with each action suitably documented, to waive competitive bidding for the purpose of buying articles for experiment, test, or trial. Grant the central purchasing authority the power to review, and approve specifications. Require that central purchasing establish and administer a formal inspection and testing program.

14. Charge central purchasing with the responsibility for overall supervision and ultimate control over both the inventory and surplus programs. Require that the using agency identify surplus items, declare them as such, and report them to purchasing. Provide that the proceeds from disposition be credited to the owning agency. Grant central purchasing the authority to dispose of surplus and scrap, or to regulate its disposal, in a manner that it deems to be in the government's best interest. Assign central purchasing the task of keeping informed of items available under federal surplus programs (state statute only). Grant central purchasing the authority to operate and regulate any state program related to federal surplus programs (state statute only).
15. Explicitly provide the authority for intergovernmental cooperative purchasing, under rules and procedures established by the central purchasing authority. Provide that cooperative purchasing be permitted only when the purchasing jurisdiction assuming administrative responsibility conducts its purchasing operations to the principles of open competition.
16. Provide a statement of intent encouraging affiliation by purchasing officials and their technical staffs with one or more professional purchasing associations. Require that government personnel have the authority to prepare and maintain position specifications for the full spectrum of purchasing jobs. These specifications should reflect the current thinking of appropriate associations as to job content and credentials. Embody as part of the policy statement in the purchasing law an affirmation of the management role of public purchasing officials.

Also available for the guidance of local jurisdiction is a model purchasing ordinance drafted in 1954 by the National Institute of Municipal Law Officers (NIMLO) in cooperation with the National Institute of Governmental Purchasing.[7] The language is specifically keyed to the municipal level. These ordinance provisions were developed long before the more inclusive work of the Council of State Governments. All of the recommended elements are included in the council's itemization.

Types of Contracts and Contractual Devices

A contract is an agreement that creates a legal obligation. Generally it requires no special form, no witnesses, no seals, and no registration. A contract consists of three essential elements: an offer, an acceptance and a consideration. An offer is a proposal either explicit or implied to exchange an act for a promise, or vice-versa. The proposal that constitutes an offer must be fairly definite to serve as the basis for a contract. For a contract to be created, the offer must be accepted. This can be communicated in a variety of ways to include actual performance of the act offered. Consideration is the act of giving something in return for an offer. Regardless of how miniscule the commitment may be, it is necessary in the creation of a contract.

With few exceptions, contracts entered into by public-purchasing officials are written. As the complexity of the product or service being acquired increases, the contracts increase in complexity because the performance desired and provided must be described in more detail. The consideration must be more specifically spelled out, reflecting the agreement reached with regard to the sharing of risks and rewards.

Over the years many variations in type of contract have evolved, each reflecting a different degree of risk relating to the circumstances surrounding the contract. Originally most of the types in use were defined in connection with military procurement. Today the terms and definitions are quite generally understood and are widely used in purchasing law and regulations. There are two broad categories of contracts—fixed-price contracts and cost-reimbursement contracts—and each has variations.

Fixed-Price Contracts

Firm fixed price (FFP) is an agreement to pay a specified price when the items called for by the contract have been delivered and found to meet the specification. No price adjustment is made for the original work after award. The contractor thus assumes all financial risk and his profit depends entirely on his ability to manage his performance of the contract. Such a contract depends upon the availability of a reasonably definite specification and full agreement at the outset as to a fair and reasonable price. The FFP contract is the preferred type in most instances.

Fixed price with escalation (FPE) is an agreement to provide for the upward or downward revision of the stated price upon the occurrence of specified contingencies. The escalation is tied to recognized indexes, such as the price indexes of basic commodities or of labor hourly rates. Usually there is a limit, a ceiling, on upward adjustment. Such indexing of prices is used more and more frequently in periods of inflation.

Fixed-price incentive with firm targets (FPIF) is an agreement to pay a dollar incentive based upon reduced costs, early delivery, or improved end-item performance. Targets are established and formulas are agreed upon by which profits will be adjusted and overruns (or underruns) will be shared, on a formula, between the government and the vendor. A price ceiling and a floor are set. This type of contract is used when exact pricing at the outset is impossible, but estimated (target) price could be agreed upon.

Fixed-price incentive with successive targets (FPIS) is similar to the FPIF, except that a series of targets and formulas apply at different stages of performance of the contract. The last target and formula, prior to final delivery, is seen as either a FFP or FPIF. This type of contract is used only in the most uncertain pricing situations.

Fixed price with prospective price redetermination (FPRP) is an agreement that at certain stated times during performance of the contract, the price will be redetermined. A supplier may be willing to place a price on only the first of many increments of a large order with a long lead time. A firm price would be stated for the initial quantity, and as the time for a second increment approached, a new price would reflect the experience gained on the initial increment supplied.

Fixed price with retroactive price redetermination (FPRR) is an agreement to reprice the contract after completion. A ceiling price would be established at time of award. The repricing would be based upon audited final cost-data.

Cost-Reimbursement Contracts

Cost-reimbursement contracts are used when the information available is not adequate to support a mutually acceptable fixed-price arrangement. Since any item of cost might be challenged, the government must have specific policy as to what costs are allowable, reasonable, and allocable to the contract. Also specific policy is necessary as to the size of the fee (profit) that will be allowed on top of the allocated costs. This is usually stated as a percentage of a target cost.

Cost-reimbursement contract (CR) is an agreement to reimburse the supplier only for the allowable and allocable costs of the job. There is no ceiling on costs, and no fee is paid as such; instead the government pays whatever the vendor's accounting system can justify. This type of contract is used only when the uncertainties of performance are of great magnitude and reasonable cost estimates are impossible.

Cost sharing (CS) is an agreement that the supplier will assume part of the cost of performance. Presumably the supplier would expect to receive some side benefits of the government contract—perhaps using the capability or skill developed in performance of the contract in connection with a related commercial venture. Such government participation in work of broader benefit to the economy should be encouraged.

Cost plus a percentage of cost (CPPC) is an agreement that the supplier will receive payment for the costs of performance plus a specified percentage of such costs as a fee. The profit increases automatically as the cost increases, thus providing an incentive to run up costs as high as possible. Historically this type of contract was used extensively in weapon procurement. Its use by federal agencies is now specifically prohibited by law.

Cost plus incentive fee (CPIF) is an agreement providing for the reimbursement of costs plus a variable fee. As with fixed-price incentive contracts, cost and fee targets and ceilings and floor would be negotiated for the various elements, but there would be no set total-price ceiling. Performance objectives would have to be quite well established for this to be used.

Cost plus award fee (CPAF) is an agreement that the contractor's final fee (profit) will vary depending upon the government's after the fact evaluation of the quality of performance. A base cost and fee is negotiated and a schedule of award fees is established. The base fee covers minimum performance, and the award fee is added onto that. This type of contract is used only where the quality and quantity of work performed cannot be measured until after performance.

Cost plus fixed fee (CPFF) is an agreement that the supplier will be reimbursed for all allowable and allocable costs plus a limited fixed fee. One form of such a contract requires a completed job; another form merely calls for a level of effort during a stated time period. Under such a contract the costs would vary, but the fee would not.

In large and complicated acquistion situations, such as a weapon system or a space probe, various combinations of these contracts are often used. Moreover there is no need for an entire project or program to be accomplished under a single approach.

Other Contractual Devices

Letter contracts are a device for authorizing immediate commencement of work on something of high priority or an emergency. It is a preliminary, temporary instrument that must be replaced by one of the definitive types of contracts within a specified time.

Time-and-materials contracts are usually used in procuring service, maintenance, overhaul, or emergency repairs. The rate per labor hour includes the price of supervision, and the prices of materials are covered by a schedule. The contractor is paid for work actually performed. Similar to this is the labor-hour contract, except here the materials are government furnished. The contractor provides only labor and supervision.

A definite-quantity, indefinite-delivery contract is used when purchasing a prescribed quantity of an item during a definite time period, but allowing for delivery or performance at designated locations on order. In one sense this is an inventory-management device because it requires the vendor to carry an inventory ready for the government's call; thus it is often referred to as a call contract. Requirements contracts are similar except that they do not specify quantity (they may set a floor and ceiling on quantity, however). The government expects the vendor to deliver whatever quantities are needed. This device is used for consumable supplies or for services that are common to many users in the proximity of the supplier. Ordinarily the government obligates itself to obtain all of its needs in an area from the single contractor. The contractor assumes inventory management and the related costs.

Indefinite-quantity, indefinite-delivery contracts are used for obtaining a vendor commitment to meet recurring needs for supplies or services when the government itself wishes to make only a minimum commitment. It is similar to a requirements contract except that minimum order quantities are specified; delivery is scheduled by the using activities.

A basic agreement is a written understanding between the procuring activity and a specific contractor as to the terms applicable to future procurement. This agreement, which facilitates and simplifies future relationships, should be periodically reviewed and updated.

Finally the basic-ordering agreement provides an itemized description of supplies and services anticipated to be procured and of term of delivery and inspection. Its use is designed to facilitate and simplify future purchases.

Governmental Purchasing and the Antitrust Laws

Public-purchasing officials must comply with the provisions of the various federal and state antitrust laws. They must recognize practices that are illegal under such laws and be alert to the detection of violations. A valuable reference is *Government Purchasing and the Antitrust Laws*, a joint effort of the National Association of Attorneys General and the National Association of State Purchasing Officers. A more general reference is *Public Policies Toward Business.*[8]

The federal and state antitrust statutes are designed to prohibit restraint of trade through the exercise of excessive market power or by unfair competitive practices. Federal laws govern transactions in or substantially affecting interstate commerce. In our present day economy, there are few transactions which can clearly be identified as not substantially affecting interstate commerce. However, there are transactions involving only interstate commerce, to which only the state antitrust laws apply.

Federal antitrust law consists of the Sherman Act (1890), the Federal Trade Commission Act (1914), and the Clayton Act (1914), which is amended by the Robinson-Patman Act (1936). Other amendments to antitrust law have been enacted, the latest being the Hart-Scott-Rodino Act (1976). Several state antitrust laws predate federal law. All states and territories have enacted antitrust legislation with the exceptions of Delaware, Guam, Pennsylvania, Rhode Island, Samoa, Vermont, and West Virginia.

Federal and state laws generally provide that violations may lead to criminal penalties, civil forfeitures, injunctions, and revocation of charter. A feature providing considerable strength in enforcement is that litigants may sue for treble damages, and many such claims have been recognized by the courts. Two types of restraint of trade are involved.

The first is horizontal restraints of trade. These include combination and conspiracies to influence prices by setting minimum prices, maximum prices, uniform markups, uniform discounts, or allowances or any other arrangement or understanding among competitors that would result in fixed prices, regardless of the fairness or reasonableness of the prices. Collusive bidding is an illegal practice frequently experienced by public purchasing officials. Also prohibited are agreements among vendors to divide or allocate business, perhaps geographically or by customer, a practice that divides the market and effectively removes competition. Evidence of this sort of collusion includes abstention from bidding. Agreements among vendors to refuse to bid or negotiate with an agency are also horizontal restraints. The vendors are, in effect, boycotting the agency in an attempt to coerce acceptance of an arrangement that might not be in the public interest. Multiple abstention from bidding or negotiating might indicate that such an agreement exists.

Restraints of trade can also be vertical. For example, a manufacturer or seller and the distributor may try to fix the resale price of a commodity. This is a complex concept because the legality of the price fixing depends upon who bears the risk of loss and who holds title to the property. Public-purchasing officials should be alert for evidence that distributors are being forced to sell at a dictated or suggested price. Attempts by a manufacturer or seller to forbid the purchase of competing products, to require purchase of a share of requirements from one supplier, or to establish sole distributorships are a second example. Buyers should be alert for situations in which a supplier does not have available competing substitute products. Yet a third example concerns attempts by a manufacturer or seller to require tie-in purchases; that is, making "item A" available only with the purchase of "item B". The often-cited sample is the computer manufacturer who requires that his machine be available only if the cards, tapes, or discs used are also obtained from him.

Under vertical restraint, purchasing officials should be alert to attempts to control a market through territorial restraints and to influence a buyer through refusal to deal unless the buyer does not deal with a competitor.

Antitrust law is complex and constantly evolving. Although the applicability of the Robinson-Patman Act, in particular, to public purchasing has been challenged, it is in the public interest to encourage competition for public business. Public buyers must act fully within federal and state antitrust laws. If they do not, they may be found guilty of inducing restraint of trade.

This chapter has concentrated on law specifically dealing with purchasing, and particularly public purchasing. Such law does not stand alone.

The public-purchasing and materials manager must be familiar with the more basic business law: the law of property, agency, negotiable instruments, patents, trademarks, copyrights, and broader aspects of the law of contracts.[9] Certain aspects of tax law—perhaps sales taxes or taxes on property and inventories—could arise. The manager should generally be familiar with traffic and transporation law and regulation and law and regulation establishing socioeconomic objectives. In all legally related matters the attitude of the purchasing manager should be preventive. He should be sufficiently aware of the law to detect and prevent potential violations and be alert to instances in which he should seek the advice of legal counsel.

Notes

1. This enumeration incorporates and integrates points from sect. II, the Federal Acquisition Reform Act, from "Federal Procurement Principles" (Washington, D.C.: Aerospace Industries Association, 1971), and from several state statutes.

2. The Uniform Commercial Code is included as an appendix in Townes Loring Dawson and Earl Winfield Mounce, *Business Law: Text and Cases*, 4th ed. (Lexington, Mass.: D.C. Heath and Company, 1979).

3. American Bar Association, *A Model Procurement Code for State and Local Governments* (final draft) (Washington, D.C.: American Bar Association, 1978).

4. U.S. Government, Public Law 95-224, The Federal Grant and Cooperative Agreement Act of 1977.

5. U.S. Congress, Senate, Committee on Governmental Affairs, *The Federal Acquisition Reform Act*, 96th Cong., 1st sess., 1979, S-5; and U.S. Congress, Senate, Committee on Governmental Affairs, *Federal Acquisition Act of 1977, Report to Accompany S.1264*, 95th Cong., 2d sess., 1978, S. Report 95-715.

6. Council of State Governments, *State and Local Government Purchasing* (Lexington, Ky., 1975).

7. National Institute of Municipal Law Officers, *NIMLO Model Purchasing Ordinance—Annotated* (Washington, D.C., n.d. [c. 1954]).

8. National Association of Attorneys General, *Government Purchasing and the Antitrust Laws* (Washington, D.C., 1977). Available from the Committee on the Office of the Attorney General, 3901 Barrett Drive, Raleigh, North Carolina, 27609; Clair Wilcox and William G. Sherherd, *Public Policies Toward Business*, 5th ed. (Homewood: Richard D. Irwin, 1975).

9. See Dawson and Mounce, *Business Law*.

6 Programming and Budgeting Considerations in Public Purchasing

As each public acquisition of goods or services is considered, two basic questions must be answered: (1) Has the requirement been clearly established? (2) Are funds available with which to purchase the needed goods or services?

Public funds to be used in the acquisition of goods, services, and construction are appropriated for that purpose by the Congress, the state legislature, the county board, or the city council.[1] The act of appropriation is based upon consideration of the budgetary requests of the many components of the governmental unit. The budgeting process involves a long series of actions, transaction, and controls. Purchasing and materials managers must have enough familiarity with the process to participate in and coordinate with it effectively. It will be seen that there are numerous interfaces between purchasing and materials-management subsystems and budgeting and financial management subsystems.

The budgeting process involves thirteen steps.

1. Authorization of the object of expenditure. The Congress and most legislatures hold that an object cannot be budgeted for unless it relates to some previously legislated purpose—perhaps the support of an army, the construction and furnishing of a hospital, or the maintenance of the price level of a farm crop. The legislature passes the several authorization acts.

2. Programming of acquisition. The agency charged by the legislature or the executive with achieving the stated purpose plans and programs the time-phased resource requirements: manpower, material, and money. The programming involves comparative analysis of alternative ways of meeting the requirements.

3. Preparation of the budget. The government's budget officer issues a call for the computation and submission of the funding needed to meet the time-phased resource requirements. The call specifies a fiscal period—either a single year or multiple years. The several budgetary inputs (funding requests) are developed and assembled.

4. Review and approval. Agency and governmental subdivision heads review the assembled budget, challenging, revising, adding, and deleting items. At the highest executive level, the total effort is approved and proposed to the legislature.

5. Appropriation. The legislature considers the proposed budget, taking such actions as it sees fit. One or more appropriation acts are passed

that authorize the requesting agencies and subdivisions to obligate the government financially. The term normally used is *new obligational authority* (NOA).

6. Appropriation accounting. The treasurer posts the additional obligational authority voted by the legislature to the accounts of each agency or subdivision, and they are formally notified by warrant of the legal limits of their spending.

7. Apportionment. Apportionment is a device that the chief executive uses to control the flow of obligational authority and to prevent overobligation. The executive (or the budget director) releases or impounds funds as that person feels appropriate.

8. Allotment, suballotment, allocation, and suballocation. Apportioned obligational authority is passed down through the chain of management, so each successive level of organization receives its share of the funding. At any level, management might hold back funds in reserve.

9. Commitment. At the operating level the manager commits the funds to a specific use and posts an estimated dollar amount as committed to that purchase.

10. Reprogramming. At any point in the process, prior to obligation, the funds may be reprogrammed (directed to some other purpose). Perhaps the original requirement has been overtaken by events, or a requirement of higher priority has arisen. Depending upon the magnitude of the reprogramming, higher executive or even legislative approval may be needed.

11. Obligation. Subsequent to commitment the buyer selects the successful bidder or negotiates the placement of an order, and a contract is signed. The government is now legally obligated to compensate the supplier upon performance.

12. Expenditure. When the contract is completed or accomplished to a point of progress payment, an invoice is presented and paid. The appropriated money has been expended.

13. Audit. The appropriate authority—for example, the General Accounting Office (GAO) or the state auditor general—examines the accounts of the contracting and disbursing officers, deals with any claims, and disciplines employees found guilty of violating funding conditions or controls.

The practical significance of this sequence is that contracting officers may not go beyond the express limitations on their obligational authority. They cannot, for example, enter into a contract in excess of an appropriation or a contract under an annual appropriation for more than the amount available in the current fiscal year. It is these statutory limitations that make it necessary to go through the annual budget process to provide express authorizations and appropriations.

At the national level, the Budget and Accounting Act (1921) establishes the national budget system. Under this act the president is required at the opening of each session of Congress to transmit a budget recommending appropriations within the several categories and identifying the substantive legislative authority for each program being funded. This is necessary because, in the absence of prior or concurrent legislative authorization, an appropriation is subject to a point of order on the floor of the House and if challenged must be stricken from the pending bill. The reason for this rule is organizational and jurisdictional: to ensure that the cognizant legislative committees have had the opportunity to review and approve or reject the program. If no point of order is raised, the appropriation act itself becomes the authority to enter into contracts and to make payments. At the state and local levels also the chief executives prepare and transmit their budget recommendations for legislative approval.

Authorization of the Object of Expenditure

Program authorizations may be permanent or recurring; if the latter, they may be annual or, less frequently, multiyear authorizations, which are provided by authorization acts each year. Permanent authorizations are found in an agency's organic legislation or other specific legislation of a continuing nature. Permanent authorizations generally are for personnel, maintenance, operations, housekeeping, repair, and minor improvement programs, as contrasted with capital-improvement or other major programs. For example, the president's budget cites permanent provisions in support of appropriations for operations and maintenance for the army, navy, marine corps, and air force. However, appropriations for construction must be preceded by specific acts authorizing such construction, item by item.

There has been a growing trend in recent years for Congress to require separate authorization acts as a prerequisite to appropriations. Thus specific authorization acts now are prescribed for the procurement of military aircraft, missiles, vessels, research and development, combat vehicles, torpedoes, and other weapons. Similar requirements have been extended to certain programs of the National Aeronautics and Space Administration, the Department of Energy, and the National Science Foundation, among others.

Other authorizations may provide formulas, such as a formula for determining a subsidy to be paid covering wage differentials, or determining the level of price supports for agricultural products. Also authorization acts often include general provisions that have a significant impact on purchasing. An act might place ceilings on the prices to be paid (for example, not more than $6,000 per passenger automobile.) Or an act might require special reporting of the economic or environmental impact of the program authorized. Recently authorization acts have required that certain vendors to the federal government report any employees of the firm who were formerly employees of the buying agency.

Many programs are authorized but not all are funded, and until they are funded, they remain in limbo. Some are deferred, some reduced, some abandoned. In addition to the intrinsic merits of each program, the government must consider the relation of total expenditures to total receipts, with an eye to achieving an overall balance between needs and resources. It, therefore, has to make a choice of priorities among competing programs, and to plan the resulting acquisitions.

Programming of Acquisition

A sequence of annual cycles of planning and programming addresses the problem of what should be acquired and when. Budgeting has been defined as a matter of allocating scarce resources. Management must take into account all of the competing demands, choose among them, and determine relative priorities. During this phase, the agency head, his advisers, and his staff examine alternatives and make decisions that will form the basis for preparation of the budget. During the programming phase, attention is focused on choice from among alternative programs to achieve objectives. For this purpose, cost and effectiveness comparisons are made, using largely statistical factors rather than the detailed information that will be developed and submitted in support of the budget submission. The subsequent budget preparation phase will concentrate on funding requirements to carry out the programming decisions.

In this phase, agency heads must examine four classes of questions by performing appropriate analyses:

1. How can the legislated purpose best be achieved? Are new organizations and methods called for, or can the purpose be accomplished with available resources?
2. If added resources are indicated, will capital expenditures be necessary? There must be identified for each major item all of the costs and the implications for effectiveness of continuing to use existing facilities and equipment, modernizing, converting, rehabilitating, or replacing.
3. What levels of operating effort will be involved, work loads and work schedules, direct costs in labor and material? How do cost and effectiveness vary with alternative levels of effort, alternative maintenance and production schedules, lower response rates? Could costs be reduced

without commensurate reduction in effectiveness by variation in activity levels?

4. Can management be improved? Are functions organized effectively? Do supporting activities appear to bear an appropriate relationship to program activities? Do programs appear well balanced and well thought out for the long range? Are there any hints of problems relating to cost and effectiveness that might later assume great importance?

Cost-Effectiveness Analysis

An integral part of programming is cost-effectiveness analysis. It can be a relatively simple quantitative comparison of data or an extensive study utilizing advanced mathematical techniques and relying upon computer calculations. Regardless of its complexity, there will be a necessary sequence of considerations: definition of objective, laying out of alternative ways of accomplishing the objective, calculation of how effectively each alternative accomplishes the objective, and calculation of how much each alternative costs. Each of these is fraught with problems. Given the generalizations of most stated objectives, it is not simple to define even the true objective of the establishment, let alone the objective of a single component or element of that establishment. Before cost-effectiveness analysis can proceed, the objective of the program under consideration must be identified and stated.

The laying out of alternative ways of accomplishing the objective requires identifying all reasonable alternatives and ensuring that none has been overlooked. This is a matter of experience and imagination. Once identified and evolved into resource requirements, the alternatives are ready for comparative evaluation. The two concepts of comparison are economically equivalent. The approach can be either to hold the budgeted cost while evaluating the relative effectiveness of the candidate systems, or to hold a predetermined level of effectiveness and determine at what cost each candidate can attain that effectiveness. The concept to be used can be selected purely on the basis of convenience.

The cost element of a cost-effectiveness analysis can be developed best in three categories: costs associated with the development of a new capability to the point where it is ready for operational use; costs beyond the development costs, required to introduce a new capability into operational use; and the costs of operating and maintaining the capability. In each of the three areas, cost determination is difficult. Costs drawn from contracting records apply only to the two categories of development and investment. Operating costs also hold some problems of cost identification.

Those considered in the analysis of each alternative should pick up all costs directly or indirectly stemming from a decision to follow that alternative. This requires an allocation of costs, some of which may be indirect and often joint or shared. Accounting judgments must be made as to the appropriateness of the many items to be charged: costs of auxiliary supplies and equipment, maintenance expense, personnel and training expense, and so forth.

Another consideration present in economic and systems analysis is that of treatment of sunk costs. These costs are not usually considered in such analysis on the ground that only future costs are relevant; decisions of the past that generated costs in the past are not relevant. Thus the cost-effectiveness analysis does not include sunk costs of the basic equipment, supporting facilities, inventories of parts and components, or anything else for which the investment has already been made. This consideration creates a bias in the direction of retention of older equipment to the extent that the initial investment value is not offset by high operating costs of the old system and the hoped-for relatively lower operating costs of the more modern system.

The effectiveness side of the cost-effectiveness function also presents several central problems. Basic to these is the fact that there is no common denominator or expression of value. Effectiveness must be measured in terms of consequences or results. To date there are no generally accepted quantitative measures of the effectiveness of most public programs.

Preparation of the Budget

The budget is prepared in support of, and within the context of, the agency's plans and programs. It must be as complete, informative, and accurate as possible. It must also be simple, concise, and understandable. In budgeting, requirements are recognized as competing with each other, and the process presupposes that all needs will not be funded. Therefore a large element of budget formulation consists of convincing superiors that requirements should be funded and that the monies can and will be used efficiently.

Budget preparation consists of a sequence of considerations progressing from plans and programs to requirements to levels of expenditure and then to compromises between the stated requirements and the desired level of expenditure. The process is linear for each fiscal period. The agency plans, programs, and budgets for, say, fiscal year 1980. It has done the same for 1978 and 1979 and will for 1981 and 1982. Therefore, at any one time, the agency is involved in one phase or another of perhaps five fiscal years.

The participants in budget preparation include the president, governor, or mayor; members of their cabinets; members of the Congress, legislature, or council; managers at all levels; and many others. These participants can be classified in the following way. Policy formulators and disseminators are those in a position to establish policy. These include the president, governor, mayor, advisers, and others who are in a position to chart the general course of the government. Agency planners and programmers are those who take whatever guidance they can get and translate it into time-phased plans and programs. They try to identify what the agency will be doing several years in the future. Agency budget officers are those who establish operating procedures and conduct the successive annual cycles of budget preparation. Requirements generators are agency operating people who take the plans and programs affecting them and compute the manpower, services, supplies, equipment, and construction needed to accomplish the parts of the plans and programs for which they are responsible. Assemblers are those who examine the requirements and put the pieces together by budget project, program, and appropriation. This is primarily an agency staff task directed by the agency budget officer. Agency approvers and forwarders are those who review and approve the agency-assembled requirements and funding request. This activity is generally done by a budget review board appointed by and/or chaired by the agency head, who approves and forwards to the central budget office her funding request for the coming fiscal period.

The funding request has four parts. The proposed appropriation includes appropriation language and dollar amounts. The second part is the schedule of proposed financial activity—lists of items to be acquired, staffing plans, and production and construction schedules—and the resulting expenditure patterns. Third is the justification supporting the proposed appropriation—prepared statements, backup information, staff studies, engineering studies, drawings, and photographs. The fourth part covers related legislative proposals, such as desired changes to authorization acts.

At the federal level, the material prepared by the agency conforms to OMB circular A-11, *Preparation and Submission of Annual Budget Estimates*. Most states and larger counties and cities have issued similar manuals.

The key individual during this phase is the agency budget officer. This person establishes and conducts the budget preparation and implementation systems, procedures, and methods; communicates to his agency policy and procedural guidance received from other sources; aids and assists in program and budget decision making; conducts budgetary reviews within the agency and subsequently assists in presenting the budget for higher review; accompanies agency witnesses testifying before the legislative committees, assisting as he can; and provides a focal point for financial management within his agency.

Review and Approval

Generally the central budget office includes teams of examiners expert in the various functions of government. Their task is to assemble, correlate, revise, reduce, or increase the funding requests of the departments and agencies. Their approach is to view the requests as having been prepared by program and function specialists—and then to apply to those requests such higher-level political and economic considerations as may seem appropriate. When agency requests are received, they are referred to the examiners, who should be thoroughly familiar with administrative policy and previous legislative action, as well as with the programs of the agency and their relationship to activities of other agencies. They give considerable attention to the bases for the individual estimates: the volume of work on hand and forecast, the methods by which the agency proposes to accomplish its objectives, the costs of accomplishment, and the estimates of requirements in terms of supplies, equipment, facilities, and numbers of people required. They review past performance, check the accuracy of factual information presented, and consider the future implications of the program. They identify program, budget, and management issues of major importance to be raised for discussion with agency representatives.

The examiners look at the detailed supporting computations and the reconciliation for each item for the past year, the current year, and the budget year. After their analysis, the examiners "mark up" the estimates with which they disagree. The agency head is allowed a brief period—perhaps two days—in which to object and ask for reconsideration. After any reconsideration, the examiners prepare their summaries of the issues and their recommendations for top executive review. This review, which concentrates on the major aspects of the requested financing, provides an opportunity for senior officials to obtain from the examiners an understanding of agency program aspirations and budget requests, an analysis of the significant issues involved, the relationship of the agency requests to any budgetary limitations set for the agency, and recommendations as to budget allowances.

Finally the central budget office prepares the budget document to go before the legislature.

Appropriation and the Appropriation Warrant

Programs can be funded by annual appropriations, multiyear appropriations, continuing appropriations, interim appropriations, or incremental appropriations. Most normal repetitive programs—such as operations, maintenance, repair, and minor improvements—are funded annually. This means that a contract must be limited to the needs of the current fiscal year, although deliveries and payments may be made later. It also means that a contract must be entered into before the close of the fiscal year, a requirement that gives rise to the so-called contract crunch at the end of each fiscal year when contracting agencies scurry to spend their remaining funds. Any annual appropriation not obligated by that time is lost to the contracting agency.

Programs involving capital expenditures, such as for construction, major items of equipment, and research and development, generally are funded by continuing appropriations, those made available until expended.

In some cases appropriations take the intermediate form of a multiyear appropriation; they are made available for a specified number of years.

Appropriations occasionally are made in the form of incremental appropriations under which a project is only partially funded, but express authorization is given to contract for the entire project. This is particularly relevant to major projects that take years to accomplish. Annual appropriations sometimes may be used as incremental appropriations in support of programs under which long-term contracts are authorized. Thus, for example, federal contracts for utility services may be made for periods up to and including ten years.

The legislature determines how much will be appropriated and for how long that amount is available for obligation. Its appropriations and/or budget committees normally conduct hearings at which agency representatives will be expected to justify the requested levels of spending. The material they present to justify the appropriation should be such as to enable the committees to understand the proposed programs, to evaluate them in the light of the need, current policies, relative worth compared with competing programs, and previous accomplishments, and to make well-informed decisions. All justifications should be complete, to the point, and readily understandable. Factual data command more attention and convey more understanding than generalities do. As explicitly and yet as briefly as possible, justifications should state the facts and the reasoning that went into the estimates.

Generally in constitutional democracies, budgets originate in the lower house of the legislature. Hearings at that level are usually thorough and searching. With the hearings completed and an appropriation bill or bills reported out, the lower house approves and passes the act or acts onto the upper house. The upper house holds less-penetrating hearings, concentrating on controversial aspects of the proposed legislation for the most part. They in turn pass their version of the act or acts. Differences between the two houses are resolved in conference, and the agreed-upon version is voted by both houses and sent to the chief executive for acceptance or veto. With the signing of the act, the additional new obligational authority is legally available to the agency.

The agency must be informed officially of this new funding. Practices throughout the several levels of government are generally similar. At the federal level, after the signing of an appropriation act by the president, the Bureau of Government Financial Operations in the Department of the Treasury prepares an appropriation warrant for the signature of the secretary of the treasury and enters the appropriation in the appropriation ledger. The signed warrant is sent to the GAO, where it is examined for legality, endorsed by the comptroller general, and sent back to the Treasury. A copy of the warrant is furnished to the Office of the Treasurer, where the amount is credited to the agency's account. Within fifteen days of the passage of the appropriation, and the almost simultaneous warranting of the new funding, federal executive branch agencies are required to request formally apportionment of those funds.

Apportionment

The release of appropriated funds by means of the apportionment process is the initial step in budget execution, which encompasses all of the actions required to accomplish effectively, efficiently, and economically the purposes for which funds were requested and approved. Effective budget execution requires procedures for control and evaluation to ensure compliance with regulations and limitations established at higher levels of the policy-making and administrative structure.

Applicable laws generally provide that appropriated funds shall be apportioned so as to prevent obligation or expenditure of an account in a manner that would require deficiency or supplemental appropriation and so as to achieve the most effective and economical use of the amounts made available.

The apportionment submission, or request to the central budget office, is basically an update of the budget request. The enacted appropriation very likely did not include exactly what the agency budgeted. Other events will have transpired in the many months since the budget was prepared; priorities and costs will have changed; and more detailed financial planning will have been done as the new fiscal year approached. The submission is studied by the analysts in the central budget office, and points of disagreement discussed with agency representatives. The central budget office has open to it at least four choices of apportionment action.

1. It can release all of the funds appropriated for the purpose. Such an action would reflect a judgment that the purpose and program was still necessary, that its implementation had been well conceived, and that the financial considerations favored the agency's having available all at one time the necessary funding.

2. It can release a fiscal fraction of the funds appropriated, such as the funds for one quarter or one month of planned activity. Such an action would indicate acceptance of the purpose and program but a desire to control the spending out of the program. In some accounts, funds are customarily apportioned by quarters. Where contracting for goods, services, and minor construction is involved, this is not a desirable practice because it leads to multiple and repetitive placement of orders.

3. It can release a token portion of the appropriated amount. This is often related to further study of the requirement. For example, the central budget office might release 5 percent of an appropriation with the stipulation that activity be limited to further planning and investigation. This method keeps the program barely alive for another fiscal period.

4. It can refuse completely to release the appropriated funds. The office may state that the program has been overtaken by events and is no longer necessary, or that it is inconsistent with or in conflict with other programs or purposes. When this position is taken at the federal level, the Congress must be informed and asked to rescind the appropriation.

The apportionment process is a powerful tool of financial management. The status of appropriations and apportionments for each agency is carefully monitored against obligations and expenditures.

Allotment, Suballotment, Allocation, and Suballocation

These four terms are inconsistently employed at all levels of government. The allotment or allocation process extends obligational authority to administrative units within the department or agency. Both are defined as the authorization to incur obligations or make expenditures. Allotment of allocation is within the jurisdiction of the agency head, who extends obligational authority to subordinate administrative units and who may limit the authority in terms of objects of expenditures, or activities, or organizational units at his discretion, as long as the allocation is in accord with the agency's apportionment. It is customary, if at all possible, to make allocations for the entire fiscal year at the beginning in order to facilitate program planning by administrative units. Allotment and allocation procedures are typically controlled by a system of internal reporting. The obligational authority is further extended to subordinate organizations, using the terms *suballotment* and *suballocation*. The process provides the organization at the operating level with the ability to carry out its assigned mission by giving it authority to obligate the government to pay for required goods and services.

Commitment

Financial management must exercise control over funds to be obligated by contract. This is generally accomplished by certifying that funds are available and committed to a specific purchasing action. Commitment reserves the funds against subsequent invoicing by the vendor. Usually a specific account reference will be cited for use in the contract and on the vendor's invoice. Most importantly the certifying of commitment of funds assures the contracting officer that she is in a position to complete the related contract and obligate the government to pay the agreed compensation. However, until the contract is actually signed, no legal obligation exists and the government may still change its mind; it may reprogram.

Reprogramming

Reprogramming consists of changing the use of funds from the purposes originally submitted to the legislative committees in support of authorizations or budget requests other than changes made to comply with the intent of legislative actions. The term *reprogramming*, however, is sometimes used to include actions on any level within the government to reallocate or redistribute resources among program and/or budget categories.

At the federal level, the congressional committees concerned with appropriations and authorizations require reprogramming hearings on all items over established dollar thresholds. When an item is of special interest to a particular committee and is discussed in its report, that committee alone will usually hold the reprogramming hearing; the other committees that might be involved waive the conduct of hearings. Although the congressional committees have the option of requiring reprogramming hearings, the exercise of that option is subject to many considerations. If the hearings are held by the members of the staff of the committee, they may be held jointly with both majority and minority staff members or they may be held by only one side or the other depending upon the congressional member with a dominant interest.

Reprogramming actions at levels requiring congressional notification may not be implemented until all relevant congressional committees have had the opportunity to review the proposed reprogramming, and the agency head has been advised in writing about the extent to which the reprogramming action may be implemented.

Reprogramming actions at lower dollar levels may be processed within the agency when not otherwise constrained by law or other policy provisions, but records must be available to provide an audit trail to the congressional committees if requested.

Obligation and Expenditure

If the programmed requirement and the commitment of funds remain intact, the contracting officer signs the contract, a step that creates an obligation. This means that when the vendor performs satisfactorily and presents an invoice, the bill will be paid. Under the many types of contracts used by governments, there may be obligation to pay progress payments or to reimburse certain certified costs at established points. Funds committed and obligated to the several programs and purposes are kept segregated for reasonable periods of time. In purchasing an off-the-shelf item, the invoice might be presented very quickly. The invoice for a more complicated and specially engineered item would be presented after a considerable passage of time. In some cases, the selected vendor never does perform as specified, and an invoice is never approved for payment. Eventually the residue of unliquidated obligation is transferred back into the agency's general accounts.

Expenditures are made by government checks issued on the basis of invoices or vouchers certified by the responsible purchasing and materials-management personnel. The checks are issued by disbursing officers, who are not responsible for determining the legality of the particular expenditure but are responsible to making the payment from the proper account and within the limits of the amounts available account by account. Thus the burden of stating that a contract has been truly met lies with the administrative officers of the agencies, and the method of payment would be that agreed upon. Several possibilities exist. Advance payments might have been established to facilitate performance of the contract or to provide an incentive to conform to a socioeconomic provision, such as pollution abatement. Advance payments are frequently authorized when dealing with small and/or minority businesses. Partial payments are often related to specific accomplishments in fulfilling the contract—for example, delivery of certain of the items specified. With progress payments, a percentage of the total contract value is paid upon reaching specified milestones—perhaps the presentation of drawings and specifications or the delivery and installation of a piece of special equipment. Payment in full is rendered when all goods or services have been delivered in a satisfactory manner, with documentation needed for full settlement of the account. Sometimes legal action against a vendor requires that payments be made to third parties to which the vendor is indebted; this is referred to as payment to an assignee.

In any case, the government checks are in due course presented to banks for payment and the financial sequence is complete, except for auditing.

Audit

The audit, the final phase of the budgetary process, is designed to ensure that administrators have complied with the provisions of authorization and appropriation legislation. It also helps to ensure honesty in dispensing public funds and to evaluate results. Many operating agencies are staffed to accomplish internal audits, a highly desirable condition. The principal auditing function, however, is performed by agencies such as the GAO and its state and municipal counterparts. The GAO is an arm of the U.S. Congress. Similarly half of the state auditing agencies report to the legislatures. Many states have elected auditors, independent of both the executive and legislative sides of government.

The genesis of the GAO lies in the U.S. Constitution, which states, "No money shall be drawn from the Treasury, but in consequence of appropriations made by law." This provision was designed to ensure that the purpose and amount of every expenditure should be ascertained by a previous law. Control over the public purse was placed in the hands of the Congress by the Constitution. Until after World War I, however, financial review of federal expenditures remained lodged in the executive branch because the Congress lacked a satisfactory and independent means of reviewing the legality and propriety of money drawn from the Treasury. Studies at that time established that accounting and auditing methods were inadequate, unsatisfactory, and expensive; that congressional investigations of the administration of laws and expenditures of funds often were partisan; that investigating committees were inadequately staffed; and that congressional efforts to obtain essential information on which to legislate or control public expenditures had largely failed.

To remedy the situation, Congress enacted the Budget and Accounting Act (1921), creating the GAO, headed by a comptroller general, who was made responsible only to the Congress. To secure the independent status of the office, the act provided for the comptroller general to be appointed for a term of fifteen years by the president, with the advice and consent of the Senate. Once installed in office, the comptroller general can be removed only by impeachment or by joint resolution of the Congress for specified cause. He is not eligible for reappointment.

The office has a number of statutory responsibilities, but its broad purpose is to provide the Congress information regarding the expenditure of authorized funds and operations of the executive branch. The comptroller general is required to investigate all matters relating to the receipt, disbursement, and application of public funds and to make reports containing recommendations for legislation and recommendations looking to greater economy or efficiency in public expenditures. The comptroller general must make investigations and reports as ordered by the Congress or any committee of the Congress that has jurisdiction over revenues, appropriations, or expenditures. The heads of all executive departments, agencies, and establishments are required to cooperate with the comptroller general and furnish that person access to and the right to examine any of their books and records.

The GAO regularly audits the contracting activities of all federal agencies and of many state and local agencies where federal funding is involved. It also audits activities of firms holding negotiated contracts with the government.

Monitoring the Flow of Funds

In accounting for the flow of appropriated funds through this process, at least five accounts have to be maintained:

1. Unapportioned appropriations. Contains the funds appropriated by the legislature but not yet released for use by the operating units.
2. Unalloted or unallocated apportionments. Contains the funds being held by intermediate levels of management, perhaps in reserve.
3. Unobligated allotments. Holds the funds committed to various acquisitions out for bids or being negotiated but not yet legally obligated to a contract.
4. Unliquidated obligations. Shows all of the funds pertaining to contracts let that had not yet been paid out to the vendors.
5. Expended appropriations. Accumulates all of the payments made to the vendors.

The five accounts, totaled, reflect the total amount appropriated. As an example, suppose that an agency has requested $900,000 for the purchase of a list of items. The funds are appropriated as requested, making the $900,000 available for obligation, but the central budget officer is unconvinced that the entire amount is needed and therefore holds back 10 percent, apportioning $810,000 to the operating division that developed the funding requirement. The operating division chief also has some doubts about the entire program and so holds back $60,000, allotting $750,000 for purchasing. Orders are placed for $650,000 worth of the needed items. Deliveries begin and within the accounting period, $500,000 worth of invoices are paid. The agency accounting for this program looks like this:

Account	Balance
Unapportioned appropriations	$ 90,000
Unalloted apportionments	60,000
Unobligated allotments	100,000
Unliquidated obligations	150,000
Expended appropriations	500,000
Total	$900,000

The terms used may vary from one governmental entity to another. For example, many organizations use the term *encumbered* to designate funds committed for obligation to a particular acquisition.

Cost Overruns

Programming and budgeting for acquisition is plagued with a persistent problem: cost overruns. The problem is most persistent at the federal level but frequently cited also at the state and local levels. Cost overruns are ascribed to, among other things, planning and programming deficiencies, organizational rivalries, premature commitment to production with resulting engineering changes, overoptimism by buyers, buy-in attempts by sellers, changes in program scope, poor estimating, and inflation.

The GAO periodically analyzes the financial status of major acquisitons, including both those financed solely with federal funds and those financed jointly with federal, state, and local funds. An attempt is made to identify baseline figures, or original cost estimates, though many of these are not available, are outdated, or later are superseded by changed congressional authorizations.

In a report of 30 September 1978, the GAO itemized 857 major acquisitions by units of government.[2] Cost overruns for the 857 acquisitons totaled $207 billion, 64 percent more than the programmed cost. None of the acquisitions reported on had yet been completed, so the eventual cost overrun is unknown. The acquisitions include development, production, and construction. Some of the more visible examples are shown in table 6-1.

Table 6-1
Examples of Cost Overruns

Project	Overrun	
	$ million	*Percentage*
Space shuttle (NASA)	2,161.0	42
Senate Office Building, U.S. Capitol	37.5	44
CGN-38, frigate (USN)	458.0	56
Diesel locomotives (AMTRAC)	43.3	63
Subway system, San Francisco (federal share)	38.4	83
F-16 aircraft (USAF)	8,982.3	148
Clinch River reactor (DOE)	1,801.0	258
Medical center, Seattle (VA)	87.3	373
Appalachian development highway	6,708.0	583
Chaparral Missile (USA)	601.0	630

Projects such as these are highly complex and difficult to manage. But there are thousands of examples of equal or greater cost overruns on very uncomplicated acquisitions. The need for more effective programming and budgeting is readily apparent.

Finally anyone entering into a contract with the government has a duty to ascertain the relevant statutory and regulatory provisions pertaining to the funding of the contract and the extent of the obligational authority of the government agent dealt with.

Notes

1. Two widely used references on public finance and budgeting are: Bernard P. Herber, *Modern Public Finance: The Study of Public Sector Economics*, 3d ed. (Homewood: Richard D. Irwin, 1975); and Robert D. Lee, Jr., and Ronald W. Johnson, *Public Budgeting Systems* (Baltimore: University Park Press, 1973).

2. General Accounting Office, *Financial Status of Major Federal Acquisitions, September 30, 1978*, PSAD 79-14 (Washington, D.C. 11 January 1979).

7 Documenting the System

The documentation of the system consists of a hierarchy of written material beginning with and taking off from the basic statutory provisions described in chapter 5. A variety of management issuances further define and prescribe the system. The rule makers are the members and committees of the legislature, the executive and that person's cabinet and advisers—particularly the comptroller or auditor general—and the purchasing and materials-management activities themselves.

The documentation is wide ranging. It begins with a body of implementing directives or regulations expanding upon the intent and purpose of the statutes, assigning responsibilities, delegating authority, and setting controls. Manuals of policies and procedures, which should be organized for easy reference by managerial and operational personnel, carry out the statutes and implementing regulations. A series of periodic information releases—usually numbered and dated memoranda, notes, or newsletters—detail changes to the law, regulations, policies, or procedures; current developments of interest; personnel announcements and appointments; and discussion of problem areas. Vendors are aided by directories of buying locations, lists of goods and services sought, and instructions. A standard set of forms is carefully integrated with the methods and procedures for purchasing and materials management and the related finance and accounting methods and procedures. A system of records and files is designed for ready access—manually or by computer—and on-line, with provisions for limited retention and periodic purging. Finally there is a system of reports to management, the executive, the auditor, and the legislature.

Implementing Directives

Historically at the federal level there have been two basic procurement regulations because there have been two statutes. The two statutes are the Armed Services Procurement Act (1947), as amended, and the Federal Property and Administrative Services Act (1949), as amended. The two regulations have been the Armed Services Procurement Regulations (ASPR) and the Federal Procurement Regulation (FPR).

In April 1976 the Office of Federal Procurement Policy (OFPP) began the long process of achieving a single regulation. Under the authority granted by the Congress, OFPP wrote and the Office of Management and Budget (OMB) issued circular A-109, "Major Systems Acquisition." The circular has the full force and effect of the law and is binding on federal executive agencies for policy purposes. This circular was the first attempt, at the level of the Executive Office of the President, to publish a procurement regulation binding on all executive branch agencies.

The circular states the national policy for federal agencies that are acquiring major systems. They must begin by expressing needs and program objectives in mission terms rather than in equipment terms to encourage innovation and competition in creating, exploring, and developing alternative system design concepts. Their emphasis must be placed on the initial activities of the acquisition process to allow competitive exploration of alternative system-design concepts in response to mission needs. Early in the system-acquisition process, they must communicate with Congress by relating major system-acquisition programs to agency mission needs. This communication is to follow the requirements of OMB circular A-10, which deals with budget estimates. The agencies must establish clear lines of authority, responsibility, and accountability for the management of major-system acquisition programs. They must also use appropriate managerial levels in decision making and obtain agency head approval at key decision points in the evolution of each acquisition program. The agencies must designate a focal point responsible for integrating and unifying the system-acquisition management process and monitoring policy. According to the circular, they are required to rely on private industry as the primary source of the products and services they need.

Circular A-109 has been described as formalizing the front end of the acquisition process. To be effectively implemented, a great many individual agency regulations will need to be rewritten, setting off a chain reaction down through the bureaus and commands.

Closely related at the federal level is the replacement of the two regulations, the ASPR and the FPR, with a set of single Federal Acquisition Regulations (FAR). The FAR is the initial attempt at uniform acquisition regulations to be followed by all federal executive agencies. They will apply to the acquisition of supplies and services, including construction, with appropriated funds. They will not cover grants or acquisition with nonappropriated funds. The basic objectives of the FAR are to reduce proliferation of regulations, eliminate conflicts and redundancies within and between regulations, and, most importantly, provide uniform regulations that are simple and clear.

The FAR will reduce and change individual agency procurement regulations to varying degrees, depending on how extensive they are now and how much of the material in them is truly agency peculiar. The FAR will still recognize a need for agency-acquisition regulations. Such regulations will be necessary to implement FAR policies and procedures and to supplement the FAR to meet specific agency needs.

The FAR is not just a broad policy document. It includes both policies and procedures that can be and should be consistent among agencies. Also the first edition of the FAR does not include any sweeping policy changes.

The basic objective in writing the regulation was to combine the existing coverage of ASPR and FPR. The FAR also attempts to anticipate provisions of the Federal Acquisition Reform Act (see Appendix B), and to include where possible the provisions of the Uniform Commercial Code. The FAR also is consistent with OMB circular A-109.

The Federal Acquisition Regulations (FAR) cover the following topics:[1]

1. *Subchapter A-General*
   Federal Acquistion Regulation System
   Definitions and Special Policies
   Ethics
   Administrative Matters
   Publicizing Acquisition Actions
2. *Subchapter B-Acquisition Planning*
   Planning
   Required Sources of Supplies and Services
   Contractor Qualifications
   Acquisition and Distribution of Commercial Products
3. *Subchapter C-Contracting Methods and Contract Types*
   Small Purchase
   Formal Advertising
   Negotiation
   Types of Contracts
   Special Contracting Methods
4. *Subchapter D-Socioeconomic Programs*
   Small Business Concerns
   Labor Surplus Area Concerns
   Minority Business Enterprises
   Labor Relations
   Environmental Protection
   Protection of Privacy and Freedom of Information
   Foreign Purchases
5. *Subchapter E-General Contracting Requirements*
   Patents, Data, and Copyrights
   Bonds and Insurance
   Taxes
   Cost Accounting Standards
   Contract Cost Principles and Procedures
   Contract Financing
6. *Subchapter F-Special Categories of Contracting*
   Major System Acquisition
   Research and Development Contracting
   Construction and Architect Engineer Contracting
   Service Contracting
   Federal Supply Schedule
   Automatic Data Processing Equipment Contracting
   Contracting of Operation of Government-Owned Plants
7. *Subchapter G-Contract Management*

Contract Administration
Contract Modifications
Subcontracting Policies and Procedures
Property
Quality Assurance
Transportation
Production and Value Engineering
Termination of Contracts
Extraordinary Contractual Actions
8. *Subchapter H-Clauses and Forms*
Contract Clauses and Solicitation Provisions
Forms

Thus, after well-over-200 years, the federal government has a comprehensive and uniform procurement regulation.

Closely related are the Federal Property Management Regulations (FPMR), which prescribe policies and procedures and delegate authority for the management of government property and records. FPMR issuances are published daily in the *Federal Register* and are accumulated in the *Code of Federal Regulations*. These regulations are developed in coordination with other agencies, primarily those represented on the Interagency Committee for Improvement in Procurement and Management of Property and with interested industrial or commercial concerns or organizations.[2]

Both the Council of State Governments and the sections on Local Government Law and Public Contract Law of the American Bar Association (ABA) have addressed the matter of implementing directives at the state and local levels. The work of the ABA is in progress, and current material may be obtained from the coordinating committee.[3] The Council of State Governments in its report on state- and local-government purchasing detailed the recommended coverage of implementing regulations at the state and local level.[4] The report recommends that, at the state and local level, written implementing regulations include:

1. As to organizational structure: delegation to others of activities to be monitored and controlled by purchasing, purchasing goals and objectives, the organizational placement of the function and its internal organization.
2. As to planning and scheduling: instructions as to scheduled submission of requirements by using activities, procedures and practices for term contracting—including documentation of ordering against such contracts.
3. As to qualification of bidders: the forms to be used by potential suppliers and the methods of evaluating the data provided, the procedures for notifying bidders judged unqualified, the procedures for maintenance of the qualified bidders list, the policy covering deletion of bidders from the qualified list and the allowable grounds for such action, the procedures for reinstatement of a previously deleted firm, the right to administrative review.
4. As to the fostering of competition: procedures for competitive bidding where the value of the purchase justifies, the definition of emergencies

under which competitive bidding might be waived, procedures for verifying the necessity of single-source procurement.

5. As to impediments to competitive bidding: the procedures for coordination with Attorneys General on suspected collusion, the requirements for records retention, guidelines for making awards when identical bids are received, procedures for maintenance of a bid-award history file and the analysis of bid-award history in detecting collusive practices, procedures governing the use of option clauses and their execution, procedures for the use of escalator clauses, procedures for the relief of contractors.

6. As to receipt, opening, and tabulation of bids: procedures for the safeguarding of bids until the time set for opening, procedures for the tabulation of bids and the retention of tabulation records.

7. As to bid evaluation and award: guidelines for determining the lowest responsive bidder, a definition of "responsiveness," procedures for handling mistakes discovered in bids, guidelines for determining "substantial conformance" and "minor irregularities," policy regarding late bids, policy regarding rejection of bids in whole or in part.

8. As to safeguards: procedures to detect and prevent collusion between buyers and sellers, procedures to detect circumvention of laws and regulations, procedures for punishment of employees who circumvent laws and regulations.

9. As to quality assurance: the procedures for handling optional items, the nature and methods of testing, the types of specifications and their use, the roll of samples, the use of performance specifications, the techniques and standards of inspection, the procedure for reporting deficiencies noted, the procedure for acting upon deficiencies and complaints against suppliers.

10. As to disposition of excess and surplus: guidelines for identifying items and determining appropriate disposition, procedures for transferring excess between agencies, conditions for bidding on and sale of surplus.

There is considerable evidence that these points are increasingly being incorporated into implementing directives of several states and major local jurisdictions.

Policies and Procedures Manuals

Established policies and procedures are best communicated to the implementing personnel through the publication of manuals, a format that provides recognition and ready reference. It also forces on management a systematic approach to the issuance of new and revised policies and procedures. To facilitate maintaining currency and ease of reference, the manuals are generally loose-leaf and decimally indexed. The larger federal agencies publish series of manuals coordinated with related regulations and other directives. The Department of the Air Force, for example, in the field of purchasing and materials management identifies the following series:

67   Supply
69   Storage and Warehousing

70   Contracting and Acquisition
71   Packaging and Materials Handling
72   Federal Supply Cataloging
74   Quality and Reliability Assurance
75   Transportation and Traffic Management
81   Specifications and Standards
167 Medical Material
800 Acquisition Management

Examples of manuals within these several series would include,[5]

67-1   *USAF Supply Manual* (9 volumes)
67-3   *Storage and Materials Handling*
67-12   *Provisioning Requirements for DLS Procured Equipment*
70-332 *Customer Integrated Automated Procurement System*
71-3   *Regulated Materials*
72-4   *Master Requirements Directory*
75-1   *Transportation of Material*

Other agencies of the federal government utilize similar publications, the extent depending upon their level of involvement in purchasing and materials management activities.

At the state level, the most comprehensive manual is published by the commonwealth of Kentucky.[6] The manual is in loose-leaf form and is decimally indexed. Policy and procedure relating to the Division of Purchases are integrated with that of other related divisions within the Department of Finance. The 1979 revised manual reflects the changes relating to Kentucky's new model procurement code.

A well-organized state or local policies and procedures manual includes sections dealing with,

1. The role and significance of purchasing and materials management in the governmental units, objectives, and standards of performance.
2. Terms and definitions.
3. Excerpts from applicable statutes and other legal references and rulings.
4. Internal operating rules and regulations.
5. Organizational relationships and internal organizational structure.
6. Types and methods of purchases.
7. Purchasing policies and procedures; including commodity assignments, buyers assignments, purchase-request preparation by agencies, improperly prepared purchase requests, noncompetitive purchase requests, funding of purchases, purchases requiring special review or approval, purchases requiring budget-division approval, authorization to

exceed dollar limits on purchases, bid preparation, formal bid-processing procedures, bid cancellation and amendment, formal bid withdrawals, price-request procedure, due-date terms, quantity terms, delivery terms, shipping terms, sample submission terms, bonds, federal excise taxes, warranty or guarantee terms, prequalification of bidders, removal of vendors from prequalified bidders lists, review of bidder questionnaire requesting prequalification, bid awards, required preferences in bid awards, determining the "responsibility" of bidders, specification compliance, analysis of unadjusted bids, processing of tie bids, processing of low bids exceeding allocated funds, rejection of low formal bids, protesting of bid, collusive bidding, purchase-order issuance, blanket purchases, purchase-order alteration, follow-up on purchase orders, vendor performance file, vendor failure to perform, approving payment of vendor, emergency purchases, and purchasing for other jurisdictions.

8. Supply policies and procedures; including stock-quality maintenance, inventory control and ordering, review of stock levels, reorder points, ordering, pricing of material in stock, receiving testing and inspection, rejection of shipments, shipping, delivery, pick-up by customer, storage practices, warehouse security, withdrawals from stock, communications with customers, handling supply complaints, central stores cataloging, and maintenance of price lists.

9. Specification and testing policies and procedures; including specification-development responsibility, use of federal specifications, standard specifications, qualified products lists, inspection and testing, plant inspection, product analysis, comparability considerations, suitability considerations, and assistance to vendors.

10. Traffic and transportation policies and procedures; including rate-structure analysis, transportation-service analysis, distribution analysis, contracting with carriers, contract review, rate negotiations, regulatory matters, liaison with transportation industry, traffic problem resolution, rates and routing guides, traffic services, maintenance of master tarriff file, audit of freight bills, rates review, shipping practices review, and loss and damage claims.

11. Surplus property utilization policies and procedures; including utilization of federal surplus property, reutilization of state surplus property, property disposition, criteria for acquisition of surplus of other agencies, determining condition, determining remaining service life, property-survey reports involving trade-in, property-survey reports proposing sale, property-survey reports proposing junking, property-survey reports (other dispositions), refurbishing of property, pricing of property for disposition, public sale, donation of property, junking of property, loans of property.

12. Standard forms, forms accomplishment, and records management; including new-form approval, reproduction, review and management, accomplishment, and routing of forms; and retention and security of records.

Many jurisdictions issue as a separate volume a manual of commodity classification—a classification index to be used by all agencies requisitioning commodities, equipment or services. Such a manual provides standard nomenclature and numbering of the item, procurement classification within which the item falls, standard units of order (unit packs), and normal frequency of requisitioning and purchase. A manual such as this would be used with a requisitioning schedule under which the flow of agency requests to purchasing would be smoothed. The State of Illinois, for example, maintains a commodity classification manual identifying the fifty-five hundred most frequently requested items.

Periodic Information Releases

The information contained in policy and procedures manuals is updated between revisions by various methods. The same information releases contain a range of related announcements and news of interest to the purchasing and materials-management community.

At the federal level, the *Federal Register*, issued five days a week, contains all orders and regulations of federal agencies. At least annually, all regulations that have been published in the *Federal Register* are published in codified form in the *Code of Federal Regulations*.

A broad range of current information is contained in the *Commerce Business Daily*, a publication of the Domestic and International Business Administration of the U.S. Department of Commerce, available by subscription[7] The coverage of the *Daily* includes a listing of proposed federal government procurements-subcontracting leads, contract awards, sales of surplus property, and foreign-business opportunities. By law, all procurement actions of $10,000 or more by military agencies and of $5,000 or more by civilian agencies are published except for those that are classified for reasons of national security, are for perishable subsistence items, are for certain utility services, are required within fifteen days, are placed under existing contracts, are made by other government agencies, are for personal professional services, are for services from educational institutions, are to be made only from foreign sources, or are not to be given advance publicity, as determined by the Small Business Administration.

The *Commerce Business Daily* classifies each procurement invitation under one of nineteen alphabetical service codes or one of ninety-nine numerical supply and equipment codes. For example, under "J" are listed all equipment repair and maintenance invitations. Under "34" are listed all metal-working machinery purchase invitations. The listing of major contract awards is included for subscribers that might be interested in subcontracting work.

Many states with large centralized-purchasing programs publish periodic information releases. One of the more enduring of these is the Commonwealth of Kentucky's *Purchasing Notes*, generally distributed monthly by the Division of Purchases.[8] As a matter of editorial and economic policy, each note is a single sheet of colored 8½ × 11 paper, printed both sides. It includes such information as announcement of availability of new publications; augmentation of instructions and new and/or troublesome procedures; reminders of schedule and cut-off dates, special documentation and approvals required, need for accuracy in preparing requisitions and purchase orders, conflict-of-interest and other ethical considerations; announcements of appointments, transfers, and promotions of personnel; supply (delivery) lead-time predictions; product-substitutability information; and new source needs.

Professional associations, and several private publishers also distribute newsletters. These are identified in the earlier discussion of professional organizations and in the Bibliography.

Aids to Vendors

The aids distributed to potential vendors should be designed to give each the information needed to qualify for the bidders' list, respond properly to invitations for bids, meet contractual requirements, and conform to federal, state and local laws, purchasing policies, and other standards of good purchasing. In addition to providing information on government policies and requirements, manuals should also advise vendors of what they are permitted, or even encouraged, to do to solicit business. Thus, a good manual recognizes the essential partnership arrangement that exists between the government as buyer and the vendor as seller and that attributes rights and courtesies to each within an open, business framework.

Currently there is a great disparity in the content, coverage, and size of vendors' manuals and their quality and treatment also vary. Some are clear and simple, others far less so; and the tone and content range from a listing of punitive measures that may be taken against errant vendors to solitications of vendors in a public relations manner calculated to encourage and stimulate them. The Council of State Governments has developed an excellent guide to the preparation of a vendors' manual.[9]

The General Services Administration publishes and periodically revises a basic forty-five-page pamphlet, *Doing Business with the Federal Government*.[10] The Small Business Administration periodically publishes a two-hundred-page book, *U.S. Government Purchasing and Sales Directory*.[11] The two together can be taken as the federal government's vendors' manual. *Doing Business with the Federal Government* briefly explains the principles and procedures of federal procurement, describes assistance available to potential vendors, describes the procurement programs of the departments and agencies, describes government sales of surplus property, and locates sources of business services across the nation.

The more extensive *Purchasing and Sales Directory* consists of eight parts. It:

1. Provides information on selling to the government and to government contractors.
2. Lists products and services bought by the major military-purchasing offices and indicates, by means of code numbers following the products or services, the purchasing offices that buy them.
3. Discusses local purchasing by military installations and gives a state-by-state listing of installations that are possible sources of business for small concerns.
4. Lists products and services purchased by the major federal civilian agency purchasing offices and indicates, by means of code numbers following the products and services, the purchasing offices that buy them.
5. Lists those federal agencies that engage in major research and development activities. Each agency has developed procedures that are designed to ensure for all organizations the opportunity to submit proposals on their research and development needs. This part of the directory also contains useful information on preparing proposals and brochures.
6. Presents a guide to government specifications: what they are, how they are used, and where they may be obtained by prospective bidders.
7. Discusses government property sales, including types of property sold and where such sales take place. Information is also provided on the assistance offered by the Small Business Administration to small firms interested in buying property being disposed of by the government.
8. Contains government forms helpful to users of the directory. Included is a copy of the standard bidders' mailing list application used by all federal agencies. Also lists of the addresses and telephone numbers of federal government offices.

Somewhat redundant to the *Purchasing and Sales Directory* is the Department of Defense's *Selling to the Military*.[12] It does provide somewhat more detail beyond that in the *Purchasing and Sales Directory*. The Department of Defense also publishes a directory of information sources available to assist small and minority business and businesses in labor-surplus areas.[13]

Vendors' guides and manuals of the states range from one-page flyers to eighteen- or twenty-page pamphlets. Only the more sophisticated cover the range of topics suggested by the Council of State Governments. The style of these publications may be seen in figure 7-1. Similarly, many cities and counties distribute guides, examples of which are included in figure 7-2. All serve the very useful purpose of orienting the potential vendor, or vendor's representative, to the buying activity.

Forms

An integrated set of printed forms is a basic element of any purchasing and materials-management system. Not only must the forms be integrated in themselves, they must be integrated with the overall management-information system described in chapter 2. All related records and files must also be integrated with both the system of forms and the management-information system. They must be subject to explicit control of design, reproduction, and usage. The control must ensure that each form fulfills a basic requirement of a specific, identified, purchasing and materials-management procedure; that each is designed for most effective use by both humans and machines; and that each is reproduced in the most economic quantities, the supply is replenished in a timely manner, and obsolete forms are pulled out of the system.

In forms design, the maximum amount of constant data should be printed, and the spaces for entry of variable data should be adequate in size and clearly identified. Every form should have a concise title and an identifying number, which should carry over from the number of the regulation or manual governing the procedure in which the form is used. As mentioned in the discussion of manuals, a decimal numbering system is recommended. Thus a range of forms for use in purchasing and materials management might include:

Form No. 1.1 Purchase Requisition
Form No. 1.2 Emergency Purchase Authorization
Form No. 2.1 Bidders Mailing List Application
Form No. 2.2 Request for Quotation
Form No. 2.3 Invitation to Bid
Form No. 2.4 Report of Bid Opening and Award
Form No. 2.5 Report of Tie Bid
Form No. 2.6 Report of Apparent Collusive Bid
Form No. 2.7 Request for Bid Withdrawal
Form No. 2.8 Report of Bid Protest
Form No. 2.9 Report of Disqualification of Vendor
Form No. 3.1 Purchase Order

Figure 7-1. Examples of Vendors' Guides for States

Figure 7-2. Examples of Vendors' Guides for Cities and Counties

Form No. 3.2   Notice of Award and Authorization to Proceed
               With Contract (Contract Certification)
Form No. 4.1   Request for Specification or Standard
Form No. 4.2   Qualification of Product
Form No. 5.1   Performance Bond
Form No. 6.1   Inspection of Vendor's Facility
Form No. 6.2   Incoming Quality Inspection
Form No. 6.3   Receiving Report
Form No. 6.4   Report of Rejection of Shipment
Form No. 6.5   Complaint to Vendor
Form No. 7.1   Report of Damage in Shipment
Form No. 7.2   Audit of Transportation Charges
Form No. 8.1   Report of Excess Property
Form No. 8.2   Property Damage Notice
Form No. 8.3   Property Loss Notice
Form No. 8.4   Property Disposition Notice; Trade-In, Sale,
               Junking, Donation

Circumstances in the various levels of government vary, so no one system of forms can be universal.

Records and Files

The records of a public-purchasing and materials-management activity are public and are open to inspection by any interested person, subject to reasonable rules as to time and place. Under the freedom-of-information concept, certified copies of records must be furnished upon request and payment of a reasonable fee.

Controls over the creation, maintenance, and use of records must be worked out. The period of active access to each record must be established, and procedures prescribed for disposition of records at the end of that period, either by destruction or by retirement to the agency archives.

Suitable protection and security must be provided for records that document organizational functions, policies, decisions, procedures, and essential transactions; and those that protect the legal and financial rights of the government and any persons directly affected by the agency's activities.

Basic to the entire records-and-files-management procedure is the determination of a retention schedule. The schedule must reflect legal, administrative, and historical criteria, and therefore could vary considerably. The National Institute of Governmental Purchasing suggests the following example of a retention and destruction schedule:

1. Purchase order files: Destroy after twenty years.
2. Purchase order case files: Destroy after ten years.

3. Formal bid case files: Destroy five years after award.
4. Purchase order transmittals: Destroy five years after orders completed.
5. Vendor performance files: Records that show deviations destroy after ten years; all others five years.
6. Purchasing commodity files: Retain permanently.
7. Cancelled bids: Destroy after ten years.
8. Purchase order register files: Destroy after ten years.
9. Rejected bid files: Destroy after five years.
10. Contracting bond files: Retain permanently.
11. Contract review files: Destroy after six years.
12. Contract termination files: Destroy after five years.
13. Debarred bidder list files: Retain permanently.
14. Contractors' insurance certificate files: Destroy after six years.
15. Open-end and call-type contract files: Destroy six years after expiration and final payment.
16. Contract case files: Destroy five years after close of contract.

Notes

1. Federal Acquisition Regulations (FAR) are available to federal agencies at no cost from the General Services Administration, Printing and Distribution Division (WBRD), Regional Office Building, 7th and D Streets, SW, Room 2076, Washington, D.C. 20407. Others can obtain a subscription for an indeterminate period of time for $50 from the Superintendent of Documents, U.S. Government Printing Office, Washington, D.C. 20402. Make check payable to the Superintendent of Documents.

2. Federal Property Management Regulations (FPMR) are available to federal agencies from their GSA liaison officers. They can be requested on GSA form 49 or form 1725 from the General Services Administration, Printing Materials Depot, Franklin and Union Streets, Alexandria, Virginia 22314. To be placed on the distribution list, contact the General Services Administration (WBRD), Regional Office Building, 7th and D Streets, SW, Room 2662, Washington, D.C. 20407. Persons not with the federal government should contact the nearest GSA Business Service Center.

3. Write to: Coordinating Committee on a Model Procurement Code for State and Local Governments, 1700 K Street, NW, Washington, D.C. 20006.

4. Council of State Governments, *State and Local Government Purchasing* (Lexington, Ky., 1975).

5. Publication of the United States Air Force, Army, Navy and Marine Corps may be obtained by writing, U.S. Naval Publications and Forms Center, 5801 Tabor Avenue, Philadelphia, Pennsylvania 19120.

6. A publication of: Department of Finance, Bureau of Administrative

Services, Commonwealth of Kentucky, 234 Capitol Annex, Frankfort, Kentucky 40601.

7. Subscription forms available from: Commerce Business Daily, Superintendent of Documents, U.S. Government Printing Office, Washington, D.C. 20402.

8. The publishing office solicits an exchange of concepts, ideas, and solutions to purchasing problems. Write to: Specifications and Inspection Section, Division of Purchases, New Capitol Annex, Frankfort, Kentucky 40601.

9. See Council *State and Local Government Purchasing*, chap. 19. The address of the council is: Council of State Governments, Iron Works Pike, Lexington, Kentucky 40511.

10. General Services Administration, *Doing Business with the Federal Government* (Washington, D.C.: Government Printing Office, 1978).

11. Small Business Administration, *U.S. Government Purchasing and Sales Directory* (Washington, D.C.: Government Printing Office, 1978).

12. Department of Defense, *Selling to the Military* (Washington, D.C.: Government Printing Office, 1976).

13. Department of Defense, *Small Business and Labor Surplus Area Specialists* (Washington, D.C.: Government Printing Office, 1976). Available from the Superintendent of Documents, Washington, D.C. 20402.

8

Material Requirements: Qualitative and Quantitative

The first of the several subsystems and procedures of the purchasing and materials-management system is that of requirements determination. It is composed of procedures for:

1. Developing engineering standards that govern the design and specifications of items entering the system.
2. Identifying the specifications that will apply in an acquisition.
3. Qualification of products and the listing of qualified products.
4. Classifying and coding items of material.
5. Identifying and cataloging items of material.
6. Standardizing items of material.
7. Establishing authorizations and allowances.
8. Computing quantitative requirements.

Overview of Requirements Determination

All material objects are subject to operational and technological obsolescence, so managers must constantly be alert for new products, new equipment, and new operational and support systems. New ideas can come from any source. Original ideas for new material-support capabilities should be encouraged and sought. A user may state a new requirement, which may result eventually in a system proposal by a research and development activity. A suppliers' research organization may produce a new device or technique and offer it for use. Regardless of the source, the materials manager should be constantly evaluating ideas in the search for the next generations of products and equipment. Items that are determined to qualitatively serve stated purposes are approved for inclusion in authorization documents and specification references.

Once a system or item that has been at least tentatively accepted as meeting the qualitative requirement has been identified, the quantitative requirement-determination process may begin. This latter process establishes the quantity required, the desired date of delivery, the estimated cost, and the fiscal period in which funding will be necessary.

For only a very few major items, it is possible to go directly from an authorization document to a procurement program for a fiscal period.

Most items require individual determination of the quantity to be funded and placed on procurement at any one time. The diversity of items used by most governmental units makes necessary sophisticated procedures for classifying, coding, and cataloging. Methods of requirements determination will differ by general categories, which can be wide ranging. Some categories are:

1. Major systems, such as a military weapon system or a municipal solid-waste disposal system.
2. Government-furnished components of systems, items are separately purchased and furnished to manufacturers to become part of an assembled system.
3. Major end items of support equipment and major assemblies or components.
4. Spare parts and maintenance supplies for the initial support of item included in 1, 2, and 3 above.
5. Continuing operating and reserve quantities of spare parts, maintenance supplies, and other items.
6. Items in general and common use in the government and in industry and normally available from commercial sources.

Requirements in categories 1, 2, and 3 generally have the greatest importance and the highest monetary value, and thus they warrant the greatest amount of attention. They should be subject to rigorous continuing analysis and review. The intensity of centralized control of a category of items is established in consideration of several factors: nature of the item, feasibility of centrally determining requirements for the item, essentiality of central accumulation of data on the item for management purposes, availability of the item in sufficient quantity to requiring activities or installations, and desirability of centralized control of the item should an emergency occur.

Requirements for major systems are generally centrally determined and fed directly into the purchasing process. Requirements for government-furnished components are similarly derived. The requirements-determination process for these items is basically straightforward. Other major end items and components are involved in a much more extensive and difficult requirements-determination process.

The objective of the requirements process is the detailed identification of material needs, establishing the input of required items into the supply system at the times, quantities, and rates that will satisfy future demands. Therefore the requirements process basically focuses on the management of individual items of supply. It involves collecting all available data pertaining to an item, balancing assets against estimated demand, and taking definitive procurement and supply action. The more important of the actions that depend upon a requirements determination follow.

1. Budget estimates. Since governmental units depend upon appropriated funds, an important step in planning to meet any future demand must be the preparation of budget estimates. In many cases the preparation and justification of a budget requires a study of the individual item to be purchased. In some instances, however, it is sufficient to budget on the basis of dollar figures for entire classes of items.

2. Purchase and repair programs. As the period for which support is being planned draws nearer, demand must be computed or estimated for each individual item of supply, assets balanced against demand, and action initiated to program procurement of any additional quantities needed to satisfy the total requirement. If an item is one that can be repaired it is necessary to determine which portion of the total requirement can be satisfied through repair and to develop repair schedules accordingly.

3. Control and distribution of stock. The estimate of demand and the analysis of asset availability, which form the basis for procurement and repair actions, are also used in the control and distribution of stocks. Although procurement and distribution are sometimes viewed as separate functions, their coordination is essential in achieving effective management of individual items of supply. This coordination should begin when buying plans are made. It carries over into the day-to-day control of stocks, when deliveries from procurement or repair lag or when demand for an item is greater than anticipated. Under such circumstances, it becomes necessary to revise stock levels or to take other action until demand and assets can be brought into balance.

4. Contract termination and disposal of excesses. Since assets in some instances may be found to be greater than total demand, the requirements process involves decisions on the disposition of excess stocks, as well as on amounts to be purchased or repaired. Some assets in long supply can be retained and used beyond the period for which demand is being forecast; others may have to be terminated from contracts or disposed of if already in the supply system.

5. Support capability studies. A fundamental consideration in estimating demand is the operational use to be made of the item. Requirements for spare aircraft engines, for example, are partly based on the flying hours planned for the aircraft in which the engine is installed, but execution of flying-hour programs depends in turn on adequate logistic support. If spare parts and equipment are not available, the planned rate of operations must be modified. It is often necessary to determine, by analysis of critical items, the portion of an operating program that can in fact be supported over a given period of time.

The quantitative-requirements segment has two phases: one for computation and one for judgment. The computation phase is systematic and logical, the judgment phase value laden and often illogical.

As a minimum, a requirements computation should be made annually for each active major item. Many items should be recomputed semiannually, quarterly, or even monthly. Ideally the annual computation should establish three positions simultaneously: a stock status position as of the cutoff date of the computation, a net procurement quantity for use in the current or imminent annual procurement program, and a budget quantity and cost for use in developing a justification of the next annual budget.

The computation begins with program documents of data elements. They may be activities to be equipped or supported; the equipment authorized each activity, stated in equipping tables referenced by the program documents; or special requirements, such as additional items needed for training, experimental use, one-time projects, or emergency use stockpiling. From these three inputs an initial allowance is computed for the item under consideration. An authorized replacement factor derived from the planned useful life of the item is then applied to the total initial allowance, considering the age of the items currently in use.

Many of the items are procured with the intention of filling an authorization, plus creating an inventory for replacement purposes and filling a supply-distribution pipeline. Factors exist from which to compute these two increments, which, when added to the total initial allowance, result in the gross quantitative requirement for the item.

The next step is to identify and apply to the gross requirement the on-hand and due-in assets. On-hand figures come from automatically maintained perpetual-inventory records. The stock-control points and the purchasing offices maintain records of items on order but undelivered. Similarly data are assembled regarding items due in from repair and overhaul facilities. The application of these quantities to the gross requirement results in the net purchase requirement.

Next it is necessary to establish when the net purchase requirement should be funded, placed on contract, and delivered. To this increasingly complex process must now be added a lead-time study, working back from the desired date of delivery all the way to the fiscal year quarter in which funds will have to be allotted. The major time elements are distribution time, production time, production lead time, contract award time, administrative lead time, and funding lead time.

The final step in the computation phase is to cost out the net requirement by funding periods. Wherever possible cost is to be based upon known prices taken from existing contracts or purchase orders. For the items that may not have been on contract at any time, an estimate of likely price is made. To the extended unit price are added the many allowances, operating manual and spare-parts costs, and shipping charges.

At this point the materials manager should have the theoretically correct quantity of each item to be procured, its cost, and the fiscal period in which funds must be available with which to make the purchase. All three of these elements—quantity, cost, and funding period—must then undergo a series of value judgments.

Value Judgments in Requirements Determination

The computed requirement has been referred to as the theoretically correct requirement. The computed requirement is seldom procured. Funding is seldom adequate to finance purchase of the theoretically correct requirement, so the first value judgment deals with the likelihood of the computed requirement's being included in a budget request. Against the basic judgment as to likely funding, several other judgments are made.

The second is that of program balance. The goal is to purchase and deliver equipment in perfect timing with the demands of the using activities, but this is an ideal not easily attained. Most likely the objective will be to achieve an adequate level of support for the higher-priority organizations, with less important organizations and programs struggling along as best they can.

The third consideration concerns the problem of whether the administration is most concerned with the long term or short term. Under pressures of many kinds, long-term programs give way to short-term ones that produce quick, visible results. Officials therefore look at individual computed requirements and ask whether an item contributes to the immediate capability or whether it relates to a long-range problem.

The fourth judgment weighs the stated requirement against the actual procurability and producibility of the item. Needs may be for items which in reality have not yet been invented. This has been particularly true of the more advanced electronics devices, computers, hospital equipment, and weaponry. Not only do individuals attempt to program requirements for items on which no specifications are available, but they also ask for quantities that are far beyond the production capability of any available source.

A final area of judgment is logistics considerations. It includes the things that can be done to manipulate those parts of the requirement based on supply pipelines, replacement factors, transportation factors, or stock levels, all of which are basically arbitrary.

The requirements function establishes the flow of materials into the supply systems and from that to the using activities. Input into the system that turns out to be inadequate to the demand results in reduced effectiveness because of inadequate equipment and supply support, and in greater costs incurred in redistribution of material and priority supply actions. Input that turns out to be in excess of demand results in waste, increased handling costs, the denying of requirements that could otherwise have been met, and criticism from many sides. In trying to arrive at the best figure, the requirements process encounters numerous problems.

A basic problem in requirements determination continues to be the lastingness of the qualitative requirement. Qualitative requirements are evaluated and approved on technological grounds. In the face of pressure to save time, engineering may have been inadequate, or even if completely engineered the users' needs and plans may have changed since the request. In view of the high likelihood of technological advance, many feel that there is too much concern with firmly stating a qualitative requirement, but if the requirement is not specifically described, cost estimates can hardly be realistic and changes in configuration could occur that would end the usefulness of the equipment for some purposes.

Two divergent considerations influence requirements planning: need and available resources (primarily money). Need motivates users to develop objectives that incur minimum risk. Limitations of manpower and money motivate the administrators to develop reasonably attainable programs within these limitations. Each should understand and appreciate the other's task, but on one point, there are divergent views: the users believe the requirements of their plans are accurate and should not be reduced to meet money limitations, but the administrators need to develop programs that are compatible with the funds likely to be made available.

Another problem concerns data inputs and factors used in the requirement process. So much depends upon the individual who prepares the allowance documents, the engineer who estimates the number of hours an item will operate between overhauls, and the stock-control clerk who reports the inventory position. All of these inputs have degrees of validity, and yet all must be accepted and applied under the pressure of tight deadlines. Among the more difficult and sensitive inputs are the logistics considerations: inventory levels, supply pipeline factors and transportation factors.

A fourth problem area is concerned with assets on hand and due in. In many cases, a requirement can be met by any one of several substitutable items or by various types, models, and series of the item. Identification of all reasonable substitute assets requires highly sophisticated cataloging and detailed knowledge of specifications. Applicability of an asset to a requirement depends also upon its condition and sometimes upon its location in the supply system. The situation often arises in which new procurement is more practical and economical than movement and reconditioning of substitutable assets already on hand.

A fifth problem is time, primarily the program-requirements-budget preparation time and the fact that successive fiscal-year cycles overlap to the extent that new requirements must be determined before the last prior proposed purchase program has been considered by the legislature or the Congress, and the preceding prior year's program is only partially implemented. For example, the U.S. government's fiscal year 1980 budget, and back-up data to include purchase requirements were submitted to the Office of Management and Budget in September 1978. Computation of procurement requirements for that submission was begun in November 1977. In the spring of 1978 the congressional appropriations committees were conducting hearings on the fiscal year 1979 budget, which contained increments of many of the same and related items involved in the FY 1980 budget. Congressional committee reaction to these items was not yet known, nor was the exact level of funding of procurement programs and objects. Also at the time requirements computations were started, in the fall of 1977, FY 1978 was in its first quarter. Only a small portion of procurement funds had been allocated, and contracting with that year's funds was just getting underway. Depending upon lead time, deliveries to units and supply depots were still being made against requirements computed for FY 1977, 1976, and 1975. Uncertainties were present in regard to all of the six fiscal-year programs, 1975-1980.

Engineering Standardization

The most basic prerequisite to the requirements-determination process is the identification and classification of the items involved. Thus the first sequence of procedures deals with identification, standardization, and cataloging.

By far the majority of items involved are well known; they have readily recognized uses and capabilities. However, some items are not, and they must be developed in response to user needs. The realm in which this most often occurs is in the armed services. When one of the armed services recognizes a need that cannot be met by an existing weapon, communication, or support system—or item of major equipment—it originates a detailed statement, called a required operational capability (ROC). The ROC describes the need, the time frame in which the capability is required, how the system wil be used, its essential characteristics (one of which is the level of reliability), and a rough preliminary cost estimate. If the requirement, the ROC, is recognized and accepted by management, the necessary research, development, testing, and engineering will be programmed and funded. Subsequently the system or item is subjected to developmental and operational testing. After satisfactory testing, full-scale production may be authorized, and in due course the system or item becomes part of the inventory.

Throughout the process, management must continually question the nature and the realism of the stated requirement. As time passes the need being responded to will change; the time values will change; and as research, development, test, and engineering are conducted, the system or item characteristics will change.

Engineering standardization is unique among standardization controls in that it does not depend on catalog data to achieve its objectives.[1] Instead it is accomplished through communication with designers on parts preferences and through parts-control programs, which assist designers in selecting a preferred part, method, or process and using it wherever possible in equipment design. This latter effort is accomplished by written specifications on part characteristics and performance, designating preferred parts as standard and encouraging manufacturers to use these preferred parts whenever feasible.

Public and industry specialists generally agree that the most effective way to restrain the proliferation of new, unneeded items is to practice standardization at the time new equipment is designed. By the time item entry controls are in operation, the government has committed itself to buying equipment that may contain many items for which the government already has cataloged preferred substitutes.

Three elements are essential in engineering standardization procedures. The first is communication to inform designers what items the government prefers to have in new equipment. Such communication must be readily available, current, and tailored to the needs of the designers. Second are incentives to encourage contractors through positive and negative rewards to use preferred items. Third is a monitoring system to ensure that contractors give sustained attention to the problem of using nonessential new parts.

Engineering standards as published by agencies of government, military groups, and trade associations are frequently referenced in the specifications cited in a contract. They are thus part of the contract and binding on the parties.

Specification

Quality to a purchasing and materials manager really means suitability to fill a need. Quality can be analyzed, measured, and described. The ways of describing quality include these:

1. Performance specifications, which describe the standards of performance of the item, its functions and capabilities, its operating limits, and its dependability or reliability.
2. Design specifications, which describe physical characteristics, such as size and shape, materials to be used, and methods of fabrication. A design specification would include or reference engineering drawings. It might also describe chemical characteristics.
3. Reference to commercial standards, such as those published by the American Society for Testing and Materials (ASTM) or the American National Standards Institute (ANSI).

4. Reference to government standards, either to federal specifications, which cover a large number of civilian-type items used by government, or military specifications.[2] Many larger state and local governments have also published series of specifications, and there are numerous specialized publications. One is the series of Law Enforcement Equipment Standards developed by the Law Enforcement Assistance Administration of the Department of Justice.

5. Reference to market grades when procuring regularly traded commodities, such as items traded on the commodity exchanges (for example, Wheat, No. 1 dark Northern). The standard general reference on commodities and materials and how they are identified is the *Materials Handbook*, which describes thirteen thousand materials.[3]

6. Reference to brand names—for example, "Tube bender, rotary, 5 HP, 1/2" to 2" capacity, digital readout selector, Richards-Multiform No. 9 or equal."

7. Reference to a sample, with the order simply stating, "Per sample furnished."

8. Reference to a qualified products list (QPL), which itemizes, by property class, products that have been prequalified by testing.

Various combinations of two or more of the eight techniques are commonly used. Design specifications are the most widely used, particularly in competitive bidding. In order to be useful, such specifications must be constantly revised and reissued. The GAO in 1976 reported that 56 percent of federal specifications were over five years old and 12 percent were over fifteen years old. The value of such old specifications is marginal. Also many specifications are so complex that they inhibit or exclude many potential bidders.

In the acquisition of major items of equipment, use would also be made of general specifications, which cover technical requirements common to a broad class of products, services, or materials and impose a set of general design requirements on that class. This technique avoids repetition of requirements in subsequently issued performance and/or design specifications. An example is the general specification for naval aircraft (SD-24K). The performance and/or detail specifications can be limited to the requirements peculiar to a single aircraft—for example, the navy's F-18. In specifying a weapon system, a whole hierarchy of specifications will be developed, including an overall system specification, development specifications, product specifications, process specifications, and material specifications. The system specification describes the technical and operational requirements for a system as an entity, allocates requirements to functional subsystems, and defines the interfaces among the subsystems. Development specifications describe the requirements during the development phases. Development specifications are generally performance specifications. Product specifications are used to describe components in production configurations, subsequent to development. Process specifications define operations that are performed on a product or materials. Material specifications are applicable to raw materials used in manufacture.

Configuration management refers to the subprocedure for ensuring that all such specifications are consistent and subject to an orderly process of review and data validation and verification. The configuration-management process must be tailored to the particular item, whether it is developed at government expense or privately developed and offered for government use. For less complex items, such as test meters, configuration management may require nothing more than the control of the applicable specification, followed by inspection of the items produced. But complex items, such as missile systems, may require a highly organized configuration-management system to ensure achievement of program objectives. The application of configuration management to privately developed items, whether simple or complex, must recognize the constraints of rights in data and the inherent absence of the government's right to control the detailed configuration of a privately developed item.

The Federal Government's System of Specifications

The federal government has exact specifications for most of the products and services it buys repeatedly.[4] These are in the form of written descriptions, drawings, prints, commercial designations, industry standards, and other descriptive references. Since they are based in part on industrial and technical society standards and specifications, they meet the requirements of the government without lessening the ability of business concerns to furnish the items or services.

Traditionally government specifications have been divided into two groups: federal and military. Federal specifications cover the civilian-type items and services purchased. Military specifications describe the items and services purchased by the Department of Defense and its many subdivisions and by other agencies concerned with national defense. Some items used by the Department of Defense, particularly ones with no special military characteristics, can be described satisfactorally by federal specifications, and in purchasing these items the Department of Defense uses federal rather than military specifications.

Federal specifications cover materials, products, or services used or potentially used by two or more federal agencies, or new items of potential general application. They are issued by the General Services Administration and are mandatory for use by all federal agencies. The director of the Standardization Division in the GSA's Federal Supply Service administers the specifications.

Federal specification numbers are made up of two nonsignificant groups of letters followed by numbers, such as, "H-R-550, Roller, kit, paint; GG-C-455, Clock, portable, watchman's; HHH-S-450, Slide, microscope." The specification symbol starts with a single, double, or triple letter, followed by a single letter, usually the first letter of the first word in the title, and then an assigned serial number.

Since specification documents are controlled by their basic number, a letter after the number is used as a revision indicator. "H-B-51" would be the first issue for "Broom, upright (corn)." The first revision would be H-B-51A; the second revision would be H-B-51B. A revised federal specification supersedes entirely the previous issue, including amendments to it.

Amendments effect minor but essential changes in technical requirements in specifications. An amendment is part of the specification document with which it is identified, and determines the date of that document for indexing purposes. Amendments are cumulative and are numbered consecutively. Each amendment bears the specification number, the amendment number, and the amendment date in the upper right corner of the specification. For example:

J-C-580A

Amendment-6 (GSA-FSS)

6 March 1979

Superseding

Amendment-5 (GSA-FSS)

10 June 1978

Military specifications cover items or services that are intrinsically military in character, commercial items modified to meet special requirements of the military, or commercial items with no present or potential use by federal agencies other than military. These specifications were originally issued under the auspices of the Joint Army-Navy Specifications Board as "JAN" specifications. The series has been continued in the same numerical sequence, with the prefix "MIL" replacing the "JAN." As the few remaining JAN specifications are revised, the prefixes will be changed to MIL, although the specification numbers will remain the same.

Military specifications are identified by a symbol composed of three parts: the letters *MIL*, a single letter that usually is the first letter of the first word in the title, and a nonsignificant serial number. An example is "MIL-M-2241, Microscope, Stage Micrometer."

A revision of a military specification supersedes entirely the previous issue, including any amendments to it. A revision is indicated by the addition of a capital letter following the symbol in the upper right corner of the first page and preceding any suffix. The first revision is indicated by the letter "A," and succeeding revisions are indicated by the other letters in alphabetical sequence except that the letters "I," "O," and "S" are not used. For example:

MIL-I-24391A

13 Jan 1979

Superseding

MIL-I-24391

16 June 1975

Brief changes in a military specification are printed in the form of an amendment, which bears the specification symbol, the amendment number, and the date in the upper right corner. Only one amendment is ever in effect for an individual specification. Subsequent amendments include the pertinent changes from the previous amendments. Superseding amendments are indicated by the figures "2," "3," and so on.

Two indexes to government specifications are available: the *Index of Federal Specifications and Standards* and *Department of Defense Index of Specifications and Standards*.

The *Index of Federal Specifications and Standards* consists of three principal sections in which the documents are listed alphabetically, numerically, and by federal supply class (FSC). In all three sections, a brief explanatory title describes each specification or standard. The index tells the price, if any, at which each document may be purchased from the GSA. It also lists canceled or superseded documents. The index is for sale on a subscription basis.[5]

The *Department of Defense Index of Specifications and Standards* has two parts: an alphabetical listing and a numerical listing with cumulative supplements to the particular edition. The index lists the unclassified federal military and departmental documents used by the defense department. A consolidation of the separate indexes formerly published by the three military departments, it greatly simplifies the search for available design, engineering, and procurement data. Copies may be purchased from the superintendent of documents.

Another helpful publication is a GSA pamphlet, *Guide to Specifications and Standards of the Federal Government*. It describes the development and use of government specifications and standards, tells how they benefit the government and companies selling to it, discusses the importance of industry participation in the development of government specifications and standards, and explains how to obtain copies or sets of specifications and standards. The pamphlet is available free from the GSA's Business Service Centers.

Since 1976 the federal government has been engaged in a long-range project to move to the use of commercial-item descriptions wherever practical. This move had long been urged by the GAO, which had ridiculed many of the federal specifications. For example, Federal Specification GGG-M-00550, Mousetrap and Rattrap, was a 102,000-word, two-pound document. The generally used commercial-item description is a one-page document.

In response to the urging of the GAO and the Congress and the recommendations of the Commission on Government Procurement, regulations are being revised to emphasize the use by federal agencies of commercial products.[6] The new regulations prescribe policies and procedures for the management of specifications, standards, and descriptions for commercial products. The regulations are intended to result in a cost savings to the government by decreasing the reliance on federal specifications and standards and providing for the use of commercial-item descriptions.

The Office of Federal Procurement Policy (OFPP) has established a goal to increase the government's reliance on commercial products as opposed to products specifically manufactured to meet government specifications. One of the specific tasks required to realize this goal is the development of a government-wide management and control system governing the development and issuance of purchase descriptions, specifications, standards, and other documents that describe commercial or commercial-type products for government procurement. The GSA has established an interagency task force to develop the required management control system. Concurrent with this effort the OFPP has called for a simultaneous systematic improvement in existing procurement specifications and standards.

In support of the goal, GSA has developed policies and procedures that provide for a new series of commercial-item descriptions (CIDs). Intended as an alternative to detailed federal specifications, the CIDs will supplement federal specifications and standards. The new policies and procedures contain substantive changes relating to specifications and standards and include definitive guidelines relating to the establishment of need and justification criteria. The policies include maximizing the use of functional or performance type requirements; eliminating unnecessary federal specifications and standards; maximizing the reliance on commercial packaging, packing, and marking; limiting reference material to that which is essential; and generally requiring that the complexity of the descriptions be substantially reduced commensurate with the legitimate needs of federal agencies.

The CIDs are a new series of documents formalized under the federal specifications and standards program and intended to be used in the acquisition of commercial off-the-shelf and commercial-type products. Commercial-item descriptions are intended to be formalized purchase descriptions stated in functional terms to the maximum extent possible to permit a variety of distinct products to qualify for award or, when a particular product must be designated in terms of performance specifications, to stipulate a range of acceptable characteristics or minimum standards. Brand-name (single model or part number references) descriptions cannot be approved for publication under the CIDs series.

A commercial off-the-shelf product is a product from regular production sold in substantial quantities to the general public and/or industry at established market or catalog prices. A commercial-type product is one peculiar to the government that, though appearing to be a commercial product, is produced in accordance with a government specification, is subject to some physical change or addition and/or packaged and identified differently from its normal commercial product counterpart, and may be but is not necessarily stocked centrally by the government.

Also involved here is the idea of established commercial-market acceptability, a judgment to be made by the government buyer for the purpose of determining a prospective contractor's ability to provide a commercial product that will conform to the governent's need. To be market acceptable, a product must be marketed to the general public in substantial quantities; sales to the general public must predominate over those to the government. Commercial products previously produced in accordance with a government specification that met the requirements of the specification may be considered acceptable for a stated period of time under solicitations requiring a product to have etablished commercial market acceptability. The period of time such products will be considered acceptable will be determined by the contracting office in light of the circumstances of specific procurements.

Thus a third index of specifications, published by the federal government, is in preparation: the *Index of Commercial Item Descriptions* (CIDs).

Qualification and Qualified-Product Listing

Qualification is the testing of products for compliance with the requirements of a specification prior to and independent of purchasing action. The qualification procedure prevents delay in delivery of items under contract that might be caused by problems in design or composition or by time-consuming tests required to prove that the specification requirements can be met. Products approved after qualification tests have been conducted are listed on qualified products' lists (QPL), which serve as procurement tools in the awarding of contracts.

When the government has determined that qualification testing is necessary, the specifications for those products include the requirements for qualification, the qualification tests, and the name of the activity responsible for qualification.

Normally after the announcement of a forthcoming procurement or the issuance of an invitation for bids, it is too late to perform qualification testing for that particular procurement. Therefore firms that are interested in supplying a product under a specification containing a qualification requirement should arrange to have their product qualified immediately.

The fact that a product has been tested and included on a QPL is evidence only that a manufacturer can make a product that meets the specification requirements. It does not in any way relieve the manufacturer of an obligation to maintain such quality. The listing also does not guarantee acceptance of the product in any future purchase, nor does it constitute a waiver of the requirements of the specification as to acceptance, inspection, testing, or other provisions of any contract. The fact that a product is listed on a QPL does not relieve inspectors or purchasing officers of the responsibility for enforcing the requirements of the basic specification of the contract as to inspection and quality performance.

A supplier who wants to be eligible for award of a contract to furnish an approved product manufactured by another firm should be required to state in a bid the name of the actual manufacturer, the manufacturer's designation for the product, and the qualification test reference number. The bid will then receive the same consideration as bids for approved products from other sources.

In general, distributors or dealers who are completely responsible for the distribution of a product carrying their brand designation but manufactured by another company are considered eligible for listing on the QPL. In such cases a particular distributor will ask the manufacturer to certify that he, as distributor, is authorized to rebrand and distribute the product. When this certification has been furnished to the activity responsible for qualification, or to its authorized agent, samples of the rebranded product may be requested from the distributor for tests. If the rebranded product has been tested previously and approved under the brand designation of the manufacturer, qualification approval may be extended to the rebranded product by the activity responsible for qualification without retest. However, the manufacturer must certify that the rebranded product is in all respects the same as the approved product. The listing of a qualified product submitted by a distributor will include the name and brand designation of the distributor and the name and plant address of the actual manufacturer. This procedure is generally not applicable to equipment that requires repair-parts support or where it conflicts with the provisions of an individual specification.

The activity responsible for qualification (preparing activity of the specification) notifies the manufacturer concerning the results of the testing and whether the product has met the qualification requirements. If the product is approved for inclusion on a QPL, the activity will prepare the list.

Item Classifying and Coding

For effective management the wide range of items moving through the system must be categorized and classified. A comprehensive procedure for classifying and coding items begins with a distinction between nonexpendable and expendable items. Nonexpendable items are neither consumed in use nor lose their original identity during periods of use; examples are vehicles, shop equipment, tools, furniture, and similar items. Normally these items are issued on the basis of allowances established in approved allowance documents or by special authorization for limited purposes. Accountability for such items is maintained by the using unit or activity to which issued. Expendable items are either consumed in use or lose their original identity during periods of use by incorporation in or attachment to another assembly. These items are issued on an as-required basis. Examples are maintenance parts and components, raw materials, fuel, and office and housekeeping supplies consumed in use. Accountability for expendable items is dropped when they are issued or attached to another item, but for expendable items that can be repaired and used again, accountability must be maintained when turned in until they are reissued or condemned.

Items are also classified as replacement-type or consumption-type items. A replacement-type item is a nonexpendable equipment-type item issued in accordance with allowances set forth in documents. This type of item maintains its identity while in use. Requirements for it are based on the number of organizations authorized to have the item and the amount that each organization is authorized. After all units are equipped with their authorizations, the requirement for such an item consists of replacements for worn or damaged equipment (hence the name replacement-type item). A consumption-type item is an expendable item that is consumed in use or loses its identity through incorporation in another assembly. Issued on an as-required basis, the consumption-type item category consists of a wide range of supplies from complete assemblies such as pumps, motors, and instruments to minor maintenance parts and consumable supplies such as paint, fuel, and chemicals. Consumption-type items can be more specifically broken down:

1. Component. A physically separable combination of assemblies, subassemblies, and parts that are electrically and/or mechanically connected to perform a specific function.
2. Assembly. A group of two or more physically connected or related parts that can be taken apart without being destroyed.
3. Spare parts. Individual pieces of a component, assembly, or end item used in the field and in depots to repair or overhaul worn or damaged material.
4. Consumable supplies. Items such as fuel, paint, and ammunition, which are consumed in use.

Since consumption-type items are issued on an as-required basis, requirements for them are usually based on past usage or demand and a projection of this demand into the future rather than on the basis of authorized allowance.

The terms *replacement type* and *consumption type* primarily identify methods of computing requirements. The two types may not always coincide with the categories of nonexpendable and expendable supplies. Even though issues on the basis of allowance documents, nonexpendable items of small-dollar value that are issued frequently may be better controlled by the consumption-type method of computation. On the other hand, major components and accessories, although consumption-type items, are considered nonexpendable when issued for special purposes on the basis of allowance documents. Other items may be issued on the basis of definite allowances, and requirements are computed accordingly. In the sound management of the requirements function, it is important that the computation method used for an item provide the desired accuracy with the minimum expenditure of time and money.

Another classification of items important for requirements purposes is their breakdown into recoverable and nonrecoverable items. Recoverable items are those that can be repaired by maintenance activities and reissued. Nonrecoverable items are consumed in use or cannot be economically repaired when they become unserviceable. In computing requirements, it is necessary to know not only whether items fall into the general categories of recoverable and nonrecoverable but also the maintenance level at which repairs can be made. Sometimes an item cannot be economically repaired except by the using unit. If such items become unserviceable and cannot be fixed by the users, they are thrown away rather than turned in to maintenance shops.

Closely related to recoverability classification is classification by condition. Serviceable items are those ready for issue. Reparable items are not ready for issue and use because of the need for minor or major repairs. Periodic-inspection items are those such as fire extinguishers or delicate laboratory devices. Condemned items, are those that have become unserviceable through use and are not suitable for repair, and those that are obsolete, unsafe, or otherwise unsuitable for use and have been administratively condemned.

In order to provide for the selective management of items in accordance with the inventory investment they represent, items are divided into various cost or demand-value categories. Under the cost-categorization program, items are placed in one of three cost categories. Cost category I items are high-value items that on the basis of unit cost or dollar turnover represent a substantial portion of dollars spent in a commodity class. Such high-value items usually account for only 2 to 3 percent of the total items within a particular commodity class, but by detailed control of these items it is possible to manage effectively anywhere from 20 percent to 80 percent of the total inventory investment for the class. Cost category II items are those with a unit price of ten dollars or more that are not in cost category I. Cost category III items are those with a unit cost of under ten dollars.

Under the demand-value system of classification, general categories of items, such as low-value cost category III and nonrecoverable cost category II items, are further subdivided according to value of annual demand (unit price times annual issues). In effect classification by demand value carries over into the field of low-cost items the concept of considering both unit cost and turnover.

Since the purpose of classification by cost or demand value is to vary the degree of control in accordance with inventory investment, any such system will usually affect nearly all phases of the requirements operation, from the collection of demand data to the determination of economical procurement quantities. The criteria for establishing such categories are consequently of great importance to materials managers.

Finally every item is classified into a commodity class. The most all-inclusive is the federal government's listing of FSCs. There are 604 classes, under one of which every item of material in public use can be classified. (The listing, developed by the federal government, is widely used and referred to at other levels of government and in industry.) Ironically, the listing begins with guns and ends with cemetarial and mortuary equipment and supplies. Of the 604 classes, those of most general interest and applicability are,

FSC

1005   Guns, through 30mm
1010   Guns, over 30mm, to 75mm
1015   Guns, 75mm through 125mm
1020   Guns, over 125mm through 150mm
1025   Guns, over 150mm through 200mm

FSC

1030	Guns, over 200mm through 300mm
1035	Guns, over 300mm
1040	Chemical Weapons and Equipment
1055	Launchers, Rocket and Pyrotechnic
1090	Assemblies Interchangeable Between Weapons in Two or More Classes
1095	Miscellaneous Weapons
1105	Nuclear Bombs
1110	Nuclear Projectiles
1115	Nuclear Warhead and Warhead Sections
1125	Nuclear Demolition Charges
1127	Nuclear Rockets
1130	Conversion Kits, Nuclear Ordnance
1135	Fuzing and Firing Devices, Nuclear Ordnance
1140	Nuclear Components
1145	High Explosive Charges, Propellants and Detonators, Nuclear Ordnance
1190	Specialized Test and Handling Equipment, Nuclear Ordnance
1195	Miscellaneous Nuclear Ordnance
1210	Fire Control Directors
1220	Fire Control Computing Sights and Devices
1230	Fire Control Systems, Complete
1240	Optical Sighting and Ranging Equipment
1250	Fire Control Stabilizing Mechanisms
1260	Fire Control Designating and Indicating Equipment
1265	Fire Control Transmitting and Receiving Equipment, except Airborne
1285	Fire Control Radar Equipment, except Airborne
1290	Fire Control Equipment, Miscellaneous
1305	Ammunition, through 30mm
1310	Ammunition, over 30mm up to 75mm
1315	Ammunition, 75mm through 125mm
1320	Ammunition, over 125mm
1325	Bombs
1330	Grenades
1340	Rockets and Rocket Ammunition
1345	Land Mines
1365	Military Chemical Agents
1370	Pyrotechnics
1375	Demolition Materials
1376	Bulk Explosives
1377	Cartridge & Propellant Actuated Devices and Components
1380	Military Biological Agents
1390	Fuzes and Primers
1550	Drones
1905	Combat Ships and Landing Vessels
1910	Transport Vessels, Passenger and Troop
1920	Fishing Vessels
1925	Special Service Vessels
1930	Barges and Lighters, Cargo
1935	Barges and Lighters, Special Purpose

FSC

1940	Small Craft
1945	Pontoons and Floating Docks
1950	Floating Drydocks
1990	Miscellaneous Vessels
2010	Ship and Boat Propulsion Components
2020	Rigging and Rigging Gear
2030	Deck Machinery
2040	Marine Hardware and Hull Items
2060	Commercial Fishing Equipment
2090	Miscellaneous Ship and Marine Equipment
2210	Locomotives
2220	Rail Cars
2230	Right-of-Way Construction and Maintenance Equipment, Railroad
2240	Locomotive and Rail Car Accessories and Components
2250	Track Materials, Railroad
2310	Passenger Motor Vehicles
2320	Trucks and Truck Tractors
2330	Trailers
2340	Motorcycles, Motor Scooters and Bicycles
2350	Tanks and Self-Propelled Weapons
2410	Tractors, Full Track, Low Speed
2420	Tractors, Wheeled
2430	Tractors, Track Laying, High Speed
2510	Vehicular Cab, Body, and Frame Structural Components
2520	Vehicular Power Transmission Components
2530	Vehicular Brake, Steering, Axle, Wheel, and Track Components
2540	Vehicular Furniture and Accessories
2590	Vehicular Components, Miscellaneous
2610	Tires and Tubes, Pneumatic, Except Aircraft
2630	Tires, Solid and Cushion
2640	Tire Rebuilding and Tire and Tube Repair Materials
2805	Gasoline Reciprocating Engines, Except Aircraft; and Components
2815	Diesel Engines and Components
2820	Steam Engines, Reciprocating; and Components
2825	Steam Turbines and Components
2895	Miscellaneous Engines and Components
2910	Engine Fuel System Components, Nonaircraft
2920	Engine Electrical System Components, Nonaircraft
2930	Engine Cooling System Components, Nonaircraft
2940	Engine Air and Oil Filters, Strainers, and Cleaners, Nonaircraft
2990	Miscellaneous Engine Accessories, Nonaircraft
3010	Torque Converters and Speed Changers
3020	Gears, Pulleys, Sprockets, and Transmission Chain
3030	Belting, Drive Belts, Fan Belts, and Accessories
3040	Miscellaneous Power Transmission Equipment
3110	Bearings, Antifriction, Unmounted
3120	Bearings, Plain, Unmounted
3130	Bearings, Mounted
3210	Sawmill and Planing Mill Machinery

FSC

3220 Woodworking Machines
3230 Tools and Attachments for Woodworking Machinery
3405 Saws and Filing Machines
3408 Machining Centers and Way-Type Machines
3410 Electrical and Ultrasonic Erosion Machines
3411 Boring Machines
3412 Broaching Machines
3413 Drilling and Tapping Machines
3414 Gear Cutting and Finishing Machines
3415 Grinding Machines
3416 Lathes
3417 Milling Machines
3418 Planers and Shapers
3419 Miscellaneous Machine Tools
3422 Rolling Mills and Drawing Machines
3424 Metal Heat Treating Equipment
3426 Metal Finishing Equipment
3431 Electric ARC Welding Equipment
3432 Electric Resistance Welding Equipment
3433 Gas Welding, Heat Cutting and Metalizing Equipment
3436 Welding Positioners and Manipulators
3438 Miscellaneous Welding Equipment
3439 Miscellaneous Welding, Soldering & Brazing Supplies & Accessories
3441 Bending and Forming Machines
3442 Hydraulic and Pneumatic Presses, Power Driven
3443 Mechanical Presses, Power Driven
3444 Manual Presses
3445 Punching and Shearing Machines
3446 Forging Machinery and Hammers
3447 Wire and Metal Ribbon Forming Machinery
3448 Riveting Machines
3449 Miscellaneous Secondary Metal Forming & Cutting Machines
3450 Machine Tools, Portable
3455 Cutting Tools for Machine
3456 Cutting and Forming Tools for Secondary Metalworking Machinery
3460 Machine Tool Accessories
3461 Accessories for Secondary Metalworking Machinery
3465 Production Jigs, Fixtures and Templates
3470 Machine Shop Sets, Kits and Outfits
3510 Laundry and Dry Cleaning Equipment
3520 Shoe Repairing Equipment
3530 Industrial Sewing Machines & Mobile Textile Repair Shops
3540 Wrapping and Packaging Machinery
3550 Vending and Coil Operated Machines
3590 Miscellaneous Service and Trade Equipment
3610 Printing, Duplicating, and Bookbinding Equipment
3611 Industrial Marking Machines
3620 Rubber and Plastics Working Machinery
3635 Crystal and Glass Industries Machinery

FSC

3650	Chemical & Pharmaceutical Products Manufacturing Machinery
3655	Gas Generating and Dispensing Systems, Fixed or Mobile
3660	Industrial Size Reduction Machinery
3670	Specialized Semiconductor, Microelectronic Circuit Device & Printed Circuit Board Mfg. Machinery
3680	Foundry Machinery, Related Equipment and Supplies
3685	Specialized Metal Container Mfg. Machinery & Related Equipment
3693	Industrial Assembly Machines
3694	Clean Work Stations, Controlled Environment & Related Equipment
3695	Miscellaneous Special Industry Machinery
3710	Soil Preparation Equipment
3720	Harvesting Equipment
3740	Pest, Disease, and Frost Control Equipment
3750	Gardening Implements and Tools
3770	Saddlery, Harness, Whips, and Related Animal Furnishings
3805	Earth Moving and Excavating Equipment
3810	Cranes and Crane-Shovels
3815	Crane and Crane-Shovel Attachments
3820	Mining, Rock Drilling, Earth Boring, and Related Equipment
3825	Road Clearing and Cleaning Equipment
3830	Truck and Tractor Attachments
3835	Petroleum Production and Distribution Equipment
3895	Miscellaneous Construction Equipment
3910	Conveyors
3920	Materials Handing Equipment, Nonself-Propelled
3930	Warehouse Trucks and Tractors, Self-Propelled
3940	Blocks, Tackle, Rigging, and Slings
3950	Winches, Hoists, Cranes, and Derricks
3990	Miscellaneous Materials Handling Equipment
4010	Chain and Wire Rope
4020	Fiber Rope, Cordage, and Twine
4030	Fittings for Rope, Cable, and Chain
4110	Refrigeration Equipment
4120	Air Conditioning Equipment
4130	Refrigeration and Air Conditioning Components
4140	Fans, Air Circulators, and Blower Equipment
4210	Fire Fighting Equipment
4220	Marine Life Saving and Diving Equipment
4230	Decontaminating and Impregnating Equipment
4240	Safety and Rescue Equipment
4310	Compressors and Vacuum Pumps
4320	Power and Hand Pumps
4330	Centrifugals, Separators, and Pressure and Vacuum Filters
4410	Industrial Boilers
4420	Heat Exchangers and Steam Condensers
4440	Driers, Dehydrators, and Anhydrators
4460	Air Purification Equipment
4510	Plumbing Fixtures and Accessories
4520	Space Heating Equipment and Domestic Water Heaters

FSC

4530   Fuel Burning Equipment Units
4540   Miscellaneous Plumbing, Heating, and Sanitation Equipment
4610   Water Purification Equipment
4620   Water Distillation Equipment, Marine and Industrial
4630   Sewage Treatment Equipment
4710   Pipe and Tube
4720   Hose and Tubing, Flexible
4730   Fittings and Specialties: Hose, Pipe, and Tube
4810   Valves, Powered
4820   Valves, Nonpowered
4925   Ammunition Maintenance and Repair Shop Specialized Equipment
4930   Lubrication and Fuel Dispensing Equipment
5110   Hand Tools, Edged, Nonpowered
5120   Hand Tools, Nonedged, Nonpowered
5130   Hand Tools, Power Driven
5133   Drill Bits, Counterbores, and Countersinks, Hand and Machine
5136   Taps, Dies, and Collets: Hand and Machine
5140   Tool and Hardware Boxes
5180   Sets, Kits, and Outfits of Hand Tools
5210   Measuring Tools, Craftsmen's
5280   Sets, Kits, and Outfits of Measuring Tools
5305   Screws
5306   Bolts
5307   Studs
5310   Nuts and Washers
5315   Nails, Keys and Pins
5320   Rivets
5325   Fastening Devices
5330   Packing and Gasket Materials
5335   Metal Screening
5340   Miscellaneous Hardware
5345   Disks and Stones, Abrasive
5350   Abrasive Materials
5355   Knobs and Pointers
5360   Coil, Flat and Wire Springs
5365   Rings, Shims, and Spacers
5410   Prefabricated and Portable Buildings
5430   Storage Tanks
5440   Scaffolding Equipment and Concrete Forms
5445   Prefabricated Tower Structures
5450   Miscellaneous Prefabricated Structures
5510   Lumber and Related Basic Wood Materials
5520   Millwork
5530   Plywood and Veneer
5610   Mineral Construction Materials, Bulk
5620   Building Glass, Tile, Brick and Block
5630   Pipe and Conduit, Nonmetallic
5640   Wallboard, Building Paper, and Thermal Insulation Materials
5650   Roofing and Siding Materials

FSC

5660 Fencing, Fences and Gates
5670 Architectural and Related Metal Products
5680 Miscellaneous Construction Materials
5805 Telephone and Telegraph Equipment
5815 Teletype and Facsimile Equipment
5820 Radio and Television Communication Equipment, except Airborne
5821 Radio and Television Communication Equipment, Airborne
5825 Radio Navigation Equipment, except Airborne
5830 Intercommunication and Public Address Systems, except Airborne
5831 Intercommunication and Public Address Systems, Airborne
5835 Sound Recording and Reproducing Equipment
5895 Miscellaneous Communications Equipment
5905 Resistors
5910 Capacitors
5915 Filters and Networks
5920 Fuses and Lightning Arrestors
5925 Circuit Breakers
5930 Switches
5935 Connectors, Electrical
5940 Lugs, Terminals, and Terminal Strips
5945 Relays, Contractors, and Solenoids
5950 Coils and Transformers
5955 Piezoelectric Crystals
5960 Electron Tubes and Associated Hardware
5961 Semiconductor Devices and Associated Hardware
5962 Microelectronic Circuit Devices
5965 Headsets, Handsets, Microphones and Speakers
5970 Electrical Insulators and Insulating Materials
5975 Electrical Hardware and Supplies
5977 Electrical Contact Brushes and Electrodes
5985 Antennas, Waveguides, and Related Equipment
5990 Synchros and Resolvers
5995 Cable, Cord, and Wire Assemblies: Communication Equipment
5999 Miscellaneous Electrical and Electronic Components
6105 Motors, Electrical
6110 Electrical Control Equipment
6115 Generators and Generator Sets, Electrical
6120 Transformers: Distribution and Power Station
6125 Converters, Electrical, Rotating
6130 Converters, Electrical, Nonrotating
6135 Batteries, Primary
6140 Batteries, Secondary
6145 Wire and Cable, Electrical
6150 Miscellaneous Electric Power and Distribution Equipment
6210 Indoor and Outdoor Electric Lighting Fixtures
6220 Electric Vehicular Lights and Fixtures
6230 Electric Portable and Hand Lighting Equipment
6240 Electric Lamps
6250 Ballasts, Lampholders, and Starters
6260 Nonelectrical Lighting Fixtures

FSC

6320 Shipboard Alarm and Signal Systems
6350 Miscellaneous Alarm and Signal Systems
6505 Drugs, Biologicals, and Official Reagents
6508 Medicated Cosmetics and Toiletries
6510 Surgical Dressing Materials
6515 Medical and Surgical Instruments, Equipment, and Supplies
6520 Dental Instruments, Equipment, and Supplies
6525 X-Ray Equipment and Supplies: Medical, Dental, Veterinary
6530 Hospital Furniture, Equipment, Utensils, and Supplies
6532 Hospital and Surgical Clothing and Textile Special Purpose Items
6540 Opticians' Instruments, Equipment, and Supplies
6545 Medical Sets, Kits, and Outfits
6605 Navigational Instruments
6625 Electrical and Electronic Properties Measuring and Testing Instruments
6630 Chemical Analysis Instruments
6635 Physical Properties Testing Equipment
6640 Laboratory Equipment and Supplies
6645 Time Measuring Instruments
6650 Optical Instruments
6655 Geophysical and Astronomical Instruments
6660 Meteorological Instruments and Apparatus
6665 Hazard-Detecting Instruments and Apparatus
6670 Scales and Balances
6675 Drafting, Surveying, and Mapping Instruments
6680 Liquid and Gas Flow, Liquid Level, and Mechanical Motion Measuring Instruments
6685 Pressure, Temperature, and Humidity Measuring and Controlling Instruments
6695 Combination and Miscellaneous Instruments
6710 Cameras, Motion Picture
6720 Cameras, Still Picture
6730 Photographic Projection Equipment
6740 Photographic Developing and Finishing Equipment
6750 Photographic Supplies
6760 Photographic Equipment and Accessories
6780 Photographic Sets, Kits, and Outfits
6810 Chemicals
6820 Dyes
6830 Gases: Compressed and Liquefied
6840 Pest Control Agents and Disinfectants
6850 Miscellaneous Chemical Specialties
6910 Training Aids
6920 Armament Training Devices
6940 Communication Training Devices
7105 Household Furniture
7125 Cabinets, Lockers, Bins, and Shelving
7195 Miscellaneous Furniture and Fixtures
7210 Household Furnishings
7220 Floor Coverings

FSC

7230 Draperies, Awnings, and Shades
7240 Household and Commercial Utility Containers
7290 Miscellaneous Household and Commercial Furnishings and Appliances
7310 Food Cooking, Baking, and Serving Equipment
7320 Kitchen Equipment and Appliances
7330 Kitchen Hand Tools and Utensils
7340 Cutlery and Flatware
7350 Tableware
7360 Sets, Kits, and Outfits: Food Preparation and Serving
7410 Punched Card System Machines
7420 Accounting and Calculating Machines
7430 Typewriters and Office Type Composing Machines
7450 Office Type Sound Recording and Reproducing Machines
7460 Visible Record Equipment
7490 Miscellaneous Office Machines
7510 Office Supplies
7520 Office Devices and Accessories
7530 Stationery and Record Forms
7610 Books and Pamphlets
7660 Sheet and Book Music
7690 Miscellaneous Printed Matter
7710 Musical Instruments
7720 Musical Instrument Parts and Accessories
7730 Phonographs, Radios, and Television Sets: Home Type
7740 Phonograph Records
7810 Athletic and Sporting Equipment
7820 Games, Toys, and Wheeled Goods
7830 Recreational and Gymnastic Equipment
7910 Floor Polishers and Vacuum Cleaning Equipment
7920 Brooms, Brushes, Mops, and Sponges
7930 Cleaning and Polishing Compounds and Preparations
8010 Paints, Dopes, Varnishes, and Related Products
8020 Paint and Artists' Brushes
8030 Preservative and Sealing Compounds
8040 Adhesives
8105 Bags and Sacks
8110 Drums and Cans
8115 Boxes, Cartons, and Crates
8120 Commercial and Industrial Gas Cylinders
8125 Bottles and Jars
8130 Reels and Spools
8135 Packaging and Packing Bulk Materials
8140 Ammunition Boxes, Packages, and Special Containers
8305 Textile Fabrics
8310 Yarn and Thread
8315 Notions and Apparel Findings
8320 Padding and Stuffing Materials
8325 Fur Materials
8330 Leather
8335 Shoe Findings and Soling Materials

FSC

8340	Tents and Tarpaulins
8345	Flags and Pennants
8405	Outerwear, Men's
8410	Outerwear, Women's
8415	Clothing, Special Purpose
8420	Underwear and Nightwear, Men's
8425	Underwear and Nightwear, Women's
8430	Footwear, Mens
8435	Footwear, Women's
8440	Hosiery, Handwear, and Clothing Accessories, Men's
8445	Hosiery, Handwear, and Clothing Accessories, Women's
8450	Children's and Infants' Apparel and Accessories
8455	Badges and Insignia
8460	Luggage
8465	Individual Equipment
8470	Armor, Personal
8475	Specialized Flight Clothing and Accessories
8510	Perfumes, Toilet Preparations, and Powders
8520	Toilet Soap, Shaving Preparations, and Dentifrices
8530	Personal Toiletry Articles
8540	Toiletry Paper Products
8710	Forage and Feed
8720	Fertilizers
8730	Seeds and Nursery Stock
8820	Live Animals, not Raised for Food
8905	Meat, Poultry, and Fish
8910	Dairy Foods and Eggs
8915	Fruits and Vegetables
8920	Bakery and Cereal Products
8925	Sugar, Confectionary, and Nuts
8930	Jams, Jellies, and Preserves
8935	Soups and Bouillons
8940	Special Dietary Foods and Food Specialty Preparations
8945	Food Oils and Fats
8950	Condiments and Related Products
8955	Coffee, Tea, and Cocoa
8960	Beverages, Nonalcoholic
8970	Composite Food Packages
8975	Tobacco Products
9110	Fuels, Solid
9130	Liquid Propellants and Fuels, Petroleum Base
9140	Fuel Oils
9150	Oils and Greases: Cutting, Lubricating, and Hydraulic
9160	Miscellaneous Waxes, Oils, and Fats
9310	Paper and Paperboard
9320	Rubber Fabricated Materials
9330	Plastics Fabricated Materials
9340	Glass Fabricated Materials
9350	Refractories and Fire Surfacing Materials
9390	Miscellaneous Fabricated Nonmetallic Materials

FSC

9420   Fibers: Vegetable, Animal, and Synthetic
9430   Miscellaneous Crude Animal Products, Inedible
9505   Wire, Nonelectrical, Iron and Steel
9510   Bars and Rods, Iron and Steel
9515   Plate, Sheet, and Strip: Iron and Steel
9520   Structural Shapes, Iron and Steel
9525   Wire, Nonelectrical, Nonferrous Base Metal
9530   Bars and Rods, Nonferrous Base Metal
9535   Plate, Sheet, Strip, and Foil: Nonferrous Base Metal
9540   Structural Shapes, Nonferrous Base Metal
9545   Plate, Sheet, Strip, Foil, and Wire: Precious Metal
9620   Minerals, Natural and Synthetic
9905   Signs, Advertising Displays, and Identification Plates
9910   Jewelry
9915   Collectors' Items
9920   Smokers' Articles and Matches
9925   Ecclesiastical Equipment, Furnishings, and Supplies
9930   Memorials; Cemeterial and Mortuary Equipment and Supplies

Thus a truck would be classified and coded as a nonexpendable, replacement-type, recoverable, perhaps reparable, Cost Category I, FSC 2320 item. A tire for the truck would be expendable, consumption-type, recoverable, perhaps reparable (to be recapped), Cost Category II, FSC 2610 item. The gasoline fueling the truck would be expendable, consumption-type, consumable, nonrecoverable, FSC 9130 item.

Item Identification and Cataloging[7]

Proper item identification is fundamental to all materials-management operations, including procurement, distribution, storage, issuance, accounting, and disposal. Cataloging establishes a uniform method of identifying material and thus underlies all other operations in the supply chain. Each item must be uniquely identified so that the same item does not appear under different names, numbers, and descriptions or that different items are not given the same designation. This requires a uniform, systematic procedure for naming, describing, classifying, and numbering items. The new entries can then be screened against existing items to avoid unnecessary duplication.

The procedure that establishes the unique character of each item is known as item identification. It is both the process and product of describing items. Its elements are item name, item description, and item classification and numbering. Each element is necessary to identify items fully and support the entry controls employed within the catalog system to keep out unneeded items. Inaccurate or incomplete identification weakens these control mechanisms and promotes duplication in the catalog.

The item name should be a noun with a generally recognized dictionary meaning. At the federal level, catalogers utilize a listing of approved item names. The noun is followed by indicators of size, form, color, style, weight, and any other characteristics of the item. If the item is designated by type, grade, or class, these will be specified in sequence. If a standard or specification exists, it will be cited. The unit pack or unit of issue will be given.

Once identified, the item will be recorded under the appropriate supply-class number. For example, in the federal system, an item would be recorded under a supply group, such as "Group 53, Hardware and Abrasives," and in one of the 604 classes, such as "Class 5305, Screws." Thus the full identification of an item would be: "5305-00-014-4791 Screw, tapping, steel, cadmium-coated, panhead, No. 6, 1/4", 48 (unit pack)."

Many items can be identified by reference to a manufacturer's part number, but a full descriptive-item identification is preferred since such a description establishes the true identity of an item and differentiates it from every other item of supply. Thus duplicate stock numbers can be recognized and eliminated, and similar items can be selected and studied for elimination of those having dispensable differences. Partially described and reference-type identifications are not complete. Because all characteristics are not documented, such items are not subject to the item entry controls operating in the cataloging procedure. As a result, new items are assigned stock numbers and added to the catalog and supply systems even though identical or similar items are already in the catalog. This duplication can remain undetected because some controls designed to identify duplicate and unneeded items depend upon the presence of characteristic data. If items are not fully described, these controls are substantially weakened.

The federal catalog system requires that each item of supply be classified in only one FSC. Accordingly cataloging handbooks are prepared and issued to help identify the appropriate class for an item of supply. Typically the manufacturer's part name or approved name can be found in such handbooks together with reference to the normally assigned FSC. By consulting such handbooks, catalogers can assign items to designated classes and thereby ensure that each item of supply appears under only one identification and in only one class. Thus cataloging an item involves five steps: selecting an item name, writing the description, classifying the item, numbering the item, and publishing the collected data.

The initial step in establishing the characteristics of an item of supply is selecting a name that answers the question, What is it? A single name must be established for each item of supply. Regardless of how many different activities use the item, they all will call the same item of supply by the same name.

Approximately 29,500 uniform item names are currently in use in the federal catalog system. These names, called approved item names (AINs), are published together with their definitions (plus exclusions and inclusions of related approved and colloquial item names) in the *Federal Item Name Directory for Supply Cataloguing*. The directory also lists thousands of colloquial names, including part names used by industry, which are cross-referenced to the AINs.

The federal catalog system, in addition to establishing uniformity of names within the government supply systems, bridges the gap in item name language between government and industry and provides a basis for increased uniformity of understanding in materials management.

For specialized or proprietary items, in which the name is governed by the design or function of the part and no AIN exists, the colloquial or part name established by the manufacturer or designer may be used. However, when more than one name exists for the same item, the single name most commonly used by government and industry is selected for use in the federal catalog system. The other name is cross-referenced.

An interesting and important practice related to proprietary or specialized item name selection is that copyrighted or trademarked names (such as Decalcomania, Frigidaire, Kleenex, Kodak, and Stainless Steel) normally are not selected or approved for use in the federal catalog system. Exceptions are product names (such as neon, nylon, and zipper) that have become a common part of the language. This emphasizes the fact that a correct name for an item of supply is vital not only for cataloging but also for administrative, legal, safety, security, and many other purposes.

The second step in establishing the characteristics of an item of supply is describing its physical and functional attributes. If possible, an item is described through the use of words, numbers, and codes that depict the essential characteristics, including physical, mechanical, electrical, chemical, material, dimensional, and performance data (descriptive method). If the item cannot be described, only the appropriate item-identifying part or reference number(s) and technical data (such as blueprints, drawings, specifications, and standards) are cited (reference method). The descriptive method results in a narrative statement of the technical characteristics of the item of supply in a predesignated sequence:

1. Item name.
2. Material of which formed.
3. Style.
4. Dimension(s).
5. Manufacturer's data, if needed.

This sequence primarily applies to single, specific items. Complete assemblies also can be described under this type of identification. For maintenance purposes, even though the end items are functionally and physically interchangeable as units, they may have different internal components. If spare-parts support is maintained for these units and all the internal parts are not completely interchangeable, then the item identification for each unit must contain the manufacturer's data, and each manufacturer's unit is assigned a different number. An example would be interchangeable diesel engine units of the same horsepower and size. Several manufacturers make such engines, but each manufacturer's engine requires different repair parts. Each manufacturer and engine designation number must be cited (in addition to the other descriptive characteristics common to all of the engines) so that correct components may be related to the proper engine. This type of item identification normally is used to describe items where a specific application, performance, or reliability requirement dictates the use of a single manufacturer's item of production.

The reference method of item identification relies solely on reference to the appropriate manufacturer(s) part number(s). Descriptive characteristics are not actually recorded but are considered to be inherent or implied in the recorded part number(s) for the item. The reference method is used in specific commodity areas where the collection and recording of descriptive characteristics would serve no useful purpose or when the manufacturer's technical data are not available to the government for various reasons; the data may be proprietary to the manufacturer, purchase charges for the technical data may be too high, or the manufacturer may refuse to furnish the information.

The third step in establishing the characteristics of an item of supply is determining its relationship to other items in the system. Considering the vast variety and number of items in the supply systems of the government and the worldwide scope of operations, it is evident that materials managers cannot effectively manage their systems in all operations on an item-by-item basis. Therefore items are organized into groups and classes.

Each item of supply that is identified in the federal catalog system is normally assigned to a unique four-digit class. An item is classified either by what it is (bolts in the bolt class, electron tubes in the electron tube class) or where it fits (typewriter platen with the typewriter). Specifically designed items are classified in the same class as their higher assemblies in the absence of an existing applicable class. For example, in the absence of classes specifically covering safety guards for power saws or agitators for washing machines, the safety guard is classified in the same one as the power saw and the agitator in the same one as the washing machine.

The fourth step in the process of item identification is the assignment of a stock number to each different item of supply. Each item of supply in the federal catalog system is assigned a different thirteen-digit stock number, for example:

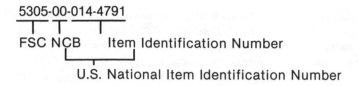

FSC: Federal Supply Class.
NCB: National Codification Bureau (the national agency that assigned the number).

The first six digits identify the group and the class and who assigned the number. The remaining seven digits are nonsignificant, serially assigned.

The fifth step in the procedure is to catalog or publish the collected data for the items of supply that have been assigned stock numbers. Basically this means to present the information in formats and media suitable for utilization by personnel involved in the materials function. Many media are available. The catalog may be a bound or loose-leaf paper volume. It may be a card file, either manually or machine prepared. It may be a magnetic disk or tape, read on a screen. The medium in most general use is microfiche. The microfiche used in federal catalog system publications is prepared at a 48:1 reduction ratio on sheets of 105-millimeter film approximately 4 × 6 inches in size. Each film sheet (fiche) contains 270 frames (269 frames of data and 1 index frame in the lower right corner to direct readers to the proper data frame). Each frame is equivalent to one printed page (10 × 14 inches maximum size) reduced to about 3/16 by 1/4 inch. Each fiche has a title line, readable without magnification and printed across the top, which includes such information as the publication designation, effective date, an indication of the first entry on that fiche, and the sequential number of that fiche in the set.

The item identification and cataloging procedure must possess these fundamental capabilities:

1. It must protect, through precise identification, the uniqueness of an item of supply in its applications throughout the government.
2. It must be stable and maintain permanence of the item identification throughout the life of the item of supply.
3. It must be flexible and capable of meeting the varying requirements of many users.
4. It must be capable of expansion to meet peak loads and new programs.
5. It must possess continuity in order to withstand any impacts, such as changes in materials-management concepts, technological improvements, or disasters.
6. It must provide ready data accessibility for management purposes.
7. It must be capable of performing effectively and economically.

Effective cataloging serves the needs of the entire purchasing and materials-management system by providing data for requirements determination, procurement, production, vendor buying, packaging, inventory management, and other essential activities.

The federal catalog system and how it fits into the total supply system at the federal level is described in the Department of Defense's *Supply Management Reference Book*. The book covers the supply-management systems and supply-supporting systems of the military services and the Defense Logistics Agency. The role of the GSA is portrayed where support of defense activities is involved. The supply systems of the Department of Transportation are also included. The book is intended to serve as a vehicle for information and discussion by professionals within government agencies, the Congress, interested individuals, and outside groups such as universities, industrial activities, and research organizations.[8]

Supply Standardization

Supply standardization is accomplished primarily through item-reduction studies and inactive-item reviews. Item reduction consists of examining items already in the catalog, grouping together those that serve the same purpose, and eliminating those that are unneeded. It is accomplished by comparing the functions and technical characteristics of similar items and selecting a preferred item from the group. Removal of the other items from the inventory and the catalog is then initiated. If all users of the items agree to the finding of the study, the unessential items are coded "not procurable," and the remaining inventory stocks are systematically depleted. Thereafter the preferred item is ordered and used. As stocks of nonpreferred items are eliminated, users withdraw their interest in the item, and it becomes inactive.

Another method of eliminating unessential items is to find and remove those no longer used. Inactive-item review programs are operated to identify unused items, prompting coordinated withdrawal of user interest and subsequent inactivation.

Supply standardization is primarily a matter of discipline. Item reduction must be a program, with responsibilities assigned and objectives stated. Procedures must halt procurement of nonstandard items, eliminate stocks of unneeded items, and deregister users of those unneeded items. The proper coding of items will support these three procedures. Schedules must be established for periodically and systematically reviewing each supply class. Safeguards must be established to ensure that nonstandard items are not simply thrown away or otherwise prematurely disposed of.

Inactive-item review must also be established as a program. Supply classes should be systematically screened for items no longer being requisitioned. Users should be asked to advise materials managers when changes in using activities will eliminate or reduce material-support needs. If users are reluctant to say that they will no longer be interested in some item, procedures should be established to flag items not requisitioned within a specified time limit.

Authorization and Allowance

Essential to the requirements determination for items of equipment and supply is a procedure for making authorizations and allowances. Every operating organization has equipment of some kind—tools, instruments, trucks, planes, desks, typewriters, and so forth. Every organization also has at its place of work an operating quantity of supplies—materials, compounds, maintenance items, and stationery are examples. The items of equipment needed by each unit are listed on a unit authorization list, and the supplies to be provided are shown in a schedule of allowances. It is easy to visualize the unit authorization list for a high school chemistry laboratory, for example. The laboratory benches, stools, burners, generators, extractors, pumps, ovens, and washers would be listed, perhaps with columns showing the quantities authorized for schools of different sizes. Hospital wards, fire stations, and military units all have unit authorizations of equipment. A schedule of allowances similarly lists the expendable items of supply each activity would normally have on hand. For example, each nursing station in a hospital would be furnished an allowance of preparation sets, enema sets, suture-removal kits, shields, bandages, and other items regularly consumed.

A newly established activity receives its initial issue of equipment and supplies. If such past issues have resulted in all units having their full allowance of an item, demand in the future will be at a much lower rate. The demand will consist of replacement and replenishment quantities only. Thus in determining the requirement, a computation would be made of all items needed to complete the initial issue to established or planned activities. Then a second additive computation would be made of replacement and replenishment needs. In the second computation, use would be made of such factors as wearout rate, time between overhauls, and consumption rates.

Requirements Computation

There are basically two types of material-requirements computations: requirements for consumption-type items and requirements for replacement-type items.

For consumption-type items, the operating cycle requirement in the computation represents the amount of stock needed to satisfy demands placed on the system until another procurement is made. If an item is procured semiannually, the operating cycle requirement is a six-month supply. If a two-year supply is bought at each procurement of an item, then the operating cycle requirement is a two-year supply.

The term *operating program* is sometimes used to denote a particular fiscal year for which buying requirements are computed. This computation serves a twofold purpose: it is the basis for apportionment of funds when the budget for that fiscal year is approved, and it forms the basis for procurement action.

Materials managers must lead their requirements by the amount of time it takes to replenish stock through deliveries from manufacturers or commercial suppliers. Procurement lead time, therefore, is an essential element of the requirements computation. It represents the time between initiation of a request to buy and delivery of goods from the manufacturer. The procurement lead time in a computation can be illustrated by an item that is procured semiannually, that has a demand rate of one hundred per month, and that has a procurement lead time of nine months. Projection of demand for this item must cover the period until the next reorder (six months), plus the period until deliveries from the next reorder enter the system (nine more months). The demand projection must therefore cover a period of fifteen months and results in a quantity of fifteen hundred, at the rate of one hundred per month.

The operating and procurement lead-time segments of the requirements computation represent a projection of user's demands on the supply system. Shipments from manufacturers, however, are not generally available to the user immediately. A supply system may consist of several distribution networks, and a certain amount of stock is always in movement within the system itself or held as safety stock at various echelons. This quantity of stock, which must be included in the computation, is known as the pipeline or stock-level requirement. The exact extent of this requirement that the manager has to consider depends on the number of echelons that report assets and demands for requirements purposes.

An important element of the requirements computation for recoverable items is the repair-cycle requirement, frequently termed the reparable side of the supply pipeline. It represents the period of time from the removal of an assembly from a piece of equipment to its return to serviceable condition through repair. There must be enough serviceable stock in the system to cover this gap. When output from repair activities begins to enter the system, the manager need only buy replacements for items condemned in the course of overhaul.

A reorder point for use in the computation of requirements can be developed. It consists of two basic elements: the procurement lead time and the stock-level requirement. Procurement made at the time assets reach the reorder point should result in deliveries when stocks are just adequate to maintain safety levels and fill the supply pipeline to the using activities.

Requirements for replacement-type items are based on a quarterly, semiannual, or annual projection of the status of requisitioning activities over a period of three to four years in the future. By knowing the equipment authorization of each organization or unit and consolidating the requirements of all units, it is possible to obtain a time-phased requirement for each replacement-type item. Assets that are in the hands of using organizations, in storage, or on order are applied against the phased requirement. Buying and budget requirements can then be developed by examining the point in time at which assets fall short of meeting requirements. An allowance is also made for that portion of the in-use assets that are expected to wear out or otherwise be lost during the period covered by the computation.

In converting the time-phased requirement to a buying or budget quantity, the procurement lead time must be considered. If the projection of assets and requirements shows a shortage in the second quarter of fiscal year 1981 and the item has a twelve-month lead time, procurement action must begin in the second quarter of fiscal year 1980. Procurement lead time is an essential element in computing requirements for replacement-type items.

The adjustment for procurement lead time permits the development of a procurement quantity for a particular operating cycle of an operating program. For major items of equipment, this period is usually one year; that is, the procurement frequency is geared to the annual cycle of funds appropriation and apportionment.

A stock-level requirement is usually not authorized for replacement-type items. In cases where it is permitted, it becomes part of the time-phased requirement to which assets are applied. Similarly a repair-cycle requirement is not a distinct element of the computation for replacement-type items. Many replacement-type items are kept in service by the replacement of major components, and a sufficient amount of such components is purchased to fill a repair pipeline to the overhaul activity.

Another element has a part in the computation of requirements for recoverable items. The repair cycle represents the time that elapses from removal of a reparable item from an assembly until it is made serviceable and ready for reissue. Many recoverable items are expensive components or assemblies that can be repaired for considerably less than the cost of buying a new item. The objective of the requirements computation is to determine the quantity needed to cover the repair cycle and maintain levels of serviceable stock and then to determine the quantity needed to replace items that are lost through condemnation in the process of repair. The repair cycle computation involves three concepts: wearout percentage, wearout rate, and recovery percentage.

Wearout percentage is the percentage of material issued that is lost to the supply system through condemnation. A wearout percentage is normally used with reference to a specific item; it indicates the percentage that has been or is expected to be lost out of total reparable turn-ins in a given period of time. A wearout percentage of 20 percent, for example, means that for every 100 reparable turn-ins, 20 are lost through condemnation, and 80 are repaired and reissued. Since each reparable generation (turn-in) normally requires a serviceable issue to replace it, the wearout percentage is customarily expressed as a percentage of issues. In the above example, issues of 100 and a wearout percentage of 20 means that every 100 issues result in 20 condemnations and 80 reparables available for repair and reissue.

Wearout rate represents the average rate of condemnation of property for a unit of program. The rate can be developed by applying the number of condemnations of an item to the program data or by multiplying the wearout percentage by the issue rate. For example, in supporting a flying program, issues of 1,200 were made in a base period, which represented 12,000 flying hours. If every 100 issues resulted in 20 condemnations, total condemnations for 1,200 issues would be 240. The wearout rate is 2.0 per hundred flying hours. The same result can be obtained by taking the issue rate of 10.0 and multiplying it by the wearout percentage (10 × .20 = 2.0).

The total or overall recovery percentage for an item represents that portion of material issued that can be restored to serviceable condition when it becomes reparable. In the example above, total recovery percentage is 80 percent; it means that for every 100 issues, 80 reparable turn-ins can be repaired and reissued.

Condemnations on which overall recovery and wearout percentages are based can occur when a reparable is removed from a higher assembly or in the course of overhaul when the reparable is further inspected and torn down for repair (condemnation in overhaul). The number of condemnations in overhaul, compared with the total number of an item going through overhaul, gives a recovery in overhaul percentage. This percentage can be applied to reparable assets on hand at the overhaul point (which have passed screening at base level) to determine the total recovery percentage. For example, if out of one hundred issues there are ten field condemnations and ninety reparable generations (returned for overhaul), and the overhaul recovery rate is 90 percent, then the total recovery rate is 81 percent:

$$\frac{\text{Reparable generations (90)} \times \text{overhaul recovery percentage (.90)}}{\text{Issues (100)}} = \frac{81,}{100} \text{ or } 81\%.$$

As issues are made in any operating cycle, reparables are turned in in exchange and are processed through repair. The repair-cycle requirements, therefore, are not added to the operating-cycle requirement but replace a portion of it equivalent to the length of the repair cycle.

Notes

1. This discussions draws from General Accounting Office, *Fragmented Management Delays Centralized Federal Cataloging and Standardization of Five Million Supply Items*, report LCD 79-403 (Washington, D.C.: General Accounting Office, 15 March 1979).

2. Federal standards and specifications are available from the GSA, Specifications and Distribution Branch (WFRI), Washington Navy Yard, Building 197, Washington, D.C. 20407.

3. George S. Brady and Henry R. Clauser, *Materials Handbook*, 11th ed. (New York: McGraw-Hill, 1977).

4. This section adapted from Department of Defense, *Selling to the Military* (Washington, D.C.: U.S. Government Printing Office, 1976), pt. V.

5. Write to: GSA, Specification and Consumer Information Distribution Branch (3FSIS), Washington Navy Yard, Building 197, Washington, D.C. 20407. Ask for *Index of Federal Specifications and Standards*, GPO 0-211-388(4).

6. See *Federal Register*, 5 March 1979, 12031 (FPMR Temporary Regulation E-59, Commercial Products).

7. This material includes passages drawn from *An Introduction to the Federal Catalog System*, U.S. Government, Department of Defense, Defense Logistics Services Center, Battle Creek, Michigan, 1978. Copies of this pamphlet may be requested from the Defense Logistics Services Center, Attention DLSC-C, Federal Center, Battle Creek, Michigan 49016.

8. Government organizations may obtain copies through normal acquisition channels, based on these official designations: Department of Army Pamphlet No. 700-1; Navy Supply Instruction No. 4400.78A; Air Force Pamphlet No. 67-2; and Defense Logistics Agency Manual 5105.1. Nongovernment organizations and individuals may purchase copies of this book from the Superintendent of Documents, U.S. Government Printing Office, Washington, D.C. 20402.

9 Inventory Policy, Procedures, and Methods

Many items pass through the purchasing and materials-management system without entering inventory; they are requisitioned by the potential user, acquired, and delivered directly to the user. But other items are subject to continuing demand, and for these it may be appropriate to establish and maintain an inventory. Inventory policy is concerned with the selection of items to be carried in inventory, and in what quantities.

Inventory management pertains to the development and administration of such policy and to the subsystems and procedures by which the policy is implemented. The objective of inventory management is to provide the required level of material support while minimizing inventory investment and operating costs.

The inventory of purchased material serves many purposes. It provides a buffer that can absorb unexpected changes in demand or interruptions in supply. It permits economies of quantity purchasing, with fewer purchase actions. It makes possible forward buying, and even speculation, in times of rising prices. And it provides flexibility in units of issue and usages, the breakdown of bulk and large-quantity packs into smaller packs.

Inventories also present problems. One is that excesses accumulate; there may be more assets on hand than can be used. Excesses are caused by abrupt changes in user programs, errors in reporting issue and asset data, technological changes in design, inaccurate usage factors, erroneous computer programs, and misinterpreted policies. Losses occur when excess items are transferred from inventory to disposal activities. Gains occur when an unexpected need is generated for items previously transferred to disposal but not yet sold and the items are returned to the inventory. Another problem is that damage occurs because items are abused in handling or are not properly protected from the elements. Some items (such as paints and photographic film) possess deteriorative or unstable characteristics to the degree that a storage time period must be assigned. These items require special management attention to ensure that they are issued to users before their useful life expires. And third, pilferage occurs. Tools, automotive supplies, clocks and watches, school and stationary supplies, foodstuffs, and drugs and medicines are particularly susceptible to theft by employees and others.

Overview of Inventory Management and Control

An organizational unit, part of the inventory-control subsystem, is the inventory-control point (ICP). The unit is assigned responsibility for the management of a group of items; this includes computation of quantitative requirements, the authority to direct procurement or initiate disposal, the development of quantitative and monetary inventory data, and the positioning and repositioning of material.

Each ICP maintains accounting for assigned items of supply showing the composition of inventories on a quantitative and monetary basis with respect to condition and purpose for which held (for example, operating stocks, safety stocks, reserve stocks, economic retention stocks, contingency retention stocks, and excess stocks). If an item is in long supply, a retention limit is established.

Generally all items held in stock are physically inventoried not less frequently than once each year. Exceptions are permitted to allow for less-frequent physical inventorying of items that are relatively slow moving, nonperishable, of low monetary value, and other types of items where storage conditions or lack of movement ensure adequate physical protection and accuracy of records. Inventory records and reports are reconciled promptly on the basis of physical inventories.

Each item of material, regardless of manner of acquisition, is under the cognizance of one ICP, which maintains an inventory of all these items. For items not included in periodic inventory status reports on a quantitative basis, the ICP makes reports and maintains data in such monetary terms and groupings, and upon such frequency, as necessary to ensure sound evaluation and control of inventory. Each ICP extends its reporting control over selected items of material under its cognizance to include items and quantities that are in the hands of users where appropriate. The ICP also channels the flow of material into and through the distribution system in such a manner as to eliminate unnecessary cross-hauling and back hauling and to minimize aggregate inventory holdings. It takes necessary steps to minimize the entrance of nonstandard items into the supply systems and vigorous action to dispose of nonstandard items currently in stock for which retention cannot be justified on the basis of known equipment or program application.

When a new substituting item is introduced into the supply system, it is phased to ensure the maximum practical and economical utilization of the obsolescent item and its repair parts. When such utilization has been accomplished, remaining stocks are promptly declared excess and removed from the supply system.

Those supply activities responsible for the control, supply, and positioning of material solicit and utilize the assistance and guidance of transportation specialists as necessary. The supply activity also stores emergency and reserve stocks in that manner and at such locations as to support emergency plans and positions stocks in such a manner as to attain minimum vulnerability.

Each ICP periodically reviews the complete inventory status of each item under its control in relation to current and future demands for it. The frequency of this review depends upon the type, importance, value, or rate of issue of the item concerned and is done not less often than once annually in the case of items of significant annual demand. It then determines the excess of items under its cognizance. Material turned in or reported as local excess by using units and activities is picked up in appropriate stock record accounts. Exceptions to this policy are made for material for which system excess has been predetermined. In such cases, material turned in may be processed directly to disposal. That quantity of an item that exceeds the authorized retention limit is declared excess without delay.

Material in the custody of supply and storage activities is subject to periodic and systematic quality evaluation in order to ensure its readiness and reliability. When quality deficiencies are uncovered, action is initiated promptly to identify nonserviceable material from serviceable stocks and to correct the causes of such deficiencies. Stock records reflect this separation of serviceable and nonserviceable stocks.

In order to attain maximum utilization of assets, each ICP determines and adheres to minimum time periods for the identification, inspection, and classification of material reported as unserviceable. Economically reparable materials, both on hand and to be generated, are considered as assets to the extent that such reparables can be returned to serviceable condition for use. Within fund limitations, these materials are scheduled for rework or are rebuilt in conformance with requirements furnished by cognizant ICPs.

Establishing Inventory Objectives and Strategy

Inventory management and control objectives include these:

1. Maintaining the investment in inventories at the lowest cost consistent with meeting user demands.
2. Ensuring an adequate supply of those items essential to an efficient level of user-activity operations.
3. Ensuring that physical quantities and dollar values of property actually on hand are those shown on inventory records.
4. Ensuring that property is protected from loss or damage.
5. Ensuring that warning is provided of understocked or overstocked positions.

6. Ensuring that surplus, excess, and obsolete material is purged from stock.
7. Ensuring that a data base is established in support of the requirements-determination subsystem.

Obviously these first two objectives are essentially in conflict. Recognition and resolution of such conflicts is the proper responsibility of management.[1] Conflicts must be resolved as they arise, but their frequency may be reduced by framing policies in the form of performance standards—for example, inventory on hand should not exceed $3 million. Management will generally concede that an increased inventory investment could have the effect of reducing operating costs associated with purchasing, or the costs and problems of stock-outs, or both. But sometimes managers will forgo this opportunity because they believe that the cost of the additional inventory investment would be greater than the other savings. Perhaps the maximum level of user support is associated with an inventory of, say, $4 million. Whatever the optimum total level, it must be achieved through the use of the optimum ordering strategy for each item.

Inventory Cost Concepts: Cost to Acquire and Hold

The guiding principle for identifying costs to be considered in selecting ordering strategies is that they shall be variable—that is, they will change as a strategy or decision is changed. Thus when a cost is used as the basis for selecting a particular strategy and that strategy is implemented, the resultant costs should be reasonably close to the estimate. The three cost factors to be identified are the cost of an order with no lines (preparing the heading apart from the order), the incremental cost of adding an item to an order, and the annual percentage cost of one dollar invested in inventory.

The most clear-cut case of potentially variable cost occurs where a vendor offers a discount for purchase of a specified quantity. Suppose that the annual dollar value of usage of an item is $6,000. If the vendor grants a 5 percent discount on orders of a certain size, the annual payment could be reduced by $300 (to $5,700) if every order placed was the requisite size. If only some of the orders placed were large enough to earn the discount, the annual cost would lie somewhere between $5,700 and $6,000. There is, then, a maximum possible payment to the vendor of $6,000, and a minimum possible payment of $5,700, as well as many possibilities between the two extremes. The exact payment will be a function of the ordering strategy employed, but there is a potential variable cost of $300.

Synonyms for variable costs are *direct*, *incremental*, and *marginal*. They are opposed to fixed, indirect, or overhead costs that will be incurred regardless of ordering strategy. Fixed costs are of interest to the cost accountant, whose normal concern is not with optimum strategies or decisions. Rather the accountant's usual objective is to present a consistent statement that necessarily includes all expenses. Such a presentation entails allocating a portion of all fixed costs, such as executive salaries, office space, and utilities, to various operations. The various techniques of doing this are not of concern here, but it should be realized that an accounting cost of ordering is likely to be quite different from the figure that is pertinent for evaluating ordering strategy. This is not to say that the cost accountant is wrong but simply that the intent differs. On the contrary, if the objectives are made clear to the cost accountant, she can be of real help.

Maintenance cost represents the cost per year of one dollar invested in inventory. It is represented as a carrying rate expressed as a percentage. Obviously it costs more to keep $150,000 of inventory than $100,000. Assigning a specific value to the difference in cost, however, is likely to be a novel concept.

Maintenance cost is the total of several components, including insurance (if carried), obsolescence and depreciation, storage and warehousing, and cost of capital (if debt financed). Insurance costs are fairly easily obtained. More effort will be required to quantify the other components.

Insurance on inventory is normally paid in proportion to the average value. It includes only the premium paid to replace destroyed or damaged inventory and not other coverages such as public liability and workmen's compensation. This figure should be available in the accounting records.

The value of goods may be gradually reduced for a variety of reasons, among them spoilage or deterioration, breakage, technical obsolescence, and pilferage. A small inventory decreases the risk and magnitude of such loss of value. The rate to be charged may differ sharply among commodities. For instance, the risk would be greater for auto parts than for basic hardware. Within groceries, as an example, canned goods are much less subject to obsolescence or depreciation than are dairy products. The decision to consider these differences in selection of ordering strategies should be based on an evaluation of their significance relative to other components of the carrying rate. Perhaps the other components of the carrying rate total 18 percent, and commodity C has an obsolescence factor of 4 percent, while the factor for all other commodities is 2 percent. Although this factor alone is twice as large for commodity C, it tends to become insignificantly different when added to the total carrying rate (22 percent versus 20 percent). The effect on the ordering strategy and the resultant costs would be negligible, so there is some justification for not going to the extra effort of treating commodity C separately. In most cases the difference in results will not justify any effort beyond that necessary to derive an average figure.

In some cases, the inventory record-keeping system provides a separate transaction code for items that have been removed from inventory for spoilage, deterioration, or obsolescence. If such records do not exist, a likely starting point for arriving at the obsolescence or depreciation rate is available from the accounting records.

These components are quite clearly variable as a function of ordering strategy, so the essential problem associated with them is the determination of a specific rate. The storage and warehousing cost component is a problem of a slightly different nature because it is first necessary to settle whether it is variable. For many agencies storage cost is fixed.

To determine the variability of storage cost, management should be asked if it would increase warehouse capacity to accommodate a 25 percent increase in inventory or release some of the present space if inventory were reduced 25 percent. If the agency is leasing space, this would imply an increase or decrease in rental. If it owns the facility, it implies either additional investment or other use of the space released. A change, if any, in either direction would come about because it yielded the minimum total of costs dependent upon ordering strategy.

Many agencies are so located physically that they cannot build or lease additional space without moving to another location. Similarly many warehouses are so arranged that it would be impossible to release unused space without major rearrangement or remodeling. The changes implied in either case could be effected only as a substantial and long-term investment, which is realistically dismissed as a possibility to be considered in the short range. Accordingly the present facilities operate as a fixed expense, and there is no variable cost of storage. Remember that the costs established will be used to set an ordering strategy for the immediate future. Any agreed-upon change in the warehouse capacity will normally be some time in coming about. It is difficult, if not impossible, to reduce the projected change in the total warehousing cost to a rate per dollar of inventory that will have any immediate effect. The only clear-cut instance of a variable-cost storage occurs where an agency uses leased warehousing routinely. It is more typical that the cost of storage is fixed.

If it is feasible to adjust the storage requirements as the inventory varies, the cost must be included. The cost and the capacity (in inventory dollars) of the present facility are determined in order to get the annual rate. Office and any other space not used for inventory is, of course, excluded.

The cost of capital can be a factor to be considered. The key concept is that money invested in the inventory is not available for other purposes. By committing capital to the inventory, other opportunities are forgone. In public purchasing and materials management, the cost of capital would be considered only if the government were significantly dependent upon debt financing. The cost of capital would be the amount of interest and debt service expense allocable to the inventory investment.

Inventory Cost Concepts: Cost to Order

Certain operating costs must be identified for balancing against the investment costs created by an ordering strategy. These operating costs, called ordering costs, include those elements of cost that increase or decrease with the number of orders placed. Included are certain elements of the costs of receiving, inspection, and putting away that are not usually thought of in connection with the cost of the purchasing department as such. These elements are included because the receiving cost will also be affected by a change in the number of orders placed per year.

Conceptually it is necessary to know the additional cost of placing one more order per year. It may reasonably be argued that placing one more order per year entails a negligible labor cost, since people have an inherent capability of absorbing increased work loads or keeping just as busy with reduced work loads. But this elasticity is true only temporarily and in the short range. A sustained increase in the activity level will exceed the capacity of people to adjust, and eventually more people or overtime will be required.

To arrive conceptually at the cost of one more order, it is helpful to think of a 25 percent change in the annual number of orders. This change will happen while the same total volume of goods is handled during the year. As a result, then, the quantities on individual orders will be reduced (or increased if number of orders is reduced).

If time were unlimited and management were indulgent, it would be possible to determine the cost of purchasing by experimentation: operating at two different levels and recording the resulting costs. The practical alternative is to isolate those costs that are potentially variable in the present operation. Thus if ten thousand orders per year are now being placed, it is hoped that the total annual variable costs of $10,000 are segregated and, thus, the same figure of $1 per order is derived.

Purchasing costs should be separated into two components: header cost, the cost of an order with no lines (an instance of header cost is the typing or printing of vendor name and address, and terms), and line cost, the cost of each line on an order. An instance of line cost is the typing or printing of item quantity and description.

The actual elements of the purchasing cost are found in several sections of the agency. It will be helpful to construct a flow diagram of events generated by the ordering process. Next, each function is examined, personnel involved are consulted for their subjective estimates, and those functions that are clear-cut are observed.

A likely result of an inventory-management implementation will be some modification in the mechanics of order preparation, which may change the costs somewhat. The greatest effect will probably be in data processing, but the cost is normally quite small in comparison to the other elements, which are less prone to change. Accordingly there is no need to be too precise in either measuring these costs under the present system or estimating them for the new system. Once the new system has operated on a substantial number of items for a long enough period, it would be worthwhile to verify the original estimates.

The costs derived for all of these will, in many cases, be estimates based on judgment, so there is no way to be completely certain of their accuracy. For this reason, only enough time should be expended to ensure that they are reasonable and that all of the significant elements have been identified. If there is confidence about a total variable cost of $10,000 developed in investigations up to some point, there need not be concern about a newly encountered and doubtful area that would add only $200 to that total. Also there is nothing final about the costs determined. The carrying rate can, and should, be used as a management-policy variable to assist in carrying out those policies that management desires.

Suppose that the present-cycle stock is $4 million and that there are 80,000 order lines per year. What are believed to be valid costs have been determined. Upon calculating order quantities, a cycle stock of $3 million and 150,000 lines results. If the cost figures are correct, this is certainly the optimum state of affairs. However, the results of such a drastic change in purchasing frequency may be chaotic and unacceptable to management. In such an extreme case, it is prudent to choose a maintenance cost to yield performance more in consonance with present levels initially and then work toward the optimum in stages. Further, within a fairly broad range of accuracy, the resultant total costs are relatively insensitive to errors (or deliberate changes) in the input values. In summary:

1. Cost-minimization formulas are based on the assumption that the costs they minimize are truly variable (marginal, incremental, direct variable).
2. Fixed or overhead costs do not depend upon ordering strategy, and hence are excluded.
3. Because of the human capacity to do more work temporarily, it is necessary to think of a sustained change to get realistic estimates.
4. Because header cost may be fixed and thus not pertinent in assessing the ordering strategy of an item, it is necessary to segregate purchasing cost into two components: header and line.
5. Cost of capital must be based on its potential use for other purposes since the investment in inventory is relatively permanently tied up.
6. The carrying rate can be used in the total system as a variable to carry out management policy.
7. There need not be an intensive search for the true costs, since minor errors in cost figures result in insignificant differences in total operating costs.

8. An optimized replenishment procedure will guarantee minimum cost for a specified user service level.

The use of these costs concepts in choosing between alternative ordering strategies is illustrated in the following example. The item under consideration has an annual demand of 112 units and a purchase price of $5. The order cost is $2 and the carrying cost is 20 percent of capital invested. Table 9-1 shows that the lowest cost ordering strategy would be to place either five or six orders per year.

Inventory Management and Control

A considerable body of procedural material, techniques, and methods of inventory management and control has been developed. Some excellent sources are *Materials Management and Inventory Systems* by Richard J. Tersine, *Purchasing and Materials Management* by Lamar Lee, Jr., and Donald W. Dobler, and *Purchasing and Materials Management for Health Care Institutions* by Dean S. Ammer.[2]

The inventory management and control subsystem includes procedures for selecting ordering strategy, setting stock levels, selectively controlling inventory, determining shelf life, determining order quantity, determining when to order, physically counting (taking) inventory, and identifying items for disposition.

Procedures for setting stock levels basically involve adding together operating stock and safety stock. The operating stock is the quantity needed to fill future user demand between stock replenishments. In most cases, future demand can be estimated based on past demand history. If an item moves one hundred units per month on the average and it has done so over the past year, it is highly likely that one hundred units will be issued next

Table 9-1
Total Costs of Various Ordering Strategies

Orders per Year	Order Cost	Order Quantity	Average Stock	Carrying Cost	Total Cost
1	$2	112	56	$56	$58
2	4	56	28	28	32
4	8	28	14	14	22
5	10	22	11	11	21
6	12	18	9	9	21
7	14	16	8	8	22
10	20	11	6	6	26

month. It is generally agreed that current history should have a greater influence on a forecast than old history, and there are a number of techniques available to weigh past history in order to achieve that effect. Past history can also be used to analyze trends and seasonal patterns of demand.

The requirements-computation procedure, described in chapter 9 identifies future demand during specific replenishment periods or lead times. The inventory-management function may be improved by employing such systematized forecasting, and a great many of the items in an inventory can be forecast automatically with little or no human intervention.

Operating stocks are drawn down to fill user demands. As this occurs, it would not be sufficient to reorder any item when the available stock has reached a level corresponding to the exact expected lead-time usage. User demands vary, and so do lead times; thus safety stocks have to be added to avoid excessive stock-outs. An extra quantity is kept on hand in addition to that required to cover the resupply time. The extra quantity is a buffer, whose presence improves the overall user service level. Nevertheless, it is still unlikely that the items that require large stocks will get enough, while it is probable that the majority of the items will be overstocked.

Stock-control procedures must be selective. Pareto's law states that in a series of elements to be controlled, a selected small fraction, in terms of number of elements, will always account for a large fraction in terms of effect. Conversely the majority of items will be of relatively minor significance in terms of effect. Pareto's law applied to inventory management relates to the cost-category classification of items. Cost categories I, II, and III are frequently referred to as categories A, B, and C, or the ABC concept of selective inventory control. Under this concept, management effort is allocated among the items to be managed in proportion to their relative dollar value and operational importance.

Stock control requires a continuing review of inventory on hand by units of issue, by days of supply, and by dollar value. Issue experience is monitored and user satisfaction is measured. The level of service achieved is compared to the service objectives prescribed. To emphasize managerial responsibility and accountability, performance measures are published for each inventory-control point and/or supply class. When the appropriate ordering strategy has been established and the service level objectives have been set, a theoretical average inventory level can be calculated by item and dollar value. These values are compared periodically with the actual amounts on hand. Significant discrepancies between actual and theoretical values are investigated and corrected.

Determination of shelf life is an important but frequently neglected procedure. The overall objective of the procedure is to establish controls that will ensure the satisfactory in-service performance of shelf-life items and to minimize losses of shelf-life items due to shelf-life expiration. To this end, inventory-control points identify items with deteriorative characteristics, assign codes that indicate the length of shelf-life, prescribe serviceability standards for items managed, and periodically reevaluate shelf-life assignments, identifying replacement items that do not require shelf-life control. Designating an item of supply as a shelf-life item sets in motion a series of management-control procedures not usually associated with most other items. Because these procedures result in additional costs, policy should limit these designations to items with known or suspected deteriorative characteristics. A technical evaluation of a new item's instability or deteriorative characteristic must be performed before the ICP designates it as a shelf-life item.

The key questions for inventory management are when to order and how much to order. The procedure to be used in determining order quantity depends upon the nature of demand. If the demand rate is reasonably constant, economic order quantity (EOQ) procedures are appropriate. The EOQ formula balances the cost of ordering against the cost of holding increasing quantities of items received with progressively larger orders so as to reach an optimum ordering quantity. The cost factors used in the formula are difficult to develop. Effective use of the EOQ formula requires a computer. Otherwise the time and cost of working the computations would be prohibitive. EOQ calculators similar to slide rules have been developed and can be purchased commercially.

If usage or price of an item is not constant, the EOQ procedure is not appropriate. Also a supplier may require minimum-order quantities or standard-pack multiples, and therefore the computed EOQ may not be a useful figure.

Determining when to order is a function of lead time and economic order frequency. The reorder point is the stock level at which the item must be reordered to ensure continuity of supply. This is influenced by several factors: The administrative time required by stock control and management to review the items and make a reorder determination, the level of usage of the item forecast for the reorder period, the average lead time involved between placing an order and the subsequent availability of the items ordered, and the economics of ordering strategy. When inventory on hand drops to the number of days supply reflected by these considerations, the time has come to place an order. If the item is subject to random or erratic demand, other procedures are available.

After a purchase order has been sent out, little can be done to raise the on-hand quantity prior to the scheduled delivery, but the safety stock covers a certain percentage of demands. The safety stock must be based on the individual item requirements for extra stock, and it in turn depends on how erratic the item demand is, as well as how reliable the lead-time estimate is. The fact that lead times can, and should be, forecast and that a lead-time fluctuation can be estimated is often ignored. Use of a maximum reasonable lead time is the prevalent technique, although lead-time measurements are as important to an inventory system as are demand measurements.

Inventory counting procedures are necessary to validate the accuracy of the paper inventory records as posted. The basic count of items is maintained on perpetual records either through manual posting of transactions or through a computer. Such records indicate the running or current balance of stock on hand and on order for each individual inventory item through the posting of each individual receiving or disbursement transaction. However, errors in posting occur, and items may be lost through pilferage, damage, or deterioration. Therefore physical counts of the items actually on hand are required. Normally the procedure involves a cycle of inventories, class by class.

The advantages of cycle physical inventories are several: shutdowns and interruptions of operations are avoided; the counting procedure is accomplished within normal work hours; correction of records to reflect differences found is accomplished within normal work hours; and the personnel who conduct the ongoing counting develop expertise and accuracy.

Perpetual inventories, mantained on either a manual or computerized basis, backed up by cycle count procedures eliminate the need for an annual physical inventory. Auditors can rely on sample counts to verify that the inventory counting procedure used was valid and that the inventory records are accurate. Once the basic inventory count procedure is established, audits are conducted periodically to determine that the procedure continues to be followed properly.

Finally procedures are needed to identify items for disposition. Excess, obsolete, and damaged stocks are bound to be generated in any purchasing and materials-management system, and these stocks must be identified and marked for disposal. Inventories for which there is no foreseeable need cannot be retained. The accumulation of holding costs can rapidly exceed the value of the items. A continuous review is needed for individual items and classes of items to detect evidence of overinvestment or obsolescence. Disposition procedures must provide for continuing activity rather than occasional housecleaning.

Although it is possible to review items manually, the use of computers facilitates rapid and frequent review with a printout of items showing no issue activity for a predetermined period of time or of balances well in excess of current rates of usage.

Notes

1. The following material is extracted, with editing, from "Executive Perspective of Computer Assisted Inventory Management," 5798-NCX,

prepared by the General Systems Division, International Business Machines Corporation, n.d.

2. Richard J. Tersine, *Materials Management and Inventory Systems* (New York: American Elsevier Publishing Company, 1976); Lamar Lee, Jr., and Donald W. Dobler, *Purchasing and Materials Management*, 3d ed. (New York: McGraw-Hill, 1977), chaps. 10, 11; Dean S. Ammer, *Purchasing and Materials Management for Health Care Institutions* (Lexington, Mass.: Lexington Books, D.C. Heath and Company, 1975), chaps. 8-12.

10 Purchasing Policy and Strategy

Purchasing and materials management is moving through a period of unprecedented and sweeping change, challenge, and opportunity. The changes affect industrial, institutional, and governmental buyers alike. All facets of the environment are involved: physical, social, economic, political and legal, and technical.

The Changing Environment of Purchasing

Purchasing is carried on in a five-aspect environment: the physical or natural environment (which includes land, water, air, plant, and animal life); the social environment (our human society); the economic environment (the world of work and money); the political and legal environment; and the technological environment, with its changing materials and methods.

The economic, political and legal, and technological environments are perhaps of overriding importance. There is, for example, greatly increased buying of foreign-finished products, components, and commodities, which requires dealing with distributors or agents and directly with foreign sources. At the same time, foreign-trade arrangements are becoming increasingly complex. There are countervailing quotas, cartel-set prices, trigger prices, and political boycotts. Other examples are an increased buying of services of all kinds—technical assistance, consulting, supporting, and maintaining; increasing concern over shortages; spiraling inflation; more aggressive federal and state antitrust, price-fixing, and market-splitting law enforcement; increased governmental demands for reporting; and increased governmental standard and specification setting for a wide range of products and services. Working in this changing environment requires a high level of sophistication, knowledge, and skill in purchasing. Managers must react correctly to material availability and purchase price changes; they must be able to develop a strategy and to plan purchases rather than simply to place orders.

Each purchasing manager must have an annual purchase plan and, in some cases, a plan for more than a single year. The plan should identify buying categories (commodities, finished items, and services) and list the environmental changes that could effect availability and price. The plan should address these objectives: to buy at competitive prices, to minimize inventory, to hold down cost to acquire or to purchase, to ensure continuity of supply and consistent quality, and to maintain favorable supplier relations.

For each buying category the manager must assess the environmental changes by drawing upon all of the data available: internal purchasing experience; industry and trade association data; NAPM, NIGP, NCMA, and NASPO data; and national trade and economic data, including such specific and directly applicable information as the vendor performance index maintained by the National Bureau of Economic Research.[1]

A well-prepared purchase plan will provide the specific timing of future purchases and the prices expected. In many cases, planning will point up the need for specific shortage plans in some areas. These are contingency plans to be used when suppliers fail to deliver as scheduled. Such plans should include the availability of alternative inventories subject to transfer, the names of alternate suppliers, the identification of substitutable materials, any expediting arrangements necessary, and any emergency rescheduling required of affected user activities.

Purchasing Policy

Purchasing policy consists of a set of predetermined attitudes toward a variety of issues:

1. The extent to which the government will provide its own needed goods or services rather than contracting out with private enterprise.
2. The extent to which the government will utilize commercially available products rather than specifying peculiar products for its own use.
3. The extent to which the government will favor suppliers within its own constituency, showing local preference.
4. The extent to which the government will speculate or engage in forward buying to protect itself against shortages or price increases.
5. The extent to which the government will negotiate with vendors rather than advertising for sealed competitive bids.
6. The extent to which the government will reply upon supplier development of a suitable product.
7. The extent to which the government will acquire complete, integrated systems rather than individual components.
8. The trade-offs between achievement of procurement objectives and socioeconomic objectives.

Make-or-Buy, Contracting Out

Make-or-buy policy decisions are based upon three criteria: relative cost, quality, and dependability of supply. For each criterion, the purchasing and materials manager must weigh internal capabilities against the outside suppliers' capabilities.

In industry make-or-buy decisions are an integral part of production planning. A manufacturer makes the item when cost analysis indicates it is cheaper to make than to buy; company know-how and equipment exists; idle capacity is available to help absorb overhead; the item is unusual or complex and its fabrication needs to be controlled carefully; making will facilitate control of changes, deliveries, and inventories; the item is difficult to transport; the design, materials, or methods of manufacture are confidential; or the item is too important to be dependent upon a single outside source of supply.

A manufacturer contracts out the item when cost analysis indicates it is cheaper to buy than to make; space, equipment, time, and skills are not available in plant; because of low volume or other considerations it is not attractive to invest in added capability; it seems desirable to transfer the seasonal, cyclical, and market risks to someone else; the potential suppliers have specialized equipment or techniques that will result in a better product; or legal (perhaps patent right) or customer-supplier relationships favor contracting out.

In governmental purchasing, particularly at the federal level, competition with private enterprise has long been a controversial issue. For over forty years, special and standing congressional committees have conducted many studies of the extent to which the government has engaged in commercial or industrial activities in competition with private enterprise. In 1932 the first extensive study was conducted by a special House committee, which found several commercial or industrial activities created expressly for World War I needs still in existence. Similar observations were made after World War II.

In September 1952, the Department of Defense issued the first in a long series of directives, detailing policy and instructions for commercial or industrial facilities operated by the military departments. The directive stated a policy against retaining and operating such facilities where required needs could be effectively and economically met by existing facilities of any other military department or by private commercial facilities. It required the military departments to survey and justify their continuation and to restrict the establishment of new facilities.

In July 1953, the Congress, in establishing the Commission on Organization of the Executive Branch of the Government, stated that its policy was to eliminate nonessential services, functions, and activities that were competitive with private enterprise. And in 1955 this commission issued a series of reports with many recommendations designed to eliminate or substantially decrease government activities that were competing with private enterprise and urging the use of private contract services. These reports pointed out several reasons why the government should not do anything that the private sector was able to do. First, it stated that the private enterprise system had been demonstrated to be the best way to organize and develop the economic resources of the nation, resulting in the maximum production of goods and services with the minimum effort. Moreover to the extent that government engages in business enterprises, the base for taxation is reduced, and larger taxes must be levied on individuals and industry. In private industry, the initiative of individuals has been developed to a greater extent than in governmental activities. Private industry can provide more adequate incentives in many instances and thus encourage new ideas and improvements while maintaining competitive costs. Finally political control of what are essentially economic activities does not produce the effective results in government business enterprises that are produced by the competitive and profit motives of private industry.

Currently at the federal level there is a basic policy of relying on private enterprise to supply the government's needs, unless it is in the national interest for the government to provide its needed products and services directly.[2] A government commercial or industrial activity is defined as one operated and managed by an executive agency that provides for the government's own use a product or service that is obtainable from a private source. The exceptions under which the government may provide a commercial or industrial product or service for its own use are instances when:

1. Procurement of a product or service from a commercial source would disrupt or delay an agency's program.
2. It is necessary for the government to conduct a commercial or industrial activity for purposes of combat support or for individual and unit retraining of military personnel or to maintain or strengthen mobilization readiness.
3. A satisfactory commercial source is not available and cannot be developed in time to provide a product or service when it is needed.
4. The product or service is available from another federal agency.
5. Procurement of the product or service from a commercial source will result in higher cost to the government.

However, the policy also states:

1. The fact that a commercial or industrial activity is classified or is related to an agency's basic program is not an adequate reason for starting or continuing a government activity.

2. Urgency of a requirement is not an adequate reason unless there is evidence that commercial sources are not able, and the government is able, to provide a product or service when needed.
3. The fact that a product or service is being provided to another agency does not justify a government commercial or industrial activity.
4. A decision to rely on a government activity for reasons involving relative costs must be supported by a comparative cost analysis.

To guide agencies in the conduct of comparative-cost analyses, the *Cost Comparison Handbook* has been prepared.[3] It provides detailed instructions for developing a comprehensive and valid comparison of the estimated cost to the government of acquiring a product or service by contract and of providing it with in-house, government resources. The *Handbook* is intended to establish consistency, assurance that all substantive factors are considered when making cost comparisons, and a desirable level of uniformity among agencies in comparative-cost analyses.

In the preparation of cost analyses, both government and commercial cost figures must be based on the same scope of work and the same level of performance. This requires the preparation of a sufficiently precise work statement with performance standards that can be monitored for either mode of performance. Standard cost factors will be used as prescribed by the *Handbook* and as supplemented by agencies for particular operations. Each agency must be able to defend any variations in costing from one case to another.

Cost comparisons are to be aimed at full cost, to the maximum extent practical in all cases. All significant government costs (including allocation of overhead and indirect costs) must be considered, both for direct government performance and for administration of a contract.

In the solicitation of bids or offers from contractors for work loads that are of a continuing nature, solicitations should (unless otherwise inappropriate) provide for prepriced options or renewal options for the out-years (beyond the period programmed). These measures will guard against buy-in pricing on the part of contractors. Although recompetition also guards against buy-ins, the use of prepriced or renewal options provides certain advantages, such as continuity of operation, the possibility of lower contract prices when the contractor is required to provide equipment or facilities, and reduced disruption of ongoing activities.

Ordinarily agencies should not incur the delay and expense of conducting cost-comparison studies to justify a governmental commercial or industrial activity for products or services estimated to cost less than $100,000 annually. Activities below this threshold should be performed by contract unless in-house performance is justified because there is no commercial source or there are overriding national security considerations. However, if there is reason to believe that inadequate competition or other factors are causing commercial prices to be unreasonable, a cost-comparison study may be conducted. Reasonable efforts should first be made to obtain satisfactory prices from existing commercial sources and to develop other competitive commercial sources.

The cost comparison will use an annual rate of 10 percent as the opportunity cost of capital investments and of the net proceeds from the potential sale of capital assets, as prescribed in the *Handbook*.

The *Handbook* provides in detail for the consideration of each element of cost on both the government's side and the potential contractor's side.

Commercial Off-the-Shelf Items

At the federal level, the stated policy is that the government will purchase commercial, off-the-shelf products when such products will adequately serve the government's requirements provided such products have an established acceptability in the commercial market. Also the government will utilize commercial distribution channels in supplying commercial products to its users.

Thousands of products are bought and used every day by the general public, industry, and nonprofit organizations, as well as by the government.[4] The policy is based on the thesis that most of the government's needs for commercial products can be acquired more effectively and cheaply by relying primarily on off-the-shelf competition than on solicitations based on government specifications.

As a result of the language used in procurement statutes and implementing regulations, it has become traditional practice in government to write purchase specifications in such a way that any potential supplier can produce the item, request bids or proposals for products that meet the description, and then award a contract to the supplier offering the lowest price.

The practice works well for special needs, but it is a costly way to buy products that are readily available on the commercial market. In addition to the cost of the process, the result is a hodgepodge of products made especially, or modified just slightly to meet the government specification. This competition by specification is also limited to firms that are willing to compete in this manner. The alternative to this practice is off-the-shelf competition for commercial products. The basic difference is that instead of asking industry to offer products meeting a government specification or description, the government acts as another customer for privately designed and developed products currently offered by industry in the marketplace. The government uses this method in making small purchases, in emergencies, and in several other indefinite delivery contract arrangements that are not expressly provided for in the procurement statutes or implementing directives.

The federal multiple-award schedule program has been in existence for over fifty years. It consists of a pricing arrangement with each manufacturer or supplier that sells commercial products in the marketplace and will provide these same products to any government ordering activity at an agreed-upon price. Initial solicitation is for offers of entire lines of off-the-shelf products at a discount from established catalog or market prices. The offers are evaluated and negotiations are conducted with each firm that has a product the government may need during the contract period. The award criterion is a price objective (benchmark) determined appropriate by the buyer in consideration of the anticipated volume of government business and the range of discounts offered by competitors for the same range of products. The resulting contracts are made available to every government activity for ordering needed items directly from the supplier without further negotiation. These using activities select the lowest-priced item that will fill their needs from the multiple sources on contract.

The multiple-award schedule program is operated by the Federal Supply Service (FSS) in support of all agencies of government. The Department of Defense uses an almost identical method of contracting for processed foods for resale in commissaries. This program is operated under the exception authority, which states, "for property or services for which it is impractical to secure competition." Examples of when this authority may be used are given in the Federal Acquisition Regulations. These examples include cases where the supplies or services can be obtained from only one person or firm ("sole source") and when it is impossible to draft adequate specifications or purchase descriptions for a solicitation for bids.

The wording of this exception and the examples for its use convey the impression that competition is not feasible when using this authority. Even the FSS refers to single-award schedules as competitive, inferring that multiple-award schedules are not. But those managing the multiple-award program recognize it as being based on off-the-shelf competition with two additional competitive steps achieved, one in the process of contract negotiations and one in product selection at point of use.

Multiple-source contracts come under the indefinite-delivery type of contract. These are prepriced arrangements for a period of time where the quantity is either indefinite or is dependent on government needs. A purchasing office can quickly place a delivery order against a multiple-source contract on a one-page form. Many companies provide for these orders to be placed with a local retail outlet for more responsive delivery and customer service. In fact the purchasing office can even place the order by telephone and confirm it by the one-page delivery order. The responsiveness of delivery is as fast as the user would receive if the agency made the purchase for its own use.

The price negotiated on multiple-source contracts is based on the terms and conditions of the solicitation. Price and discount offers are solicited for the commercial line of products. In the case of the FSS multiple-award schedules, no total quantities are established, orders are placed by thousands of ordering units throughout the United States, and destination delivery is required to each user. A frequent criticism of multiple-source contracts is that the system does not ensure the lowest possible price for a given delivery and that the lowest-priced item is not always selected for the specific need. Also transportation costs, which cannot be determined at time of contract negotiation, are averaged. The total cost of an item is therefore its price plus the allocated transportation cost.

Selection of the least-total-cost item at the point of use is a judgment that can best be made at the local site to fit the specific need. These decisions have to be justified to the satisfaction of the contracting officer; the discipline for making the right decision is a responsibility of management.

A great many questions arise in deciding the appropriate acquisition method for items of this type. What is the total value of the procurement? How many items are normally ordered at one time? How often are they ordered during a given time? What is the nature of the market situation for the product? Is it a highly competitive market? Is technology moving quickly, or is it marked by gradual changes in product function and design? Is there a recognized commercial distribution system? Can the product be purchased economically in numerous locations? What are the needs of the user agencies, and how specific are they? How have the government's requirements previously been supplied? Are small or minority businesses dependent upon the government business? What is the most cost-effective system to supply government users, considering all costs to acquire and deliver an item to the ultimate user?

In some cases, it will be more efficient for the government to utilize specifications and make a single award. In others, multiple-award schedules will make more sense. In still others, agencies should purchase on an open-market basis.

The policy of the federal government in regard to the acquisition and distribution of commercial off-the-shelf items is equally applicable at other levels of government. In summary, the policy is that the government will acquire commercial, off-the-shelf items when such items will serve the government's requirement adequately, provided such items have an established commercial market acceptability. It will use commercial distribution channels in supplying commercial items to users when it is economically advantageous to do so and the impact on level of user support is acceptable. It will encourage, recognize, and evaluate technological innovations in commercial items that are applicable to government needs. This policy also eliminates unnecessary government specifications for commercial products and enables nongovernment specifications and standards to be adopted where feasible. When government specifications are used, their application must be tailored, where possible, to reflect the best commercial practices in form, fit, function, or performance. Acquisition procedures designed to optimize the government's advantage, while minimizing the administrative burden to the contractor and government, should be implemented. Finally the policy fosters competitive industrial sources for the acquisition, distribution, and support of government requirements.

Favoring Constituent Suppliers

Historically political interests have imposed purchase restrictions that favor constituent suppliers. An example at the federal level is the Buy American Act (1933) and at the state and local level the several local-preference laws.

The Buy American Act establishes as a policy of the federal government that manufactured materials, supplies, or articles acquired for public use shall be substantially constituted from domestically mined or manufactured articles or supplies. Implementing regulations provide that products shall be considered to be of foreign origin if the cost of foreign products used in them is 50 percent or more. The price of a domestic product competing with a foreign product shall be deemed to be unreasonable if that price exceeds the bid or offered price of the foreign product by an amount determined as the foreign-product bid price plus 6 percent or by an amount determined as the foreign product bid price, less customs duty and applicable costs incurred after arrival in the United States, plus 10 percent. If the foreign-bid price is less than $25,000, the 10 percent shall be added to the bid price less only customs duty, not less costs incurred in the United States.

A general exception is made to the application of the Buy American Act where the purchase is deemed to be inconsistent with the public interest or the cost is unreasonable after application of these percentage differentials. Also agency and department heads are allowed broad discretion in making administrative determinations as to the reasonableness of price differentials.

Articles for use outside the United States do not fall within the act restrictions. And, if articles, materials, or supplies are not mined, produced, or manufactured in sufficient quantities in the United States, an exception is made. Prospective contractors to the federal government are advised in invitations for bids and requests for proposals that specific information relating to exceptions under the act is available. When bids or proposals are submitted, the bidder must include certification that the end product is a domestic-source item except as shown in the required listing of excluded items.

In evaluating bids where both domestic and foreign bids have been submitted, preference must be given to the domestic bid unless it is determined that the acquisition of such domestic end products would be unreasonable in cost or inconsistent with the public interest.

Multinational trade negotiators working under the auspices of the General Agreement on Tariffs and Trade (GATT) are close to agreement on the International Code on Government Procurement. (It will enter into force on 1 January 1981 if approved by Congress.) Provisions of this code are designed to discourage discrimination at all stages of the procurement process and to provide potential foreign suppliers with treatment no less favorable than that accorded domestic producers and suppliers. There are specific rules for advertising prospective purchases. Technical specifications must be prepared with the view to avoid the creating of obstacles to international trade. Procurement agencies must prepare specifications in terms of performance rather than design, and such specifications must be based on international standards, national technical regulations, or recognized national standards. The code will be applicable to any procurement that exceeds the value of $150,000.

Because of the code, the federal Buy American rules and preferences will have to be changed. This code will also raise questions as to the need for changing similar buy-national, -state, and -local policies when federally assisted projects are involved.

Many state and local laws also direct the preferential treatment of constituent suppliers. Virginia's law, for example, states, *"Preference to materials, etc., produced or sold in Virginia. The Director shall, in the purchase of materials, equipment and supplies, give preference, so far as may be practicable, to materials, equipment and supplies produced in Virginia or sold by Virginia persons, firms and corporations."*[5]

The policy of South Carolina is very explicit:

> In the event two or more bidders are tied in price, while otherwise meeting all of the required conditions, awards are determined as follows: 1. Should there be a South Carolina firm tied with an out-of-state firm, the award will be made automatically to the South Carolina firm. 2. Tie bids involving South Carolina produced or manufactured products, when known, and items produced or manufactured out of the State will be resolved in favor of the South Carolina commodity. These are the only conditions under which any in-state preference is shown.

The statutes of the commonwealth of Kentucky (reproduced in appendix C) do not include a preference clause. This is consistent with the Model Procurement Code. The desired policy is to award contracts to the lowest responsive and responsible bidder. Usually the margin of bidding is very small, indicative of good pricing and close competition. The omission of out-of-state suppliers from bidders' lists drastically reduces the number of bidders for state contracts, restricts competition, and escalates the costs of purchases. Preferences based solely upon the location of a bidder cause an unreasonable restraint of trade and invite retaliation by others. This does not serve the best interests of the state.

Forward Buying

Managers can purchase according to the current requirement or according to market conditions. Purchasing to requirements is the usual, and generally more conservative, approach, but at times market conditions may dictate use of the second alternative.

Purchasing during periods of unstable pricing presents many problems. In certain commodity areas, purchasing managers make use of the futures market as a purchasing tool. If the item is a hedgeable commodity or if it is manufactured primarily from a hedgeable commodity (copper, for example), the manager establishes a price and reduces risk by buying a futures contract.

Public purchasing managers are not expected to speculate in the cash market or to trade in the futures market. In periods of unstable pricing, they therefore have recourse to either hand-to-mouth buying or forward buying. In hand-to-mouth buying, orders are placed for quantities smaller than requirements justify and smaller than would normally be considered economical. A hand-to-mouth buying policy would be followed in three circumstances. If prices are falling or are expected to fall, high-priced inventory is not accumulated, and the series of small orders would be priced at about the average for the period. If demand is expected to change, an inventory of obsolete or no-longer-wanted items can be avoided. Or if the agency is in a drawn-down financial condition, funds can be stretched to last until the next funding period.

Forward buying involves the placing of orders larger than current requirements justify. A forward-buying policy would be followed when prices are rising or are expected to rise. Needs are thus filled at what is seen as a favorable price, and savings are generated by not ordering soon again at the higher price. The availability of quantity discounts, large unit-pack prices, or volume freight rates that generate savings makes this policy favorable. It is also useful if risks of interruption—such as a material shortage, a labor strike, or a transportation breakdown—can be avoided. Of course the advantages of forward buying could be offset by increased inventory carrying costs.

Forward buying should be based upon careful study of requirements and of the market. Particularly useful are the individual commodity committee reports published periodically by the National Association of Purchasing Managers. Current and detailed information is included on both availability and price of the more commonly used commodities and materials.

Formal Advertising and Negotiation

The source for a purchase may be identified through formal advertising and the resultant competitive bidding or through negotiation. The choice is much more than a legal or procedural matter; it is a matter of purchasing strategy. Stanley N. Sherman, in *Procurement Management: The Federal System*, develops four alternative strategies.[7]

1. Price-directed strategy. The manager approaches the procurement in a manner calculated to force the market to act as the decision maker through competitive bidding. He attempts to take advantage of vital market forces in which price directs source selection. There are three alternatives under this strategy: one employs the familiar auction, the second abhors the auction but employs the sealed bid, and the third is a variation of the sealed-bid alternative. The first two alternatives are widely used, but only where pertinent to the procurement objective and competitive situation. The variation of price-directed strategy found in the life-cycle costing substitutes life-cycle cost guarantees for price guarantees but still employs competitive bidding.

2. Negotiation strategy, classical competitive model. The manager uses competitive price bidding but not as the central source-determining force. She designs the procurement to allow nonprice considerations to enter into, and potentially to govern, source selection. In this strategy, a number of variations may be discerned such that a manager may formulate decision criteria unique to the nature of the procurement. Fundamental in each case is the existence of viable competitors seeking the award.

3. Negotiation strategy, limited-source models. This strategy addresses the problem of a limited choice as to source. The essence of it is that a particular source is so dominant that only an extraordinary set of events would cause the manager to employ a new source. The several models under this strategy tend to employ cost-based pricing processes. The most widely recognized models are the unsolicited-proposal model, the solicited-proposal model, the change-process model, and the regulated-industry model.[8]

4. Negotiation strategy, technological-conceptual model. This strategy is associated with major undertakings of substantial complexity. The source-selection processes under this strategy are based on employment of a set of contracts with alternative sources, each source is funded through a se-

quence of contracts requiring the source to develop and refine its technological-conceptual system designed to meet the buyer's mission. Final source selection is based upon a choice from the alternatives thus developed. This strategy is the subject of Office of Management and Budget (OMB) circular A-109.

In each procurement, the public-purchasing officer first considers the use of the price-directed strategy: formal advertising and competitive bidding. Only after determining that formal advertising and competitive bidding are inappropriate may he consider negotiation.

At the federal level the Congress has clearly established its preference for competition in the award of contracts by formal advertising procedure, with negotiation being allowed only under exceptional conditions:

The various exceptions to the requirement or the use of formal advertising methods are,

1. National emergency. Purchases and contracts may be negotiated without formal advertising if it is determined that such action is necessary in the public interest during a national emergency declared by Congress or the president.
2. Public exigency. Purchases and contracts may be negotiated without formal advertising if the public exigency will not permit the delay incident to advertising. To justify this authority to negotiate, the need must be compelling and of unusual urgency—for example, when the government would be injured, financially or otherwise, if the services or supplies were not furnished by a certain date and such date will not allow time to advertise.
3. Purchases not in excess of $2,500. Purchases and contracts are authorized for negotiation without formal advertising if the aggregate amount involved is not more than $2,500.
4. Personal or professional services. Purchases and contracts may be negotiated without formal advertising if they are for personal or professional services (with some qualifications).
5. Services of educational institutions. Purchases and contracts may be negotiated without formal advertising for any service to be rendered by any university, college, or other educational institution.
6. Purchases outside the United States. Department of Defense purchases and contracts may be negotiated without formal advertising for property and services to be procured and used outside the United States, its territories, possessions, and Puerto Rico, with some qualifications.
7. Medicines or medical supplies. Purchases and contracts may be negotiated without formal advertising for medicine or medical supplies. Medicine and medical supplies include technical equipment such as surgical instruments, surgical and orthopedic appliances, X-ray supplies and equipment, and similar items. Prosthetic equipment such as artificial limbs, etc., is not included.

8. Property procured for resale. Purchases and contracts may be negotiated without formal advertising if the property is to be procured for authorized resale through commissaries or similar facilities.

9. Subsistence supplies. Purchases and contracts may be negotiated without formal advertising if the purchases are for the procurement of perishable or nonperishable subsistence supplies. When procuring such subsistence supplies, however, competitive proposals must be solicited from sufficient qualified sources of supply to assure full and free competition.

10. Competition impracticable. Purchases and contracts may be negotiated without formal advertising for supplies and services if it is impracticable to secure competition. Situations in which this authority may be used include cases in which there is only one source of supply; situations in which patent rights, copyrights, control of basis raw materials, or similar circumstances preclude competition; when no responsive bid had been received from a responsible bidder through formal advertising; or when adequate specifications for competitive procurement cannot be written.

11. Experimental, developmental or research work. Purchases and contracts may be negotiated without formal advertising for property or services determined to be for experimental, developmental, or research work or for making or furnishing property for experiment, test, development, or research. This includes contracts relating to theoretical analysis, exploratory studies, and experiment in any field of science or technology; developmental contracts calling for practical application of findings and theories of a scientific or technical nature; contracts for supplies, equipment, parts, accessories, or patent rights thereto, and drawings or designs thereof, as required for experiment, development, research, or test; and contracts for services, tests and reports necessary or incident to experimental, developmental or research work.

12. Classified purchases. Purchases and contracts may be negotiated without formal advertising for property or services which it is determined should not be publicly disclosed because of their character, ingredients, or components.

13. Standardized and interchangeable technical equipment. Purchases and contracts may be negotiated without formal advertising for equipment determined to be technical equipment whose standardization and the interchangeability of whose parts are necessary in the public interest and whose procurement by negotiation is necessary to assure that standardization and interchangeability.

14. Technical or specialized supplies. Purchases and contracts may be negotiated without formal advertising for technical or special property which require substantial initial investment or an extended period of preparation for manufacture and for which advertising would be likely to result in higher cost because of duplication of necessary preparation.

15. Negotiation after advertising. Purchases and contracts may be negotiated after formal advertising if the bid prices received after advertising are unreasonable as to all or a part of the requirements or were collusive, i.e., not independently reached in open competition. However, notice must be given to each responsible bidder of the intention to negotiate and each must be given a reasonable opportunity to

negotiate. Also, the negotiated price must be the lowest negotiated price offered by any responsible supplier.

16. Purchases for national defense or industrial mobilization. Purchases and contracts may be negotiated without formal advertising if it is determined that such negotiation is necessary to keep vital suppliers or facilities in business to make them available in national emergencies.

17. Other legal authorization. Purchases and contracts may be negotiated if otherwise authorized by law. An example would be a small business set aside as authorized by the Small Business Act.

The use of any of these exemptions in any instance requires a departmental determination and finding that negotiation is appropriate. Although these determinations and findings are intradepartmental, failure to make the determinations can result in cancellation of the requests for proposals or quotations. Determinations and findings are required not only to justify the use of negotiation but also to permit advance payments under negotiated contracts, to determine the type of contract, or to waive requirements for cost or pricing data.

Prototyping

In the purchase of complex equipment involving technical uncertainties, there should be assurance, prior to a commitment to production, that the equipment will perform as desired. An item of equipment may exist on paper, or it can exist as a working model (a prototype). This is particularly important in the acquisition of weapon systems, security equipment, or water and waste equipment, for example.

Regardless of whether it is a matter of advancing the state of the art, making sure all is well before tooling up for production, or finding out which of several options is best, the real purpose of prototype development is to put theories, analyses, and laboratory data to the test in a full-scale functioning model. The model must incorporate only those aspects that are essential for answering the vital questions that the prototype program must address. For this reason, it is imperative that the specific objectives of a prototype program be clearly defined and understood by all concerned.

Ideally prototypes should be developed competitively with no specific production commitment. Contractors are motivated by the knowledge that if their entry wins a rigorous competitive evaluation, their chances for getting further contracts are improved significantly.

On the basis of prototype evaluation, a wise decision is possible about whether to buy and, if so, what and how many. Sometimes the decision not to buy is the best result of prototype development.

If systems and equipments turned out exactly as planned and estimated, prototypes would not be needed. Prototypes, at relatively modest cost, reduce the risk of making gross errors that produce large cost overruns.

System Acquisition

A system is defined here as a combination of elements that will function together to fulfill a need. The elements may include equipment, spare parts and supplies, related hardware, software, real property, construction, test devices, maintenance arrangements, transportation, technical data, and operator training. The policy decision addresses the question of the extent to which all of the elements can be combined into a single well-integrated and well-coordinated procurement program and how the program can best be managed. The system could be a military weapon, a trauma-treatment center, or a metropolitan waste-disposal capability. System acquisition is approached on a life-cycle basis; considerations cover everything from the earliest identification of need on through to the ultimate disposition of the obsolete remains.

Management of system acquisition begins with a carefully developed statement of the need. The determination of a mission need is at the heart of OMB circular A-109.[9] The mission-need statement:

1. Identifies the mission area and states the need in terms of the task to be performed. The mission need is not stated in terms of capabilities or of characteristics of a hardware or software system.
2. Identifies existing capability to accomplish the task.
3. Assesses the need in terms of a deficiency in the existing capability, a projected physical obsolescence, or a technological or cost-savings opportunity.
4. States the known constraints to apply to any acceptable solution, including operational and logistics considerations, requirements for standardization, limits on the resource investment to be made, and timing. These constraints will constitute boundary conditions for the exploration of alternative solutions.
5. Assesses the impact of not acquiring or maintaining the capability.
6. Provides a program plan to identify and explore competitive alternative systems extending through to the next milestone decision.

After acceptance by top management of the stated need, the program is initiated and subsequently managed and controlled through four critical points, referred to as milestones.

Milestone O—program initiation. Upon making a determination that a valid need exists and a major system-acquisition program is required to acquire a new system capability, or a modification to an existing capability, authority is granted to proceed with identification of alternative system-design concepts.

Milestone I—demonstration and validation. As a result of the competitive identification and exploration of alternative design concepts, management may conclude that the demonstration and validation phase should involve several alternatives; be limited to a single system concept; involve alternative subsystems only and not be conducted at the system level; or there should be no demonstration and the program should proceed directly into full-scale engineering development. The preferred alternative is identified.

Milestone II—full-scale engineering development. Upon successful completion of the demonstration and validation phase, full-scale engineering development and production is directed. The milestone II decision is a commitment to continue the program through the engineering development phase. It includes long-lead-time procurement items and such limited production as required to support an operational test and evaluation.

Milestone III—production and deployment. Upon completion of the engineering development phase, including the initial operational test and evaluation leading to the milestone III production and deployment decision, management makes a commitment to production and deployment of the system.

This management process is designed to meet the agency objectives laid down in circular A-109. A department or agency is expected to ensure that each system fulfills a mission need, operates effectively in its intended environment, and demonstrates a level of performance and reliability that justifies the allocation of resources for its acquisition and ownership. Whenever economically beneficial, it must depend on competition between similar or differing system-design concepts throughout the entire acquisition process. It must ensure appropriate trade-offs among investment costs, ownership costs, schedules, and performance characteristics. It is important for the agency to provide strong checks and balances by ensuring adequate system test and evaluation. Where practicable, it must conduct such tests and evaluation independent of developer and user. Another goal is to accomplish system-acquisition planning built on analysis of agency missions, which implies appropriate resource allocation resulting from clear articulation of agency mission needs. It must tailor an acquisition strategy for each program and refine the strategy as the program proceeds through the acquisition process. The strategy, which must encompass test and evaluation criteria and business-management considerations, typically includes: the contracting strategy to be employed; a schedule of essential steps in the acquisition process; demonstration, test, and evaluation criteria; planned content of solicitations for proposals; potential suppliers to solicit; the method for obtaining and sustaining competition; guidelines for the evaluation and acceptance or rejection of proposals; goals for design-to-cost; methods projecting life-cycle costs; guidelines for use of data and for use of warranties; methods for evaluating contractor and government risk; the need for developing contractor incentives; selection of the type of contract best suited for each stage of the acquisition; and methods for the administration of the contracts.

During this process, the agency must maintain the capability to predict, review, assess, negotiate, and monitor system costs; assess schedule and performance experience against predictions; reassess where significant cost, schedule, or performance variances occur; reassess life-cycle costs to ensure appropriate trade-offs among investment costs, ownership costs, schedules, and performance; and obtain independent cost estimates, where feasible, for comparison.

Achieving Nonprocurement Objectives

The overall effect of legislation designed to attain socioeconomic objects upon purchasing policy and strategy is clearly to superimpose a great many additional requirements and pressures. The major socioeconomic programs are those to protect workers employed in the performance of the contract, those favoring groups viewed as economically, socially, physically, or mentally disadvantaged, and those designed to protect the quality of life or the natural environment and to encourage conservation of scarce resources.[10]

The federal government provides broad coverage under its contracts for the protection of workers employed in the performance of the contract. These provisions mandate minimum wage levels, provide for overtime restrictions, and set standards for working conditions.

The Walsh-Healey Public Contracts Act generally applies to government contracts for the manufacture or supply of materials, items of supply, or articles or equipment costing in excess of $10,000.[11] It also covers all employees engaged in or connected with the manufacture, fabrication, assembling, handling, supervision, or shipment of materials, supplies, articles, or equipment required under a covered contract except executive, administrative, professional, office, custodial, and maintenance employees. The provisions of the act require that the prevailing minimum wage as established by the secretary of labor for similar work in the particular or similar industries or groups of industries currently operating in the locality be paid. The secretary of labor has issued both minimum-wage determinations for specific industries and determinations that prescribe the minimum-wage rates for all other industries where no specific industry determinations have been made. Additionally overtime pay at time and one-half of at least the basic minimum hourly rate is required, with any hours worked in excess of forty per week or eight per day considered to be overtime. The act prohibits contractors performing covered contracts from employing either child or convict labor in the performance of the contracts. Child labor is defined as any person under sixteen years of age. Convict labor includes all persons actually serving prison sentences. It thus excludes those on parole or otherwise not physically in prison.

Contracts subject to the act contain a stipulation that work not be performed under conditions that are unsanitary, harzardous, or dangerous to the health and safety of the employees. Uniform national safety and health standards for such contracts are set forth in considerable detail in regulations issued under the act and the Occupational Safety and Health Act (1970). Evidence of compliance with this portion of the act is provided by the contractor's passing an inspection conducted by state officials acting as authorized representatives of the Department of Labor.

The Walsh-Healey Act requires contractors supplying or furnishing materials, supplies, or equipment to enter into a representation that they are manufacturers of or regular dealers in the commodities being supplied. Although it is not necessary that a contractor performing a contract subject to the Walsh-Healey Act keep separate records for complying with the record-keeping requirements of the act, the employment records that he does maintain must show the hours worked and the rates of pay for each employee. The records must include the name, address, sex, and occupation of each employee, the date of birth of all employees under nineteen years of age, certificates of age or work permits of minors, amounts of pay to each employee for each pay period, and hours of work for each day and for each week for each employee during the periods employed on work for the government contract. The original time and earnings cards, wage-rate tables from which compensation is computed, and work-time schedules must be retained for a period of two years. All other records must be preserved for a period of three years from the date of last entry.

The Davis-Bacon Act, as amended, requires that all laborers and mechanics employed on contracts of over $2,000 for public-works projects be paid at least the prevailing minimum wage.[12] This guarantee is accomplished through the statutory requirement that all such contracts specify minimum wages to be paid as determined by the secretary of labor as being the prevailing wage for corresponding classes of laborers and mechanics on similar projects in the city, town, or other civil subdivision in which the contract is to be performed. Employees must be paid at least weekly regardless of the existence of any contractual agreement to the contrary between the contractor and the employees.

To implement this requirement, solicitations for contracts for the construction, alteration, and/or repair of public buildings or public works contain a specification of the minimum wages and fringe benefits that must be paid by the contractor as determined by the secretary of labor. Two types of wage determinations are issued: (1) a general wage determination for use by governmental agencies in a designated geographical area, having a 120-day duration but issued on a continuing basis and published in the *Federal Reg-*

ister, and (2) an area or installation determination for the specific geographic area or installation when no general determination has been issued, issued by the secretary of labor upon the request of the federal agency.

Several actions must be accomplished in implementing Davis-Bacon. For example, in addition to paying at least the specified minimum wage and time and one-half for time worked over eight hours per day or forty hours per week, contractors are required to post the schedule of minimum wages determined to be applicable by the secretary of labor in a prominent and easily accessible place at the work site. Contractors must submit to the government within seven calendar days after each payday copies of weekly payrolls, which contain the names and addresses of all employees, their job classifications, rates of pay (including fringe benefits), daily and weekly hours worked, deductions made, and actual wages paid. The original records must be maintained by the contractor for three years.

Enforcement rests with the individual procuring activity. In addition to the receipt and maintenance of payrolls, compliance checks must be accomplished by the procuring agency. These include:

1. Frequent employee interviews conducted by the inspector and contracting officer (or a representative) to determine correctness of classification and rate of pay, including fringe benefits.
2. On-site inspections to check type and classifications of work performed, number of workers, and fulfillment of posting requirements.
3. Payroll reviews to ensure that payrolls of prime contractors and subcontractors have been submitted on time and that such payrolls are complete and correct.
4. Comparison of this information with available data, including daily inspector's reports and daily logs of construction, to ensure consistency.

If apparent violations are discovered during any of the compliance checks, the procuring activity must conduct an investigation and forward its report to the Department of Labor. Sums must be withheld from amounts due the contractor, which may later be used to pay employees who have not been paid the full amounts required under the act.

The McNamara-O'Hara Service Contract Act provides for employees working on service contracts many of the minimum labor standards afforded employees of construction and supply contractors by Davis-Bacon and Walsh-Healey, respectively.[13] The Service Contract Act applies to all service contracts in excess of $2,500. This includes basic ordering agreements and blanket-purchase agreements entered into by the United States or the District of Columbia for the principal purpose of securing services in the United States through the use of service employees. Exceptions are provided on contracts for transportation, communications, public utilities, individual personnel services, postal contract stations, and contracts covered by Davis-Bacon or Walsh-Healey. The act provides, however, that regardless of contract amount, no firm performing work under any federal service contract furnishing services through the use of service employees will pay any of its employees engaged in work under the contract less than the minimum wage specified in the Fair Labor Standards Act, as amended. The act requires all government service contracts in excess of $2,500 to contain provisions specifying the minimum wages and fringe benefits to be paid under the contract, to provide for safe working conditions, and for posting of notices of compensation due to employees under the prevailing wage determination.

Prior to the issuance of an invitation for bids or the commencement of negotiations, a procuring activity must file with the Department of Labor a full description of the intended service contract and its terms. With the application, which must be filed at least thirty days prior to issuing a solicitation, the contracting officer must include all known payroll data relevant to the contract. Such data could include government wage scales or existing collective-bargaining agreements applicable to any existing contract. The Department of Labor, based on this and its own information, determines the minimum wages and fringe benefits that must be paid in the performance of the prime contract or any subcontract. In the event of apparent violation, the Department of Labor itself investigates apparent violations under the Service Contract Act.

Record-keeping requirements are imposed under the Service Contract Act. The contractor must maintain records for three years from completion of the contract. The records must be by workweek and must contain employee names and addresses, work classifications and compensation, daily and weekly hours worked, and deductions taken.

The Contract Work Hours and Safety Standards Act provides for maximum working hours and time and one-half for overtime in excess of eight hours per day or forty hours per week for service and construction workers who work at jobs that are also covered either by the Service Contract Act or the Davis-Bacon Act, respectively.[14] Not included are contracts of $2,500 or less, contracts subject to the Walsh-Healey Act, and transportation contracts. Since Walsh-Healey covers supply contracts in amounts of more than $10,000, supply contracts for items other than those available in the open market in amounts between $2,500 and $10,000 are subject to this act. In addition to the time and one-half for overtime requirement originally set forth, the act also promotes health and safety in the construction trades by requiring that construction contractors ensure that laborers and mechanics not be required to work in any place under any working conditions that are unsanitary, hazardous, or dangerous to their health or safety. With the legislation of these standards for the construction industry, coverage that already existed on supply and service contracts was extended to construction workers.

Violations are investigated by the procuring activity in a fashion similar to that followed with Davis-Bacon Act violations. The act also requires that each contract administration office submit a semiannual report on compliance actions taken under the Contract Work Hours and Safety Standards Act.

The Fair Labor Standards Act is the overall wage and hour law; it has general application with respect to minimum wage and maximum standards for employees.[15] Under the act, the Wage and Hour Division within the Department of Labor has the responsibility for interpreting and enforcing the provisions of the act, which include investigations and inspections of government contractors. The act prohibits oppressive child labor and covers all employees engaged in interstate or foreign commerce, the production of goods for such commerce, or in any related process or occupation essential to such production. The act applies to all contractors and establishes a minimum wage per hour that all employees covered by the statute must be paid. The act provides for overtime pay at the rate of time and one-half for hours worked in excess of forty hours per week. Additionally the act prohibits the employment of children in certain designated jobs. The ages at which children must not be employed are classified either administratively or by statute and vary according to particular job types. Finally, the statute requires equal pay for equal work. Every employer subject to any provision of the act or any regulation issued under it is required to make and preserve records of wages, hours, and other terms of employment.

The Fair Labor Standards Act applies to government contracts despite the fact that there may be simultaneous coverage under other statutes. The act that contains the highest benefit to the employee prevails.

It is national policy to favor certain disadvantaged groups through the public-purchasing process. Groups include black, Hispanic, and native Americans, as well as other minorities and the handicapped, who have been either economically or socially disadvantaged. Preferential treatment can take the form of specifying the labor-force composition of government contractors, the targeting of contracts directly to disadvantaged groups, or the requirement that government contractors target subcontracts to disadvantaged groups.

A major policy of the federal government is to ensure equal opportunity for all qualified persons, without regard to race, color, religion, sex, age, or national origin, employed by or seeking employment within government contractors. A series of executive orders declare it to be against national policy to discriminate on the basis of age, except upon the basis of a bona-fide occupational qualification, retirement plan, or statutory requirement; or because of race, creed, color, or national origin; or on the basis of sex.[16]

The administration of these executive orders for federal agency contractors has been vested in the director of the Office of Federal Contract Compliance Programs (OFCCP) of the Department of Labor. The OFCCP is charged with issuing rules and regulations and determining the extent of contractor compliance with these programs. Compliance with these orders occurs in several ways. For example, a written assurance must be obtained from each offerer on awards over $10,000 that he does not and will not maintain any facilities for his employees in a segregated manner and that he will not require his employees to use segregated facilities at any location under his control. For each contract greater than $10,000 or for those contracts under $10,000 when the contractor has contracts that aggregate over $10,000 in a twelve-month period, an equal-employment opportunity clause must be inserted into the contract. The clause requires contractors not to discriminate against any employee, or anyone seeking employment, because of race, creed, color, or national origin. The duty is an affirmative one, requiring the employer to take positive action to ensure nondiscrimination with respect not only to hiring but also to the terms and conditions of employment. One mandatory step is that all advertisements for employees shall state that job applications will be considered without regard to race, creed, color, or national origin. In addition the contractor must inform, by notice, all employees and unions of their nondiscriminatory and procedural commitments under the executive orders. The contractor is required to post on the job site the equal employment opportunity (EEO) poster and standard form 38, "Notice to Labor Unions or Other Organization of Workers—Nondiscrimination in Employment." Each federal nonconstruction contractor or subcontractor with a contract of $50,000 or more and fifty or more employees must develop an affirmative-action program with respect to equal-employment opportunities in each of its facilities. The affirmative-action program must ensure that all employees have equal chances for employment, promotion, training, pay, and equal work areas and recreational facilities. Employers must maintain separate affirmative-action compliance records for each facility and must submit an affirmative-action program within 120 days from the commencement of a covered contract and annually thereafter, with updates as required.

In the process of developing an affirmative-action program, the Equal Employment Opportunity Commission (EEOC) has suggested eight specific steps to be accomplished by contractors:

1. Issuance of a written EEO policy and affirmative-action commitment.
2. Appointment of a top company official with responsibility and authority to direct and implement the program.
3. Publicizing of the policy internally and externally.
4. Surveying present minority and female employment by department and job classification to determine whether equal-employment opportunity is being afforded in the company hiring, upgrading, transfer, and promotion practices.

5. Development of specific goals and timetables to improve utilization of minorities and females.
6. Development of specific programs to achieve goals.
7. Establishment of an internal audit and reporting system to monitor progress toward goals.
8. Development of supportive in-house and community programs.[17]

It is also national policy to ensure that a fair proportion of government contracts are awarded to small business.[18] This preference achieves a dual purpose of ensuring the continued existence of small businesses, and thus a healthy competitive environment, and of providing a broad base of capable suppliers in the event a national emergency should require the expansion of the nation's productive capacity. To achieve this purpose, the Congress passed the Small Business Act, which created the Small Business Administration (SBA) and provided for the preferential treatment of small-business concerns in the award of government contracts.[19]

Definition of what constitutes a small business in a particular industry has been delegated to the SBA. Generally as defined in the statute, a small-business concern is one independently owned and operated and not dominant in its field. The SBA, as a rule, uses annual receipts and the number of employees of a firm to determine whether in a particular industry a firm meets the standard of a small business. These standards are set industry by industry and range from five hundred or fewer employees in the food canning and processing industry to the passenger car industry where the following classification is used:

> Passenger cars—A company is classified as small if it is bidding on a contract for passenger cars: Provided, that (i) the value of the passenger cars which it manufactured or otherwise produced in the United States during the preceding calendar year is more than 50% of the value of its total worldwide manufacture or production of such passenger cars, (ii) the value of the passenger cars which it manufactured or otherwise produced during the preceding calendar year was less than 5% of the total value of all such cars manufactured or produced in the United States during the said period, and (iii) the value of the principal products which it manufactured or otherwise produced or sold during the preceding calendar year is less than 10% of the total value of such products manufactured or otherwise produced or sold in the United States during said period.[20]

The SBA issues a certificate when the criteria for a small business in its industry have been met by a particular firm. After receipt, the firm can certify itself as a small business for purpose of contract award.

The small-business preference is implemented in a variety of ways. Among them are the use of small-business-restricted advertising; the requirement for government prime contractors to utilize small-business subcontractors to the maximum extent possible; the requirement for contracts with prime contracts greater than $500,000 to have a formal small-business subcontracting program; and a procedure whereby the contracting agency can award contracts direct to the SBA.

Small-business restricted advertising is accomplished in accordance with federal statutes that provide for the setting aside by the government of a procurement for exclusive bidding by, and award to small business.[21] To accomplish a procurement, a joint determination must be made by the procuring contracting officer and the small-business specialist or representative assigned to the procurement activity that the procurement can be made from small-business concerns. Any individual procurement or class of procurements, regardless of dollar value, may be set aside for the exclusive participation of small-business firms, as determined by these individuals. A decision not to set aside a procurement for small-business exclusive participation must be documented as to the reason why, signed by the contracting officer and the small-business specialist.

Under a class set-aside, both current and future procurements of selected items or groups of related items are totally set aside for procurement from small-business concerns only. The class set-aside is recommended by the small-business specialist and requires the concurrence of the contracting officer. In contrast to an individual set-aside, which is made for a single purchase, this class arrangement does not depend on the present existence of a procurement but can be made for present or future procurements. Total set-asides are those in which the entire procurement, be it a class set-aside or an individual procurement set-aside, is set aside for award to small-business concerns. Partial set-asides are those in which only part of the total procurement is required to be awarded to small-business concerns; the balance is available for award to either large- or small-business concerns under the nonset-aside portion of the procurement.

Increased emphasis on awards of contracts to small businesses is apparent in the 1978 amendments to the Small Business Investment Act.[22] Under this act, each purchasing installation must appoint a small- and disadvantaged-business utilization specialist, who will be reviewed at the department level prior to hiring. Additionally the department will comment and contribute to annual performance appraisals of field-level specialists, including the establishment of rates of pay under the Civil Service Reform Act (1978). Moreover, the law establishes a requirement that procuring agencies report monthly to the Congress on awards to small business.

The SBA also becomes involved in direct awards to small business by government-procuring activities. If the bid or proposal of a small-business concern is to be rejected by the government contracting officer solely because the contracting officer believes the bidder is incapable of performing the contract, he must notify the SBA of his proposed rejection. The SBA will determine whether the business in question possesses the capability, competency, capacity, credit, integrity, perseverance, and tenacity to perform. If the determination is favorable, the SBA will issue a certificate of competency (COC). The COC is conclusive of the fact that the bidder has the overall ability to meet quality, quantity, and performance requirements and has or will be able to obtain the necessary financial resources to perform the contract. If the contracting officer has substantial doubts regarding the contractor's ability to perform, he must appeal the issuance of the COC to his higher headquarters.

The commitment to small business can also be fulfilled under what is referred to as "Section 8(a) Authority."[23] Under this provision, the SBA has the authority to enter into contracts with other government departments and agencies for supplies, services, construction, and research and development required by those departments and agencies. Using this method, the procuring activity contract award is made directly to SBA, which then enters into subcontracts with small-business concerns it has selected. In fulfillment of its responsibilities, the SBA is authorized to provide technical and administrative assistance to its subcontractors, as well as financial assistance and liaison activities to coordinate the accomplishment of the contract requirements.

Implementation of the 8(a) program requires the procuring activity to refer susceptible procurements to the SBA for consideration. The SBA must notify the procuring activity of its acceptance or rejection of referred procurements within ten days. A fair-market price is then negotiated with the procuring activity and an 8(a) contractor of SBA choice for the required goods or services. If the total proposed price is greater than the estimated current market price, the SBA is authorized to fund the difference as business-development expense.

Several acts and an executive order establish policy and authority for the use of the acquisition process to aid parts of the country classified by the Department of Labor as labor-surplus areas (LSAs).[24] This policy is implemented through the Federal Preparedness Agency of the GSA by the government's both awarding contracts to LSA concerns and having prime contractors target subcontracts to firms in these areas. An LSA is defined as a labor market area in which the unemployment rate is 120 percent of the national average and at least 6 percent, or a labor market area having a 10 percent unemployment rate. An area also can be classified as eligible for preference if it encompasses a smaller area, or areas, or labor surplus, if the unemployment rate for the overall area is at least equal to 6 percent; each qualifying subarea has a population of at least 50,000; and together the qualifying subareas account for at least 25 percent of the overall area unemployment.

To be eligible for a preference for direct award of a government con-tract, the contractor must agree to perform a substantial proportion of the contract in an LSA. Substantial performance is achieved if manufacturing and production costs incurred from performance in the labor surplus area amount to more than one-half of the contract price. Awards by the govern-ment can be made under either total or partial set-asides where firms agree-ing to have substantial performance in an LSA are given preference for award. Total set-asides for LSAs are authorized if offers from a sufficient number of eligible concerns can be expected. Partial LSA set-asides can be made if the procurement is severable into at least two or more economic production runs or lots and one or more LSA concerns are anticipated to have the competency and capacity to fulfill a portion of the procurement at a reasonable price.

To be eligible for award under the procedures for the set-aside portion of a partial set-aside, an offerer must submit an offer on the nonset-aside portion of the solicitation. After award has been made on that portion, of-fers are requested from concerns in the order of their offers on the nonset-aside, beginning with the lowest responsive offer within each priority groups as follows:

1. Concerns located in LSAs, and which are small-business concerns, on the basis of a total set-aside.
2. Small-business concerns, on the basis of a total set-aside.
3. Small-business concerns, on the basis of a partial set-aside.
4. Concerns located in LSAs, on the basis of a total set-aside.

Generally, award on the set-aside portion will be made on a negotiated basis at the highest unit price for each item awarded on the nonset-aside portion, adjusted to reflect transportation and other cost factors used in evaluating offers on that portion.

It is also national policy that minority business enterprises (MBE) be utilized as much as possible.[25] To implement this policy, each government procuring activity must establish a program to facilitate the participation of MBEs in government procurement. Such programs must provide for the following:

1. To seek out MBEs and facilitate the placement of such concerns on source lists.
2. To solicit offers from the MBEs on source lists.
3. To counsel MBEs with respect to business opportunities for the purpose of enhancing their potential participation in government procurement.
4. To ensure that MBEs have an equitable opportunity to compete for contracts, particularly by arranging solicitations, time for the prepara-

tion of bids, quantities, specifications, and delivery schedules to facilitate their participation.

5. To establish operating procedures that accomplish these requirements.
6. To maintain records showing with respect to MBE enterprises concerns on source lists, concerns solicited, and dollar value of awards to such concerns.
7. To obtain data on subcontract awards to MBEs from prime contractors who have the Minority Business Enterprise Subcontracting Program clause in their contracts.[26]

These criteria reveal that the MBE program is implemented through government procuring activities procuring direct from minority businesses and the requirement that government prime contractors target subcontractors to minority businesses. Firms responding to government solicitations greater than $10,000 must certify that they either are, or are not, an MBE. Additionally government contracts between $10,000 and $500,000 must contain a clause requiring the contractor to use MBEs to the maximum extent possible. Finally contracts greater than $500,000 require the development of a formal subcontracting program that enables the contractor to fulfill requirements of the MBE program.

A 1979 executive order directs federal agencies to take affirmative action to promote greater participation of women-owned businesses in supplying the government.[27] The order directs that each department and agency designate a high-level official to act as a focal point in implementing the order and one to serve on the Interagency Committee on Women's Business Enterprise. Reports of activities under this program are directed on a yearly basis. The order encourages agencies to develop incentives to promote women-owned businesses. The order was accompanied by the establishment of a goal to award contracts of $150 million to women-owned business in FY 1980 and to double this amount in FY 1981. The OFPP was directed to explore the use of incentive provisions to encourage contractors to award subcontracts to women-owned businesses.

National policy also requires government contractors and subcontractors to take affirmative action to employ and advance in employment qualified handicapped individuals without discrimination as to their physical or mental handicap.[28] Provisions of this requirement are enforced by the Department of Labor for contracts of $2,500 or more. Regulations require that the contractor not discriminate against and take affirmative action to employ and advance those qualified employees or applicants physically or mentally handicapped. Notices stating the contractors' obligations must be posted in conspicuous places. Contractors must notify labor unions or other representatives of workers with whom they have collective-bargaining agreements of the requirements. For those employers with contracts over $50,000 and that employ fifty or more people, the contractor must have a written affirmative-action program to employ and advance in employment those with handicaps. This plan is similar to the plan required under the EEO regulations, except that it omits goals and timetables. It must include actions to be taken in hiring, upgrading, demotion or transfer, recruitment, layoff or termination, rates of pay or other compensation, and selection for training. State employment security agencies must be requested to refer qualified handicapped individuals for employment consideration. The Office of Federal Contracts Compliance Programs of the Department of Labor is responsible for review and enforcement of these provisions. Each individual who falls under this program is self-identifying; that is, the contractor must solicit employees or applicants to apply for the program voluntarily. Subsequent to this identification, the contractor must keep records of each promotion or training program the handicapped individual was considered for. Records must be annotated for each hire, promotion, or training action as to why or why not the individual was selected and accommodations made to facilitate the action.

Contractors to the federal government must also show special consideration for Vietnam veterans.[29] Firms holding contracts that exceed $10,000 may not discriminate against any employee or applicant because of that person's status as a disabled veteran or a veteran of the Vietnam era. Moreover, firms must take affirmative action to employ or advance these individuals. They must make an accommodation for physical and mental limits of applicants unless business necessity or financial cost prohibits such accommodation. Suitable employment openings must be listed with the state employment service system. The government also requires quarterly reports on personnel actions to be filed with the state employment service system. The contractor must post in a conspicuous place notices outlining the contractor's obligations under the contract. The contractor must also notify each laborer or representative of the worker who holds a collective-bargaining agreement of his obligations under these provisions. The contractor must designate by name an individual to implement and monitor the program. For those contractors holding contracts over $50,000 and employing fifty or more employees, the contractor must develop and maintain an affirmative-action plan. This plan must be reviewed and updated annually and must include actions to be taken in hiring, upgrading, demotion or transfer, recruitment, layoff or termination, rates of pay or other compensation, and selection for training. This plan is similar to that required under the EEO provisions except that there are no established goals or timetables. The Office of Federal Contract Compliance Programs of the Department of Labor is responsible for evaluation and enforcement of these provisions. Compliance reviews conducted by OFCCP concentrate on systematic restrictions not job related, which tend to discriminate against this class of protected worker. Each individual who falls under this program is self-identifying; that is, the contractor must solicit employees or applicants to apply for the programs voluntarily. Subsequent to this identification, the contractor must keep records of each promotion or training program the veteran was considered for. Records must be annotated for each hiring, promotion, or training action as to why the individual was (or was not) selected and accommodations made to facilitate the action.

It is also national policy to show degrees of preference for products made by the blind, native Americans, and prisoners. The Wagner-O'Day Act, as amended, created the Committee for Purchase from the Blind and other Severely Handicapped.[30] The committee is presidentially appointed and consists of fifteen members. Eleven of them represent various government agencies, and four are private citizens knowledgeable of problems in employing blind and other handicapped persons. According to the act, it is the function of the committee to establish a list of commodities and services provided by any qualified nonprofit agency of the severely handicapped. Agencies listed become a priority source of supply to government users for those products and services contained in the *Schedule of Blind-Made Products*. Orders for those products are placed with the National Industries for the Blind. The Department of Interior also identifies items that are to be obtained through open-market purchase from native American-owned industry.[31] Another mandatory source is the *Schedule of Products Made in Federal Penal and Correctional Institutions*. An organization known as the Federal Prison Industries, Inc. (FPI) was created in 1934 as a wholly owned government corporation.[32] Products available are listed in the schedule, which is distributed to and maintained by all procuring activities. Orders are placed directly with the FPI.

The third group of programs setting nonprocurement objectives is concerned with the quality of life, the natural environment, and the conservation of scarce resources. Concern for protection of the environment has brought a relatively large number of programs, recently implemented, that affect the acquisition process. Starting with the Clean Air Act (1970), coverage has expanded with the passage of the Clean Water Act (1972), the Noise Control Act (1972), the Resource Conservation and Recovery Act (1976), and the Energy Policy and Conservation Act (1976).

Federal policy in the area of environmental protection has been set out in the Clean Air Act, as amended,[33] and the Federal Water Pollution Control Act.[34] The policy, as stated by executive order, is to improve and enhance environmental quality.[35] In fulfillment of this policy, except in limited circumstances, purchasing offices are prohibited from entering into, renewing, or extending any contract for the procurement of goods, materials, or services to a firm proposing to use in the performance of the contract a facility that appears on the Environmental Protection Agency's

(EPA) *List of Violating Facilities.* This requirement is valid for contracts or subcontracts greater than $100,000. In all solicitations greater than $100,000, the offerer must certify in her solicitation that she is (or is not) listed on the list. If the otherwise successful offerer informs the contracting officer that the EPA is considering listing a facility proposed to be used for contract performance, the contracting officer must notify EPA that the firm is under consideration for award. The EPA may then request the contracting officer to delay award of a contract for a period not to exceed fifteen working days until a determination is made of the nature of the violation.

The Humane Slaughter Act (1958) prohibits the purchase by the government of livestock products produced or processed by any slaughter or processor which in any of its plants slaughters livestock by any method other than humane as set forth in the act.[36] Livestock products consist of articles of food intended for human or animal consumption that are derived from slaughtered cattle, calves, horses, mules, sheep, swine, or goats. Proposed suppliers of livestock products are informed of the provisions of the act through solicitation of a statement of eligibility (Human Slaughter Act), under which the contractor agrees that his products are derived from carcasses that have been slaughtered in compliance with the act.

The Noise Control Act (1972) contains a provision relating to the procurement of products as they relate to the control of noise detrimental to the human environment.[37] As implemented by the EPA, a three-step certification procedure is involved that gives a monetary preference to low-noise emission products. If a product is certified as one that emits noises in amounts significantly below noise standards, is a suitable substitute for items currently procured, and costs no more than 125 percent of the retail price of the least expensive type of product for which it is being substituted, it is required to be procured in lieu of alternative products. The preference is obtained by the granting of a certificate that a product is a low-noise-emission product and is applicable to any manufactured article or component except aircraft and aircraft components, military weapons and equipment, rockets and equipment used by NASA, or equipment used by government for experimental work. "Buy quiet" purchasing criteria are being widely adopted at all levels of government. The National Institute of Governmental Purchasing provides as one of its many services a "buy quiet" data clearinghouse.

The Resource Conservation and Recovery Act (1976) mandates certain requirements with respect to the purchase of an item whose purchase price exceeds $10,000 or where the quantity of items acquired during the preceding fiscal year totaled $10,000 or more.[38] Requirements include the procurement of items composed of the highest percentage of recovered materials practicable, consistent with maintaining a satisfactory level of competition; and the certification by vendors of the percentage of the total material utilized for the performance of the contract that is recovered. Additionally government specifications are to be reviewed and made consistent with the statute. Finally OFPP must report annually to the Congress the actions and progress made in the implementation of this policy.

The Energy Policy and Conservation Act requires the president to develop mandatory standards with respect to energy conservation and energy efficiency to govern the procurement policies and decisions of the government.[39] By executive order the president delegated this responsibility to the OFPP.[40] Generally the act requires that federal procurement policies governing requirements determinations and source-selection decisions provide for the consideration of energy conservation and the relative energy efficiency of alternative goods or services capable of satisfying the government's needs. For example, under this policy, energy conservation and efficiency criteria are to be considered along with price and other relevant factors in the preparation of solicitations, the evaluation of offers, and the selection of bids and proposals for award. In the procurement of consumer products, executive agencies are directed to take cognizance of energy use-efficiency labels and prescribed energy-efficiency standards as they become available from the Department of Commerce.

The acquisition process has also been used as a vehicle to help achieve a variety of other political, economic, social, and ethical purposes. Examples include sanctions imposed under contract for improper conduct of government or contractor personnel, the prohibition of trading with selected foreign countries while encouraging trade with other ones, the forbidding of the use by contractors to the government of persons undergoing sentences of imprisonment or hard labor, the equitable geographic distribution of contract and subcontract spending, and the holding of price adjustments within anti-inflation guidelines.

All of these nonprocurement objectives have added a great many requirements and pressures to the purchasing subsystem:

1. Increased costs to the government and to the contractors of verifying and certifying the several conditions.
2. Increased costs of reviewing and reporting compliance.
3. Increased costs of staffing to provide the many specialists and liaison officers in the several fields.
4. Higher prices paid for goods and services acquired because of price differentials recognized and higher wage rates encouraged.
5. Increased effort and expense of set-aside procedures resulting in multiple contracts.
6. Delays while making determinations of eligibility and compliance.
7. Total default or delay in performance by marginally capable disadvantaged firms.

8. Need to increase inventory levels due to longer administrative and performance lead times.
9. Higher costs to acquire and hold material.

The positive view must prevail that these requirements and pressures are justified by the public good accomplished in the many socioeconomic problem areas.

Notes

1. Available from: National Bureau of Economic Research, 1050 Massachusetts Avenue, Cambridge, Massachusetts 02138.

2. The discussion that follows is drawn from the comptroller general's report to the Congress, "Development of a National Make-or-Buy Strategy—Progress and Problems," PSAD-78-118 (Washington, D.C.: General Accounting Office, 25 September 1978).

3. Executive Office of the President, OMB, *Cost Comparison Handbook*, Supplement No. 1 to OMB Circular No. A-76, *Policies for Acquiring Commercial or Industrial Products and Services Needed by the Government* (Washington, D.C.: Office of Management and Budget, March 1979).

4. The discussion that follows is drawn from a presentation by George S. Ostrowski at the Seventh Annual Acquisition Research Symposium, Hershey, Pennsylvania, 31 May-2 June 1978.

5. Code of the Commonwealth of Virginia, 1950, sec. 2-258; 1958, c. 124; 1966, c. 677.

6. State of South Carolina, Central State Purchasing, *Purchasing Policies and Procedures* (Columbia: State of South Carolina Division of General Services, 1974), p. 36.

7. Stanley N. Sherman, *Procurement Management: The Federal System* (Bethesda, Md.: SL Communications, 1979).

8. For a full development of these four models, see ibid., chap. 8.

9. Executive Office of the President, Office of Management and Budget, "Major System Acquisition," Circular A-109 (Washington, D.C.: OMB, 5 April 1976).

10. The taxonomy and the basic descriptions of the programs are taken from research by Richard J. Hampton, a graduate student at The George Washington University.

11. 41 U.S.C. 35-45.

12. 40 U.S.C. 276a.

13. 41 U.S.C. 351-358.

14. 40 U.S.C. 327-330.

15. 29 U.S.C. 201-219.

16. Executive Order 11141, 12 February 1964; Executive Order 11246, 24 October 1965; Executive Order 11375, 13 October 1967.

17. General Services Administration, *Code of Federal Regulations*, chap. 41, pt. 60.

18. 15 U.S.C. 637.

19. Ibid., 631.

20. General Services Administration, *Code of Federal Regulations*, chap. 13, pt. 127.

21. 10 U.S.C. 2304(a)(1), 15 U.S.C. 644.

22. Public Law 95-507, amendments to the Small Business Investment Act of 1958, 92 Stat. 1757 (24 October 1978).

23. Sec. 8(a) of the Small Business Act, 15 U.S.C. 637.

24. The Defense Production Act of 1950, 40 U.S.C. App. 2061-2166, Defense Manpower Policy No. 4A (DMP 4A), a 1977 amendment to the Small Business Act (P.L. 95-89), and executive order 12073, as of 16 August 1978.

25. Executive Order 11458, 5 March 1969; Executive Order 11625, 13 October 1971.

26. Example of criteria taken from Department of Defense, Defense Acquisition Regulation, 1-332, and General Services Administration, Federal Procurement and Regulation 1-1.13.

27. Executive Order 12138, 18 May 1979.

28. Sec. 503 of the Rehabilitation Act of 1973 as amended, 29 U.S.C. 793, implemented by Executive Order 11758, 15 January 1974.

29. Sec. 402 of Vietnam Era Veterans' Readjustment Assistance Act of 1974, as amended, 38 U.S.C. 2012, and Executive Order 11701, 24 January 1973.

30. 41 U.S.C. 46-48.

31. 25 U.S.C. 47.

32. Established under provision found at 18 U.S.C. 4121-4128.

33. 42 U.S.C. 1857 et seq.

34. 33 U.S.C. 1251 et seq.

35. Executive Order 11738, 10 September 1973.

36. 7 U.S.C. 1906.

37. 42 U.S.C. 4914.

38. Ibid., 6962.

39. Ibid., 6361.

40. Executive Order 11912, 13 April 1976.

11 Purchasing: Preaward Activities

Purchasing, by definition, is the buying of goods and services. It therefore is one of the many means of procurement, among them, purchase, loan, barter, exchange, and even theft.

The Preaward and Postaward Concepts

The purchasing subsystem can be conveniently divided into preaward and postaward activities. The issuance of a purchase order or the awarding of a contract marks the dividing line. Prior to making the award, the following activities occur, depending upon the complexity of the purchase:

1. Receiving, in the purchasing department, the requisition or purchase request describing the items needed and citing the funds to be obligated in placing the order.
2. Identifying potential sources and making a preliminary evaluation of the capability of the potential sources.
3. Issuing invitations to bid or otherwise asking for expressions of interest in doing business.
4. Communicating with potential vendors, clarifying terms, establishing working relationships.
5. Evaluating the bids or proposals, analyzing price and cost.
6. Conducting negotiations as appropriate and where allowed.
7. Awarding the order or contract to the vendor found to be most responsive and capable.

Postaward the following activities occur, or may occur, depending upon the complexity of the purchase:

1. Modifying the order or contract to correct errors or accommodate unforeseen developments.
2. Adjusting prices.
3. Conducting inspections and assuring quality of vendor performance.
4. Following up and expediting.
5. Handling discrepancies or deficiencies in the goods or services provided.
6. Dealing with default, terminating the contract for default.

7. Handling claims, disputes, and appeals.
8. Administering payment provisions.
9. Auditing the purchase.

Requesting and Authorizing Purchase

Statements of purchase requirements are passed from using activities or agencies to the purchasing unit by means of a purchase requisition or purchase authorization. No purchasing action is undertaken without such an authorization. The authorization may be for a one-time purchase of a single line item, or several line items shown on a prescribed form, or it may be a schedule of purchases for an entire fiscal period. A typical purchase requisition is shown in figure 11-1. The essential information to be provided consists of:

1. The date of initiation.
2. The requisition number, often a controlled one preprinted on the form.
3. The originating agency or activity.
4. The account or project to be charged.
5. The urgency or priority of the purchase, if any.
6. The complete description of the material desired and quantity.
7. The date of delivery desired.
8. The method of shipment recommended and the shipping address.
9. The source recommended or previously used.
10. The authorizer's signature.
11. The budget officer's approval and fund citation.

The form often also provides for subsequent notations by the purchasing activity, such as the purchase order number used, the delivery data specified or arranged, and the buyer's signature.

The purchase request is prepared in multiple copies so that the several offices concerned—the originator, the budget office, and possibly others—may each receive a copy. Also each originating office maintains a journal of purchase requests issued to facilitate follow-up actions and inquiries.

When the same item is ordered repeatedly, a traveling request or requisition is often used. This usually takes the form of a durable card on which the necessary information is entered, and the card is used over and over. Each subsequent transaction is entered in sequence.

More complicated acquisitions are authorized by letter directives, providing all of the instructions needed to carry out the purchase. Whatever the form used, management must ensure that each purchase to be made has

COUNTY OF MONTGOMERY

PURCHASE REQUISITION

No. 041632

DATE _____

SHIP TO: _____

DATE WANTED _____

BUDGET NO. _____   FUND _____

QUANTITY	DESCRIPTION	
		Total

APPROVALS

PURCHASING DEPT. _____

BUDGET DEPT. _____

COUNTY COMMISSIONER _____

APPROPRIATION LEDGER _____

PURCHASE ORDER NO. _____

PLACE ORDER WITH: _____

REMARKS: (Give any special data regarding the above to aid in procuring)

_____

_____

_____

_____

_____

_____

_____

DEPARTMENT

Figure 11-1. Representative Purchase Requisition Form

been authorized by the responsible operating official and that funds have been committed to the purchase by the responsible fiscal official.

Source Identification and Preliminary Evaluation

Government purchasing activities are under no obligation to give all potential suppliers an opportunity to bid; in fact there is no uniform way by which to decide what suppliers should have an opportunity to bid. However, the requirement for full and free competition requires that the procurement action reach as many potential bidders as possible. This is done mainly in four ways: using a bidders mailing list of known producers of the item to be procured, publishing a description of the proposed procurement, posting of notices in public places, and use of commercial advertising.

Bidders mailing lists, which specify firms that have indicated their interest as manufacturers or suppliers, are used extensively. A suggested way to initiate a bidders list is to obtain names of potential bidders from various trade directories and to contact other agencies that purchase similar items.

When a bidders mailing list is extremely long, a great deal of expense and delay can be saved by sending a brief procurement notice to bidders announcing in general terms that a specified procurement will take place at a certain time. Distribution of full and formal invitations, with all supporting data, can then be limited to those who indicate an intention to bid. Also the buyer may adopt a system of rotating the number of invitations sent to prospective bidders. This does not in any way bar other potential suppliers from submitting bids.

In federal purchasing use is made of the *Commerce Business Daily*. It lists all military procurement invitations of $10,000 or more, all National Aeronautics and Space Administration procurement invitations exceeding $25,000, and all other procurement invitations of $5,000 or more. The *Daily* is published by the Department of Commerce and is available on a subscription basis.

Paid advertising is seldom used for the solicitation of bids in public purchasing, and the practice is prohibited in many jurisdictions. However, paid advertisements may be used in certain exceptional circumstances when it is necessary to secure effective competition. Publishing an announcement of a proposed purchase in trade journals and magazines is generally permitted when no charge is made to the government for the service.

Under certain circumstances, a purchasing agency may specify that only bids that offer products qualified before the opening of the bids shall be considered in making a contract award. This means that a product must have passed the tests listed in the specification and be included on the qualified products list for the specification before the government will consider purchasing it.

Orders and contracts should be awarded only to responsible firms.[1] "Responsibility" refers to potential ability to perform successfully under the terms of the proposed contract. This requires a prediction by the contracting officer of future performance. Obviously no absolute assurance of successful performance can be guaranteed, but the chance it will occur can be appreciably increased by careful consideration of a number of factors. Before a contract is awarded, the contracting officer must be in a position to make a positive judgment that the contractor will perform the contract in complete compliance with its terms, and this determination should be in writing. In this regard, the signing of a contract may be deemed to be a determination that the prospective contractor is responsible with respect to that contract.

Although it is important that purchases be made on the basis of bids that are most advantageous to the government, price and other factors considered, this does not require absolutely that an award be made to the firm that submits the lowest bid. In order for a contractor to receive an award, the bid must not only be responsive to the requirements of the invitation but must also affirmatively demonstrate his responsibility and, when necessary, the responsibility of his subcontractors. Although the contracting officer must determine responsibility in each case, the burden of proving responsibility is placed on the prospective contractor.

A contracting officer unable to obtain enough information to permit an affirmative finding must make a determination that the contractor is not responsible. The award of a contract to a bidder who subsequently defaults, is late in deliveries, or otherwise performs unsatisfactorily is a disservice to the government. Such awards are also unfair to other bidders who are capable of satisfactory performance, and they tend to discourage them from submitting bids on future procurements. This responsibility in government contracting has been defined as "a firm having the capacity to perform, the financial ability to perform as well as possessing the integrity, perseverance, and the tenacity to properly comply with all of the requirements of the contract in a timely manner." The contracting officer has broad discretion in determining responsibility. In the absence of bad faith or a reasonable basis for the determination, the decision is solely within his jurisdiction. In a formally advertised procurement, responsibility is not considered until the apparent successful bidder has been designated. Rejection at this point would require consideration of the next eligible bidder.

A prospective contractor must have adequate financial resources or the ability to obtain such resources as required during performance of the contract. He must be able to comply with the required or proposed delivery or performance schedule, taking into consideration all existing business commitments, commercial as well as governmental. The contractor needs a satisfactory record of performance. Those who are or have been seriously deficient in current or recent contract performance, when the number of contracts and the extent of deficiency each are considered (in the absence of evidence to the contrary or circumstances properly beyond the control of the contractor), shall be presumed to be unable to meet this requirement. They also must have a satisfactory record of integrity and business ethics and be otherwise qualified and eligible—that is, not in violation of any law or order that requires contractor compliance (such as the Walsh-Healey Public Contract Act, the Davis-Bacon Act, or other regulatory requirements). Additionally, a small business concern must show a certificate of competency and/or a determination of eligibility from SBA if the prospective contractor has been otherwise determined as not responsible and/or ineligible.

Financial strength is as important as technical competency, facilities, or any other aspect of the company's operations. Effective financial analysis often will provide an insight into other important factors: backlog of commitments, efficiency of contractor management, labor resources, and skills. Information on these other factors may also assist in evaluating financial strength. The scope, depth, and detail of the analysis of the contractor's financial capability varies with the circumstances of the proposed purchase. Certainly a history of past or current delinquencies in business or serious indebtedness indicates that a more detailed analysis of the contractor's financial situation is desirable. The fact that the contractor has never done business with the government is another factor to be considered.

In appraising proposed delivery of performance, all existing business commitments, both commercial and government, should be analyzed. The relationship between past performance and future performance is highly subjective, and it is solely within the discretion of the contracting officer. The important consideration is the cause of unsatisfactory performance. Causes within the control of the contractor should properly be considered in the responsibility determination. Conversely causes outside the control of the contractor ordinarily are not considered. Performance history is maintained on all firms with which the agency has done business. The number of years of data accumulated is not necessarily the most important factor. What is important are the trends that are indicated as the causes of past deficiencies, the corrective actions taken, and relevancy to the proposed procurement. Unsatisfactory performance need not have resulted in a formal termination for default in order to support a determination of nonresponsibility. Where the purchase involves production, maintenance, construction, or research and development, a prospective contractor must have the necessary organization experience, operational controls, and technical skills, or the ability to obtain them, and the necessary production, construction, and technical equipment and facilities, or the ability to obtain them.

Finally a negative determination may be made for lack of integrity for causes or conditions that could result in debarment or suspension. The determination that a contractor lacks integrity must be based on substantial evidence of the contractor's deficiencies rather than a mere accusation. Defining integrity is not easy, and no absolute criteria can be established. In general, however, questions of integrity involve those same conditions that may result in the more drastic actions of debarment or suspension of contractors.

Depending on the availability of information, it may be necessary to perform or to have performed a preaward survey during the preliminary evaluation phase. This survey usually involves an on-site visit and inspection of plant facilities. Depending on the dollar value or technical aspects involved in a procurement, the preaward survey may be a very detailed and comprehensive inspection of facilities or just a verification of data submitted at the contractor's plant. The depth of the survey also depends on the government's experience in dealing with the contractor previously. Maximum practicable use should be made of current information on file within the agency. Each agency should maintain records and experience data readily available for use by contracting officers in the placement of new procurements. This file is sometimes referred to as a contractor experience list or bidders performance record. Data obtained from a preaward survey for the purpose of determining the responsibility of a prospective contractor may not be released outside the government and should not be available for inspection by other individuals, firms, or trade organizations.

Most jurisdictions provide that prospective contractors and subcontractors may be excluded from the opportunity to compete by being formally debarred, suspended, or declared ineligible, measures that may be invoked by the government. Suspension or debarment is a serious action and should not be invoked without good cause; however, the determination of responsibility is also a serious matter and should not be treated lightly. Each agency should establish and maintain a consolidated list of concerns and individuals to whom contracts will not be awarded and from whom bids or proposals will not be solicited.

Debarment may be based upon prior violations by the firm of applicable procurement statutes, on the basis of criminal conviction or other serious misconduct of the principles in the firm, or on the basis of prior violation of contract provisions of a character regarded by the agency involved to be so serious as to justify debarment action. At the federal level regulations provide that such debarments shall be for a reasonable period of time, generally not to exceed three years.

Suspension is solely an administrative action. It results in a temporary disqualification from government contracting because a concern or individual is suspected upon adequate evidence of engaging in criminal, fraudulent, or seriously improper conduct. A less formal procedure is the compilation of the contractor experience list, which brings to the attention of contracting officers the names of contractors who have demonstrated poor performance on prior contracts, thus requiring a more careful review of such contractors before a determination of responsibility is made.

The "Consolidated List of Current Administrative Debarments by Agencies of the Federal Government" is compiled and distributed by the GSA's Office of Investigations. Generally this listing is for information purposes only and is not intended to take the place of, or be an addition to, debarment lists maintained by the various agencies. A copy of the notice reflecting the basis for debarment of any contractor on the list may be obtained upon request.[2]

A contracting officer who deems it necessary should require a prospective prime contractor to provide written evidence regarding the responsibility of the proposed subcontractors, or show that he has an acceptable and effective purchasing and subcontracting system, which includes a method for determining subcontractor responsibility. Any information furnished may be verified by the contracting officer.

Dun & Bradstreet offers a vendor analysis service for firms and government agencies that is similar to its commercial credit-rating system. If provides from clients' vendor files the following data:

1. Alphabetical listing of all vendors.
2. The parent corporations of each vendor.
3. The D&B identification number for each vendor.
4. The home address of each vendor.
5. The vendor's branch locations.
6. The number of employees by location.
7. The vendor's gross annual sales.
8. The client's purchases (in dollars) by vendor location.
9. The commodities (by code) the client purchased from each location.
10. The client's division or branch purchases from the vendor, by location.

Additional information is optional.[3]

Sometimes an agency finds itself in a single-source purchase situation which in many jurisdictions requires prior approval of higher management. Kenneth F. Medaris, director of the Division of Purchases, commonwealth of Kentucky, suggests that before a contracting officer makes a single-source purchase, the officer should ask these questions: How did I determine there was only one source? Did I research and evaluate other systems or products? What makes this particular system or product so unique and not available from other sources? Are the component parts of the system or product patented? What product or system has my agency been using, up until now? There should be plenty of careful deliberation before going to a single source because this type of purchase eliminates competition and places the agency at the mercy of a single vendor for price and delivery.

In regard to certain items, a jurisdiction may wish to make it mandatory that agencies use a designated source of supply. This is done through the use of term contracts and the publication of supply schedules. For example, federal supply schedules (FSS) represent contracts that are executed to provide, at reasonable prices, a ready source of quality products and services to meet the normal day-to-day needs of government departments, agencies, and other authorized users. The history of these schedules dates back to the eighteenth century. Alexander Hamilton, the first secretary of the treasury, was the first advocate of centralized procurement. In 1795 he established in the treasury department the Office of the Purveyor of Public Supplies, "to conduct the procuring and providing of all arms, military and naval stores, provisions, clothing, Indian goods, and generally all articles of suppy requisite for the service of the U.S."

These schedules today furnish government agencies with articles or services not normally available from GSA supply distribution facilities. GSA has entered into contracts for articles and services, at a stated price, for a given period of time, available directly from the contractors listed. Each FSS contains the names of the contractors, their addresses, the contract period, delivery or shipment time, dollar limitation on orders, price, and other essential ordering information. Certain agencies are obligated to order needed commodities or services available from these schedules; this is the mandatory or primary-use concept. Additionally other activities authorized by law to purchase through GSA may use schedule to procure supplies and services. In these cases, use of the schedules is optional for both the agency and the contractor. Contractors, in most cases, honor optional orders. Each schedule lists the agencies that are mandatory users of the schedule and also delineates the geographic coverage of the schedules, determined on the basis of the location of the consignee, not the ordering office.

Most jurisdictions also identify a category known as small purchases, for which simplified purchasing procedures may be used. The objectives of such simplified methods are to reduce the administrative costs in accomplishing small purchases, improve opportunities for small-business concerns and minority business enterprises to obtain a fair proportion of government purchases and contracts, and eliminate costly and time-consuming paper processes. Dollar ceilings are set for various categories of small purchases. For example, for a purchase not in excess of $500, a buyer may be authorized to act on a single quotation if it is considered reasonable.

For purchases between $500 and $10,000, a buyer should be required to obtain a sufficient number of quotations from qualified sources of supply to ensure that the procurement is fair to the government, price and other factors considered, including the administrative cost of the purchase. In arriving at the number of quotations to be considered, due consideration should be given to the administrative costs associated with the proposed solicitation in relation to the potential benefits to be derived by the government. The number of quotations should be determined by the buyer considering the nature of the article or service to be procured, and whether it is highly competitive and readily available in several makes or brands, or relatively noncompetitive; information obtained in making recent purchases of the same or similar items; the urgency and dollar value of the proposed purchase; and past experience concerning specific dealers' prices.

Once the number of sources to solicit has been determined, the buyer must decide from whom to solicit quotations. The buyer should be encouraged to obtain competition from within the local trade area, but solicitations should not be limited to suppliers of well-known brands or be done on a personal-preference basis.

Procuring activities should ensure that proposed small purchases are publicized to the maximum extent practicable consistent with the dollar value of the actions and any applicable time constraints. Such intentions could be displayed on bulletin boards in the purchasing office and/or other public areas. Handouts listing proposed purchases could be prepared and displayed. The information could be publicized in local newspapers or other mass communication media. And local trade associations could be encouraged and assisted in disseminating information about the purchases to their members.

In small purchases the buyer must decide on the fairness and reasonableness of the price that will be paid. How much detail the buyer gets into will depend chiefly on dollar value and the time available. Unit price as well as total dollars should be considerd in deciding how much time to spend on analysis. Typical actions the buyer may take in such a price analysis include:

1. Reference to price history. Comparison of prior quotations and contract prices with current quotations for the same or similar end items.
2. Adequacy of competiton. Comparison of competitive price quotations.
3. Reference to established catalog and price lists. Comparison of prices on published price lists issued on a competitive basis and published market prices of commodities, together with discount or rebate schedules.
4. Established market prices. Current market conditions on the same or similar items.

5. Similar items. A comparison of the prices of similar items.
6. Visual analysis. Visual inspection of an item or the drawings of an item to enable an estimate of the probable value.
7. Government estimates. Comparison of the purchase request or other government estimate to establish reasonableness of price.
8. Trade discounts. Any regular or special discounts offered by vendors for the commodity being purchased.
9. Quality breaks. The economic purchase quantity for a particular item.
10. Prompt payment discounts. Discount offered by a supplier in order to induce early payments after deliveries have been made and accepted.

When evaluating quotations, the buyer should consider the possibility of conducting negotiations with the vendors. Although negotiation is not mandatory on a small-purchase transaction, some form of it is often conducted. The objective is to reach an understanding and an agreement on all terms and conditions of the requirement, including the specifications and price to be paid for the item or the cost of the work to be done.

Selection of source in major system procurement is extremely complex. The objective is the same as in lesser purchases: to ensure selection of the vendor whose proposal and whose capability offer the optimum prospect for satisfaction of the government's objectives in the areas of cost, schedule, and performance. If the objectives of source selection are to be met, there must be a clear definition of the requirement and of a contracting plan under which the system is to be developed and acquired. Proposals for developing the equipment that will satisfy the requirement in accordance with the contracting plan must be obtained and evaluated. A decision must be reached as to which proposal, either as submitted or as modified by subsequent negotiations, offers the greatest promise of fulfilling the requirement. This proposal must then be written into a contract, under which the actual work will be performed.

In the selection of contractual sources for major defense systems the Department of Defense prescribes a four-step procedure.

First, separate technical proposals are solicited and evaluated and discussions held with all offerers. The solicitation advises that any proposals that are unrealistic in terms of technical or schedule commitments or unrealistically low in cost or price will be deemed reflective of a inherent lack of technical competence or indicative of failure to comprehend the complexity and risks of the contract requirements and may be grounds for the rejection of the proposal.

In step two, a cost-price proposal is obtained from each offerer together with any necessary revisions to correct any deficiencies in the technical proposals. Subsequent to the receipt of the cost-price proposals and any technical revisions, the competitive range will be established. Proposals outside of this range may be eliminated and the offerers so notified. Discussions are held with the remaining offerers in connection with the respective proposals, either on an element-by-element basis or in their entirety.

Following such discussion, a common cutoff date for the receipt of final revisions to technical and cost-price submittals is established and the remaining offerers so notified. After receipt of any revisions, the proposals are evaluated based upon each offerer's total proposal, and a contractor is selected for negotiation of the contract. The evaluation considers each competitor's assessment of the technical and financial risks involved and the credibility of proposed approaches to eliminate, avoid, or minimize those risks, including plans to perform and utilize the results of test and evaluation.

In step four a definitive contract is negotiated with the selected offerer. The selection reflects an integrated decision, involving consideration of technical approach, capability, management, historical performance, price-cost, and other factors. Following selection, all competitors are notified of the firm to be awarded the contract, subject to negotiation of a satisfactory definitive contract.[4]

Invitations to Bid or Submit Proposals

All jurisdictions—federal, state, and local—require that bids be solicited from all qualified sources in order to ensure full and free competition consistent with the procurement of the required property or services. Governments thus publicize their intentions to buy through advertisements and announcements in various media and by sending invitations for bids to business firms enumerated on applicable mailing or bidders lists. Procurement offices find that the most effective means of soliciting bids and publicizing procurement actions is through direct mailing of solicitations or notices of procurements to prospective bidders. All eligible and qualified concerns that have submitted applications or firms that are considered capable of filling requirements are placed on the appropriate bidders' lists. In addition, many contracting officers maintain lists for bidders that have not yet been included on the master lists.

A brief announcement of the proposed procurement or copies of invitations may be made available for free publication to newspapers, trade journals, and magazines. Many registers and directories listing manufacturers, vendors, equipment suppliers, and industries are available. Trade journals, suppliers' catalogs, and publications such as the *Thomas Register* are valuable aids to buyers during the source-selection process. Even the yellow pages of the telephone directory can serve as a convenient source. It is important that potential bidders be encouraged to submit bidders' mailing list applications to the procurement office.

In order to keep the bidders mailing list current, the names of concerns failing to respond to an invitation to bid or preinvitation notice should be removed. Concerns that have been removed can be reinstated upon request or by filing a new application.

Many agencies find the use of preinvitation notices effective in keeping administrative costs within reason. Rather than forwarding complete bid sets to all firms on the master lists, the contracting officer prepares and forwards preinvitation notices to listed firms. The notices describe the item or service required with enough information to provide an intelligible basis for judging whether a firm has an interest in the procurement. If no bid is to be submitted, the firm is asked to advise the issuing office in writing if future invitations are desired for the types of supplies or services involved. The notices also state the date by which bidders should return the notice in order to receive a complete bid set. The return date must be sufficiently in advance of the mailing date of the invitation for bids to permit an accurate estimate of the number of bid sets required.

Four conditions must be present if formal advertising is to be a satisfactory method of procurement:

1. Adequate time to carry out the necessary procedures prescribed by the regulations. In many cases, however, formal advertising may take no more time than competitive negotiation.
2. Adequate competition—that is, an adequate number of sources that can pass the tests of responsibility must be able to bid on the basis of the invitation. In addition, there should be no other factors present that may destroy the effects of competitive bidding. Examples are full or nearly full capacity in an industry from which the government makes repetitive purchases, and collusion, or restrictive pricing practices, on an area-wide or industry-wide basis.
3. Adequate specifications so that bidders may bid and have their bids evaluated on a common basis. If the specifications are vague or poorly written, bidders will not know what is required, and, as a result, may bid too high or too low. Also specifications should not be so restrictive as to limit competition unnecessarily.
4. Price as an adequate basis for award. Other factors that may be significant in some procurement (such as best technical competence) may not be considered.

By definition, formal advertising means procurement by competitive bids and awards and involves several steps. The first is the preparation of the invitations for bids (IFB) describing the requirement of the government clearly, accurately, and completely but avoiding unnecessarily restrictive specifications or requirements that might unduly limit the number of bidders. The IFB must be publicized through distribution to prospective bidders, posting in public places, and such other means as may be appropriate in sufficient time to enable prospective bidders to prepare and submit bids. The next step is the submission of bids by prospective contractors, followed by the award of the contract to the responsible bidder whose bid conforming to the IFB will be most advantageous to the government.

The preparation of the IFB is much more than a simple clerical function. Ideally it states the requirements of the procurement activity in such a way as to provide the same meaning to all concerns competing for award. It sets forth all of the factors that will be considered in determining the lowest acceptable bidder and complies with agency regulations concerning clauses to be included and factors to be considered in establishing such things as bidding time, acceptance period, and delivery requirement.

The IFB begins with a full description of the item or items to be procured, calling attention to any special considerations or requirements. This is followed by instructions for return of the completed bid or no-bid response. If there is to be a prebid conference, the time and place will be specified. Next is a section of standard terms and conditions. The IFB then specifies any applicable maximum and minimum order limitations, guaranteed minimums, standby stocks, priority of orders, or permissible variations in the quantities specified.

Since the IFB must specify the bid evaluation factors, close attention is given to provisions concerning aggregate awards, progressive awards, government-furnished property, or any other special basis for evaluation of bids. Additional items included in an IFB are delivery terms, packing and marking requirements, samples and descriptive literature requirements, inspection and acceptance procedures, and information to be furnished by the bidders and by the contractor after award.

The next consideration is the amount of time to allow before bid opening. At one time, fourteen days was the normal period, but with the general slowing of postal services, most jurisdictions are using twenty-one days for standard commmercial articles or services and thirty days for other than standard items. In some cases more time or less time should be provided for bid preparation. Procurement documents should not refer to daylight time or daylight saving time. Rather the statement of the time designated as bid opening time should use the phrase "local time at the place of bid opening."

The IFB should employ recognized specifications and standards to the maximum practical extent. Brand-name or equal-purchase descriptions should be used to describe the item being procured only under special circumstances. When their use is approved, brand-name or equal-purchase descriptions should reference all brand-name products known to be acceptable and of current manufacture. The description must list the salient characteristics of the brand-name item(s) that are essential to the intended use.

Another important part of the IFB is the time allowed the contractor for making delivery or performing the service under the terms of the contract. Unreasonably short delivery terms tend to restrict competition and may result in higher contract prices. They also are inconsistent with the move to favor small-business concerns.

The IFB must specify a period of acceptance by the government and provide that bids offering less than the minimum stipulated acceptance period will be rejected as nonresponsive. If any government costs or expenditures other than bid prices are to be considered in evaluation of bids, the IFB must state what those factors will be and how they will be evaluated. Directions for obtaining copies of any documents such as plans, drawings, and specifications that have been incorporated by reference must be included in the IFB. Any applicable notices concerning set-asides for small-business or labor-surplus areas must be included. When needed for the purpose of preaward surveys or inspection, bidders must state the place from which the supplies will be furnished. When bids are solicited free-on-board (FOB) origin, the IFB must state that bids will be evaluated on the basis of bid price plus transportation cost to the government. The bidder will also be required to furnish such information as necessary to allow the government to evaluate transportation costs.

If no award will be made for less than the full quantities advertised, or if it is to be made by specified groups of items or in the aggregate, statements to that effect must be included in the IFB.

When certain characteristics of the item being procured cannot be adequately described in the applicable specification or purchase description and bid samples are required, an appropriate clause must be included in the IFB.

Buyers and vendors under time pressure often resort to telegraphic bids. When in the judgment of the contracting officer, the date set for the opening of bids will not allow bidders sufficient time to prepare and submit bids on the prescribed forms or when prices are subject to frequent changes, telegraphic bids may be authorized. In this case the IFB shall require bidders to include in the telegraphic bid specific reference to the invitation, the items or subitems, quantities, and unit prices for which the bid is submitted, the time and place of delivery, and a statement that the bidder agrees to all of the terms included in the IFB.

In a conventional formally advertised procurement, it is essential that all bidders have a complete understanding of the price requirements of the specifications or purchase descriptions before submitting their bids. Since the bidders must be responsive to the invitation, they must prepare their bids in accordance with the precise requirements of the specifications or purchase descriptions described in the invitation. It is not always possible for the contracting officer to obtain an appropriate specification or even a good purchase description for a particular procurement. In these situations a hybrid form of procurement is sometimes utilized, known as two-step formal advertising. The two-step method is a flexible method especially useful in obtaining complex or technical products and in preventing the elimination of potentially qualified producers from the competitive base of supply. An additional objective of the two-step method is to permit the development of a sufficiently descriptive statement of the government's requirements, including the development of a technical data package so that subsequent procurements can be made by conventional formal advertising.

Two-step formal advertising is conducted in two phases. The first step of this process consists of the request for and the submission, evaluation, and if necessary, discussion of the technical proposals without pricing to determine the acceptability of the supplies or services offered. *Technical* has a broad connotation here; it includes engineering approach, special manufacturing process, and special testing techniques. Also during this step, basic technical requirements and other related requirements such as management approach, manufacturing plan, or facilities to be utilized are clarified. During this step it is necessary for the contracting officer to work closely with technical personnel. The officer must rely on specialized knowledge in determining the technical requirements of the procurement and the criteria to be used in evaluating the technical aspects of the proposals.

Upon completion of step one, a formally advertised procurement is conducted except that IFBs are issued only to and considered only from those sources where technical proposals have been evaluated and determined to be acceptable under the first step. The invitation for bids should prominently state that the supplies or services to be produced will be in accordance with the specifications and the bidder's technical proposal, as finally accepted, under the request for technical proposals. Upon completion of step two, the award is made under the same conditions as used in formal advertising.

The use of formal advertising, either inviting bids or through the two-step procedure, can be avoided in federal purchasing by making a determination that an exception applies.

A third method of identifying potential suppliers is through a request for proposals (RFP), which provides formal documented contact between the government and industry on a contemplated procurement. It is the medium by which potential sources are introduced to the job. The RFP provides a frame of reference for the contemplated purchase, including proposal evaluation, source selection, and contract definitization.

Whenever property or services are to be procured by negotiation, RFPs should be sent to the maximum number of qualified sources consistent with the nature of and requirements for the supplies or services to be procured.

Because of the highly technical nature of some procurements, presolicitation conferences are frequently held to permit technical personnel to discuss the proposed work with prospective contractors and to elicit their interest in pursuing the task. The conference procedure is designed to develop sources for procurement; to permit the government to solicit preliminary information based on a general description of the supplies or services involved; to permit prospective offerers to submit proposals without undue expenditure of effort, time, and money; and to explain complicated specifications and requirements to interested firms. As a minimum, presolicitation conference notices should contain a request for an expression of interest in the contemplated procurement and an indication of the time for submission of responses. The notice should define the information to be furnished by the offerer and whether the notice will be followed by a conference and a formal solicitation. Detailed drawings, specifications, or plans are not normally included in the notice. All prospective contractors should be furnished with identical information in connection with the proposed procurement.

Following presolicitation conferences, a formal request for proposals is issued. Copies are sent to all known interested concerns and provided on request to anyone else having a legitimate interest. At the federal level contemplated procurements must be publicized ten calendar days before issuance of the request for proposals. If this is not feasible, a synopsis should be forwarded to the *Commerce Business Daily* to arrive not later than the date of issuance of the RFP.[5]

A preproposal conference may be used as a means of briefing prospective offerers after the solicitation has been issued but before offers or proposals are prepared. Ordinarily the conference is held in connection with a complex procurement to give the government an opportunity to explain or clarify complicated specifications and requirements to interested firms. Determination to hold a conference may be made as a result of questions and problems raised by prospective offerers. The contracting officer should make all the necessary arrangements and notify all those to whom solicitations have been issued concerning the time, place, and general nature of such conference. Similarly all prospective offerers should be furnished identical information in connection with the proposed procurement. Remarks and explanations at the conference should not qualify the terms of the solicitation and specifications.

Before the closing date for receipt of proposals, it may be necessary to issue an amendment to the RFP. There may have been a change in requirements, an ambiguous specification pointed out in a preproposal conference, or questions raised by a prospective offerer. Amendments increase administrative effort and cost and may delay award and performance of the contract. But if the amendment is necessary to make significant changes or to correct a defect or ambiguity, the potential impact on effective competition and pricing certainly will outweigh the cost of issuing an amendment. If the changes are not complex, an oral amendment (followed by a confirming written statement) may be given, provided all prospective contractors are notified simultaneously and a record of the advice is made.

Offerers must feel that they will be treated fairly and impartially by the government. Thus in formal advertising all submitted bids are held unopened, in a locked bid box or safe. They are opened publicly at the specified time. Most procuring activities follow similar procedures for negotiated procurements. The offers are generally kept in a locked file cabinet or safe until the date for submission. The proposals are not opened publicly, however, and only those with a need to know may have access to the quotations or proposals.

A late proposal will be considered for award only if it is received before award is made, and (1) it was sent by registered or certified mail not later than the fifth calendar day prior to the date specified for receipt of offers, (2) it was sent by mail (or telegram if authorized) and it is determined by the government that the late receipt was due solely to mishandling by the government after receipt at the government installation, or (3) it is the only proposal received.

A late modification of a proposal is subject to the first two conditions provided it is not a modification resulting from a request for "best and final" offer. The latter, received after the time and date specified in the request, is not considered unless it is received before award, and the late receipt is due solely to mishandling by the government after receipt at the government installation. In any case, however, a late modification of an otherwise successful proposal that makes its terms more favorable to the government will be considered at any time it is received and may be accepted. After receipt of initial proposals, written or oral discussions are conducted with all responsible offerers who submitted proposals within a competitive range, price and other factors considered. The determination as to which proposals are in this range is made on the basis of price or cost, technical, or other salient factors and includes proposals that have a reasonable chance of being selected for award. When there is doubt as to whether a proposal is within the competitive range, that doubt should be resolved by including it. The initial number of proposals considered as being within the range may be reduced when, as a result of the written or oral discussions, any such proposal has been determined no longer to have a reasonable chance of being selected for award.

No indications should be given to offerers in discussions of a price that must be met to obtain further consideration; such practice constitutes an auction technique, which must be avoided. Also no offerers should be advised of their relative standing with competitors as to price or be furnished information as to the price offered by others.

Proposal revisions that result from the conduct of written or oral discussions may be made at any time prior to the closing date for negotiations. A common closing date must be established and controlled to preserve the competitive system. All those in the competitive range must be given notice of the closing date. Offerers then submit written best-and-final offers.

Once negotiations have been held and best-and-final offers received, negotiations should not be reopened unless it is clearly in the best interest of the government, since this practice in the absence of a valid reason tends to undermine the integrity of the competitive negotiation process.

After receiving the best-and-final offers, the government buyer performs a final evaluation, and then source selection is made.

Communicating with Potential Vendors

General communication with potential suppliers includes vendors manuals, which tell generally how to do business with the government and how to be placed on bidders lists, the schedule or index of commodities and services regularly purchased, the coding of the listed items, which informs potential offerers how, and by whom, each item is purchased, and guidance in specific areas of concern, such as preparation for preaward surveys, negotiating techniques, interpreting specifications, and auditing of contract performance.[6]

The most widely referenced publication is the *Commerce Business Daily*, which is published Mondays through Fridays (except on federal legal holidays) by the Department of Commerce in cooperation with government purchasing agencies. This publication provides a daily list of U.S. government procurement invitations for bid, subcontracting leads, contract awards, sales of surplus property, and foreign business opportunities.[7]

The effort to communicate with vendors goes beyond these written publications. Briefings held by various agencies are among the most valuable methods of keeping vendors up to date. In some jurisdictions and agencies the briefings take the form of a show presented across the entire country or state. This is usually done at the request of a legislator and sponsored by a local group, which also advertises the meeting. In addition to the briefing, representatives of major purchasing offices attend and are available to answer questions.

Federal Small Business Administration (SBA) representatives are stationed at major buying centers of the federal government to assist firms with contracting problems and advise them on how to do business with the government. They also ensure that appropriate procurements are set aside for small business, provide additional opportunities for small firms to participate in unrestricted procurements, request changes in specifications that are too restrictive, initiate breakouts on sole-source purchases, and review and evaluate the overall small-business programs of purchasing centers. SBA representatives carry out the same type of program at smaller buying installations on a liaison basis.

A very specific form of assistance to vendors is the issuance of a certificate of competency. Sometimes a contracting officer proposes to reject the low bid of a small-business firm because of questions as to whether the firm is sufficiently responsible to perform the contract. In that event, the case is acted upon by the SBA representative. If the investigation reveals that the business is competent to perform the contract, SBA issues the certificate. SBA's certification is sent to the government purchasing officer responsible for award of the contract. By law, the officer is directed to accept these findings as conclusive as far as any and all elements of responsibility are concerned. Responsibility has been statutorily determined to be inclusive of, but not limited to, capability, competency, capacity, credit, integrity, perseverance, and tenacity.

Certificates of competency are issued by SBA when (1) the small concern applying for a certificate has submitted the lowest responsive bid on an advertised purchase or the lowest proposal on a negotiated purchase, (2) the government official responsible for making the purchase does not believe the bidder is able to carry out the particular contract, or (3) a survey by SBA's specialists has convinced the agency that the business is capable of performing the contract satisfactorily.

When a contract has been awarded as a result of issuance of a certificate of competency, SBA follows the progress of the contract until it is completed. If the contractor has difficulty in meeting production schedules because of technical or other problems, the agency offers assistance.

SBA also maintains a register of small firms interested in supplying goods and services to government purchasing agencies and to their prime contractors.

When looking for small-business concerns that might be interested in bidding on government procurement opportunities or subcontracting opportunities offered by major prime contractors, SBA offices do not confine their searches to their own areas; they obtain sources from each other as well. Consequently a small plant that registers in the facilities inventory may be referred as a source to a procurement center of a prime contractor located in a different part of the country.

Most of the means of communication are initiatives of the federal government. Principal reliance at the state and local level is on the use of bidders lists. Although state and local government do advertise in the newspapers, purchasing officials state that they get very little response from these advertisements. Potential vendors usually wait until they receive a notice from the purchasing agent of a contract suited to them.

Evaluating Bids and Proposals

The integrity of the sealed competitive-bid system depends upon all bids being submitted without knowledge of competing bids. Therefore the procedure employed must provide for maintaining the security and secrecy of all bids until they are opened, opening of all bids at the prescribed time and in public, recording all bids, and examining of all bids by interested persons. It is essential that the procedure be followed carefully to avoid administrative mistakes that may require cancellation and readvertising the procurement. All bids (including modifications) received prior to the time set for opening must be kept unopened and placed in a locked bid container. When bid samples are submitted, they also should be secured to prevent disclosure of bidders' information. Before bid opening, information concerning the identity and number of bids received should be made available only to government employees who have need for such information.

Bids that are not properly identified externally may be opened solely for the purpose of identification and then only by an authorized official. If a sealed bid is opened by mistake, the person who opens it should immediately write his signature and position title on the envelope and deliver it to the proper official. This official should immediately write on the envelope an explanation of the opening, the date and time opened, the invitation for bid number, and his signature. Bids opened by mistake or for identification purposes must be resealed in the envelope and no information contained therein disclosed prior to the public bid opening.

Bids received in the office designated in the invitation after the exact time set for opening of bids are late bids and shall not be considered unless received before award and sent by registered or certified mail not later than the fifth calendar day prior to the date specified for the receipt of bids; or sent by mail (or telegram if authorized) and it is determined by the government that the late receipt was due solely to mishandling by the government after receipt at the government installation.

Any modification or withdrawal of a bid is subject to the same rules. The date of mailing of a late bid, modification, or withdrawal sent either by registered or certified mail is the U.S. Postal Service postmark on both the envelope or wrapper and on the original receipt from the Postal Service. If neither postmark shows a legible date, the bid, modification, or withdrawal shall be deemed to have been mailed late. Late hand-carried bids are not considered for award; neither are telegraphic bids that are late for any reason other than mishandling at the government installation.

Under ordinary contract principles, an offerer may withdraw or modify an offer any time prior to acceptance, but a distinction has been drawn when an offer in the form of a bid is made to the government under formal advertising procedures. In that situation when there is no mistake or unreasonable delay, the offer may be withdrawn or modified as a matter of right only until the date and hour set for opening of bids. Subsequent to bid opening, the government has the power to award a contract on the basis of the offer submitted for a specified period of time. This is known as the firm-bid rule. It is an exception to the common law that an offer can be withdrawn or changed at any time before acceptance. The evaluation of bids takes a certain amount of time; so does responsibility determination. If a bidder could withdraw or modify his bid during this period, the system of awarding government contracts on the basis of competitive bidding would deteriorate. This would be obviously unfair to the other bidders. It would put a bidder in a position where he could gamble on the invitation. Also after the opening, a bidder would know the prices quoted by others, as well as any changes in market conditions. He could then get a change by asking to modify or withdraw his bid. Modifications or requests for withdrawal of bids received after the exact time set for opening are handled as late modifications or late withdrawals. If the successful bidder wishes to make a change favorable to the government and not prejudicial to other bidders, it may be considered. Otherwise the rules that cover late bids apply to late modifications and late withdrawals.

The firm-bid rule has certain limitations. It does not apply when a bidder establishes that he has made an honest mistake in his bid. Nor can bidders be held to their bids beyond the period specified for award in the invitation.

The official designated as the bid-opening officer must decide when the time set for bid opening has arrived and shall so declare to those present at the opening. This officer publicly opens each bid received (when practical), reads the bids aloud and has them recorded. At most bid openings only the important elements of the bid are read aloud, such as prices offered, discounts, delivery terms, quantity bid, and so forth. It is important that the original of each bid be carefully safeguarded. It is the duty of the bid-opening officer to ensure that the bids are not changed in any way. Bidders who desire to examine original bids may do so, but only under government supervision. The bid-opening officer must also make sure that any descriptive literature included with a bid is not disclosed beyond the limits set by the bidder. Copies of bids may be placed in the bid-opening room for examination by bidders. After bids have been opened and recorded, the designated officer signs the certificate of the abstract. The original of all bids and the abstract of bids are subject to examination by authorized personnel.

The invitation number, bid-opening date, general description of the procurement item, names of bidders, prices bid, and any other information required for bid evaluation must be entered in an abstract or record that, except in the case of a classified procurement, shall be available for public inspection. When the items are too numerous to warrant the recording of all bids completely, an entry should be made of the invitation number, opening date, general description of the procurement items, and the total price bid where definite quantities are involved. The record or abstract should be completed as soon as practicable after the bids have been opened and read. The bids-opening officer certifies the accuracy of the record or abstract. If the invitation for bids is cancelled before the time set for bid opening, this fact should be recorded, together with a statement of the number of concerns invited to bid and the number of bids received.

After bid opening the contracting officer examines all bids for possible mistakes and to determine if they are responsive to the terms of the IFB. Those that are not responsive may not be considered for award. Some deficiencies in a bid, referred to as minor informalities or irregularities, do not require rejection of the bid. A minor informality or irregularity is one that is merely a matter of form and not of substance or pertains to some immaterial or inconsequential defect or variation of a bid from the exact requirements of the invitation for bids, the correction or waiver of which would not be prejudicial to other bidders. The defect or variation is immaterial and inconsequential when its significance as to price, quantity, quality, or delivery is trivial or negligible when contrasted with the total cost or scope of the supplies or services being procured.

If the contracting officer believes that a mistake in the bid may have been made, he is required to request verification from the bidder. This request must include the specific reasons for the contracting officer's suspicion. The use of such vague terms as *discrepancy in the bid*, *disparity in prices*, or *prices are out of line* should be avoided. If the bidder verifies the bid, it shall be considered as submitted. If he alleges a mistake, he shall be advised to furnish pertinent evidence to support his allegation.

Unless all bids are rejected, award must be made by the contracting officer by written notice within the time for acceptance specified in the bid or extensions to the responsible bidder whose bid conforming to the invitation for bids will be most advantageous to the government, price and other factors considered. If two or more bidders are tied, most jurisdictions provide that the award be determined by a drawing of lot limited to such bidders.

In some instances a bid is protested. Jurisdictions should require contracting officers to consider all protests or objections regarding the award of a contract whether submitted before or after the award. At the federal level the rules and regulations of the GAO prescribe formal procedures for handling bid protests both before and after award, which recommend and urge protesters to seek solutions of their complaints initially with the contracting officer. In many situations the contracting officer will be able to handle the complaint and satisfy the protester. It may also be possible for other individuals within the agency at a level higher than the contracting officer to resolve the protest. It is generally good practice for agencies to designate officials to resolve protests at a sufficiently high level that detachment from the immediate controversy and independence of judgment are assured to the maximum practical extent.

Protests usually occur when a bidder believes she has been treated unfairly or some other bidder has obtained an unfair advantage at some point in the process. The most common reasons for protests are submission of late bids, alleged improprieties, mistake in bids, minor informalities or irregularities, and ambiguity and restrictiveness of specifications. Misunderstandings on the part of the bidders, and at times poor judgment on the part of the contracting officer, all too often contribute to the problem. Contracting officers have a duty and an obligation to protect the interest of the government, but that does not mean that the bidders' rights should be violated in any way. Considerable skill, tact, and diplomacy must be employed if conflict is to be avoided.

If a protest on a federal bid is not resolved at the agency level, the concerned party may protest to the U.S. comptroller general. When a written protest before award is lodged directly with the comptroller general, a copy of the protest is sent to the government agency involved with a request that the agency's position on the protest be furnished to the comptroller general, together with all relevant documents, such as a copy of the IFB. The comptroller general will resolve the protest on the basis of the administrative report and submissions, often including a legal brief or relevant documents from the protester. Regulations require the contracting officer, upon learning of the lodging of a protest directly with the comptroller general, to withhold making award before the resolution of the protest, unless the contracting officer can justify the need for an immediate issuance of an award. In appropriate cases, other persons, including bidders, involved in or affected by the protest must be given notice of the protest and the basis for it. They should also be advised that they may submit their views and relevant information on the protest to the contracting officer within a specified period of time, normally one week. When a protest against the making of an award is received and the contracting officer determines to withhold the award pending disposition of the protest, those whose bids might become eligible for award should be requested before expiration of the time for acceptance of their bids to extend the time for acceptance (with consent of sureties, if any) to avoid the need for readvertisement. Timely action on protests is essential to avoid undue delay in procurements and to ensure fair treatment to protesting firms and individuals. Accordingly protests should be handled on a priority basis.

With regard to protests after award and when it appears likely that an award may be invalidated and a delay in receiving the supplies or services is not prejudicial to the government's interest, the contracting officer should consider a mutual agreement with the contractor to suspend performance on a no-cost basis.

The comptroller general may refuse to decide any protest where the matter involved is the subject of litigation before a court of competent jurisdiction or has been decided on the merits by such a court. This does not apply where the court requests, expects, or otherwise expresses interest in the comptroller general's decision.

When a GAO decision contains a recommendation for corrective action on the part of the procuring agency, copies of the decision are transmitted to congressional committees, and the agency's attention is directed to section 236 of the Legislative Reorganization Act (1970), which requires the agency to submit written statements of the action to be taken on the recommendations contained in the report.

The issuance of an RFP initiates a much more involved sequence of evaluation procedures. The effectiveness of any evaluation is dependent, in large measure, on the quality of the RFP and whether it will lead to the submission of comparable proposals. Therefore special care and attention should be devoted to the development of the RFP. The complete statement of work, specifications, project objectives, and schedule are the primary responsibility of the operating agency or office, while the business aspects are primarily the responsibility of the purchasing office. In the development of the RFP, special consideration must be given to the qualification criteria, evaluation criteria, and the requirements for price and cost information.

The RFP contains a covering letter of transmittal to prospective offerers and the following enclosures as appropriate: description of work or services, qualification criteria, evaluation criteria, price-cost considerations, representations and certifications of compliance, proposal format, and proposed draft contract.

The evaluation criteria consist of those elements that the board must examine in each proposal to determine an offerer's understanding of the work to be performed; technical, business, and management approach; potential for completing the job as specified in the RFP; probable cost based upon offerer's approach; relative qualifications and experience of both the proposer and key individuals proposed; and comparative competitive status. There are no restrictions on the kinds of evaluation criteria that may be used, as long as they are disclosed in the RFP and relate to the purpose of the procurement. The specific criteria used will depend on the particular circumstances, however, and will generally fall into the major categories of technical, business and management, and price.

The extent of the technical evaluation will depend on the nature and complexity of the proposed procurement. Evaluation of a proposal for a major weapon system might require many months, whereas proposals received in response to a solicitation for minor components may be evaluated in a much shorter time. The technical evaluation must establish that the offerer clearly understands the engineering, scientific, and operational requirements of the RFP.

The basic determination to be made during the business and management evaluation is that of responsibility. Specific factors that might need to be rated are management structure, make-or-buy programs, a contractor's purchasing procedures, and past experience. The standards for determining responsibility require that a prospective contractor must:

1. Have adequate financial resources or the ability to obtain such resources as required during performance of the contract.
2. Be able to comply with the required or proposed delivery or performance schedule, taking into consideration all existing business commitments, commercial as well as governmental.
3. Have a satisfactory record of performance. Contractors who are or have been seriously deficient in current or recent contract performance, when the number of contracts and the extent of deficiency of each are considered, in the absence of evidence to the contrary or circumstances properly beyond the control of the contractor, shall be presumed to be unable to meet this requirement. Past unsatisfactory performance will ordinarily be sufficient to justify a finding of nonresponsibility.
4. Have a satisfactory record of integrity and business ethics; have a certificate of competency and/or a determination of eligibility from SBA if the prospective contractor is a small-business concern and is determined to be nonresponsible and/or ineligible by the contracting officer.
5. Be otherwise qualified and eligible to receive an award under applicable laws and regulations.

Additional standards are applicable where the procurement involves production, maintenance, construction, or research and development work (and in other procurements as appropriate). These standards require a prospective contractor to have (or the ability to obtain) the necessary organization, experience, operational controls, and technical skills. Also required are the necessary production, construction, and technical equipment and facilities.

When the situation warrants, special standards of responsibility may be established, with the assistance of technical personnel or other specialists, to be applicable to a particular procurement or class of procurements.

Before a determination of responsibility can be made, the contracting officer must have sufficient information to be satisfied that a prospective contractor currently meets the minimum standards. Maximum practicable use should be made of information on file within the agency, providing it is currently valid. Other sources of information relating to contractor responsibility include any list of debarred, suspended, or ineligible concerns or individuals; publications, trade and financial journals, business directories and registers; suppliers, subcontractors, customers, banks, commercial credit agencies, and so forth; the prospective contractor; and financial data, current and past production records, personnel records, lists of equipment and facilities, and written statements or commitments concerning financial assistance and subcontracting arrangements.

Depending on the amount of subcontracting, the responsibility determination of the prime contractor may require a similar determination for the subcontractor. Such determinations are generally made by the prospective prime contractor, but in certain situations it may be in the interest of the government to make a direct determination of the responsibility of one or more prospective subcontractors prior to award of the prime contract.

The price evaluation, the determination that the price is fair and reasonable, must be based on some form of analysis, either price or a combination of cost and price analysis. Price analysis is a broad term; it includes whatever actions the contracting officer takes to reach a price decision, without recourse to cost analysis. Cost analysis involves evaluating elements of the contractor's detailed estimate of his cost of contract performance.

Price analysis is accomplished in a number of different ways, including the following:

1. Comparison of the price quotations submitted.
2. Comparison of prior quotations and contract prices with current quotations for the same or similar items.
3. Use of rough yardsticks (such as dollars per pound, per horsepower, or other units) to point up apparent gross inconsistencies that should be subjected to greater pricing inquiry.
4. The comparison of prices set forth in published price lists issued on a competitive basis, published market prices of commodities, and similar material, together with discount or rebate arrangements.
5. The comparison of proposed prices with estimates of cost independently developed by personnel within the contracting activity.

The government is constrained by the concept of a fair and reasonable price (it should not pay unfair prices and the contractor should not realize exorbitant profits) and the fact that the competition fostered may be imperfect. Both the procurement situation and the offers must be analyzed to determine that there is competition and that the competition is effective. Four conditions must have been met: (1) there are at least two offerers; (2) both can satisfy the government's requirement; (3) both are independently contending for a contract award to the offerer who submits the lowest evaluated price; (4) and both have submitted priced offers responsive to the expressed requirements of the solicitation.

Contract cost analysis is the element-by-element examination of the estimated or actual cost of contract performance. It involves analysis of cost-accounting data furnished by the offerer or contractor. It also involves analysis of design features, manufacturing processes, organization and manning, materials and estimating assumptions, and all cost factors that make up the total cost of a procurement.

Cost analysis includes verification of cost data and evaluation of specific elements of cost and projection of these data. It looks into such factors as necessity for certain costs, reasonableness of amounts estimated for necessary costs, extent of uncertainties involved in contract performance and realism of any allowances for contingencies, bases for allocation of overhead costs, and appropriateness of allocations of particular overhead costs to the contract.

Without knowing how the contractor arrived at his proposed price, what contingencies he included, or how he made his cost projections, the government would have no basis upon which to refute the contractor's price in a noncompetitive situation. In order to overcome this problem and strengthen the federal government's bargaining position, the Congress passed the Truth in Negotiations Act.[8] It requires the contractor to submit cost or pricing data and to certify that they are complete, accurate, and current at the time agreement is reached on price. The law provides for an adjustment in price if it is later found that the data were not complete, accurate, and current and gives the government audit rights to ensure the data were as certified. These requirements apply to all negotiated contracts and contract modifications expected to exceed $100,000 unless the price negotiated is based on adequate price competition, established catalog or market prices of commercial items sold in substantial quantities to the general public, or prices set by law or regulation. The law permits the head of the agency or an authorized designee to waive the requirements in exceptional cases, and it places the requirements on both prime and subcontractors.

The objective of cost analysis is to arrive at a realistic, or reasonable, price. The judgment that a price is reasonable is based on a cost estimate that it is attainable—that is, what it should cost if the contractor operates with reasonable economy and efficiency. "Should cost" is a concept, not a technique. How one reaches a conclusion that the cost is reasonably attainable and reflects the best deal under the circumstances is not important. There is a relatively old concept in cost analysis that says one should attempt to establish what it should, not what it will, cost to do a job. What is important is that the method used results in a price that is based on what it should cost in the environment and under the conditions predicted for the performance of the contract.

Closely related to cost analysis is the concept of value analysis, sometimes called value engineering, a procedure for systematically analyzing functional requirements of systems, equipment, and material to achieve the essential functions at the lowest total cost of ownership consistent with requirements for performance, reliability, quality, maintainability, and safety.

Value analysis is frequently a team effort of personnel drawn from purchasing, engineering, production, maintenance, and any other specialties that might contribute. In federal government, contracting procedure provides for value-engineering incentive clauses designed to motivate contractors and subcontractors to conduct value analysis. The incentive in this case is a negotiated share of the savings resulting from a value analysis.

In its simplest form, value analysis consists of answering five questions: What is it? What does it do (what is its basic function)? What does it cost? What are the alternative ways of accomplishing the function? What do the alternatives cost? The concern is with function, or utility, versus cost. The heart of the analysis is a systematic exploration of every conceivable aspect: the design of each part and component, the tolerances specified, the materials used, the machine process involved, the assembly techniques used, the finish prescribed, the packaging prescribed. Each suggested alternative is discussed with the user, product engineer, and vendor. Viable alternatives are then carried through to design and specification changes. Detailed guidance on value analysis procedures can be found in the standard references.[9]

Conducting Negotiations

Negotiation by definition is the deliberation and discussion that takes place between parties touching a proposed agreement. Out of the discussion will come the terms and conditions of purchase. Negotiation usually involves a series of offers and counteroffers, continuing until a mutually satisfactory conclusion is reached.

Wherever possible public purchasing should be accomplished under competitive, formally advertised conditions. But when such procedures cannot be used, both the buyer and the seller must know when and how to negotiate. Negotiation may be required in establishing the initial price and terms of the contract, in repricing the contract under incentive or redetermination-type contracts, in the pricing of change orders, or in contract administration activities with technical, audit, inspection, and property personnel.

The importance of negotiation cannot be overstated. It is the principal means by which buyers and sellers achieve their objectives, both in the initial contract and during contract performance. It is a difficult art that requires a knowledge of the psychology of individuals, small groups, and large organizations and the exercise of judgment, tact, and common sense.

Negotiating a public contract covers such factors as these:

1. Comparison of prices quoted and consideration of other prices for the same or similar property or services, with due regard to production costs and any other factor relating to the price, such as profits, cost of transportation, and cash discounts.
2. Comparison of the business reputation, capacity, and responsibility of the respective persons or firms who submit offers.
3. Consideration of the quality of the property or services offered, including the same or similar property or services previously furnished with due regard to conformance with specification requirements.
4. Consideration of delivery requirements.
5. Discriminating use of price and cost analysis.
6. Investigation of price aspects of any important subcontract.
7. Consideration of cost sharing.
8. Effective utilization in general of the most desirable type of contract.
9. Consideration of the size of the business concern.
10. Consideration as to whether the prospective supplier requires expansion or conversion of plant facilities.
11. Consideration as to whether the prospective supplier is located in a surplus- or scarce-labor area.
12. Consideration as to whether the prospective supplier will have an adequate supply of qualified labor.
13. Consideration of subcontracting, with the use of small-business subcontractors being considered a favorable factor.
14. Consideration of the existing and potential work load of the prospective supplier.
15. Consideration of broadening the source base by the development of additional suppliers.
16. Consideration of whether the contractor requires the use of government-furnished property, machine tools, or facilities.

The most important prerequisite to effective negotiation is thorough preparation. The buyer must make sure the offerer submits the necessary cost or pricing data, checks the facts, prepares the case, has an objective, anticipates arguments, and develops responses. Sooner or later the buyer will have to discuss price with an individual who will be arguing that the offer is reasonable and probably too low. The buyer may view the price as too high, but even if right, the buyer must have valid arguments ready to convince the seller that he will not lose everything but will make an adequate and equitable return at the buyer's price. The seller will have strong feelings about his own self-interest and future. His first interest must be perpetuation of his company and job and furtherance of his career. The seller begins knowing more about his own proposal than the government does. He knows the assumptions underlying the cost estimate or proposed price, the contingencies that have been included, and, most importantly, the actual cost or price level at which his company will be willing to accept the contract. Only thorough preparation on the part of the government negotiator can balance this advantage of the seller.

Thorough preparation takes time. In most cases the government representative is handling many purchasing actions simultaneously, so there will be a limited amount of time to analyze the offerer's proposal and develop a strategy. There may also be cases where the approaching end of the agency's fiscal year shortens available time for preparation. Some actions can be taken to lessen the effect of time pressures. If contractual action is necessary for urgent delivery, for example, a letter contract may offer a partial solution, allowing the government adequate preparation time before completing the negotiations. Where a negotiator is burdened with several cases at once, careful judgment should be used to establish priorities and to allot preparation time where it can be best used. Equally important, the negotiator should make maximum use of the specialists available: field representatives, auditors, technical personnel from the requisitioning activity, legal counsel, and estimating and statistical personnel.

The negotiator must have a thorough grasp of the characteristics of the industry and of the specific requirements. She must have a clear and comprehensive understanding of what is being bought. To some degree the nature of the requirement controls price, contract type, contract terms, and bargaining position. The selection of an appropriate contract type and the negotiation of prices are related and should be considered together. The respective contract types vary as to the degree and timing of responsibility assumed by the contractor for the costs of performance, and the amount and type of profit incentive offered the contractor to achieve or exceed specified standards or goals. A negotiation objective is to arrive at a contract type and price that includes reasonable contractor risk and provides the contractor with the greatest incentive for efficient and economical performance. Those who write the RFP must specify the type of contract so that proposers base their price or cost estimates in terms of the requirements of the type of contract. Specifying the contract type in an RFP provides uniformity to permit comparisons, but this does not bind the negotiators subsequently to agree on the basis of the specified type.

It is not enough merely to request and receive cost or pricing data. The data must be separated into various elements, with close examination of each factor. For example, the actual costs of doing the same kinds of tasks should be established to measure the probable future costs of performing under the upcoming contract. The assumptions and judgments the offerer has actually made in getting from the indicated current costs to the probable future costs should also be isolated and examined. Price or cost analysis is one of the most important tools of contract negotiators. Without an adequate analysis of the material submitted, negotiators will not be able to perform effectively at the negotiation table.

In the prenegotiation planning stage, it is essential to assess the position of each party in negotiation. Each party's strengths and weaknesses will influence the course of negotiation and must be understood to be counteracted. Perhaps the major factor of influence is the number of qualified firms competing for the contract. The greater the competition, the stronger the government's position. A seller's need or desire for a particular contract may also affect the relative bargaining position of the two parties, as will the amount of time the buyer or seller has in which to reach agreement. Time pressures (restrictive delivery schedules, for example) usually work to the seller's advantage and the buyer's disadvantage.

In preparing for negotiations, the buyer should attempt to anticipate the seller's specific objectives and their relative importance. This knowledge can be used as leverage to win concessions. In any case a comparison of opposing objectives will highlight major areas of disagreement. The buyer can then prepare effective counteroffers. An effective way to anticipate the seller's objectives is to role play the seller. The buyer tries to imagine himself in the seller's position, deciding what is important and how to reach that particular result. Then he compares his own case, keeping the seller's case in mind.

The negotiation session is opened by the buyer. At this point the seller's attitude is that he has presented a proposal based on the best estimate and will stand by it until the buyer can convince him to do otherwise. The approaches open to the buyer depend on how close the seller's price is to the buyer's objective. The buyer may begin with a series of questions that cover the proposal part by part. Or the buyer might present counterproposals designed to make the seller see the unreasonableness of his position.

It is important that the negotiations be conducted in a relaxed and friendly atmosphere; the objective, after all, is to reach an agreement that is fair and reasonable to both parties. Successful negotiation demands that the buyer establish and maintain sound, cooperative, and mutually respectful relationships with the offerers. Merchandise cannot be sold in an atmosphere of distrust and deception; neither can ideas, opinions, and objectives. Successful negotiation depends on the buyer's ability to sell himself and his position; therefore the tone set for the conference is important. Any indication of distrust or any unsupported statements that the price is too high or that the offerer is trying to cheat the government are clearly out of order. They will weaken the buyer's position and his chances of success.

The physical environment in which the negotiation takes place may also have a significant effect on the outcome. The room should be well lighted and airy, with comfortable chairs in reasonable proximity. Blackboards and calculators may be helpful. Either a conference room or a separate office should be made available to the seller for use during recesses.

Some very unprofessional tactics are known to have been used by negotiators: splitting up a team by the seating arrangement, deliberately raising room temperature, adusting blinds so that the sun shines in the eyes of the opponents, and providing only the hallway for private conferences. These practices have no place in government contracting. If a government negotiator is confronted with any such tactics, he should call for their correction and refuse to carry on negotiations until the situation has been rectified.

In federal contract negotiations, six rules must be followed:

1. Whenever negotiations are conducted with more than one offerer, no indication shall be given to any offerer of a price that must be met to obtain further consideration; such practice constitutes an auction technique.
2. No offerer shall be advised of his relative standing with other offerers as to price or be furnished information as to the prices offered by others.
3. After receipt of proposals, no information regarding the number or identity of the offerers participating in the negotiations shall be made available to the public or to any one else whose official duties do not require such knowledge.
4. Whenever negotiations are conducted with several offerers, while such negotiations may be conducted successively, each offerer selected to participate in such negotiations shall have an equitable opportunity to submit such price, technical, or other revisions in proposals as may result from the negotiations.
5. All offerers shall be informed of the specified date of the closing of negotiations and that any revisions to their proposals should be submitted by that date.
6. All offerers shall be informed that after the specified date for the closing of negotiations, no information (other than preaward notice of unacceptable proposals or offers) will be furnished to any other offerer until award has been made.

Awarding the Order or Contract

Unless all bids or proposals are rejected, an award should be made by the contracting officer, by written notice, within the time for acceptance specified, to that responsible offerer whose bid or proposal, conforming to the invitation, will be most advantageous to the government, price and other factors considered. The award is made by mailing or otherwise furnishing to the successful offerer a properly executed award document or notice of award. When an advance notice of award is issued, it must be followed as soon as possible by the formal award. When more than one award results from any single invitation, separate award documents must be executed, each suitably numbered. When an award is made for less than all of the items offered and additional items are being withheld for subsequent award, the first award should state that the government may make subsequent awards on those additional items within the acceptance period. All provisions of the invitation for bids or request for proposals, including any additions or changes, should be clearly and accurately set forth (either expressly or by reference) since an acceptance of the bid or proposal and the award constitute the contract.

The purchase order is the most widely used of all purchase methods. This technique provides the greatest documentation, but it is expensive. Various agencies have estimated the cost of processing a small purchase requisition through to completion using the purchase order to be about fifty dollars. Because of this cost the purchase order should be used only when additional documentation is necessary to establish a record of the funds being obligated, because the vendor insists on a written order, because the order covers a long list of items or the item descriptions are complex, because the vendor is in a remote location, or where delivery, payment, inspection, packing, or other aspects of the purchase are facilitated. A representative purchase order form is shown in figure 11-2.

A purchase order can be used in a number of different ways. As a delivery order, it is a request for delivery of articles or services in accordance with the terms of an existing contract. As an award document, it is a form for making award on a bid or offer submitted on a standard contract form. As a buy order, it is a written request to a supplier to furnish articles or services in accordance with specified terms.

The blanket-purchasing arrangement can be defined simply as a charge account since it is similar in nature to a commercial charge account. This type of arrangement eliminates the necessity of issuing individual purchase orders by allowing the purchases to be placed orally. The terms and conditions for this procedure must be mutually agreed upon by the vendor and the agency in advance of its implementation. The primary objectives in establishing a blanket-purchasing arrangement are to reduce duplication of paperwork when making repetitive purchases from the same vendor, simplify the total documentation of the purchase, and reduce the administrative costs per order. This reduction of administrative costs makes this arrangement one of the least expensive purchasing procedures. It also provides for consolidated billing and, if utilized correctly, results in better agency-supplier relations.

Blanket-purchasing arrangements are most appropriate when a wide variety of items in a broad class of goods, like hardware, are generally purchased from local suppliers but the exact items, quantities, and delivery requirements are not known in advance and may vary considerably; when there is a need to provide local commercial sources of supply for one or more agencies or projects in a given area that do not have or need authority to purchase otherwise; or in any other case where the writing of numerous purchase orders can be avoided through the use of this procedure.

The blanket-purchasing arrangement is not a contract; it is simply a prearranged understanding as to how an activity will buy, if it buys. The fact that the arrangement has been established creates no contractual obligation on either the government or the vendor.

The oral purchase is another method designed to save time, paperwork, and money. Under it an order is placed by telephone, with no confirming paperwork of any kind. All the documentation required is handled on the vendor's original invoice. Usually the following limitations are placed on the use of the oral purchase technique: the amount of any one purchase is $500 or less, a purchase order is not required by either the supplier or the government, or appropriate invoices are obtainable from the supplier. The success of this method rests on the care with which the transaction is handled. When an oral order is placed, the vendor is asked to make delivery with no confirming paperwork from the government. A vendor is willing to comply only if she knows payment will be made promptly, so to facilitate payment of invoices, ordering offices should advise the vendor to make delivery with the invoice attached. The original invoice is then endorsed by the buyer, showing that the item has been received as ordered. The buyer might also include a funding symbol, activity or job number, and time discount. The ordering office signs the invoice and forwards it to the appropriate office for expedited payment.

The unpriced purchase order is another method of accomplishing small purchases. It should be used when all of the following conditions are present: the transaction will not exceed a set dollar ceiling (in federal purchasing, $2,500), only one delivery and one payment will be made, it is impractical to obtain pricing prior to the issuance of the purchase order, and the procurement is for repairs to equipment requiring disassembly to determine the nature and extent of such repairs, sole-source material not currently in production for which the cost cannot be readily established, or supplies or services where prices are known to be competitive but for which exact prices are not known.

Each unpriced purchase order is issued on a purchase order form and should include a realistic monetary limitation. This dollar figure becomes an obligation subject to adjustment when the firm price is established and also acts as a control on the vendor. The supplier is notified that if the total price will exceed the estimated limitation or if materials or services cannot be furnished in exact accordance with the requirement set forth, then performance is to be withheld pending advice from the ordering office. A supplier who

Obverse

Form No. DA-PC-10

STATE OF NORTH CAROLINA
DEPARTMENT OF ADMINISTRATION

PURCHASE AND CONTRACT DIVISION

RALEIGH, N. C. 27603

DATE

PURCHASE ORDER
578346
REQUISITION NO.

BOTH ABOVE NUMBERS MUST APPEAR
ON ALL INVOICES, SHIPPING PAPERS
AND SHIPMENTS. SEE REVERSE SIDE
FOR ADDITIONAL INSTRUCTIONS.

BILLING INSTRUCTIONS

Separate invoices in quadruplicate must
be rendered for each order or shipment.
The title of the account must be exactly
as shown under "Charge To". If nothing
appears under "Charge To", charge as
shown under "Ship To". All invoices
and shipping papers should be mailed to
Purchase and Contract Division, Administration Building, 116 West Jones
St., Raleigh, N. C. 27603

ALL APPLICABLE N. C. SALES & USE TAX
SHALL BE SHOWN AS A SEPARATE ITEM
ON INVOICE.

PLEASE ENTER OUR ORDER AS FOLLOWS.

SHIP TO   CHARGE TO

SHIP VIA

F. O. B.

DELIVERY

TERMS

IMPORTANT
FOUR COPIES OF INVOICE REQUIRED.
MUST BE MAILED DIRECTLY TO PURCHASE
AND CONTRACT DIVISION ON DATE
SHIPMENT IS MADE.

QUANTITY	DESCRIPTION	PRICE	AMOUNT

ORIGINAL PREPAID TRANSPORTATION RECEIPT MUST BE ATTACHED
TO INVOICES BEFORE THEY WILL BE APPROVED FOR PAYMENT.
SEE REVERSE SIDE FOR ADDITIONAL INSTRUCTIONS.

PURCHASE AND CONTRACT DIVISION

PURCHASING AGENT

Reverse

CONDITIONS AND INSTRUCTIONS

1. This order is placed subject to shipment at prices, amounts and transportation rates not in excess of those indicated on the face of this order.

2. Each shipment must be shipped to address and marked to the attention of the individual indicated on the face of this order, labeled plainly with our Order and Requisition Numbers and show gross, tare and net weight.

3. Complete packing list must accompany each shipment.

4. Drafts will not be honored.

5. Materials received in excess of quantities specified herein may be, at our option, returned at Shipper's expense.

6. Invoices in quadruplicate, showing Order and Requisition Numbers, terms of payment, and routing, must be mailed to us on date of shipment.

7. On all invoices subject to discount, the discount period will be calculated from date correct invoice is received in this office.

8. Each invoice must be accompanied by the following papers: —

   (A) Original bill of lading when shipment is made by freight or express.
   (B) Signed delivery receipt when delivery is made by passenger or truck.
   (C) Parcel post insurance when shipment is made by parcel post and value is over $1.00.

9. All invoices and shipping papers are to be sent to Purchase and Contract Division, Administration Building, 116 West Jones St., Raleigh, N. C. 27603

10. In cases where materials are shipped against this order by parties other than yourselves, shipper must be instructed to show our Order and Requisition Numbers on all packages and shipping manifests to insure prompt identification and payment of invoices.

Figure 11-2. Representative Purchase-Order Form

performs anyway and invoices a dollar amount above the ceiling established takes the risk of being held to be a "volunteer" and going unpaid above the ceiling.

The supplier is also advised to submit an invoice to the ordering office for approval so that the fairness and reasonableness of the price can be ascertained. The buyer then endorses the invoice as to the receipt of the article or service and forwards it for payment.

Care must be used in the application of this technique. Unpriced purchase orders should be issued only to reliable vendors. The estimated monetary limitation should be conservative since there may be a tendency on the part of the supplier to invoice up to the stated ceiling amount. Finally the buyer should again take whatever steps are necessary to ensure that the supplier is paid on time.

Notes

1. The material that follows incorporates and integrates instructional matter developed by the GSA's Acquisition Training Facility.

2. Request from: General Services Administration, Office of Investigations, General Services Building, Washington, D.C. 20405.

3. For information, contact: Marketing Services Division, Dun & Bradstreet, 99 Church Street, New York, N.Y. 10007.

4. Department of Defense, *Selection of Contractual Sources for Major Defense Systems*, directive 4105.62 (6 January 1976, rev. 3 March 1977).

5. Notices are sent to: Department of Commerce, Office of Field Operations, *Commerce Business Daily* Section, P.O. Box 5999, Chicago, Illinois 60680.

6. Examples of publications available from Federal agencies include: "How to Prepare for a Pre-Award Survey," *Management Aids* no. 215; "Termination of DOD Contracts for the Government's Convenience," *Management Aids* no. 211; "Pointers on Negotiating DOD Contracts," *Management Aids* no. 204; "A Tested System for Achieving Quality Control," *Technical Aids* no. 91; and "PERT/CPM Management System for the Small Subcontractor," *Technical Aids* no. 86. All are available free from SBA, Washington, D.C. 20416 (or nearest SBA office).

7. Copies of the *Commerce Business Daily* are available for reference purposes at SBA and Department of Commerce field offices or may be obtained on a subscription basis for $80 per year by second-class mail or $105 by first-class mail from the Superintendent of Documents, "Commerce Business Daily," Government Printing Office, Washington, D.C. 20402. Purchase order must be accompanied by payment. All remittances (check or money order) shall be made out to the Superintendent of Documents, Government Printing Office, Washington, D.C. 20402. Copies may also be ordered through any Department of Commerce Field Office.

8. Public Law 87-653, Truth in Negotiations Act of 1962.

9. The most frequently cited reference is Lawrence D. Miles, *Techniques of Value Analysis and Engineering*, 2d ed. (New York: McGraw-Hill, 1972).

12 Purchasing: Postaward Activities

After the purchase order is issued or the contract let, management's attention shifts to matters of performance and accomplishment. It hopes that the selected vendor will perform well, and the object of the purchase will be accomplished in a timely fashion.

Overview of Contract Administration[1]

The efficient administration of purchase orders and contracts is an extremely important function. Too often a purchasing activity will consider that the job is done when the contract is awarded, but responsibility does not end until both parties to the contract have performed in strict compliance with the terms of the contract, compensation has been paid, and the record closed.

The terms of a contract and the manner of performance may be altered by an agreement of the parties; however, a representative of the government cannot waive a vested contractual right of the government without adequate consideration. As a result, a party to a contract assumes the full risk of performing his obligation and undertakes the risk of compensating the other party by way of damages for any failure to perform. This strict rule of performance is often modified in government contracts by including clauses that allocate certain performance risks and allow the government unilaterally to change, delay, or terminate performance of a contract.

When a contract is in force between the government and a contractor, an important phase of materials management has begun. All of the preceding actions are, in effect, tested now. A good purchase request, a satisfactory solicitation, and a careful analysis of the contractor's proposal has led to the moment when the parties to the agreement are ready to begin their respective obligations under the contract. The contract represents the whole agreement of the parties, and its performance by both parties now becomes important. Both the contractor and the government have obligations under the contract. Contract administration is the process by which the parties ensure their respective performances. The government accomplishes its contract administration function through a contracting officer who ensures that both the contractors and the government perform all of their contractual obligations.

In large purchasing operations, a distinction is sometimes made between the officer who accomplishes the preaward activities, and the one responsible for the postaward activities. The first is called the procuring contracting officer (PCO), and the second is the administrative contracting officer (ACO). Also there are often specialists who assist the contracting officers. The scope of situations and potential problems in the postaward period can be almost as great as in the preaward period. The monitoring of the contractor's performance, the acceptance of the material being produced (or the services rendered), and the capabilities of the material to meet the changing requirements of the government will necessitate close relationships between contracting officers and agency technical and requirements personnel.

The difficulty of administration of a contract is a function of its size and scope, although at times a relatively small transaction will require a large amount of contract administration. It has been said that contract administration is not a large problem but rather the progressive solution of thousands of small problems. Law, regulations, and policy establish the manner in which the administration of a contract is performed. Regulations and policy, however, do not alter the established basic contractual relationship. The degree and the extent of the administration efforts will be dependent upon the type of contract, the complexity of the item or service being procured, and, to some extent, the efficiency and the cooperation of the contractor. Regulations seldom give full and complete directions as to what actions are required in the administration of contracts. The simplest contract requires the assumption of responsibility and the exercise of judgment by the administrator. The contract administrator should realize that she is a member of a unified administration effort and that she must rely upon other members of the materials-management team for their special skills and knowledge. Lacking special skill and knowledge does not, however, relieve the contracting officer from the responsibility of making decisions and taking action in those areas where such special skill or knowledge may be required. Actions in these areas must be based upon the analysis of the situation and the recommendations pertaining to it, furnished by the team members who are trained and skilled in the respective areas. The contract administrator must always remember that the ultimate goal of any contract is the delivery of the goods or services required.

Only a properly designated contracting officer has the authority to commit the government contractually in connection with the administration of contracts. Federal purchasing activities and large state and local jurisdictions also use contracting officer representatives (CORs) selected by contracting officers to act as their authorized representative in administering contracts. It should be required that each designation of a COR be in a writing that should clearly identify the scope and limitations of his authority. The authority exercised by a COR must be clearly distinguished from that exercised by a properly designated contracting officer. CORs are not authorized to agree to or sign contracts or modifications that in any way obligate the payment of money by the government. Normally CORs can issue administrative-type change orders (those not affecting price, delivery, quantity, or quality), change shipping and marking instructions, and take any other action under a contract that could lawfully be taken by the contracting officer, with two important exceptions; they cannot obligate monies or sign contractual instruments, and they cannot do anything specifically prohibited by the contract itself.

Contract administration involves a multitude of tasks and problems. A good contract administrator, whether working for the government or for the contractor, must be a kind of all-purpose person: part accountant, part lawyer, part engineer, part negotiator, and part financier.

The volume of contract administration actions varies greatly from contract to contract. In many cases, particularly in the procurement of standard products, the only action by the government during contract performance may be inspection of the product and payment of the contract price. On the other hand, in a cost-reimbursement contract the government representatives may take actions on a daily basis, including subcontract and overtime approvals, issuance and pricing of changes, continuing surveillance of the contractor's performance, and specification interpretation, as well as the normal contract administration duties.

The contract is a delegation of a government job to another organization, and with that delegation goes the right to make decisions on actions taken during contract performance. Therefore the question becomes one of how much authority has been delegated by the contract and how much has been kept by the government. The first source for an answer to this question is the contract itself. It normally reserves to the government those rights that are not reserved or are thought to be given to the contractor. Thus a partial answer is that the role of the government representative is to perform those tasks assigned by the contract.

There is a broader role for the government representative to play, however. Even if the contract is silent on the subject, the government representative has the duty to protect the interest of the government during contract performance. This means ensuring that the contractor is performing in a manner that demonstrates that he will meet the contract schedule, that government funds are not being spent wastefully, and that the contractor is in full compliance with properly interpreted specifications. In this area the government representative has the most difficult task since he must attempt to protect the rights of the government while not infringing on the rights of the contractor to make basic management decisions in his work. The role of the government representative in this area might be thought of as one of monitoring without directing.

The conflict between the government's and contractor's interests is most clearly demonstrated in the cost-reimbursement contract. There the government is not only interested in obtaining performance but is also vitally interested in the method of performance since the method used will greatly influence the amount of cost that the government will be required to reimburse the contractor. The amount of money that the contractor pays his employees, the type of facilities utilized for the contract, and the extent of subcontracting are just a few of the many areas where a contractor's decision will affect the amount that the government will have to pay for the performance of the contract. Therefore during the performance of a cost-plus-fixed-fee contract, it is not unusual for a contracting officer to disagree with a contractor's method or manner of performance because he thinks that a particular expenditure is not necessary or is excessive. In such cases the contracting officer may attempt to direct or order the contractor to perform in the manner considered proper. If the contractor fails to comply, the contracting officer may resort to a disallowance of cost. The contractor may in turn object that the manner of performance ordered increases the cost incurred. Basically when the government gives the responsibility for doing a job to a contractor, it also gives him the discretion to determine the method to be used in accomplishing that job. The only limitations would be those identified in the contract. Thus the role of government representative is a difficult one. He must be careful not to interfere with the contractor's performance of the contract and must attempt to avoid directions to the contractor that usurp the management prerogatives of the contractor. On the other hand, the government is entitled to compliance with the terms of the contract, and it is the duty of the government representative to insist on such compliance.

A contractor administrator is also responsible for seeing that the government performs those acts to which it has promised in the contract. This may involve the furnishing of drawings, plans, specifications, or models, the delivery of government-furnished property, or a wide variety of duties. These requirements are expressly set forth in the contract, and the obligation to perform them is usually evident. Since these promises are common to many contracts, they are often covered by clauses that contain standard language and that also obligate the contracting officer to adjust the contract price, the delivery schedule, or the terms and conditions of the contract in the event the government fails or does not wish to keep its promises. If no such provisions are incorporated, the contractor would be able to recover damages for any breach of contract.

The contracting officer also has an implied duty not to do anything that will prevent or hinder the contractor from carrying out part of the contract. For example, the contract might require that certain work be done in the presence of a government inspector. The contracting officer could not so schedule the time of the inspector as to reduce her availability when needed.

A third area of responsibility of the contracting officer to the contractor is in the performance of duties that require the exercise of discretion. This is most evident where the contract requires the approval of the contracting officer as a condition to such things as the right of the contractor to receive payment, to issue a subcontract, to work overtime, to be permitted to start production, or to take some other action necessary under a contract. For example, if the contract calls for approval of subcontractors, the contracting officer must make a timely determination.

A final area of responsibility of the contracting officer is in reference to the determination of disputes under the contract. The responsibility in this regard is to decide the questions presented with impartiality. The duty of the contracting officer is similar to that of a judge deciding questions of fact, and the fact that he is employed by the government should not bias his decision. The real goal is to determine the actual facts. Moreover the contractor is entitled to receive the contracting officer's personal and independent decision and not that of some other officer of the government, whether of higher or lower authority.

The magnitude of contract administration in the Department of Defense (DOD) is significant enough to justify a separate agency, the Defense Contract Administration Services (DCAS), a part of the Defense Logistics Agency. DCAS was formed in 1964 as part of a DOD reorganization under Secretary of Defense Robert S. McNamara. In 1979 DCAS employed seventeen thousand people located throughout the United States in nine DCAS regions. Regions, subdivided into DCAS management areas (DCASMAs) and DCAS plant representative offices (DCASPROs), are staffed according to the scope and complexity of the contracts under administration.

DCAS supports more than eleven hundred military and civilian purchasing activities in obtaining products and services when and where needed and at the contract price and specified quality. Although DCAS has been designated as the principal contract-administration organization within the DOD, it does not administer all DOD contracts. Under the Defense Plant Cognizance Program, certain contractor plants are assigned to the military departments, and the cognizant department is responsible for contract administration at such plants. Other exceptions include navy shipyards, universities, and army ammunition plants. Notwithstanding these exceptions, DCAS in 1979 was administering 250,000 contracts valued at nearly $73 billion.

Upon request DCAS also assumes administration of contracts let by nondefense agencies. Examples include the National Aeronautics and Space Administration, the Department of Energy, and several foreign governments.

Modifying the Order or Contract

Many types of actions taken by the government representative during the performance of a contract affect the contract price, the time of contract performance, and other terms and conditions of the contract. Most of these actions are taken under a specific clause of the contract giving the government the right to take such actions. The government includes a changes clause in the contract for the specific purpose of being able to take such actions and agrees to give the contractor an equitable price adjustment if such action increases the cost. Other actions by the government representative during contract performance are taken without the authority of such a clause. Examples are delays in giving approvals or interference with the work. In these cases the government action is legally a violation of the contract, but there is no readily apparent method of administratively adjusting the contract price, delivery schedule, or terms and conditions.

All of the types of contract modifications discussed here are unilateral modifications on the part of the government; they are actions that the government takes by itself during the performance of the contract. This is an important factor because almost all such actions could be taken on a bilateral basis by agreement of the contractor and the government before the action is taken. In such a case the only question would be one of consideration: was there a benefit to each of the parties of the contract to support the bilateral amendment of the contract?

A changes clause normally says:

> The contracting officer may at any time, by a written order, and without notice to the sureties, make changes, within the general scope of this contract, in any one or more of the following: (i) drawings, designs, or specifications, where the supplies to be furnished are to be specially manufactured for the government in accordance therewith; (ii) method of shipment or packing; and (iii) place of delivery. If any such change causes an increase or decrease in the cost of, or the time required for, the performance of any part of the work under this contract, whether changed or not changed by any such order, an equitable adjustment shall be made in the contract price or delivery schedule, or both, and the contract shall be modified in writing accordingly. . . . Failure to agree to any adjustment shall be a dispute concerning a question of fact within the meaning of the clause of this contract entitled "Disputes." However, nothing in this clause shall excuse the contractor from proceeding with the contract as changed.

Thus the contractor must accept the change and proceed with the work even in the absence of an agreement about the effect of the change on contract costs, schedules, and technical requirements.

Such a clause is unnecessary where the government is purchasing standard items, but it is mandatory where the object of the procurement is services or custom-made items that are produced to meet government requirements. The presence of the changes clause therefore provides a very necessary privilege to the government in its contract.

There are many types of changes for which a need may arise. The most important ones are:

1. Configuration changes that alter dimensions or delete or add a part to a piece of equipment. These are sometimes referred to as engineering changes.
2. Procedure changes that alter the way in which the product is formulated or tested.
3. Support changes that alter the requirement to provide spare parts, change warranty provisions, or modify maintenance and follow-on service needs.
4. Requirements changes that alter quantities, delivery schedules, and completion dates.
5. Fiscal and financial changes that alter the level and timing of funding.

Such changes are usually interrelated. Any of the first three would certainly involve the last two.

In a major systems procurement the number of changes may run into the hundreds or thousands. Individually the changes may not warrant the time and expense of negotiation. Therefore they are accumulated, and at some point a supplemental agreement to the contract is negotiated.

An important concept in the changes clause is that of constructive changes. Boards of contract appeals have often found that actions of government representatives were changes even if not so intended. Such changes are described as constructive changes, and it is clear that in this area the boards are using the changes clause as a vehicle to compensate the contractor for an action that the government representative should not have taken. For example, if the government inspector enforces a standard of quality that is above that set forth in the specifications, the extra work has been considered to be change. Of course, the board must sustain the interpretation of the specification that is proposed by the contractor and must find that the contracting officer had delegated full inspection authority to the inspector.

Adjusting Prices

When the performance terms of an order or contract are modified, the price most likely will need to be adjusted. Concerned boards and courts have consistently held that such adjustments are a required corrective measure when the government modifies a contract. The adjustments must be equitable; they must credit the proper party. The party feeling it should be credited has the burden of proving its entitlement to an adjustment; thus it must establish and maintain such records as might be necessary to support a claim.

Price also might require adjustment because contingencies provided for in the contract arise. A price-adjustment clause refers to the changes and contingencies (if any) clauses. For a fixed-price contract, it will specify:

If any such change causes an increase or decrease in the cost of, or the time required for, the performance of any part of the work under this contract, whether changed or not changed by any such order, an equitable adjustment shall be made in the contract price or delivery schedule, or both.

For a cost-reimbursement-type contract the clause might require:

If any such change causes an increase or decrease in the estimated cost of, or the time required for, the performance of any part of the work under this contract, whether changed or not changed by any such order, or otherwise affects any other provision of this contract, an equitable adjustment shall be made: (1) in the estimated cost or delivery schedule, or both; (2) in the amount of any fixed-fee to be paid to the contractor; and (3) in such other provisions of the contract as may be affected.

Similar language may be written into other types of contracts.

There are two theories—subjective and objective—on the proper techniques for determining an equitable adjustment. These theories deal with the type of information that is necessary to substantiate properly the amount of the adjustment given the contractor. The type of information that can be obtained is largely a product of the time when the adjustment is determined. If it is established before the work is accomplished, much of the backup data would necessarily be estimated rather than actual.

The clauses quite clearly contemplate that the adjustment will be made soon after the occurrence of the event calling for the adjustment (the adjustment can, of course, be made at the time the alteration in the contract is ordered). At such time the contractor and the contracting officer will be provided both known and estimated information. For instance, if the adjustment covers a deletion of work, that work may be on a fixed-price subcontract and hence the price of the work may be readily ascertainable. On the other hand, the contractor may have planned to do the work himself, in which case his estimate of the cost of the work will be the only available information. If the adjustment calls for an addition or substitution of work, there may only be estimated information on the cost of the work. Thus when the contracting officer initially undertakes the negotiation of the equitable adjustment, she will usually be obliged to rely on estimated cost information to some extent; however, she certainly should insist on any actual cost information that is available to the contractor to enable an accurate determination of the amount of the adjustment.

If the equitable adjustment is made by a board of contract appeals or by a court, the situation is quite different. By the time such adjudication occurs, the work is usually completed, and the costs have been incurred. Hence the problem becomes one of determining what those costs were in order to arrive at a fair amount for the adjustment. This is a problem of accounting detail to a large extent. For example, can the costs of the work that has been added be segregated from the other costs of the job? If not, what techniques can be used to determine with some degree of accuracy what these costs were? Even if a contractor has segregated the costs, in many cases he will not have actual costs of work that has been deleted because the work was never done. Hence, even in the case of an equitable adjustment after the work has been performed, the availability of actual costs is problematical.

For years considerable confusion has existed concerning the proper standard to be applied in establishing an equitable adjustment. The subjective theory holds that the proper measure of the adjustment is the cost impact on the contractor; the objective theory holds that the proper standard is the reasonable value of the change.

Under the subjective theory, the actual or historical costs incurred, if reasonable, are the measure of the equitable adjustment. Since the equitable-adjustment language of the changes clause contemplates an adjustment for an increase or a decrease in cost, the actual purpose of the language is to keep both parties whole (that is, legally in the same position) when the contract is modified. The adjustment should neither increase the contractor's loss nor decrease it at the government's expense. If the contractor had a certain profit potential before the change was ordered, she should come out with the same relative profit potential after the change has been priced. On the other hand, if she was in a loss position before the change was ordered, the change should not permit her to recover such losses.

Under the objective theory, often espoused by contractors, it is argued that the change increases the value to the government of the item being supplied. It is difficult to prove the market value of an item unless similar items have been currently bought and sold. Therefore the subjective theory usually prevails.

There are basically three techniques used for establishing the amount for an equitable adjustment. The approach used depends on the types of information available at the time the adjustment is made. These approaches are the specific-, or directly related, cost approach, the total-cost approach, and the jury-verdict approach.

The specific-cost approach involves determining basically with accounting detail the amount of impact the change order has on the contract costs. This approach is appropriate for use in those cases where a formal change order is used and the contractor establishes an account to cover the costs that flow directly from the change order. If the change involves only a substitution of a higher quality of material or an increase in the amount of work, then this approach can be comparatively easy to apply. Even if the change order involves a deletion of work, the specific-cost approach can be used if the contractor had a binding commitment from the subcontractor for that portion of the work deleted.

In many cases, however, the cost impact of a contract modification cannot be readily identified. For instance, if the adjustment flows from a constructive change order, it may be impossible for the contractor to prove, with accounting-type detail, the exact amount of entitlement. This might also be the case where multiple change orders generate overlapping and ripple-effect costs. Under these circumstances, other approaches must be used to provide equitable treatment for both the government and the contractor.

The total-cost approach for determining an equitable adjustment takes the total cost of the work done and subtracts the estimated cost of the work that would have been done had it not been for the change. This is clearly a comprehensive method of pricing an equitable adjustment that may have very little relation to the change that is being priced. This is so because the approach is based on two shaky premises: that the actual cost incurred is proper for the work and that the estimate is a fair approximation of what it would have cost to perform this work. To correct the first difficulty, the boards and courts have closely scrutinized the costs incurred, subtracting those that they believe to be the fault of the contractor and not caused by the change. To correct the second difficulty, averaged estimates of other bidders and the government estimate have been used in an attempt to overcome the possibility that the contractor may have underbid the price.

The jury-verdict approach is one of hearing all of the evidence, including opinions of qualified experts, and basing the equitable adjustment on a total view of the evidence. The essence of the approach is that it uses estimates of the cost effect of change rather than actual costs. The contracting officer, board, or court considers the opinions of qualified experts on the reasonableness of the costs claimed by the contractor and reaches an equitable adjustment.

Inspection and Quality Assurance

Every purchase order or contract requires that at some point the contractor will tender performance for acceptance by the government. The contract establishes time and place of performance and, for material items, quality and quantity. Time and place of performance are set in a delivery schedule. Quality is established by the specification and standards cited in the purchase order or contract.

When specifications are accurate, complete, and realistic, the issue becomes merely one of performance of or attributing the responsibility for a performance failure. In the cost-type contract, the government undertakes the responsibility for reimbursing the contractor for the cost of meeting the specifications. The government selects or drafts specifications in the form of design or performance requirements (or a combination of the two). Where the government has selected or drafted a detailed set of specifications to be followed by the contractor in fulfilling the contractual obligation, this in essence guarantees that if the specifications are followed, the expected result will be obtained. This warranty may be limited by notifying prospective contractors that the specifications may be defective. Defective specifications may entitle the contractor to additional compensation if the cost of performance is increased. To recover the extra cost of performance, the contractor must show that the contract did not allocate to her the risk of such a mistake and that the government received a benefit from the extra work for which it would have been willing to contract had the facts been known.

In extreme cases of defective specifications, the contractor may claim impossibility of performance. If the contractor cannot meet a design specification, she might attempt to trace her difficulties to some specific defects in the specifications, and the best avenue of relief would be to assert that the government has by implication warranted the specifications. On the other hand, in the case of a performance specification that a contractor cannot meet, it is very unusual that the government would be held to have warranted the specifications. The use of performance specifications in itself is an indication that the government does not know the exact way to achieve the desired results and is relying on the contractor to provide that way. Hence the contractor in such a case is usually left only with the argument of impossibility of performance.

The doctrine of impossibility of performance states that when two parties have entered into a contract calling for something that subsequently turns out to be impossible to achieve, both parties are relieved of the obligations under the contract. In a sense, such a contract is void; neither party can enforce the contract against the other, and the only rights remaining are those to be compensated for any benefit rendered to the other party.

After resolution of any differences concerning specifications, work proceeds and inspection of that work is necessary. The inspection clause of the contract generally provides for two distinct types of inspection; in-process and acceptance inspection. The in-process inspection during contract performance allows the contracting officer to direct correction prior to delivery. The inspection conducted at this stage does not prevent subsequent rejection for defects discovered prior to formal acceptance. However, under certain circumstances where the inspector's acts imply waiver of a defect, the government may be stopped from later rejecting the performance.

The government has the right to conduct inspections, but this does not mean the right will always be exercised. In many procurements, the contractor is required to establish a quality-assurance program, and the government will limit its inspection to a review of that program. When the government does inspect, it has broad latitude in selecting the type of inspection to be conducted. However, the inspection may not impose a higher standard of quality than that required by the specifications. When conducting an inspection, the inspector may delay the performance of a contract for a reasonable time for that purpose; however, unreasonable delay might be viewed as a breach of contract.

If the government chooses to inspect and discovers defects, two courses of action are available: it may reject, or refuse to accept, the contractor's tendered performance, or it may direct correction of the defects. The government is entitled to strict compliance with the specifications. Alternate relief through correction of the defects, or price reduction for defects, is discretionary and does not affect the determination to reject performance. The government's right of partial rejection has been limited to particular items where the inspection conducted was not sufficient to be a reasonable basis to reject the whole lot. In any case, the contractor must be notified of rejection and the reason(s) for the rejection within a reasonable time. In the absence of such notice, implied acceptance may result.

As an alternative to rejection of defective performance, the government may require the contractor to replace or correct the defective material and, if that is not done promptly, it may do so by contract or otherwise at the expense of the contractor who failed to perform. This avenue also allows the government to obtain timely performance in accordance with the specifications. If the time for delivery has passed, the government may accept defective performance with a corresponding reduction in contract price. This does not constitute a waiver of those defects for any subsequent performance. In the absence of a contract provision to the contrary, the government must accept the performance when tendered by the contractor or reject it as nonconforming. If the government fails to give notice of rejection within a reasonable time, this may be construed as a waiver of defects and acceptance of the otherwise nonconforming performance.

The actual inspection may vary from relatively simple methods such as comparing the salient characteristics of an item offered in response to a brand name or equal purchase, to more complex procedures involving the use of special testing equipment. By whatever means it is accomplished, inspection is the key to the government's enforcing the technical requirements of the contract.

The inspection clause provisions or references establish who inspects, when and where the inspection is to be accomplished, what method is to be used in the inspection, and who pays for the inspection. In determining by whom and when an inspection can be made, the inspection clause gives the government the right to inspect at various times and places, including the period of manufacture. Problems could arise when the government wishes to inspect at a certain time or place, but it would be inconvenient to the contractor. The inspection provision touches on this problem by stating, "All inspection and tests by the government shall be performed in such a manner as not to unduly delay the work." This statement recognizes the fact that it may be necessary for the inspector to interfere somewhat with the work in order to inspect properly, but it leaves the extent to which this is permitted to be determined under the circumstances existing under each contract. The inspection clause should also state that if any inspection or test is made by the government on the premises of the contractor or a subcontractor, the contractor, without additional charge, must provide reasonable facilities and assistance for the safety and convenience of the government inspectors in the performance of their duties.

For a discussion of detailed methods of inspection, sampling plans, and related statistical methods, the reader is referred to the standard works in the field.[2]

Follow-up and Expediting

During performance of the government contract, a contractor may encounter many situations that will delay the work. Some of these will be due to the fault or negligence of the contractor, some will be generated by acts of the government in administering the contract, and others will be caused by factors beyond the control of either government or contractor. The government assumes no responsibility for delays that fall into the first category, of course, but if the delay is caused by the government or if it can be classified as an excusable delay, the contractor has certain remedies available. In general, the government is liable for the additional costs incurred by the contractor if the government unreasonably delays the contractor's work. The type of adjustment to the delivery schedule the contractor receives will depend upon the nature of the event that generated the delay and the contract language applicable to that event. In some cases the contractor will be entitled to a time adjustment only for the delay, and in other cases a monetary adjustment is provided as well. These differences are significant to the contractor since in many cases an adjustment of time for a government-caused delay will not be at all adequate to compensate for the actual damage caused by the delay.

When delay occurs, follow-up action becomes necessary if user needs are to be met. Follow-up and expediting are closely related activities. Follow-up applies to the monitoring of the contractor's delivery schedule to ensure compliance. Expediting pertains to attempting to improve upon the contractually stipulated delivery times.

Follow-up procedure includes identifying, at or before the date of award, which contracts need to be monitored. Such early identification permits preparation of a follow-up plan, which includes: verification with the contractor of the delivery schedule, establishing liaison with appropriate vendor representatives, notification of shipments (for items of material), alerting the receiving room staff, providing transportation and handling assistance, authorizing substitutions or specification waiver, and taking contingency action with alternate sources.

Handling Discrepancies and Deficiencies

It is extremely important that discrepancies and deficiencies be fully documented. This need becomes apparent during the discussion that follows of claims, disputes, and appeals. Government activities that receive goods or services from contractors must carefully document: (1) discrepancies or deficiencies in material received or services rendered, (2) inspections made and results observed, (3) warranty provisions in effect, (4) adjustments made to financial or inventory records, (5) loss or damage claims against suppliers or carriers, (6) instances of over, short, or damaged freight noted in connection with prepared bill of lading, (7) requests of billing adjustments, and (8) actions taken to resolve claims. Federal agencies and larger state and local jurisdictions utilize standard forms for these purposes.

Warranties are important in dealing with discrepancies and deficiencies. The promises of a contractor, usually set forth in drawings, specifications, and work statements either drafted into the contract or incorporated by reference, warranties may involve the ability of the delivery item to perform a particular function, to conform to specific design, or to be the equivalent of an item whose description is furnished. Generally these warranties refer to three factors that determine whether the goods are satisfactory: design, materials, and workmanship. When a contract contains such promises and they are not fulfilled, the government must complain and be prepared to back up its complaint.

Dealing with Default, Termination

Since the contractor has promised to deliver in accordance with the contract requirements, an unexcused failure to do so will be considered a breach of contract, for which the government has certain remedies available. There are two types of failures to perform in a timely manner. The most common is the simple failure to tender work that conforms to the contract requirements at the required time. In such a case, the determination of whether the time for delivery has arrived is usually accomplished by consulting the delivery schedule included in the contract. It is the second type of failure to perform that causes the difficulty: anticipatory breach or repudiation. If an event has occurred that will likely lead to failure to tender work at the time due and the contractor is not acting to respond to the event, a breach of contract would be anticipated. For example, work might have stopped over an inspection problem. The government changes its inspection procedure, but the contractor does not resume work.

When it has been established that there is a default, the contract administrator's decision is very important since it will establish the basis for determining the respective rights of the government and the contractor. Basically the choice is between two alternatives: to terminate the contract for default or allow the contractor to continue to perform. In deciding to terminate, the contracting officer must carefully consider these factors:

1. The provisions of the contract and applicable laws and relations.
2. The specific failure of the contractor and the excuses, if any, made by the contractor for such failures.
3. The availability of the supplies or services from other sources.
4. The urgency of the need for the supplies or services and the period of time that would be required to obtain the supplies or services from other sources as compared with the time in which delivery could be obtained from the delinquent contractor.
5. The degree of essentiality of the contractor in the government procurement program and the effect of termination for default upon the contractor's capability as a supplier under other contracts.
6. The effect of a termination for default on the ability of the contractor to liquidate guaranteed loans, progress payments, or advance payments.
7. The availability of funds to finance repurchase costs that may prove to be uncollectible from the defaulted contractor, and the availability of funds to finance termination costs if the default is determined to be excusable.

The intent of these considerations is to ensure that the decision to terminate is not against the interest of the government. For example, if the contracting officer were certain that he could get the items within two weeks from the defaulting contractor, it would be common sense to decide not to terminate if the best delivery from other sources would be three months. Another case where it could be in the best interest not to terminate the contract could be if such action would result in the contractor's bankruptcy. However, where the contractor is in default, the contractor has no legal basis for complaint if the contracting officer decides to terminate. This is a discretionary matter, and the boards of contract appeals continually hold that as long as the government has the right to terminate for default, they will not look into the wisdom of that course of action.

Repurchasing pertains to the likelihood that the government will have to repurchase from another vendor the material originally ordered from the defaulting vendor. If upon termination, the government still needs or desires the completion of the work that was terminated, it has a right to charge the excess costs of completing such work to the contractor. This right is not without limitation, however, because the courts will protect the rights of a defaulting contractor, as well as those of the party against whom he has defaulted. These limitations stem from the rule that an injured party has the duty to mitigate his or her damages. It has been held that these considerations require that the government establish that the repurchase was made within a reasonable time, the repurchase price was reasonable, the one item on the reprocurement contract is similar to the item on the defaulted contract, and the government attempted to mitigate its damages.

The government is also entitled to damages caused by the breach of contract. These damages are designed to compensate the party against whom the default was committed for the costs occasioned thereby. The government's right to damages is not dependent on whether it has terminated a contract. Whether the contract is terminated or not, the contractor is liable for damages resulting from his default. And where the government loses its right to excess costs of repurchasing by delaying the repurchase, it still may recover common-law damages. This is so because the default clauses specifically provide that the specified rights and remedies are not exclusive and are in addition to other rights provided by the contract or law. However, it is up to the government to prove the extent of its damages, and it may recover only for actual damages. Thus if it has sustained no damages, there is no recovery against the contractor.

In addition to termination for default, the contracting officer also might resort to termination for convenience of the government. This clause gives the government the right to cancel a contract when this action is in the best interest of the government, notwithstanding the contractor's ability and readiness to perform. Also the default clause provides that an erroneous default termination is considered a termination for convenience. The real effect of the termination-for-convenience clause is to establish the measure of compensation the contractor may recover for the government's termination of the contract. In the absence of this contract right, the unilateral repudiation of a contract would be a breach of contract, in which the aggrieved party may recover expected or anticipated profits as damages. However, under the termination-for-convenience clause, the contractor recovers only costs and the profit earned on work actually accomplished and the latter only if he is in a profit position at time of termination.

The cumulative effect of the termination-for-convenience and the default clauses is to give the government extraordinary control over the performance of its contracts and establish by contract the measure of reimbursement to be given to contractors when it exercises these rights. This power becomes even more remarkable when coupled with the disputes clause of the contract, which establishes the contracting officer as the initial arbiter of any disputes arising under the contract and makes his decision final on questions of fact subject to an appeal to an appropriate board of contract appeals. More importantly, it requires the contractor to perform in accordance with the contracting officer's decision pending final decision of a dispute.

Handling Claims, Disputes, and Appeals

A whole range of clauses in a contract are specific about disagreements from which claims of one type or another can emerge, such as changes, suspension of work, differing site condition, termination for convenience, and default. In addition there are a limitless number of occasions in which the contractor may believe that she has a claim against the government. The contractor has a right, an obligation, to come forward with her claim whenever she feels that one exists. There is no intention on the part of the government that the contractor lose money on a contract or be forced into bankruptcy. Therefore while claims from the contractor should not be encouraged, the contractor should not feel that the agency is actively inhibiting her ability to make a claim where it is warranted.

The contracting officer should request the details upon which the contractor bases her claim. The claim must be fully supported by such facts as relevant documentation, opinions of experts, and the cost elements present. On receipt of the claim, the contracting officer should have the cost data audited.

After the claim is submitted, the negotiations between the contractor and the government can result in a contract modification, allowing some or all of the claim, or a final decision of the contracting officer from which the contractor can pursue further remedies under the disputes clause. The contracting officer must fully understand his rights, obligations, and authorities to settle claims submitted by the contractor and to document his decisions in supplemental agreements. In some jurisdictions, the dollar value of the claim might require review by higher management, but it is still the contracting officer's responsibility and legal right to amend the contract. The failure of this officer to settle at the lowest level when such a settlement is possible has a major effect on the cost of procurement: it causes the contractor to go through the disputes process, it involves reams of paper and the services of both government and private attorneys, and it involves the boards of appeals and possibly a court of claims. Failure to make the decision at the lowest level raises the decision ultimately to a level perhaps divorced from an understanding of the facts and the equities of the situation.

In any event, the contractor is entitled to the contracting officer's independent judgment in the matter under contention. A matter settled by mutual agreement of the contracting agency and the contractor is not legally viewed as a dispute. However, within a prescribed period, a contractor who objects to the judgment may appeal to higher authority.

Claims work both ways. A government claim can be made against a contractor. For example, the government can request a price reduction in a contract for such reasons as the changes clause, the termination for default clause, and many others. The government in this case determines the amount of money that it feels is due from the contractor and the basis for the claim. It presents its claim through the contracting officer and attempts to negotiate with the contractor. There will either be agreement to settle locally or a final decision by the contracting officer that will specify a certain amount of money that the government feels is due from the contractor.

At this point the contractor can accept the reduced price or obtain a final decision and go into dispute under the disputes clause. As in the claim by the contractor, the contracting officer can attempt to negotiate and arrive at a figure that is below that which the government originally claimed. The contracting officer must keep in mind the possible expense of litigation, the possibilities of prevailing before the board, and the time and expense to him and to the agency in preparing for the case.

The parties to a federal government contract dispute have a choice of forum in which to present a case. An appeal may be made to the comptroller general for settlement or adjustment in the GAO. A case may be taken to the federal district courts (this is seldom done). Normally a claim goes before a board of contract appeals or the court of claims.

Recent legislation has responded to some of the criticism of federal disputes procedure.[3] This legislation incorporated many of the recommendations of the Commission on Government Procurement. Under present federal law, if the contractor and the contracting officer cannot reach a mutual agreement on a claim, the Disputes Act requires that the contractor submit a claim in writing to the contracting officer for a formal decision. The act also provides that claims of the government against the contractor are subject to a formal decision by the contracting officer. The act imposes time limits on a contracting officer in making the decision. For claims of $50,000 or less, the contracting officer is required to render a decision within sixty days after receipt of a written request from the contractor that a decision be rendered within that period. The burden is on the contractor to request the expedited decision. If she does not request that the decision be rendered within sixty days, the contracting officer is required only to render a decision within a reasonable time.

For claims in excess of $50,000, the procedures are somewhat more formalized. In this case the contractor is required to certify that the claim is made in good faith, that the supporting data are accurate and complete to the best of her knowledge and belief, and that the amount requested accurately reflects the contract adjustment for which the contractor believes the government is liable. (The act provides for certain sanctions against a contractor who intentionally misrepresents the amount of the claim.) Within sixty days after receipt of a certified claim, the contracting officer must either issue a decision or notify the contractor of the time within which a decision will be issued. If the contracting officer fails to issue a decision within a reasonable time, the contractor may request the agency's board of contract appeals to establish a time frame within which the contracting officer must issue a decision. Failure to meet the deadline established by the board may be deemed a decision denying a claim, thus giving the contractor the right to file an appeal with the board of contract appeals or to initiate a suit in the court of claims. When the contracting officer issues his decision, he must set forth in writing the reasons for the decision. In addition the written decision must advise the contractor of the right to appeal.

Under the provisions of the act, a contractor has a choice of actions regarding an unfavorable decision from the contracting officer. She may appeal the decision to the agency board of contract appeals or bring action directly in the court of claims. If she decides to appeal to the board of contract appeals, she must do so within ninety days after receipt of the contracting officer's final decision.

Depending on the size of the claim, the contractor may request that the appeal be handled before the board in one of three ways.

1. Small claims procedures. If the amount in dispute is $10,000 or less, the contractor may request that the claim be handled through an expedited procedure. The act requires each agency board to establish a procedure that provides for simplified rules to facilitate the decision. The appeal may be decided by a single board member, with such concurrences as may be provided by rule or regulation. Appeals under this procedure must be resolved whenever possible within 120 days from the date on which the contractor elects to use the procedure. If the contractor uses the small claims procedure, she will be waiving her right to appeal further should the decision be unfavorable. The act provides that a decision against the government or the contractor reached under this procedure shall be final and conclusive and shall not be set aside except in cases of fraud.

2. Accelerated procedures for claims for $50,000 or less. In addition

to the small claims procedure, the act requires each board to establish procedures for the accelerated disposition of any appeal from a decision of a contracting officer where the amount in dispute is $50,000 or less. The act provides that the decision to use this accelerated procedure shall also be at the sole election of the contractor. Agency boards are required to render their decision, whenever possible, within 180 days from the date the contractor elects to utilize such procedure. Under this procedure, the contractor preserves all of the appeal rights that she would have under the regular board procedures.

3. Regular board procedures. If the contractor's claim exceeds $50,000, it will be subject to a full board hearing in accordance with the formal procedural requirements established by each board of contract appeals. Contractors with claims of less than $50,000 may also have their claims handled through these more formal procedures if they so desire.

The act specifically gives the boards of contract appeals the authority to grant any relief that would be available to a litigant in the court of claims. With the exception of those cases handled under the small claims procedure, however, the board's decision can be appealed by either party to the court of claims.

The decision of an agency board of contract appeals is final unless appealed by either the contractor or the government within 120 days from the receipt of the board's decision. The act places one limitation on the agency with regard to an appeal to the court of claims: The agency head is required to obtain the prior approval of the attorney general before appealing the agency's board decision to the court of claims.

When a board's decision is appealed to the court of claims, the case is not processed de novo. The act provides that the decision of the board on any question of fact shall be final and conclusive and shall not be set aside unless the decision is fraudulent, arbitrary, capricious, or so grossly erroneous as to imply bad faith, or if such decision is not supported by substantial evidence. The court of claims has, however, been given the authority to take additional evidence or to remand the case to the agency board for further evidentiary hearings.

Instead of appealing a contracting officer's final decision to the agency's board of contract appeals, contractors may go directly to the court of claims for relief. If the contractor decides on this avenue she must file the claim with the court within twelve months from the date of receipt of the decision of the contracting officer. Claims submitted directly to the court of claims are processed de novo, a factor that may influence the contractor's decision concerning the forum she selects in pursuing her claim since appeals of board of contract appeals decisions to the court of claims are not processed de novo. Thus the only way a contractor can ensure full judicial treatment of her claim is to go directly to the court of claims. The act gives the agency boards of contract appeals the power to require, by subpoena, the attendance of witness, and production of books and papers, for the taking of testimony or evidence by deposition or in the hearing of an appeal by the agency board. Since the decisions of the boards of contract appeals on questions of fact are usually final, this provision of the act provides equitable treatment to the parties to the dispute because it gives the board the ability to obtain a full record on the matter.

For claims in excess of $50,000, the contractor must certify that the claim is made in good faith, that supporting data are accurate and complete to the best of her knowledge and belief, and that the amount requested accurately reflects the contract adjustment for which she believes the government is liable. The act provides for certain sanctions against a contractor who submits a claim that does not meet those standards. That section provides: "If a contractor is unable to support any part of his claim, and it is determined that such inability is attributable to misrepresentation of fact or fraud on the part of the contractor, he shall be liable to the government for an amount equal to such unsupported part of his claim in addition to all costs to the government attributable to the cost of reviewing said part of his claim." The act gives the government six years to establish liability under this section.

Administering Payment Provisions

A major activity in contract administration is the administering of payment provisions. Although the initial negotiations and contract award establish the basis for payment, it is up to the contract administrator to follow through and make certain that the contractor is paid only what she is entitled to receive. If this only involved the payment of a previously established firm-fixed price, the task of the contract administrator would be somewhat simple. However, many of the types of contracts in use today require consideration of the cost of performance in order to determine the price. The different payment provisions can be illustrated by examining three major types of contracts involved in government contracting: firm-fixed-price contract, the fixed-price incentive or redeterminable contract, and the cost-reimbursement contract.

Under firm-fixed-price contracts, the price is established at the time of award of negotiation, and the contract administrator will not be involved in any price negotiation or determination efforts except to the extent that the contract provides for escalation. Under this type of contract, the duties of the contract administrator are to see that the contractor has properly performed her part of the contract prior to making payment. This involves the performance of work according to the specifications and other terms of the contract. Thus under a fixed-price supply contract, delivery and acceptance will precede the payment of the contract price to the contractor.

Provision is made for progress payments; the contractor is paid "as the work progresses from time to time upon request of the contractor." The clause also provides that in order to be subject to progress payments, the cost must be reasonable, properly allocable, and consistent with generally accepted accounting principles and practices. In addition, the aggregate of progress payments under the clause is limited to a certain percentage of the total contract price. This provision prevents the contractor from recovering any amounts in excess of the contract price when she is in a loss situation. Progress payments are considered a method of financing the contractor in supply contracts, and so the clause provides that the contractor must repay the government for progress payments made out of the contract price. This procedure, called liquidation, is ordinarily accomplished by applying the same percentage as authorized for progress payments to the price of the articles delivered. If, for example, progress payments are stipulated at 80 percent of costs incurred, the government will apply the same percentage in liquidation of the payments already made through progress payments. Since progress payments represent a method of financing the contractor, any payments made under the progress-payments clauses will not be considered as an acceptance of the work of the contractor by the government.

Most of the principles relating to the payment of contractors under firm fixed price contracts apply to fixed-price incentive and redeterminable contracts (hereafter referred to as redeterminable contracts). The important difference is that in redeterminable contracts, the initial price is not firm; it is to be redetermined on the basis of cost incurred in the performance of the contract. The most common redeterminable contract is the fixed-price-incentive contract where a target cost, a target profit, and a target price are initially negotiated into the contract, as are a ceiling price and a sharing formula. The ceiling price is a maximum limitation on the price of the contract. The sharing formula usually provides that the contractor will be paid a cost of performance of the contract plus a target profit, less a stipulated percentage of any amounts the cost of performance exceeds the target cost. In the event the cost of performance is less than the target cost, the sharing formula provides that a stipulated percentage of the difference will be added to the contract price. This procedure is set forth in an incentive-price revision clause, which is incorporated in the contract.

The most commonly used clause provides that within a certain period of time after completion of work under the contract, the contractor is required to submit a statement of the costs incurred in the performance. On the basis of this statement, the contractor and the contracting officer attempt to agree upon a final negotiated cost of the contract. The incentive formula is then applied to the final negotiated cost to determine whether the contractor has earned or lost profit. The consideration of cost in determining the final prices under the incentive contract is of utmost importance. It would, therefore, appear that prior to final redetermination, the contract has the attributes of a cost-reimbursement contract. After final redetermination, the prices are fixed, and the contract is similar to that of a firm fixed price.

Under the cost-reimbursement contract, the contractor is reimbursed for expenditures that are allowable under the contract and, if stipulated in the contract, either a fixed or incentive fee. In either event, the administration of this type of contract requires constant attention. Since the government agrees to reimburse the contractor for this expenditure, it is natural for the government to be concerned with the manner of and reasons for a contractor's costs incurred. Even so, it is the contract that governs, and both the government and contractor's rights are to be determined in accordance with it. Payment is covered in a clause regarding allowable cost, fixed fee, and payment. Under this clause, the payment of the contractor is not discretionary; the contracting officer shall pay the contractor to the extent that the costs are allowable. Payment of the fixed fee is made in increments as the work progresses. Out of the fee due to the contractor, the government withholds a portion until the completion of all of the work under the contract.

One of the problems encountered with payment on all types of contracts is in determining the proper party to be paid. Both fixed-price and cost-reimbursement contracts contain an assignment of claims clause that permits the contractor to assign his right to payment to a bank, trust company, or other financing institution. Some contracts contain requirements for performance bonds and payment bonds. When there are conflicting claims for the money due under the contract, the contracting officer must be careful to avoid taking any action that would change the government's position as simply a stakeholder in the dispute between the surety and the assignee. Legal assistance should be obtained when making any decision in this area.

Final payment of government contracts is important not only because it completes the obligations of the government under the contract but because it serves to cut off certain of the potential remedies of the contractor under the contract. For example, the contractor has no right to an equitable adjustment under the changes clause unless she has made a claim or given notice of the claim prior to final payment. Final payment under the various types of contracts differs as to the formalities and methods by which it is accomplished. To draw a parallel, under the payment provisions in construction contracts, the contractor and his assignee, if any, are required to give a release of all claims against the government arising out of the contract. The clause does provide that if there are unsettled claims, they may be excepted for the release. The boards have repeatedly held that the contractor loses any right to recover claims that are not excepted from the release.

In comparison under a firm-fixed-price supply contract, contractors are not generally required to sign a release of claims form. Typically the contractor submits his final voucher or invoice upon completion of the job, and the government, upon determining that the contract has been performed according to its terms, makes payment of all money due the contractor.

Evaluating Vendor Performance

Several elements of performance evaluation are present in public purchasing and materials management. The concern here is with building and using a record reflecting the historic effectiveness of individual contractors in meeting their contractual commitments.

The existence of such a record and the knowledge that it will be used in making future source selections puts the contractor on notice and perhaps stimulates him to make more rational commitments. It indicates that submission of a low-cost estimate, early-delivery proposal, and promise of high technical achievement may result in award of the current contract, but in the long run could prejudice his ability to obtain future government contracts. The contractor therefore must be constrained to be realistic and objective in pitting his capability against the proposal requirements and in estimating the costs of his performance under the contract. He should also be inspired to improve his managerial capability to ensure meeting his contractual obligations within the technical, schedule, and cost parameters established. He will be rewarded for doing so by being placed in a favorable position for selection as a source for future contracts.

If the contractor is to be rewarded or penalized on the basis of his performance, it is incumbent upon the government to ensure that the bases for evaluation are well defined and that a mutual understanding of intent and meaning is held by both the government and the contractor. The evaluations cannot be merely subjective, narrative assessments. The record must consist of succinct and objective data. A recent U.S. Air Force study suggests that data be gathered in four areas:

1. Administrative. A listing of the vendor, the contract number, dollar value, procuring agency, acquisition phase involved, brief description of work, names and telephone numbers of government project manager, PCO, and ACO, dates of contract, and type of contract.
2. Cost. Percentage over or under target and dollar amount (actual for completed and estimated at completion for active contracts). Number and dollar amounts of claims submitted and claims approved or disapproved.

3. Schedule. Months the contract has been delinquent/total contract months. Reasons for delinquencies. Changes made to original schedule and reasons.

4. Performance. Number of acceptances; numbers of major deficiencies and conditional acceptances. Numbers of deviations and waivers. Numbers of specifications and test plans/reports resubmitted for approval.[4]

The method and form in which this information is used can be standardized to a simple report for presentation to source selection authorities. The cost information reflects the number of contracts that met or were over or under target costs. Schedule information reflects total months of original contracts and the number of months delinquent and/or of schedule extension, and the performance portion reflects the quality of the products delivered by indicating the number of deviations or conditional acceptances on a percentage basis relative to the total items delivered. Dollar values would be totaled to show gross overrun or underrun for the total contracts charted. Where such a procedure is used, requests for proposals must clearly state the manner in which past performance will be considered as part of the criteria for contract award.

A less involved procedure, applicable to the more usual supply contract, entails making a monthly tabulation of the invoices from each supplier and the value of the supplier's materials that were rejected during the month.[5] This figure is then divided by the value of the materials shipped. The resulting percentage indicates the rate of rejection for the period. Comparison of rates among competing suppliers or against an average of the rejection rates shows which suppliers are achieving the desired level of quality.

Along with the rating of quality performance, delivery and service performance can be rated by making a continuing tabulation for each supplier covering the following points:

1. Excellent. Meets delivery dates without expediting.
2. Good. Usually meets shipping dates without substantial follow-up.
3. Fair. Shipments sometimes late, substantial amount of follow-up required.
4. Unsatisfactory. Shipments usually late, delivery promises seldom met, constant expediting required.

In addition, the buyer records an opinion of the technical help the supplier is able to furnish, the willingness to furnish such help, and the general attitude in meeting any situation that may arise.

Notes

1. The material that follows incorporates and integrates instructional matter developed by the U.S. General Services Administration, Acquisition Training Facility, and used in their course in government contract administration (supply contracts). Also incorporated here is instructional matter developed by the U.S. Office of Personnel Management, Workforce Effectiveness and Development Group, Management Science Training Center.

2. The standard international reference on detailed methods of inspection, sampling plans, and statistical methods is Joseph M. Juran, ed., *Quality Control Handbook* (New York: McGraw-Hill, 1974, 3d ed.). See also Juran and Frank M. Gryna, Jr., *Quality Planning Analysis* (New York: McGraw-Hil, 1970), which references the *Handbook*. The most recent publication is Dale H. Besterfield, *Quality Control: A Practical Approach* (Englewood Cliffs, N.J.: Prentice-Hall, 1979). Besterfield includes a chapter on computer uses in inspection and quality control.

3. Public Law 95-563 (Contract Dispute Act of 1978).

4. From a presentation by Michael A. Nassr, Colonel, USAF, Air Force Systems Command, Proceedings of Seventh Annual Acquisition Research Symposium, 31 May 1978, at Hershey, Pennsylvania.

5. Adopted from Wilbur B. England and Michiel R. Leenders, *Purchasing and Materials Management*, 6th ed. (Homewood, Ill.: Richard D. Irwin, 1975), pp. 442-443.

13 Physical-Distribution Activities

The physical-distribution subsystem embraces the activities that take place between the point of production and the point of use of an item of material. The item is moved, received, stored, perhaps packaged or repackaged, and issued or disposed of. The procedures relate closely to those for inventory management and control.

Involved in physical distribution are a sequence of procedures for transporting and receiving of income shipments, warehousing and location control, packaging and preserving, order filling from stock, and disposing of excess and surplus. With the disposition of surplus, the purchasing and materials-management sequence is completed.

Much of the subject matter of this chapter is treated in the literature under the subject of logistics. For detail not included here the reader is referred to standard references in the field.[1]

Overview of Physical Distribution

The distribution subsystem exists for one purpose: the effective movement of materials from producer to user.[2] The movement of materials must be done economically and in as nearly a straight line as possible, using a minimum number of stops from source to destination. Distribution systems consist of a series of echelons of supply, which extend through a depot system and subsidiary storage points to the ultimate consumer in the field. To be efficient, the subsystem must be responsive to the customer, have the ability to react rapidly in periods of emergency, be resistant to disruption in periods of disorder, and be economical to operate.

Once requirements have been determined and materials have been procured, they enter the distribution subsystem and are the responsibility of the system until they have been issued to the ultimate user. During this period of responsibility, certain basic activities must be performed.

The process of accepting materials into the system entails inspection for quality and conformity to specifications. Frequently technical inspection is performed in the contractor's plant; in this case, a physical check of quality and condition to detect damage in shipment must be made at the initial destination. Bills of lading or waybills are made out for payment of the transportation agent. Finally the quantities of supplies actually accepted must be entered on control records for future issue, the supplies dispatched to the proper storage location or delivered directly to the ultimate consumer, and the transactions entered in appropriate financial records.

Holding and caring for supplies before they are issued is another common distribution activity. Supply managers determine the proper storage location by considering many factors: the length of time items may be expected to stay in storage, the sources of anticipated demand, the amount of space available, the expected frequency of issue, and the anticipated size of issue. Some commodities require preservation or packaging before they are put in storage; others require refrigeration, humidity and temperature control, or periodic inspection and rotation to prevent deterioration while in storage. An adequate system for locating stocks must be established and maintained so that items can be found and issued quickly. Materials-handling equipment is used to promote effective, economical storage operations.

All systems have procedures for formally releasing supplies to using activities or to another echelon in the distribution system. The general procedure is for a unit or installation requiring supplies to submit a request using standard ordering and issue procedures. Requests for major items and components are usually based on established tables of allowances or allowance lists, which in themselves constitute a control on the type and number of items that may be issued. For repair parts, consumables, and other common items of supply, the user must "pay" for the stocks requisitioned; therefore he cites an allotment of consumer funds on the request to the supplier. If the request is within the authorized allowance, there are no other restrictions and funds are properly cited, the requested quantities are issued from available inventories. If the quantities requested are not available, the request may be back ordered against a quantity due in from contract or from another supply source, immediate procurement may be initiated, or the request may be passed to another supply unit that can fill the need. For major items, supply response may involve overhaul of available assets in unserviceable condition or assembly of the requested item from components held in stock.

At times operating conditions are such that requiring activities cannot follow normal requisition procedures, and some means of automatic supply must be established. The function itself is basically unchanged; the difference is that a directive from higher authority, instead of the request from the user, then constitutes the authority for issue.

A significant portion of procurement dollars and supply operational costs go for preservation, packaging, packing, unitizing loads, blocking, and bracing. Materials are often exposed to varying temperatures, rain, and heavy humidity and must be properly protected. The cost of packaging is secondary to the legitimate need for protection, but adequate levels of protection and safe delivery to required destinations in a serviceable condition must be assured at the lowest reasonable cost. Different modes of transportation and different destinations often dictate special packing and packaging specifications. Management must ensure that supplies are properly packed and packaged without being overpacked. This applies to packing for shipment, as well as for protection of items retained in warehouse storage.

Records must be maintained to ensure that adequate stocks are available to fill customer requirements. Stock levels may be stated quantitatively, but more often they are stated in days of supply. Considerations that influence the levels of stocks to be maintained in the distribution system include time required to obtain replenishment, shipping time, reserves, essentiality of units or equipment supported, perishability of the commodity, availability of storage facilities, and predictability of requirements.

Records of receipts and issues are maintained to keep a running balance of quantities in store. These inventory records serve as the basis for reorder or replenishment decisions. Frequently they also serve as the basis for financial control of inventories.

It is neither effective nor economical to stock all authorized items at all levels of the system. Excessive inventories increase operating costs and require an unnecessarily high inventory investment. Not all types of items actually move through the entire system. Some can best be obtained by procurement or fabrication at local activities; others that are centrally stocked because of special characterisics or other requirements are not carried at all levels of the distribution system. Overdispersion of available stocks can create a situation in which some activities could not provide needed items, while others would have excesses of the same items. This situation could occur even though total supply were in balance with demand.

Most record keeping is accomplished through the use of computer systems. The accountable balance file for each inventory-control point or supply-distribution activity provides intricate record-keeping possibilities. The computerized balance file records all appropriate catalog information for each item managed, and stocks on hand are recorded by account and condition (that is, by the various ownership or reserved purposes for which portions of the inventory are held and the condition or issuability of the stocks on hand). Presumably most of the inventory on hand is serviceable, issuable, and available for general issue, but it is likely that some percentage of any item or reparable component will show some unserviceable or suspended balances and some portion of the available stocks will be reserved for planned supply programs or specific customer requirements. All of these programs and their associated records are maintained as part of the inventory process. Other subsidiary computer records carry transaction histories for each item to help maintain accurate inventory records and requisition history to show that proper and complete action has been taken on each request received. All of these records become the basis for other activities, such as requirements computations and supply performance evaluations.

Incoming Transportation and Receiving

The means of incoming transportation selected must be that which meets agency requirements satisfactorily at the lowest overall cost from point of origin to the final destination. A buyer has the right at any time to suggest the carrier and routing of an incoming shipment and to specify the carrier and routing for a shipment that has been purchased FOB point of origin. The buyer must take advantage of the differences that exist between the rates charged for different modes of transportation and of the differences in services provided.

Where movement is entirely by for-hire carriers, transportation activity consists of purchasing transportation services and movement control. If a jurisdiction owns and operates its own transportation equipment, the transportation unit administers and schedules that equipment. In both cases the objective is to provide a service that meets the requirements of the physical-distribution subsystem relating to speed or service, size of order to be shipped, and assignment of the specific warehouse to make the shipment. It is the responsibility of the transportation activity to identify the appropriate freight classification, obtain the lowest rate for a given movement consistent with service requirements, schedule the use of transportation facilities and equipment, document the shipment, trace and expedite shipments as necessary, audit freight bills, and file claims in instances of loss or damage.

Freight classification of materials and products is based on a relative percentage index of 100. As a general rule, the higher the class rating, the higher the freight rate of the material or product being transported. But numerous items do not fit clearly into a single classification, and therefore interpretation and judgment often play a significant role in the assignment of a classification number to a given item. Thus through careful attention to item descriptions, it is often possible for alert purchasers to influence the reclassification of many materials and products into lower-rated classes.

Motor and rail carriers have separate classification systems. The motor carrier system's is the *National Motor Freight Classification*, and rail classifications are published in the *Uniform Freight Classification*. The motor classification has twenty-three classes of freight; the rail thirty-one. In addition, individual groups of carriers in local or regional areas publish classification listings. A request for reclassification is made in writing to the appropriate classification board. The board reviews the proposal with respect to minimum weights, commodity descriptions, packaging requirements, and general rules and regulations. All changes other than corrections require public hearings, where interested parties are provided an opportunity to be heard. After the proposal is accepted or rejected, methods of appeal are provided.

Materials management must take an active interest in freight classification. Neglect of this activity leads to substantial unnecessary expense.

Freight rates are established and published for each method of movement: rail, air, motor, pipeline, parcel post, United Parcel, and the several freight forwarders. The transportation unit maintains a library of rates in effect, which must be kept up to date. For any given shipment it is the responsibility of the transportation unit to obtain the lowest possible rate consistent with delivery requirements.

Another major responsibility is facility and equipment scheduling. A common problem is the building up of carrier equipment waiting to be loaded or unloaded at a shipper's dock. All carriers have special charges for equipment delay beyond normal times allowed. Demurrage charges are penalties assessed by a carrier for holding cars or trucks beyond a designated free period. In order to reduce demurrage charges, an agency may wish to enter an average demurrage agreement with a carrier whereby the receiver is given one demurrage credit for each car or truck released within an established free period. The receiver is also assessed one demurrage debit for each car or truck held beyond the allowable free period. The agency is then billed monthly for the debits in excess of its credits.

Documentation of transportation services consists primarily of the bill of lading and the freight bill. The bill of lading is the basic document used in the purchase of transportation; it is also the means by which title to the material is transferred upon delivery. Because it serves as a receipt for goods shipped, accurate description and count are essential. In case of loss or damage, the bill of lading provides evidence for claims resulting from inferior carrier performance. It also specifies the terms and conditions under which the carrier is liable and includes all possible causes of loss or damage except those defined as acts of God.

A negotiable bill of lading is also a credit instrument. It provides that delivery shall not be made unless the original bill of lading is surrendered. The seller sends the bill of lading to a third party, usually a bank or credit institution. Upon payment of the invoice, the credit institution releases the bill of lading to the buyer, who presents it to the carrier, who releases the goods.

The freight bill, derived from the bill of lading is the carrier's method of charging for transportation services. It may be either prepaid—paid for by the vendor prior to transportation performance—or collect—paid for by the buyer, usually within a tightly prescribed time period.

Expediting and tracing of purchasing actions are also significant activities in transportation management. The transportation network is vast, and shipments do become delayed or go astray. When this happens, the intended recipient of a shipment notifies the vendor, who initiates the tracing or expediting action with the carrier.

Freight classifying, rating, and billing is a highly complicated affair, so freight bills are routinely audited to verify their accuracy. Auditing ensures that the goods shipped were properly classified, that the proper rates were applied, and that the proper rate calculations were made. The purchaser must audit freight bills and file claims for overcharges. Auditing may be done internally or externally. Specialized freight-auditing companies exist whose personnel are assigned to work with specific commodity groupings. Payment for an external audit is usually based upon the rate of recovery of the overcharges in the original payment.

Two types of claims might arise in transportation activities: those of loss or damage and those of overcharging. Receiving-room personnel must be aware of the proper procedure for handling incoming shipments. When there is visible loss or damage or shortage, the consignee must make appropriate notation on the delivering carrier's freight bill, confirmed by the driver's signature, and the vendor must be notified immediately in writing.

Sometimes the loss or damage is not apparent until the item is unpacked; this is called concealed loss or damage. The contents may have been damaged in transit even though the outside carton does not indicate rough handling. When this is discovered, the consignee must stop further unpacking and save all packing materials for the carrier's inspection. It then becomes the vendor's responsibility to investigate, request a concealed-damage inspection report, file a claim either with the originating or delivering carrier, and promptly provide the purchaser with a replacement for the lost or damaged items.

All of the efforts of purchasing personnel are wasted if haphazard receiving procedures and methods result in products being delivered and used that do not meet specifications. As a physical-distribution activity, receiving inspection would be responsible for determining the quality of materials, parts, or assemblies purchased from vendors; items sent outside for maintenance, rework, or overhaul and being returned to the inventory; items that may have been drawn from stock but were not used and are being returned to inventory; and items that have been previously accepted but because of shelf life or engineering considerations must be withdrawn from stock and reinspected. Uniform and consistent inspection procedures must apply in all four instances.

Warehousing and Location Control

Warehousing basically involves two functions: movement and storage. The relationship of the functions can be visualized from this description of the

U.S. Air Force's warehouse for small items at Kelly Air Force Base in Texas. The warehouse covers more than eleven acres and stocks approximately 275,000 items, such as nuts, bolts, transistors, resistors, and small motors and pumps, which individually weigh no more than fifty pounds. Contained in the warehouse are 350,000 low-structured shelves divided into eighty-two work stations. A major feature of the warehouse is a two-level storage arrangement and two highly mechanized materials-handling systems. Serving the lower level is a below-the-floor, motor-driven, chain system, which pulls 54 × 40 inch flat carts. On the mezzanine level, a belt-driven roller system moves 30 × 18 inch trays swiftly to their destinations. Both the carts and trays can be programmed to divert automatically onto a siding upon reaching the designated work station. This warehouse handles 30,000 incoming shipments and 70,000 outgoing shipments or issues per month.

A warehouse is a facility providing for the bulk and bin storage of supplies and equipment pending issuance to using activities. It includes such space as required for the receipt and shipment, preservation and packaging, and handling and storage of supplies and equipment, and warehouse office space required to support these functions. It is lighted, heated, and air-conditioned and it might be humidity controlled.

Open storage sheds are used to store supplies and equipment that are not authorized for open storage and do not need closed warehouse space but require covered protection from the weather because of the nature of the materials or the manner in which they are packed.

Open storage is often used to accommodate heavy equipment and items of supply that are packaged to withstand the elements. In order to operate materials-handling equipment in the movement of these materials, paving or some other suitable form of improvement of the area is required. Security fencing and lighting would also be necessary.

Incoming material is inspected and accounted for in a receiving area. After acceptance by the inspector, the items are placed on pallets or in tote boxes or trays. By forklift or conveyor, the container is moved to the work station responsible for the class of supply involved. At the work station, outgoing orders on hand are filled, and items not immediately needed are routed to storage location. Subsequently outgoing movement occurs in which items needed to fill requisitions are picked from stock, assembled, and packed for shipment or issue. A shipping unit consolidates item and turns the loads over to outgoing carriers.

The storage function holds and cares for the inventory pending disposition. The property in storage must be protected from deterioration, damage, and theft, and it must be locatable.

Each item in storage has a location address. The entire storage facility is laid out in blocks similar to city blocks; each aisle is numbered, and each bin row is identified horizontally and vertically. In a large installation the thousands of location addresses are recorded in a computer. An item might be recorded as stored at E22 8 C3 to indicate warehouse E, bay 22, aisle 8, bin column C, shelf 3.

Deterioration of property in storage is a problem in cases where the item, because of physical or chemical properties, could become unusable. An example is a magnetized instrument or a device incorporating a delicate membrane made of neoprene and subject to rot. Such items are said to have shelf life, so management must make provision for the minimizing of expiration of material in storage by issuing first those stocks with the earliest expiration date plus necessary surveillance to ensure that items are in a ready-for-issue condition in accordance with applicable service-ability standards or other appropriate technical documentation.

Fire is also a problem. Local codes should be consulted before laying out a storage area. Where the local fire code is silent on the matter, the following fire prevention and protection standards should be used:

1. Floor and aisle area. Maximum permissible floor area between fire walls, or between fire walls and exterior walls: 40,000 square feet. Main transportation aisles, minimum width: 10 feet. Fire aisles, minimum width: 4 feet.
2. Height of stowage. Maximum height of stowage; at least 18 inches below sprinkler heads, trusses, pipes or fixtures, but not to exceed 20 feet.
3. Area of stowage. Maximum area of stowage pile: High-combustibility materials: 2,000 square feet. Medium-combustibility materials: 4,000 square feet. Low-combustibility materials: 6,000 square feet. Noncombustible materials: Unlimited.
4. Separation between buildings. Minimum separation between warehouse buildings: 80 feet.

Theft is a major problem. Much of it is employee pilferage. The commonwealth of Kentucky's *Purchasing Notes* includes the following precautions and suggestions:

1. Reduce temptation by isolating and storing "desirable" items in a separate location under tight security.
2. Maintain a visual perpetual inventory record of their receipt and usage.
3. Take periodic "spot-check" physical inventory of them. Investigate book and physical variances immediately. Make it known that an investigation is being conducted.
4. Review the background of an employee before you assign him a position of trust to safeguard supplies.
5. Set an example of honesty, yourself, as a department head.
6. Take tactful decisive action when you have definite proof.[3]

Packaging and Preserving

The packaging of purchased items is covered in their specifications, which note the processes and procedures used to protect materials from deterioration and/or damage. This includes cleaning, drying, preserving, packing, marking, and unitization. Packaging specification should be coordinated with industry groups, standardization organizations, and trade associations. Maximum consideration should be afforded recommendations of these industry segments for the use of commercially available materials or processes.

Since the way in which material is packaged influences the risk involved in transportation, it is often possible to reclassify materials into a lower class as a result of changing packaging specifications. Thus the packaging of all materials should be reviewed in order to determine whether the use of boxes, skids, crates, or banding would result in the material being assigned to a lower freight classification and therefore a lower freight rate. However, there can be no compromise with safety requirements in packaging. Safety requirements must be in compliance with the Occupational Safety and Health Act and local safety and health laws and ordinances.

Packaging policies and procedures should require that:

1. All material be afforded the packaging required to prevent damage and deterioration and to ensure efficiency in handling at the lowest overall cost.
2. Packaging requirements be prescribed in standards, specifications, and similar documents.
3. Marking be uniformly developed and applied and held to the minimum necessary to facilitate safe handling and efficient receipt, storage, and shipment.
4. Unitized loads be used where they will result in overall economy or when specifically required by the requisitioning activity. The packaging requirement for unitization should be made a part of procurement actions where practicable and economical.
5. Supplemental protection provided by containers be considered in determining whether protective measures that would otherwise be taken should be reduced or eliminated for material shipped or stored therein; however, the protection required for material in transit to a consolidation point or after removal from containers will not be compromised.
6. Criteria be established for the development of modular pack sizes and weights compatible with systems for mechanized materials handling, storage, and shipment.
7. Automated equipment be installed to facilitate packaging operations if the use of such equipment can be supported by cost-benefit analyses.

8. Environmental pollution-preventive measures be incorporated into standards, specifications, and other instructions covering materials and processes used in packaging; also the design and selection of packaging systems and materials shall include consideration of reuse, biodegradability, and recycling when appropriate to promote environmental quality and the conservation of resources.

9. Maximum reuse be made of packaging material to the extent it is economically feasible.

10. Maximum use be made of commercial packaging.

Packaging technology is one of the most rapidly changing aspects of materials management. New materials and new processes are constantly being introduced. Costs of packaging materials are changing dramatically. This is an area in which management must constantly review and update specifications and practices.

Order Filling from Stock

The economics of purchasing and supply dictate that certain items be provided from stock in inventory established for that purpose. When this is the case, orders are received at the warehouse and dispatched to work stations, where items are picked, assembled, and issued to the requisitioning activity.

The using activity's order, often called a supply requisition or an issue slip, for a routine supply action would be submitted in accordance with a schedule. The purpose of the schedule, published by the purchasing and materials manager, would be to level the issue work load throughout the year and to discourage uncoordinated and reptitive requests for the same item. Emergency requests can be submitted at any time. The ordering schedule lists for each class of supply the frequency and the timing of requisitioning. The prescribed frequency could be biweekly, monthly, quarterly, triannual, semiannual, or even annual. The timing could specify, for example, that quarterly requisitions be received in the stock control unit on the tenth of January, April, July, and October or that biweekly requisitions be received on alternate Tuesdays.

Very few large agencies today depend upon manual methods of order processing. Federal agencies use what are known as the federal standard requisitioning and issue procedures (FEDSTRIP). FEDSTRIP is applicable to all civil agencies, including their contractors, and is mandatory except where GSA has approved an agency request for a deviation or waiver or has prescribed other requisitioning procedures for certain supply items. FEDSTRIP is compatible with the military standard requisitioning and issue procedures (MILSTRIP) of the Department of Defense. Civil agencies authorized to requisition from military sources, and the military services requisitioning from GSA, follow comparable procedures.

The two procedures form the basis for the processing of agency requisitions by the use of automatic data-processing equipment and involve the use of various standard forms. Larger state and local jurisdictions have established similar systems. The procedures provide for processing both single and multiline manually or machine-prepared requisitions or proposed returns of items, requesting and receiving status information on requisitions in process, filling orders under a standard priority system, and furnishing other requested standard information.

FEDSTRIP operates through the use of codes to represent standard information. Once the coding structure is understood, the system itself is relatively easy to follow. The codes used in the FEDSTRIP system are identified and described in a handbook.[4]

FEDSTRIP is designed to communicate requisitions and their follow-on transactions and documents in any of the following methods: data transceiver; other electrical media such as administrative message, TWX, dispatch, or teletypewriter (whichever media is used, the message must be prepared in the format described); telephone (when time, distance, or economy are considerations); or airmail, regular mail, or courier. The originator of the requisition selects the medium of communications by using the proper media and status code.

The procedure allows for clear-language remarks in circumstances not covered by the code. The entering of remarks can cause delays in supplying materials because each document containing such data must be withdrawn from routine processing, reviewed for the exception, and continued in process after a decision has been made. The procedure also accommodates requests for supply assistance. Requests for earlier than normal shipping dates or for special status may be made by message, letter, or telephone. Responses to such requests are made in the medium in which received or by interpreted status cards. Copies of each written response are provided to all designated recipient activities cited in the request. Responses to telephone requests are accomplished in the manner agreed to during the conversation.

Disposing of Excess and Surplus

The problem of determining what portion of inventory can be economically retained and what should be declared excess belongs to the inventory control points. Basically excesses are generated through two conditions. The first is obsolescence, or the decrease in utility of inventory assets due to technological changes that have brought about development of a new item or end equipment. Largely this management problem starts with the phaseout of systems or other major end items. The item manager has to decide when to classify as excess the older equipment and the associated parts held in inventory to support repair and overhaul of the parent item. Her decisions differ for parts that are peculiar to the end item being replaced from those in common use with other end items. Each situation must be analyzed on its own merits and the decision rendered accordingly. The manager has to consider disassembly of the unneeded equipment to reclaim required components for other systems still in use. She may want to cannibalize selected parts considered critical before disposal action. All of these considerations must be made on the basis of costs involved: the cost to reclaim parts through disassembly or cannibalization, the cost to retain inventory, or the cost of disposal through sales.

The second cause of excesses is long supply, or the quantity of an item in inventory that exceeds the retention limit for the item in question. What quantities should be retained for future use? What stocks exceed foreseeable needs and should be purged? Questions of this nature would pose only a minor problem if we could calculate precisely the anticipated life of parts, if our equipment were not subject to loss or destruction, and if errors in human judgment could be eliminated.

Excesses are determined by the inventory control points by using economic retention criteria, as part of the process of requirements determination. The retention formula shows at what point the cost of retaining an item is equal to the cost of disposing of it, with the knowledge that possible procurement might still be necessary at a later date. Retention costs include storage space, care and preservation, stock surveillance, deterioration in storage, and obsolescence. A retention quantity is identified, and balances above that quantity are declared excess.

Declaration of property as excess is a department or agency determination. The property exceeds the amount the agency can logically or economically retain. Later if no other agency within the government is found able to utilize the property, it is declared surplus to all known needs.

In ensuring the best possible use of property that has been declared excess, a sequence of determinations is made:

1. Can the property be reutilized by other activities within the department or agency?
2. Can the property be withdrawn and transferred to another unit of government?
3. Can the property be donated to an institution, perhaps a school, that has a valid need?
4. Can the property be sold and realize a return above the expenses of the sale?
5. Must the property be abandoned or destroyed?

Some property, because of its peculiar nature, its potential influence on public health, safety, security, or its adverse impact on private industry, must be disposed of in other than a normal fashion. Examples are explosives, including ammunition, dangerous gases, radioactive material, items containing precious metals, and strategic or critical materials. Each of these products should be disposed of in accordance with special instructions.

As a first choice, property declared excess by an individual agency should be utilized in its present configuration by other agencies of the government. Each materials-management activity must review available excess asset information to determine if requirements can be taken care of by stocks already in the system. Screening activities, before deciding whether to use or reject available excess assets, must consider the utility and desirability of excess property. They must take into account the cost of packaging, crating, handling, transportation, and rehabilitation to preclude uneconomical transfer when compared to the cost and lead time involved in new procurement.

Screening of excess property is an ideal application of automatic data-processing capability. The materials manager employs the data-processing system to receive, store, and screen asset and requirements data submitted by departments and agencies. Only after complete screening and issue or transfer of any required property will the residue become surplus and become available for donation for sale.

Upon completion of the utilization and donation cycles, the residue is sold. Sales and merchandising responsibility rests with the activity's property disposal office, which maintains property accountability, determines types of sales to be conducted, and handles merchandising responsibilities.

Methods of sale for surplus property are sealed bid, spot bid, negotiated sale, or auction.

A sealed-bid sale is a formal sale in which sealed bids are required on all items to be purchased. A guarantee deposit is required, and all bids must be submitted prior to advertised time of bid opening. Invitations to bid are sent to prospective bidders describing the property to be sold, where it may be inspected, place, conditions, and date of sale, and names of the person to see or contact for further information. The sealed bids are opened publicly at a stated time and place, and the award is made on the basis of the highest acceptable bid.

The spot-bid procedure is an assembled sale in which bidders place written offers in the bid box on site. Bids for each item are compared, and the high bid is announced for each successive item or lot before the next item is read, permitting bidders to submit a new bid on ensuring items at any point in the sale up to the time the offers on any particular item are compared. No guarantee deposit is required.

Negotiated sales are resorted to when no satisfactory bid is received by means of the sealed-bid or spot-bid procedure.

Auction sales are used when a substantial quantity and wide variety of materials with extensive commercial application are offered for sale. Catalogs that describe the property, give inspection and sales dates, and specify the conditions of sale are distributed well in advance.

Most jurisdiction specify that all individuals or organizations are entitled to purchase surplus property, except auctioneers and associates conducting sales, personnel employed by the selling agency and their families, and persons on the debarred bidders' list.

When property is not utilized, donated, or sold, it may be destroyed or abandoned. Techniques usually employed to destroy property are crushing, dumping, burying, and burning. No abandonment or destruction should take place that is considered detrimental or dangerous to public health and safety or that will harm local ecology. The file is then documented on the facts and methods used, including a certification by a disinterested party who witnessed the abandonment or destruction.

The federal government actively promotes the sale of its surplus personal property. Buying instructions and conditions are available on request.[5]

Notes

1. Two references are Donald J. Bowersox, *Logistical Management* (New York: Macmillan, 1974), and John J. Coyle and Edward J. Bardi, *The Management of Business Logistics* (St. Paul: West Publishing Company, 1976).

2. The material that follows incorporates and integrates instructional matter used by the Department of Nonresident Instruction, Industrial College of the Armed Forces, and published in *Supply Management* (Washington, D.C.: Department of Defense, Industrial College of the Armed Forces, 1974).

3. Commonwealth of Kentucky, *Purchasing Notes* (Frankfort, Ky., December 1975). p. 2.

4. U.S. General Services Administration, Federal Supply Service, *FEDSTRIP Operating Guide*, FPMR 101-26.2 (December 1977).

5. Write for: *How to Buy Surplus Personal Property*, Defense Property Disposal Service, Federal Center, Battle Creek, Michigan 49016, and *How State and Local Governments May Purchase Surplus Personal Property from the Federal Government*, General Services Administration, Property Management and Disposal Services, Washington, D.C. 20405.

14 Award and Administration of Grants

The award and administration of grants is included here for two reasons: a grant is made for the accomplishment of a public purpose, and funds granted to a state or local government often are subsequently used in purchasing goods or services relating to the public purpose involved. Because of the many similarities between grants and contracts and because the funds committee to a contract might well have had a grants origin, purchasing and materials managers should be familiar with the concept and process.

Public Law 95-224, appendix A, distinguishing federal grant and cooperative-agreement relationships from federal procurement relationships, was enacted in response to a recommendation by the Commission on Government Procurement:

> Enact legislation to (a) distinguish assistance relationships as a class from procurement relationships by restricting the term "contract" to procurement relationships and the terms "grant," "grant-in-aid," and "cooperative agreement" to assistance relationships, and (b) authorize the general use of instruments reflecting the foregoing types of relationships.[1]

The Report of the Commission discusses the considerations leading to this recommendation.

In the congressional hearings preceding enactment of the law that established the commission, it was recommended that grants be studied by the commission.[2] Because of the importance of federal grant activities and the uncertainty of their relationships to procurement, a limited review of federal grant-type assistance was conducted. The purpose was to gain an understanding of the significance, if any, of the interchangeable use of grants and contracts and of the extent to which procurement rules and regulations should apply to grant-type assistance.

As data on federal grant-type programs were examined by the commission, the focus was enlarged to include other questions. What is the nature of the grant-type assistance relationships that exist between the government and the recipient? Can and should grant-type assistance be distinguished from procurement? Can the confusion that seems to beset grant-type programs be reduced by giving relationship-based definitions for government-wide use to terms such as *contract*, *grant*, and *grant-in-aid*? These efforts led to the recognition of certain needs and the development of proposals to deal with them.

Federal grant-type activities are a vast and complex collection of assistance programs, functioning with little central guidance in a variety of ways that are often inconsistent even for similar programs or projects. This situation generates confusion, frustration, uncertainty, ineffectiveness, and waste. This disarray was traced to three basic causes: confusion of grant-type assistance relationships and transactions with procurement relationships and transactions, failure to recognize that there is more than one kind of grant-type relationships or transaction, and lack of government-wide guidance for federal grant-type relationships and transactions.

To deal with this confusion, the commission concluded that legislation was required to distinguish assistance from procurement by restricting the term *contract* to procurement relationships and by requiring the use of other instruments to implement assistance relationships; distinguish among grant-type relationships by introducing a new instrument (cooperative agreement) to accommodate the assistance relationships requiring substantial federal-nonfederal interaction during performance; override statutes that prevent the agencies from using the most appropriate instrument in each grant-type and procurement situation; and give the agencies new authority to use grant-type instruments in situations that call for them.

The commission concluded also that federal assistance programs require guidance on program implementation and a greater degree of standardization and consistency. The commission saw a need to provide basic assistance policies and procedures in the way that procurement regulations define basic procurement policies and procedures, and it suggested a framework for doing so. Such a body of policies and procedures is emerging; its base is OMB circular A-102, *Uniform Administrative Requirements for Grants-in-Aid to State and Local Governments*, and attachments A-O.[3]

Historical Development of the Use of Federal Grants

Since the early 1950s federal grants to state and local governments and to nongovernment recipients have grown significantly in both relative and absolute terms. Measured by the national income accounts, federal grants to state and local governments increased from $2.2 billion in 1950 to $82.9 billion in 1980. This growth resulted largely from the highway program (initiated in 1957) and the expansion of socially oriented programs administered by the departments of Health and Human Services (HHS), Labor, and Housing and Urban Development (HUD). HHS dominates federal grant programs; it funds the bulk of the totals to both governmental and nongovernmental grantees. The largest grant programs are those of the HHS Social and Rehabilitation Service for programs assisting the welfare of individuals, and the Department of Education, with its grants benefiting largely the educational systems of the country. The next largest program is in the Department of Transportation (DOT), with grants largely for the construction programs of the Federal Highway Administration. Other large grant programs are administered by the departments of Labor, Agriculture, and HUD. Grants to states and local units dominate in all of these programs. Also a considerable flow of state assistance to local governments has developed during this period. The Advisory Commission on Intergovernmental Relations (ACIR) estimates this to be as much as $50 billion a year. There could well be some double counting of the federal-to-state and the state-to-local grants.

Over these years the term *grant* has carried no single or precise meaning. Grant transactions have ranged from simple to complex. Grants are used by agencies such as HUD, the National Institutes of Health (NIH), and the National Science Foundation (NSF) for support of research and demonstration projects that require little or no agency involvement or direction. An agency such as the Urban Mass Transportation Administration (UMTA) of DOT, however, has exercised as much or more control over its grants, which it calls grant-contracts, than is customary in many procurements. The Office of Saline Water of the Department of the Interior has issued both grants and contracts for research but has treated them in a fashion that makes them relatively indistinguishable; its decision to use a grant or a contract has been based on the type of recipient rather than on the nature of the research or the agency's purpose in funding it.

The term *grant-in-aid* was originally used to describe grants to state and local governments, but now it is also used to describe grants to other types of recipients. It is usually associated with the large formula-type assistance programs of HHS and DOT. The Department of Agriculture (USDA) has used the term *formula grant* instead of *grant-in-aid*. The Public Health Service (PHS) Act authorizes NIH to award grants-in-aid in support of research and training projects but authorizes other PHS units to award grants in support of similar activities.

Grants and contracts have been used interchangeably (within and among agencies) for the same types of projects. For basic research, NIH and NSF have used grants; the Office of Naval Research (ONR) has used contracts; and the Atomic Energy Commission (AEC) has used a special research-support agreement, which is operationally similar to the ONR contract. The interchangeable use of grants and contracts has been most widespread when significant agency involvement occurs during performance of the assistance activity. In such cases, the older agencies, such as AEC and the National Aeronautics and Space Administration (NASA), have tended to use contracts, but the newer agencies, such as DOT, HUD, and EPA, have tended to write complicated grants; NSF and others have done both.

Some agencies admit that they used grants to avoid the requirements, such as advance payment justifications, that apply to contracts. Some agencies apparently have used more grants as the end of the fiscal year approached to obligate funds before the end of the year because grants are quicker to process than are contracts. Some program officials having responsibility for negotiating and administering grants, but not contracts, have tended to shift to contracts when they are busy in order to place the work-load elsewhere.

There has been wide variance in agency administrative (and presumably technical) involvement in similar kinds of projects. NSF has applied less administrative effort to its basic research grants than ONR has to its basic research contracts. The Department of Commerce has closely monitored construction under its grants-in-aid; HHS tried to do so but has not always succeeded; the Office of Economic Opportunity has stated that it does not have the staff to worry about construction under its grants-in-aid. UMTA procedures for administering research, development, and demonstration grants provided for very detailed government oversight. UMTA officials state that such procedures were necessary because the agency often deals with small municipalities and transit authorities that lack expertise in project management. HUD officials, however, report that they have imposed a minimum of administrative control on their model cities grants because the municipalities have their own rules and regulations for fiscal, procurement, and other matters. HUD and UMTA sometimes deal with the same municipalities.

The tendency of the executive branch either to overadminister or underadminister grant-type programs is generally recognized. A 1971 OMB report noted:

> Federal programs still are too often cluttered by unnecessary controls, regulations, clearances, reports and other impediments. . . . Wide variations in agency requirements, each of which may have some logic by itself, result in serious workloads on state and local governments with few or no national benefits which could not be realized under government-wide standardized procedures and requirements.[4]

The GAO and congressional committees have often noted inadequate administration of grant-type programs. Too much, too little, or the wrong kind of federal involvement has demonstrated uncertainty concerning the relationships of the government and the recipient in many of these programs over the years.

Grant-type assistance instruments in the past have revealed wide variances in agency requirements. The instruments used by some agencies have explicitly covered particular subjects; those used by other agencies in similar circumstances have not. A comparison of clauses ordinarily used in procurement contracts with those ordinarily used in grant-type instruments is revealing. It shows, first, that statutory authorizations for grant-type assistance have seldom required clauses such as Buy American, Walsh-Healey, Davis-Bacon, Convict Labor, Officials Not to Benefit, and Covenant against Contingent Fees in grant-type instruments. In the absence of government-wide guidance on the use of such clauses, some of the agencies have used such clauses in grant-type instruments even though their utility in most such instruments is doubtful. Second, some program authorizations have contained requirements such as Davis-Bacon, although the organic statutes did not apply the requirements to grant-type transactions. The resulting government-wide uncertainty could have been reduced if statements of the applicability of requirements had been written into the organic statutes and not the individual program statutes. Third, the clause requirements for grant-type instruments could have been, but not always, much simpler than those in procurement contracts. Government-wide guidance on procurement-type clause requirements for grant-type instruments would have been useful and relatively easy to provide.

The Emerging Federal-Assistance System

Learning from the experiences of the 1950s, 1960s, and early 1970s and following the recommendation of the Commission on Government Procurement, the federal government has begun the task of providing more consistent and appropriate guidance. Assistance is similar to procurement in some respects but significantly different in others. Assistance is intended to help a recipient organization carry out its functions or meet a particular need, the support or stimulation of which accords with prevailing public policy; or bring about social, administrative, or technological change by the provision of federal funds or other resources to help or encourage recipients to pursue recognized objectives.

Congress normally has preferred that the functions and objectives supported through assistance be carried out by state and local governments, educational institutions, other nonprofit organizations, and individuals rather than by or under the direct control of the federal government. One reason for this policy is the belief that the participation of organizations and individuals tends to ensure that the programs consider and serve local or public requirements, values, and needs in the most desirable and direct manner while accomplishing the broader purposes or objectives of Congress.

Congress, by statute, generally establishes basic program objectives, requirements, and standards and then appropriates funds to be awarded by the agencies under arrangements such as grant or grants-in-aid. Thus congressional intent and particular program purposes distinguish grant-type assistance from procurement.

In addition to the differences in basic intent and purpose between assistance, which is to support, stimulate, or aid another party's activities, and procurement, which is to purchase or buy goods and services primarily for government use, other differences help to distinguish assistance from procurement.

In many, if not most, grant-type assistance relationships, the government asks the recipient to define what it will do to achieve the objectives of the program. This often is accomplished through submission of a proposal or through a state or local plan. The recipient usually is responsible for deciding what it will do or how it will do something. In most procurements, the government specifies what it wants or how it wants something done as clearly and in as detailed a fashion as it can, thus assuming responsibility for specifying the project scope.

In assistance, price or estimated cost plays a small role in the selection of the recipient. Many assistance funds are awarded on a geographical or per-capita basis by formula; others are awarded according to need or capability. The reasons for selection of an assistance recipient are in large part a reflection or a function of the objectives of the program. Competition, if it exists, differs considerably from competition in the traditional procurement sense where proposers or bidders compete on the basis of price and other factors for one specific award and where basic regulations require, for example, that a procurement be awarded to the lowest responsive and responsible bidder. Under procurement, a determination must be made that an organization is responsible—that is, capable of performing. Assistance awards sometimes are made with knowledge that the recipient needs some form of aid or help in order to perform.

Under procurement, a basic buyer-seller relationship generally is expressed in a formal manner, with the rights and duties of the government and the performer defined in detail. The government, in the role of a buyer, has many rights, which it may choose to exercise. The government may control or direct the work through its specifications, changes, inspection, and acceptance procedures; and it can terminate for its convenience and, where appropriate, for default. In assistance, however, the government's role is not that of a purchaser but rather that of a patron or partner. For this reason, the relationship is more of a cooperative one; responsibilities for ensuring performance rest largely with the recipient or are shared with the government. Assistance relationships tend to be less formal and expressed in less detail. The differences in the roles of the parties in assistance and procurement shape the different understandings and expectations of the parties.

Procurement relationships can and do vary in the extent of formality, rights, and control. Cooperative and fairly informal arrangements can be found, especially in the procurement of research; nonetheless, procurement processes are colored by the basic purposes they serve—the obtaining of goods and services for government use. The procurement process is made up of policies, procedures, and requirements to serve that purpose. It involves requirements that seldom apply in assistance—for example, use of formal advertising or requests for proposals, price competition, competitive evaluation of bids or proposals for a specific project, competitive negotiation and selection of a contractor, and use of determinations, findings, and other justifications.

Section 8 of public law 95-224, appendix A, directed the OMB to undertake a study of alternative means of developing and administering federal assistance programs. A report to the Congress was required not later than 3 February 1980. Out of the report could emerge a truly comprehensive approach to the award and administration of grants and similar instruments.

**Procedures for Use by Grantees
in Effecting Procurement**

When a state or local government accepts a federal grant under one of the 1,075 existing assistance programs, it becomes bound by the attachments to OMB circular A-102. Attachment O, "Standards Governing State and Local Grantee Procurement," significantly affects public purchasing at the state and local level. Its conditions have been very controversial, so much so that the National Association of State Purchasing Officials (NASPO) at its annual conference in October 1978 passed a resolution finding that the then proposed regulation would erode grantee procurement programs and would prevent grantees from using their own procurement regulations reflecting applicable state and local laws, rules, and regulations.

Revision of attachment O is a continuing process. The 1 October 1979 version attempts to clarify the procurement responsibilities of the grantor and the grantee, conceding more authority to the grantee and limiting the federal agency grantor's power to impose agency-specific requirements. At the same time, the attachment sets norms of procurement management, which can be clearly identified as coming from the Model Procurement Code.

The 1979 revisions respond to much of the criticism generated by earlier versions. The methods of procurement are clearly distinguished: small purchases, formally advertised purchases, competitive negotiation, and noncompetitive negotiations. Helpful guidance is provided in choosing among prescribed methods. The extent of competition expected is spelled out, as are practices viewed as restricting competition. The nature of federal agency review of grantee purchasing practices is described. Forms of cost and price analysis are identified, and it is made clear that federal cost principles apply to procurement under grants.

The revisions also deal specifically with conflicts of interest, citing examples that would be in violation of the Model Procurement Code. Positive actions are prescribed for contracting with small and minority firms, women's business enterprises, and labor-surplus-area firms. Perhaps most significantly, the attachment calls for grantor agency reviews of grantee procurement systems. An overall system may be certified, after which the individual review of grantee contract action is not considered necessary.

Procedures for Use by Grantees in Property Management

Attachment N to OMB circular A-102, "Property Management Standards" states:

> 1. This attachment prescribes uniform standards governing the utilization and disposition of property furnished by the federal government or acquired in whole or in part with federal funds or whose cost was charged to a project supported by a federal grant. Federal grantor agencies shall require grantees to observe these standards under grants from the federal government and shall not impose additional requirements unless specifically required by federal law. The grantees shall be authorized to use their own property management standards and procedures as long as the provisions of this attachment are included.
>
> 2. The following definitions apply for the purpose of this attachment:
>
> (a) Real Property. Real property means land, including land improvements, structures and appurtenances thereto, excluding movable machinery and equipment.
>
> (b) Personal Property. Personal property of any kind except real property. It may be tangible—having physical existence, or intangible—having no physical existence, such as patents, inventions, and copyrights.
>
> (c) Nonexpendable Personal Property. Nonexpendable personal property means tangible personal property having a useful life of more than one year and an acquisition cost of $300 or more per unit. A grantee may use its own definition of nonexpendable personal property provided that such definition would at least include all tangible personal property as defined above.
>
> (d) Expendable Personal Property. Expendable personal property refers to all tangible personal property other than nonexpendable property.
>
> (e) Excess Property. Excess property means property under the control of any federal agency which, as determined by the head thereof, is no longer required for its needs or discharge of its responsibilities.

(f) Acquisition Cost of Purchased Nonexpendable Personal Property. Acquisition cost of an item of purchased nonexpendable personal property means the net invoice unit price of the property including the cost of modifications, attachments, accessories, or auxiliary apparatus necessary to make the property usable for the purpose for which it was acquired. Other charges such as the cost of installation, transportation, taxes, duty, or protective in-transit insurance, shall be included or excluded from the unit acquisition cost in accordance with the grantee's regular accounting practices.

(g) Exempt Property. Exempt property means tangible personal property acquired in whole or in part with federal funds, and title to which is vested in the recipient without further obligation to the federal government except as provided in subparagraph 6a below. Such unconditional vesting of title will be pursuant to any federal legislation that provides the federal sponsoring agency with adequate authority.

3. Real Property. Each federal grantor agency shall prescribe requirements for grantees concerning the use and disposition of real property funded partly or wholly by the federal government. Unless otherwise provided by statute, such requirements, as a minimum, shall contain the following:

(a) Title to real property shall vest in the recipient subject to the condition that the grantee shall use the real property for the authorized purpose of the original grant as long as needed.

(b) The grantee shall obtain approval by the grantor agency for the use of the real property in other projects when the grantee determines that the property is no longer needed for the original grant purposes. Use in other projects shall be limited to those under other federal grant programs, or programs that have purposes consistent with those authorized for support by the grantor.

(c) When the real property is no longer needed as provided in a and b above, the grantee shall request disposition instructions from the federal agency or its successor federal agency. The federal agency shall observe the following rules in the disposition instructions:

(1) The grantee may be permitted to retain title after it compensates the federal government in an amount computed by applying the federal percentage of participation in the cost of the original project to the fair market value of the property.

(2) The grantee may be directed to sell the property under guidelines provided by the federal agency and pay the federal government an amount computed by applying the federal percentage of participation in the cost of the original project to the proceeds from sale (after deducting actual and reasonable selling and fix-up expenses, if any, from the sales proceeds). When the grantee is authorized or required to sell the property, proper sales procedures shall be established that provide for competition to the extent practicable and result in the highest possible return.

(3) The grantee may be directed to transfer title to the property to the federal government provided that in such cases the grantee shall be entitled to compensation computed by applying the grantee's percentage of participation in the cost of the program or project to the current fair market value of the property.

4. Federally owned nonexpendable personal property. Title to federally owned property remains vested in the federal government. Recipients shall

submit annually an inventory listing of federally owned property in their custody to the federal agency. Upon completion of the agreement or when the property is no longer needed; the grantee shall report the property to the federal agency for further utilization.

If the federal agency has no further need for the property, it shall be declared excess and reported to the General Services Administration. Appropriate disposition instructions will be issued to the recipient after completion of the federal agency review.

5. Exempt property. When statutory authority exists title to nonexpendable personal property acquired with project funds shall be vested in the recipient upon acquisition unless it is determined that to do so is not in the furtherance of the objectives of the federal sponsoring agency. When title is vested in the recipient the recipient shall have no other obligation or accountability to the federal government for its use or disposition except as provided in 6a below.

6. Other nonexpendable property. When other nonexpendable tangible property is acquired by a grantee with project funds title shall not be taken by the federal government but shall vest in the grantee subject to the following conditions:

(a) Right to transfer title. For items of nonexpendable personal property having a unit acquisition cost of $1,000 or more, the federal agency may reserve the right to transfer the title to the federal government or to a third party named by the federal government when such third party is otherwise eligible under existing statutes. Such reservations shall be subject to the following standards:

(1) The property shall be appropriately identified in the grant or otherwise made known to the grantee in writing.

(2) The federal agency shall issue disposition instructions within 120 calendar days after the end of the federal support of the project for which it was acquired. If the federal agency fails to issue disposition instructions within the 120 calendar-day period, the grantee shall apply the standards of subparagraph 6(b) and 6(c) as appropriate.

(3) When the federal agency exercises its right to take title, the personal property shall be subject to the provisions for federally-owned nonexpendable property discussed in paragraph 4, above.

(4) When title is transferred either to the federal government or to a third party, the provisions of subparagraph 6(c)(2)(b) should be followed.

(b) Use of other tangible nonexpendable property for which the grantee has title.

(1) The grantee shall use the property in the project or program for which it was acquired as long as needed, whether or not the project or program continues to be supported by federal funds. When no longer needed for the original project or program, the grantee shall use the property in connection with its other federally sponsored activities, in the following order of priority:

(a) Activities sponsored by the same federal agency.

(b) Activities sponsored by other federal agencies.

(2) Shared use. During the time that nonexpendable personal property is held for use on the project or program for which it was acquired, the grantee shall make it available for use on other projects or programs if such other use will not interfere with the work on the project or

program for which the property was originally acquired. First preference for such other use shall be given to other projects or programs sponsored by the federal agency that financed the property; second preference shall be given to projects or programs sponsored by other federal agencies. If the property is owned by the federal government, use on other activities not sponsored by the federal government shall be permissible if authorized by the federal agency. User charges should be considered if appropriate.

(c) Disposition of other nonexpendable property. When the grantee no longer needs the property as provided in 6b above, the property may be used for other activities in accordance with the following standards:

(1) Nonexpendable property with a unit acquisition cost of less than $1,000. The grantee may use the property for other activities without reimbursement to the federal government or sell the property and retain the proceeds.

(2) Nonexpendable personal property with a unit acquisition cost of $1,000 or more. The grantee may retain the property for other uses provided that compensation is made to the original federal agency or its successor. The amount of compensation shall be computed by applying the percentage of federal participation in the cost of the original project or program to the current fair market value of the property. If the grantee has no need for the property and the property has further use value, the grantee shall request disposition instructions from the original grantor agency.

The federal agency shall determine whether the property can be used to meet the agency's requirements. If no requirement exists within that agency, the availability of the property shall be reported, in accordance with the guidelines of the Federal Property Management Regulations (FPMR), to the General Services Administration by the federal agency to determine whether a requirement for the property exists in other federal agencies. The federal agency shall issue instructions to the grantee no later than 120 days after the grantee request and the following procedures shall govern:

(a) If so instructed or if disposition instructions are not issued within 120 calendar days after the grantee's request, the grantee shall sell the property and reimburse the federal agency an amount computed by applying to the sales proceeds the percentage of federal participation in the cost of the original project or program. However, the grantee shall be permitted to deduct and retain from the federal share $100 or ten percent of the proceeds, whichever is greater, for the grantee's selling and handling expenses.

(b) If the grantee is instructed to ship the property elsewhere the grantee shall be reimbursed by the benefiting federal agency with an amount which is computed by applying the percentage of the grantee participation in the cost of the original grant project or program to the current fair market value of the property, plus any reasonable shipping or interim storage costs incurred.

(c) If the grantee is instructed to otherwise dispose of the property, the grantee shall be reimbursed by the federal agency for such costs incurred in its disposition.

(d) Property management standards for nonexpendable property. The grantee's property management standards for nonexpendable personal property shall include the following procedural requirements:

(1) Property records shall be maintained accurately and shall include:

(a) A description of the property.

(b) Manufacturer's serial number, model number, federal stock number, national stock number, or other identification number.

(c) Source of the property including grant or other agreement number.

(d) Whether title vests in the grantee or the federal government.

(e) Acquisition date (or date received, if the property was furnished by the federal govenrment) and cost.

(f) Percentage (at the end of the budget year) of federal participation in the cost of the project or program for which the property was acquired. (Not applicable to property furnished by the federal government.)

(g) Location, use, and condition of the property and the date the information was reported.

(h) Unit acquisition cost.

(i) Ultimate disposition data, including date of disposal and sales price or the method used to determine current fair market value where a grantee compensates the federal agency for its share.

(2) Property owned by the federal government must be marked to indicate federal ownership.

(3) A physical inventory of property shall be taken and the results reconciled with the property records at least once every two years. Any differences between quantities determined by the physical inspection and those shown in the accounting records shall be investigated to determine the causes of the difference. The grantee shall, in connection with the inventory, verify the existence, current utilization, and continued need for the property.

(4) A control system shall be in effect to insure adequate safeguards to prevent loss, damage, or theft of the property. Any loss, damage, or theft of nonexpendable property shall be investigated and fully documented; if the property was owned by the federal government, the grantee shall promptly notify the federal agency.

(5) Adequate maintenance procedures shall be implemented to keep the property in good condition.

(6) Where the grantee is authorized or required to sell the property, proper sales procedures shall be established which would provide for competition to the extent practicable and result in the highest possible return.

7. Expendable personal property. Title to expendable personal property shall vest in the grantee upon acquisition. If there is a residual inventory of such property exceeding $1,000 in total aggregate fair market value, upon termination or completion of the grant and if the property is not needed for any other federally sponsored project or program, the grantee shall retain the property for use on nonfederally sponsored activities, or sell it, but must in either case, compensate the federal government for its share. The amount of compensation shall be computed in the same manner as nonexpendable personal property.

8. Intangible property.

(a) Inventions and patents. If any program produces patentable items, patent rights, processes, or inventions, in the course of work sponsored by the federal government, such fact shall be promptly and fully reported to the federal agency. Unless there is a prior agreement between the grantee and the federal agency on disposition of such items, the federal agency shall determine whether protection on the invention or discovery, including rights under any patent issued thereon, shall be allocated and administrated in order to protect the public interest consistent with "Government Patent Policy" (President's Memorandum for Heads of Executive Departments and Agencies, August 23, 1971, and statement of Government Patent Policy as printed in 36 FR 16889).

(b) Copyrights. Except as otherwise provided in the terms and conditions of the agreement the author or the grantee organization is free to copyright any books, publications, or other copyrightable materials developed in the course of or under a federal agreement, but the federal agency shall reserve a royalty-free nonexclusive and irrevocable right to reproduce, publish, or otherwise use, and to authorize others to use, the work for government purposes.

9. Excess personal property. When title to excess property is vested in grantees such property shall be accounted for and disposed of in accordance with paragraphs 6(c) and 6(d) of this attachment.

Federal Evaluation and Surveillance

HHS, the largest grantor, has taken the lead in establishing grantee management-evaluation programs. It has formally described the essentials of management: by system, subsystem, and measure of performance.[5] Eight systems are identified: (1) fiscal administration system, (2) procurement system, (3) property management system, (4) personnel system, (5) facilities management system, (6) planning and budgeting system, (7) management information system, and (8) inventions and patents system.

The procurement system states that the objective is to obtain the property and services needed for the organization to carry out its planned objectives. Measures of performance are written procurement policies, which consider such matters as cost, quality, delivery, competition, source selection, and subcontract administration; and written procurement procedures, which cover competitive bidding, negotiation practices, follow-up on unfilled orders, receiving, inspection, and acceptance. The authority to procure and to sign requisitions is also formally established.

The property management system is described as two subsystems. The first is equipment and supply management, whose objective is to have equipment and supplies of the desired type, quality, and amount available, without overstocking, and to provide for maintenance. Proposed purchases are reviewed selectively to avoid acquisition of unnecessary or duplicative items; records are maintained that provide a description of equipment, acquisiton cost, and location; a procedure exists to minimize underutilization of equipment; and the organization has procedures for purchases of supplies and for central storage and distribution. The second subsystem is salvage, reassignment, and disposal, whose objective is to identify and dispose of property no longer required or utilized. The organization has a system for periodic evaluation of equipment and supplies with a view toward economical salvage or disposal of items that are no longer required because of obsolescence, excessive wear, excessive cost of maintenance, or lack of further need. Authority for effecting disposal or salvage is limited to designated individuals.

Another activity at the federal level has been the GAO study of procurement practices of cities under federal grant funds.[6] GAO is studying state and local purchasing for two reasons: to increase knowledge of what purchasing practices are being used and which are most effective and efficient and to evaluate the effect of federal grantor agency procurement requirements on the local purchasing function. The stated goal is to encourage the development of more efficient purchasing programs among state and local governments. A report, one phase of the overall program, presents the results of a questionnaire sent to 949 city governments. Its purpose is to provide an overview of city procurement practices and problems experienced in spending federal grant funds.

The GAO found its point of departure in *State and Local Government Purchasing*, the first comprehensive research effort on state and local procurement, published by the Council of State Governments.[7] The study was funded by a grant from the Law Enforcement Assistance Administration and was done cooperatively by the National Association of State Purchasing Officials and Peat, Marwick, Mitchell and Company. It developed the general procurement principles used by the GAO as guidelines to compare and contrast city procurement practices.

Notes

1. Commission on Government Procurement, *Report of the Commission on Government Procurement* (Washington, D.C.: Government Printing Office, 1972), 3:162.

2. U.S. Congress, House, Committee on Government Operations, *Government Procurement and Contracting, Hearings* on H.R. 474 before a Subcommittee of the Committee on Government Operations, 91st Cong., 1st sess., 15-21 May 1969, pt. 6, pp. 1636-1637.

3. *Federal Register*, 12 September 1977, vol. 42, no. 176, pt. VII, pp. 45828-45891.

4. Office of Management and Budget, *Basic Plan for the Federal Assistance Review (FAR) Program, 3rd Year* (1 July 1971), pp. I-2, D-16.

5. Department of Health, Education and Welfare, *A Program for Im-*

proving the Quality of Grantee Management (Washington, D.C.: Government Printing Office, 1970).

6. General Accounting Office, Procurement and Systems Acquisition Division, *Procurement Practices of Cities*, PSAD 77-88 (Washington, D.C.: General Accounting Office, 1977).

7. Council of State Governments, *State and Local Government Purchasing* (Lexington: Ky, 1975).

15 Intergovernmental Cooperative Purchasing

The Model Procurement Code includes provisions that facilitate cooperative purchasing endeavors. Usually such endeavors involve groups of adjacent political jurisdictions, such as the 114 self-governing municipalities and school districts in Bergen County, New Jersey, or the 28 county and city buying units which comprise metropolitan Washington, D.C. The agreements take many forms, but all are intended to achieve economies through larger-scale buying and to improve quality and service.

Historical Background of Cooperative Purchasing[1]

The earliest known cooperative purchasing system in the United States was established about 1930 in Alamosa, Colorado. It included eight school districts. It is questionable whether this was truly an intergovernmental purchasing effort, since only schools were concerned. Perhaps it should be considered a move toward greater centralization of the purchasing effort. In any event, the venture was soon abandoned.

The city of Cincinnati and Hamilton County in Ohio joined in a cooperative purchasing effort in 1931. This plan, or venture, is still in existence. It is managed by a coordinating committee of purchasing agents of Hamilton County and is made up of the purchasing agents of the Cincinnati Board of Education, the city of Cincinnati, the Public Library of Cincinnati, Hamilton County, and the University of Cincinnati. It is strictly a voluntary cooperative effort. In the first year of the plan's existence, cost savings of $50,000 (15 percent) were reported on purchases of coal and $10,500 (15 percent) on purchases of gasoline. In the early years of the plan, savings supposedly averaged about 14 percent, with some as high as 50 percent. Such saving reflects the differences between the prices paid by individual jurisdictions and the prices paid in the cooperative purchase.[2] The Cincinnati plan, as it is called, is pointed to as one of the more successful early ventures in cooperative purchasing.

Also in the 1930s the Kansas Schools Purchasing Association was formed; it is now defunct. Perhaps the best-known examples, other than Cincinnati, of cooperative purchasing ventures in the 1930s were those of state municipal leagues. These began with the Michigan League's purchase

317

of fire hose for six cities in 1930. By 1938, eleven leagues were engaged in cooperative purchasing efforts, but their cost savings were not reported to be significant. A survey of cooperative purchasing efforts in 1938 revealed that only five states—Michigan, New Hampshire, Virginia, West Virginia, and Wisconsin—had provided a workable system whereby counties and municipalities could purchase cooperatively with or through the state purchasing agency. In addition Pennsylvania had just passed a statute permitting a similar arrangement. And although some interest in intergovernmental purchasing was demonstrated in California, Kansas, Nebraska, and New York State, nothing developed immediately from that interest. During the early 1940s, Milwaukee, Wisconsin, formed a venture in cooperation with other public buying jurisdictions in Milwaukee County, including the Board of School Directors, the Metropolitan Sewerage Commission, the county, and the Milwaukee Auditorium Arena.

The late 1950s brought a revival of the concept. Fort Lauderdale and Broward County, Florida, initiated a cooperative purchasing venture in 1956. In addition to the county and Fort Lauderdale, it included two other communities located in the county: Hollywood and Pompano Beach. Over the following ten-year period, eighteen units of government participated. Participation was strictly voluntary, and cost savings were reported to be in the range of 4 to 18 percent. These savings were reported as amounting to over $200,000 for Fort Lauderdale and over $600,000 for all eighteen participants. Orange County, California, launched a cooperative purchasing effort in its school districts in 1958, which was later expanded to other school districts and cities in the county. The city of Tacoma, Washington, and its surrounding municipalities and school districts also entered into a cooperative purchasing effort in 1957.

An acceleration of the movement toward greater intergovernmental cooperative purchasing which has continued to the present, began in the 1960s. Not all of the ventures have been successful. One that was short-lived was in the Dayton, Ohio, metropolitan area. It was launched in 1962 and abandoned in 1966 because officials felt that the savings reflected were not of sufficient volume to warrant the time and effort involved. A successful effort was made in Hennepin County, Minnesota, which entered into a venture with several cities in the county in 1968. The county purchasing agent was designated as the purchasing agent for all governmental units participating. In 1965, Monroe County, Michigan, also initiated a venture with municipalities in the county. In its first eighteen months of existence, savings of over $18,000 in direct costs were reported. A highly successful venture has been the Lehigh Valley Council, organized in 1965. The council centers around the city of Bethlehem and five other municipalities in Pennsylvania. Perhaps the outstanding example has been the Bergen County, New Jersey, venture, which includes the county and 113 municipal and public school district governments and reports savings to taxpayers approaching $500,000 annually.

Several other intergovernmental cooperative purchasing efforts got underway in the 1960s. Los Angeles County and forty-three California cities launched a cooperative effort early in the decade, as did Suffolk County, New York. Later in the decade, several cities in Rhode Island and towns in the capitol region of Connecticut, and York County, Virginia, the cities of Newport News, Hampton and Williamsburg, the town of Poquoson, and the city of Hampton Schools launched cooperative ventures.

The 1970s have seen the trend continue, with such arrangements as that in the metropolitan Washington, D.C., area reporting significant savings on joint purchases of fire and rescue equipment, highway maintenance supplies, cars and buses, automotive accessories, and library, office, photo, and custodial supplies; $200,000 was reported saved in the first ten months of operation.

The tangible benefits, the direct cost savings, are not all that can be realized from an intergovernmental cooperative purchasing agreement. The jurisdictions participating report many other by-product benefits. Through the exchange of information, individual jurisdictions find that they are much more knowledgeable of the market; they are aware of more sources and of prices being paid by adjoining jurisdictions. Accordingly their own independently placed orders are more advantageously handled. Through their interagency contacts, they learn how others are handling various problems. Specifications and other technical data are exchanged. In the frequent meetings of the steering groups and of the procedural and commodity working groups, many issues of mutual concern are raised. Information is shared on inventory policies, order sizes, contract duration, packaging, marking, shipping instructions, vendor performance, delivery times, and quality assurances. Procedures are freely shared, saving some jurisdictions the time and expense of separately developing methods and procedures of their own. Participants have frequently stated that even without the dollar savings, cooperative agreements would be worthwhile because of the value of the professional and technical information exchanged.

The experiences to date with the concept of intergovernmental cooperative purchasing illustrate the importance of certain prevailing conditions. State and local laws and ordinances must encourage and facilitate the effort. The publication in 1978 of the Model Procurement Code is an important step in this regard. One jurisdiction, or one individual, must take the initiative to promote the concept and see the arrangement through its developmental stages. A relatively small nucleus of jurisdictions should pioneer the effort; later neighboring jurisdiction can be invited to join. A comprehensive plan and operating procedure must be developed and staffed through the participating jurisdictions. The first items to be cooperatively purchased should be relatively simple, facilitating agreement on specifications and terms of delivery. They should be items where savings are expected to be readily apparent. All participants in the agreement should share in the planning and operation. Each should take the lead in one or another commodity area.

The fact that some participating jurisdictions are much larger than others should not result in the smaller jurisdictions's being allowed to be carried along. Special regard must be shown to the size-related differences between governmental units. The individual jurisdictions should all practice centralized purchasing. It is difficult for a purchasing manager to participate in a cooperative agreement when his own purchasing activity is fragmented. A guiding body, such as a purchasing officers' committee, must be formed. It should be assisted by task forces made up of jurisdiction employees to work on individual commodity and procedural matters. The cooperative agreement should be firmly backed by the heads of the member jurisdictions: the mayors, county board chairmen, school board presidents, city and county managers, and superintendents. Their support should be active, continuing, and visible.

Legal Considerations in Cooperative Purchasing

All of the cooperative agreements currently existing were formed prior to the publication of the Model Procurement Code. The code addresses the standing legal barriers and problems and in doing so encourages further intergovernmental cooperation. A major issue has been that many states have not passed a specific statute permitting interlocal joint purchasing. The provisions of the code are permissive, allowing purchasing units to decide for themselves whether to enter into cooperative arrangements.

According to the code, any public procurement unit may participate in, sponsor, conduct, or administer a cooperative agreement for the procurement of any supplies, services, or construction with one or more public procurement units or external activities (such as the Federal Supply Services) in accordance with an agreement entered into between the participants. It may also enter into an agreement to sell to, acquire from, or cooperatively use any supplies or services belonging to another unit, or enter into one for the common use or lease of warehousing facilities, capital equipment, and other facilities. The unit may provide personnel to another unit, with reimbursement of the direct and indirect costs of furnishing the personnel.

Informational, technical, and other services may be made available to other units, with reimbursement for the expenses of the services so provided. Units may make available to each other standard forms, manuals, specifications and standards, testing methods, qualified products' lists, source data, supplier performance ratings, bidders' lists, contract provisions, and pricing information. They may also provide technical services to each other, for agreed-upon fees. Any fees received for the use of facilities, personnel, or services will be available for the use of the public procurement unit (as opposed to crediting the general treasury).

Information concerning the type, cost, quantity, and quality of commonly used supplies, services, or construction may be collected and made available to any unit upon request. And special agreements with procurement appeals boards are authorized to resolve controversies arising from cooperative purchasing agreements.

Organization and Procedures in Cooperative Purchasing

A cooperative purchasing agreement among a group of jurisdictions is implemented by the heads of the public purchasing units, who form a purchasing officers' committee, made up of the unit heads themselves or their designees. If the jurisdictions fall within an organized council of governments or a general regional cooperative arrangement, that council should be asked to provide administrative support to the committee. The committee prepares its charter, with each member ensuring that charter provisions are not inconsistent with his own parent jurisdiction's ordinances, regulations, and policies. The charter would be consistent with the provisions of the Model Procurement Code.

Two types of working groups—procedural and commodity—would be formed. One procedural group would prescribe uniform identification and stock numbering methods, if not already in existence; a second would prescribe uniform requirements reporting and consolidating methods; another the uniform contract terminology and standard clauses; and another uniform computer terminology and programming. As necessary, groups would be formed to deal with other procedural matters that might arise, such as administrative cost sharing, handling of protest, or redistribution of excess supplies.

Commodity groups would be formed to plan and accomplish acquisition in each commodity area: fuels and lubricants, automotive equipment and parts, school supplies, custodial supplies and equipment, and the many others that might develop. Each of the commodity working groups would normally be chaired by the official whose purchasing unit was the designated buyer of that commodity. Figure 15-1 depicts an organization based on this concept. The central element is the purchasing officers' committee, shown as reporting to a sponsoring group, usually a council of governments or a league of jurisdictions. The council or league would most

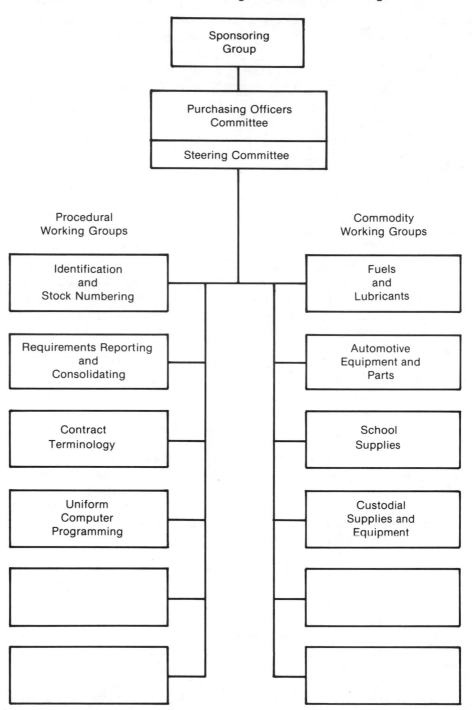

Figure 15-1. Organization for Management of Intergovernmental Cooperative Purchasing

likely be involved in other ventures—cooperation in police and fire protection, water and sanitary services, or solid waste disposal, for example.

The purchasing officers' committee would serve as the policy-making and planning body, meeting perhaps quarterly or semiannually. A group within the committee would be designated as a steering group, charged with overseeing operational aspects of the cooperative agreement. They would meet more frequently, perhaps monthly, to see to the staffing of the working groups and to draw upon the expertise of all participating jurisdictions. The working group structure should be viewed as fluid. The groups shown are representative only; in actuality groups would be formed and disbanded as need indicated. Some of the more likely groups are shown. On the procedural side, an identification and stock numbering group would ensure that all jurisdictions used compatible systems of identification. The separate jurisdictions would undoubtedly have been using various cataloging systems or perhaps none at all. Now, under the cooperative agreement, the commodities subject to the agreement will need standard nomenclature if errors in identification are to be minimized. Requirements reporting and consolidating will be a new function and procedure. Formats will be needed on which the jurisdictions report their purchasing needs. An example of such a format is shown in figure 15-2. Schedules will be necessary to ensure that all requirements are in hand by established due dates.

On the commodity side, the groups will be concerned with selecting the actual items to be purchased cooperatively. Specifications for the items will need to be studied and agreed upon; delivery conditions and schedules will have to be worked out; sources will need to be identified and evaluated; the jurisdiction selected to issue the invitation to bid and to award the contract must be agreed upon. Fuels and lubricants is shown on the organization chart as the first example of a commodity working group because historically this has been the commodity first subject to cooperative purchasing.

Two variations in purchasing procedure are commonly used: the joint-bid procedure and the price-extension procedure.

Under the joint-bid procedure the requirements of all participating jurisdictions are consolidated into a single total. The participating jurisdictions and each's share of the total pooled requirement are specified in the solicitation. The bidders are expected to respond with a price based upon the pooled requirements. The nature of the solicitation is explained in the conditions attached to the invitation to bid. These conditions state that the invitation comprises the requirements of the several listed jurisdictions. Further, each member jurisdiction named reserves the right with respect to its own requirements: to award in part or in whole, to reject any or all bids, to waive any informalities in bids, and to award so as to serve its own best interests. Also, in case of default of the contractor, the jurisdiction(s) involved may, after notice has been given in writing providing reasonable time for corrective action, procure the articles or services from other sources and hold the defaulting contractor responsible for any excess cost occasioned

METROPOLITAN WASHINGTON COUNCIL OF GOVERNMENTS

COOPERATIVE PURCHASING PROGRAM

COMMODITY REQUIREMENTS

JURISDICTION:	COMMODITY:		
BUYER:	CONTRACT PERIOD:		
COMMODITY DESCRIPTION:	ESTIMATED ANNUAL USAGE		
	QUANTITY	UNIT	CURRENT UNIT PRICE
DELIVERY LOCATION(S):	DELIVERY DATE(S):		

PREVIOUS SUPPLIERS RECOMMENDED FOR BIDDERS LIST:

SIGNATURE

TITLE   DATE

Figure 15-2. Form for Reporting Cooperative Purchasing Program Requirements

thereby. If public necessity requires the acceptance of materials, supplies, or services not conforming to the specifications, they may be accepted and payment shall be made at a proper adjustment in price. The conditions provide that a contract shall be deemed executory only to the extent of appropriations available to each jurisdiction for the purchase of such articles.

Under this procedure, the purchasing agents of each jurisdiction reserve the right to increase or decrease by a stated percentage the given quantity of their respective jurisdiction's requirement within the contract period, and, upon mutual agreement, purchase quantities more or less than this limitation.

It will be recognized that these procedures are peculiar to a joint bid solicited under an intergovernmental cooperative purchasing arrangement. Other general conditions would be the same as those found attached to any single solicitation.

Under the price-extension procedure one of the cooperating units serves as the host buyer. Only the requirements of the host unit are identified. However, a condition of the invitation to bid specifies that the successful bidder must extend the prices offered to any jurisdiction that desires to take advantage of the bid price and is in a legal position to do so. The jurisdictions are then listed.

Under the joint-bid procedure a great deal of coordination among units is necessary to set the total pooled requirement. This effort should result in a more favorable price. Under the price-extension method, little coordination is required but because the full requirement is not identified, the price offered might be less favorable.

Selection of Commodities

The experience of the several operating intergovernmental cooperative purchasing agreements indicate that certain commodity classifications lend themselves to this type of buying:

1. Motor vehicle gasoline and oil, diesel fuel, lubricants.
2. Automotive and heavy equipment tires, batteries, spark plugs, belts, hoses, air, gas, and oil filters.
3. Antifreeze, coolant, fluids.
4. Automobiles, trucks, special-purpose vehicles, plows, graders.
5. Heating oil, coal.
6. Chemical agents, calcium chloride, sodium chloride, rock salt.
7. Traffic signs, sign components, traffic paint.
8. Lamps, incandescent, fluorescent, vapor
9. Paints, varnishes, refinishing supplies.
10. Fertilizer, lime, mulch, sod, seed.
11. Concrete, concrete shapes, pipes, stone, gravel, sand.

12. Sewage treatment chemicals.
13. Fire extinguishers, refills, fire hose.
14. Custodial supplies, paper products, towels, tissues.
15. Office supplies, stationary, correspondence sets.
16. Office furniture and machines, typewriters, duplicators, dictating devices, calculators.
17. Library supplies, book covers, binding.
18. School supplies.
19. Dairy products.
20. Carpeting.
21. Uniforms, fire, police, hospital, custodial.

No one agreement covers the entire range of commodities listed here.

Problems in Cooperative Purchasing

Early attempts at intergovernmental cooperative purchasing were fraught with problems. As experience has been gained and with the publication of the Model Procurement Code, most have been resolved. However, three persistent issues remain. One is the effect of cooperative buying upon local suppliers. Many jurisdictions have local-preference policies that are either explicit or implied. Constituent suppliers complain to elected officials that the pooling of requirements deprives them of orders or that the quantities on which bids are solicited are too large for small, local businesses to handle. Local-preference provisions are discouraged under the Model Procurement Code, but many still exist. Political heads must be convinced that local-preference policies hamper purchasing units in their efforts to make the best possible buy.

A second pervasive problem concerns the sharing of administrative and technical overhead costs. The effort involved, particularly in a joint-bid procedure, is great. Requirements must be assembled from the several participating units. Term and specifications must be drafted and coordinated. Bidders lists must be prepared and solicitations drafted, reproduced, and mailed. Responses must be tabulated and evaluated. The costs of all of this must be equitably shared. The code suggests that fees may be charged, but the details as to the amounts and any sharing formula need to be worked out case by case.

The last and most difficult problem area is the chronic matter of interagency and intra-agency communication. Cooperative purchasing is a departure from the established and understood procedure. Considerable parochialism appears to exist, and there is always inherent resistance to change. In such situations, people frequently fail to gain a full understanding.

Notes

1. This section draws from research done by Raleigh F. Steinhauer while a student at The George Washington University and reported in his doctoral dissertation, *The Intergovernmental Cooperative Purchasing Arrangement in the Metropolitan Washington Area*, 1972. Used with permission.

2. Savings reported by Herbert M. Gladstone, "A Survey of Cooperative Governmental Purchasing in the United States, with Particular Emphasis on the State of New Jersey" (Master's thesis, New York University, 1969). Cost savings reported by most IGCP arrangements apparently represent differences between previous prices paid by individual jurisdictions and prices paid in the cooperative purchase.

16 Performance Evaluation and Audit

A general checklist for a management review of performance includes these: Is there an internal or external audit of the system? Are performance goals established? Is management required to measure the organization's performance periodically. Are standards (indexes) maintained against which to measure performance?

There is wide agreement that no single set of standards or measurement techniques can be used in evaluating performance. At each organizational and activity level, a selection must be made from the available quantitative and qualitative techniques of measurement.

The most widely used quantitative technique for measuring efficiency is the collection of data on output, such as dollar volume purchased or number of purchase orders or requisitions processed. The most widely used quantitative techniques for determining effectiveness are interunit comparisons of prices paid, savings generated, and lapsed time to process requisitions and orders. Such factors can be combined into ratios or units of measure, such as operating cost per dollar spent. Standard estimates can be developed of time required to perform stated tasks. On the qualitative side, the only technique in general use is the management audit. Scattered use is being made of user and vendor questionnaire-type ratings of the perceived quality of purchasing and materials-management performance.

Evaluations can be made on a periodic or as-needed basis. A periodic, perhaps annual, evaluation might be timed to precede required annual personnel reviews. As-needed evaluations might be triggered by specific developments—perhaps a pattern of user or vendor complaints of inadequate and/or inefficient service or one of budget overruns and evidence of excessive cost of purchases and/or material-support operations. There might be evidence of understaffing or overstaffing of the function, a pattern of challenges of the integrity of the department, general internal dissension and employee dissatisfaction, or a demonstrated failure to meet an agreed-upon objective or goal.

Two environmental conditions make performance evaluation perhaps more difficult in government than in industry. One is the added responsibility of achieving prescribed socioeconomic goals. Directed preferential treatment, for example, could sometimes be contrary to obtaining the best buy. The other condition is the small size of the purchasing and materials function in many cases. Half of the counties and three-fourths of the cities

329

have departments of fewer than nine persons, rendering any fairly sophisticated evaluation system difficult to justify. But larger counties and cities, state agencies, and federal bureaus can and should develop internal evaluation programs.

Quantitative Measures

Two recent studies sponsored and funded by the National Science Foundation have concluded that a management-information system and adequate data base are essential to measurement systems for purchasing and materials management.[1] In the combined studies, fourteen elements were found susceptible to quantitative measurement:

1. Price effectiveness.
2. Cost savings.
3. Work-load and work-force adequacy.
4. Purchasing output efficiency.
5. Vendor performance.
6. Material flow.
7. Socioeconomic performance.
8. Planning and forecasting.
9. Degree of competition.
10. Inventory efficiency and effectiveness.
11. Inspection efficiency.
12. Stores efficiency.
13. Transportation expense and effectiveness.
14. Standardization and specification savings.

Price-effectiveness measures are used to measure actual versus planned purchase price or market purchase price and price differentials among buying groups or locations. Purchase price variances from plan are calculated on an individual line item and on a total purchasing budget basis. The indicators are the price variances measured in terms of actual unit cost minus planned cost, the price variance percentage (actual unit cost over planned cost), and the extended price variance (actual unit cost minus planned cost multiplied by the estimated quantity for the measurement period).

The key element in measuring price effectiveness against plan is the manner in which the plan is established. The planning process generally begins with the establishment of purchase requirements and line-item purchase price forecasts for the next budget period, usually a year. In some cases, forecasts are also made for comparison purposes by a cost accounting and/or industrial engineering group independent of purchasing. These forecasts are reviewed by purchasing and nonpurchasing management, such as finance and manufacturing. After management review and acceptance and/or revision, the purchase price plan is incorporated into the operating plan. Price effectiveness is measured and reported, usually monthly, at each level of control: the departmental level, the buying-group level, and the item level. Other indicators of price effectiveness are comparison of actual purchase costs to market and comparison at multiple buying locations. Market comparisons can be made using published data, such as the prices of the same or similar items included in the wholesale price index, or the wholesale price index in total.

Cost savings measures include indicators of both cost reduction and cost avoidance. Cost reduction requires that the new unit cost be lower than the old one on a line-item basis. Cost avoidance is more loosely defined and could be obtained, for example, by buying at a price lower than the average price being quoted, even though the new unit price would be an increase over the old price.

Cost reduction or avoidance is measured on the basis of an absolute unit cost or an annual cost reduction or avoidance, or by comparing actual cost reduction or avoidance to a budgeted or targeted cost reduction or avoidance. Cost savings data are usually collected and reported on a monthly basis by buyer, buying groups, and department.

Work-load and work-force adequacy measures include work-load-in (a measure of new work coming in to the department), work-load-current (a measure of the backlog of actions), and work-load-completed (a measure of work accomplished). Measures of the work-load-in class include purchase requisitions received, purchase information requests received, number of protests received, and number of pricing requests received. These counts can be reported on a weekly, monthly, or year-to-date basis. Work-load-in measures should be reviewed regularly by management to help predict and explain changes in other departmental measures. For example, an increase in work-load-in could lead to a corresponding increase in purchasing's administrative lead-time if work-force size and efficiency stayed the same.

Measures of the work-load-current category consist of counts of the backlog of work in the department. The two most common counts are purchase requisitions on hand and line items to be processed on hand. Another approach to measuring work-load-current is to convert the work load into numbers of days of work at a standard rate.

Measures in the work-load-completed category include purchase orders placed, line items placed, dollars placed, contracts written, and price proposals written.

The planned size and composition of the work force is determined by projecting these work-load measures in proportion with the amounts budgeted for material acquisition in future periods. The most commonly used techniques is to establish a standard work load per buyer, based on historical performance or time studies. Projected work load is then divided by the standard to calculate the total number of buyers required. The projected number of buyers needed is then multiplied by another ratio to get the number of secretarial and clerical employees needed. Finally a fixed number of managers and other staff members would be added to reach the total work force for the department.

Another technique is to set the standards in terms of hours per document and to establish how much time a buyer spends in buying activity each week. This time is then translated into a standard number of documents per year per buyer, and a specific number of buyers is established, based on the level of work load anticipated.

Purchasing-output efficiency measures relate outputs, such as line items placed, to inputs, such as buyer hours expended. These measures range from two-factor measures that have one input and one output, to multifactor measures that relate several outputs to several inputs. Two-factor measures are calculated by dividing a count of some output by a count of a resource input. Among the more common two-factor measures are purchase orders per buyer, line items per buyer, dollars committed per buyer, change notices per buyer, contracts written per buyer, worker hours per line items, worker hours per purchase order, worker hours per contract, administrative dollars per purchase order, administrative dollars per contract, and administrative dollars per purchase dollar.

Purchasing administrative lead time, another measure used, is generally defined as the elapsed time from arrival of the purchasing requisition at the purchasing department to the placing of the requisition with a vendor. Lead time is tracked with an emphasis on keeping it below some standard. The requisitions with the longest elapsed time in the department are routinely identified and monitored until finally placed.

Each unit must develop a data base and a set of standards. Methods of doing so include time and motion studies, work sampling, methods-time measurement, statistical analysis, historical performance, and administrative judgment. The city of Detroit study includes examples of cost-to-purchase and cost-to-issue data for departments of various sizes. Some private-sector data have been published.[2]

Material flow measures are concerned with the flow of requisitioned material to the requesting and using activities. Material flow reports identify open purchase orders and their delivery due dates, past-due orders, urgent or other priority orders, and individual buyer and vendor performance against due dates. These elements are often combined. For example, a buyer might receive a weekly listing of all open purchase orders, with overdue orders as a percentage of the total orders.

Socioeconomic performance measures record achievement of objectives other than material support. Examples include purchase dollars or percentage of purchase dollars placed with small-, minority-, or women-owned and managed businesses; purchase dollars or percentage of purchase dollars placed in labor-surplus areas; and dollar value of waste material recycled.

Planning and forecasting measures are used to monitor the amount of planning and research activity and its accuracy. These measures include the number of procurement plans established per year (including availability and price forecasting), price forecasting accuracy (actual to forecast), lead-time forecasting accuracy (actual to forecast), and number of make-buy studies completed.

Degree of competition measures provide information about the extent to which the buying organization is developing competition in the supply marketplace and improving purchase prices and terms. Measures include purchase dollars or percentage of purchase dollars awarded through formal advertising and bidding, numbers of bids solicited and received, percentage responsiveness of bids, purchase dollars or percentage of purchase dollars awarded sole source, and number of second sources developed.

Inventory efficiency and effectiveness measures include stock turnover by commodity group (times per year); dollar value of issues as a percentage of average value of inventory on hand; stock-outs as a percentage of requests for stock items; dollar value of inventory overages or underages after physical inventory as a percentage of book value; and inventory management cost as a percentage of dollar value of issues. Inspection efficiency measures include dollar value of items inspected per inspector man-hour, dollar value of items inspected as a percentage of purchase value, and dollar value of defective incoming material (quality and/or quantity) detected as a percentage of total cost of the inspection activity.

Stores efficiency measures include warehouse operating cost as a percentage of dollar value of issues, line-item transactions per storekeeper man-hour, and average time lapsed in filling a request for a normally stocked item.

Among the transportation expense and effectiveness measures are dollar cost of premium transportation of priority shipments, transit time and reliability of performance (by carrier), and incidence of shipment loss or damage (by carrier).

Standardization and specification savings are measured by sophisticated systems. The objective is to increase effectiveness by reducing near redundancy in items supplied and by reducing specification-related errors. The measures include the number of standard specifications developed within a buying group against man-hours expended, the dollar value of items acquired covered by standards as a percentage of total dollar value of purchases, estimated annual savings attributed to standardization, and incidence of errors attributed to specification deficiencies.

Of the fourteen elements identified as measurable by quantitative techniques, five are in general use: price effectiveness, cost savings, workload and work-force adequacy, vendor performance, and material flow. But use of the other elements is increasing, particularly in the larger jurisdictions.

Auditing at the Federal Level

U.S. law requires that all negotiated government contracts and subcontracts include a clause providing that the comptroller general and his or her representatives have the right to examine "any books, documents, papers or records of the contractor, or any of his subcontractors, that directly pertain to, and involve transactions relating to, the contract or subcontract."[3] This requirement is implemented by inclusion in the contracts and subcontracts of a clause, "Examination of Records by Comptroller General."

Firms doing business with the federal government as either a prime contractor or a subcontractor are subject to both preaward and postaward audits of proposals, direct costs, overhead costs, and management systems and procedures. These audits are conducted by the GAO, headed by the comptroller general, and by agency audit units. The principal audit unit in the executive branch is the Defense Contract Audit Agency (DCAA), which provides contract audit services for the Department of Defense, the National Aeronautics and Space Administration, the Department of Energy, the Department of Transportation, the Department of Health and Human Services, and several other executive departments. Auditing outside the Department of Defense is conducted under formal interagency agreements.

The GAO was established by the Budget and Accounting Act of 1921 to strengthen congressional control over the public purse. The Congress recognized that our form of government, with its separation of powers, needed an organization that could provide unbiased information about executive branch activities. Thus GAO, headed by the comptroller general, was established as an independent, nonpartisan agency in the legislative branch of the federal government.

Over the years, the needs of the Congress have expanded enormously because of the increasing size and complexity of the nation and its governments. GAO's services have been enlarged to help meet these needs. Its major functions now are to assist the Congress in its legislative and oversight activities; provide legal services; audit and evaluate the programs, activities, and financial operations of federal departments and agencies; help improve the financial management systems of federal agencies; and settle claims and collect debts.

Auditing is a major responsibility. The purpose of audits is to evaluate the legality, efficiency, economy, and effectiveness with which federal agencies carry out their financial, management, and program responsibilities; and to provide the Congress and agency officials with objective information, conclusions and recommendations that will aid them in carrying out their responsibilities.

Audits involve over half of the professional staff of GAO, working in almost every federal agency in the United States and in numerous other countries. Assignments are performed in the United States. Puerto Rico, the Virgin Islands, Guam, American Somoa, the Panama Canal Zone, the Trust Territory of the Pacific, and seventy-five countries. GAO generally has about fifteen hundred audit assignments underway all the time.

The organization includes eleven audit divisions. One of them, the Procurement and Systems Acquisition Division, is responsible for GAO's work in the areas of federal procurement of goods and services and of science and technology policy and programs. Most of this division's work is concentrated in the Department of Defense, the National Aeronautics and Space Administration, the defense-related activities of the Department of Energy, and the Federal Supply Service of the General Services Administration. It also has responsibility for government-wide procurement and science and technology matters.

The GAO operates under a set of published standards, intended for application to audits of all government organizations, programs, activities, and functions—whether they are performed by auditors employed by federal, state, or local governments; independent public accountants; or others qualified to perform parts of the audit work contemplated.[4] The standards also apply to both internal audits and audits of contractors, grantees, and other external organizations performed by or for a governmental entity. The standards relate to the scope and quality of audit effort and to the characteristics of a professional and meaningful audit report.

The American Institute of Certified Public Accountants (AICPA) has adopted standards and procedures that are applicable to audits performed to express opinions on the fairness with which financial statements present the financial position and results of operations. Those standards are generally accepted for such audits and have been incorporated into the GAO standards.

The comptroller general holds that government and agencies entrusted with public resources, and the authority for applying them, have a responsibility to render a full accounting of their activities. This accountability is inherent in the governmental process and is not always specifically identified by legislative provision. This governmental accountability should identify not only the objects to which public resources have been devoted but also the manner and effect of their application. The standards therefore describe an audit of broad scope, consisting of three elements:

1. Financial and compliance. Determines whether financial operations are properly conducted, whether the financial reports of an audited entity are presented fairly, and whether the entity has complied with applicable laws and regulations.
2. Economy and efficiency. Determines whether the entity is managing or utilizing its resources (personnel, property, space, and so forth) in an economical and efficient manner and the causes of any inefficiencies or uneconomical practices, including inadequacies in management-information systems, administrative procedures, or organizational structure.
3. Program results. Determines whether the desired results or benefits are being achieved, whether the objectives established by the legislature or other authorizing body are being met, and whether the agency has considered alternatives that might yield desired results at a lower cost.

The audit standards are structured so that each of the three elements can be performed separately.

The comptroller general recognizes that a concurrent audit of all three parts would probably be the most economical manner of audit, but often this may not be practical. Furthermore it may not be practical or necessary to perform all three elements of the audit in particular circumstances. For most government programs or activities, however, the interests of many potential government users will not be satisfied unless all three elements are performed.

Seven basic premises underlie the standards.

1. The term *audit* is used to describe not only work done by accountants in examining financial reports but also work done in reviewing compliance with applicable laws and regulations, efficiency and economy of operations, and effectiveness in achieving program results.

2. Public office carries with it the responsibility to apply resources in an efficient, economical, and effective manner to achieve the purposes for which the resources were furnished. This responsibility applies to all resources, whether entrusted to the public officials by their own constituency or by other levels of government.

3. Public officials are accountable to those who provide the resources they use to carry out governmental programs. They are accountable both to other levels of government for the resources such levels have provided and to the electorate, the ultimate source of all governmental funds. Consequently they should provide appropriate reports to those to whom they are accountable. Unless legal restrictions or other valid reasons prevent them from doing so, auditors should make the results of audits available to other levels of government that have supplied resources and to the electorate.

4. Auditing is an important part of the accountability process since it provides independent judgments of the credibility of public officials' state-

ments about the manner in which they have carried out their respon-sibilities. Auditing also can help decision makers improve the efficiency, economy, and effectiveness of governmental operations by identifying where improvements are needed.

5. The interests of individual governments in many financially assisted programs often cannot be isolated because the resources applied have been commingled. Different levels of government share common interests in many programs. Therefore an audit should be designed to satisfy both the common and discrete accountability interests of each contributing government.

6. Cooperation by federal, state, and local governments in auditing programs of common interests with a minimum of duplication is of mutual benefit to all concerned and is a practical method of auditing intergovernmental operations.

7. Auditors may rely upon the work of auditors at other levels of government if they satisfy themselves as to the other auditors' capabilities by appropriate tests of their work or by other acceptable methods.

An inherent assumption that underlies all of the standards is that governments will cooperate in making audits in which they have mutual interests. For many programs that are federally assisted, it would be neither practical nor economical to have every auditor at every level of government do her own background research on the laws, regulations, and objectives of her segment of the program. Therefore to provide the auditor with the necessary background information and to guide her judgment in the application of the standards, federal or state agencies that request other levels to make audits are expected to prepare comprehensive audit instructions that are tailored to particular programs or program areas.

The full scope of an audit of a governmental program, function, activity, or organization should encompass an examination of financial transactions, accounts, and reports, including an evaluation of compliance with applicable laws and regulations; a review of efficiency and economy in the use of resources; and a review to determine whether desired results are effectively achieved. In determining the scope for a particular audit, responsible officials should give consideration to the needs of the potential users of the results of that audit.

The auditors assigned to perform the work must collectively possess adequate professional proficiency for the tasks required, and they must maintain an independent attitude regarding their work. In conducting the audit and in preparing related reports, they are required to use due professional care.

Examination and evaluation standards required that work be adequately planned and assistants properly supervised. There must be a review of compliance with legal and regulatory requirements and an evaluation of the system of internal control to assess the extent it can be relied upon to ensure accurate information, to ensure compliance with laws and regulations, and to provide for efficient and effective operations. Sufficient, competent, and relevant evidence is to be obtained to afford a reasonable basis for the auditor's opinions, judgments, conclusions, and recommendations.

According to the reporting standards, written audit reports are to be submitted to the appropriate officials of the organizations requiring or arranging for the audits. Copies of the reports should be sent to other officials who may be responsible for taking action on audit findings and recommendations and to others responsible or authorized to receive such reports. Unless restricted by law or regulation, copies should also be made available for public inspection. Reports are to be issued on or before the dates specified by law, regulation, or other arrangement and, in any event, as promptly as possible so as to make the information available for timely use by management and by legislative officials. The reports must be as concise as possible while being clear and complete enough to be understood by the users; present factual matter accurately, completely, and fairly; and present findings and conclusions objectively and in language as clear and simple as the subject matter permits. Moreover they must include only factual information, findings, and conclusions that are adequately supported by enough evidence in the auditor's working papers to demonstrate or prove, when called upon, the bases for the matters reported and their correctness and reasonableness. Detailed supporting information should be included in the report to the extent necessary to make a convincing presentation.

When possible, reports should include the auditor's recommendations for actions to effect improvements in problem areas noted in the audit and to make improvements in other areas of operations. Information on underlying causes of problems reported should be included to assist in implementing or devising corrective actions. The primary emphasis of reports should be on improvement rather than on criticism of the past. Any critical comments should be presented in balanced perspective, recognizing any unusual difficulties or circumstances faced by the operating officials concerned. Noteworthy accomplishments, particularly when management improvements in one program or activity may be applicable elsewhere, should be recognized, as should the views of responsible officials of the organization, program, function, or activity audited on the auditor's findings, conclusions, and recommendations. Except where the possibility of fraud or other compelling reasons may require different treatment, the auditor's tentative findings and conclusions should be reviewed with such officials. When possible, their views should be obtained without undue delay in writing and objectively considered and presented in preparing the final report.

The report should clearly explain the scope and objectives of the audit, identify and explain issues and questions needing further study and consideration by the auditor or others, and state whether any significant, pertinent information has been omitted because it is deemed privileged or confidential. The nature of this last information should be described, and the law or other basis under which it is withheld should be stated.

Each audit report containing financial reports must include an expression of the auditor's opinion as to whether the information in the reports is presented fairly in accordance with generally accepted accounting principles (or with other specified accounting principles applicable to the organization, program, function, or activity audited), applied on a basis consistent with that of the preceding reporting period. If the auditor cannot express an opinion, the reasons should be stated. The report must also contain appropriate supplementary explanatory information about the contents of the financial reports as may be necessary for full and informative disclosure about the financial operations of the organization, program, function, or activity audited. Violations of legal or other regulatory requirements, including instances of noncompliance, and material changes in accounting policies and procedures, along with their effect on the financial reports, must be explained.

Among the auditing activities operating under these premises and standards is the DCAA, by far the largest and most widely based contract audit agency in the world. It performs 95 percent of all contract auditing for the federal government. Its formal auditing agreements cover two dozen nondefense departments, administrations, and commissions. When it was formed, on 12 December 1964, it brought together the scattered activities of thirty-six hundred people from the Office of the Secretary of Defense, the military departments, and the military services.

DCAA operates under a total audit concept guided by a detailed manual of policies and procedures, the *Contract Audit Manual*.[5] The concept is designed to meet the auditing standards of the American Institute of Certified Public Accountants (AICPA) and the GAO. Those standards require a scope of audit that includes not only the traditional financial and compliance considerations but also economy and efficiency of operations and effectiveness of programs in achieving desired results.

The fundamental principle of this audit concept is that a contractor's organization must be viewed in its entirety rather than as a series of unrelated activities. All significant auditable activities that affect the costs of government contracts are identified by a comprehensive survey of the contractor's organization. Each auditable area is then considered in relation to all others in planning the work of a field audit office. Consideration consists of six basic steps:

1. Identifying auditable areas of the contractor's organization.
2. Evaluating the audit risk in each area and establishing priorities for accomplishing the audit based upon the assessed risk.
3. Preparing an annual audit plan for the contractor location.
4. Continually assessing results and replanning in the light of evolving circumstances throughout the year.
5. Managing and performing all audit activities considering the interrelationship(s) between and among such activities.
6. Establishing a documentation process for identifying the interrelationships.

At each field location, the audit effort is organized into work packages, defined as natural subdivisions of the total audit that are clearly distinguishable and of manageable size. For each work package two estimates are made: the hours of audit activity involved and the potential dollar impact in terms of savings to the government. Generally the DCAA does not audit a function unless the estimates show possible savings of $300 per audit hour expended. The work packages showing the highest possible savings per audit hour receive priority.

In addition to the planned annual audits of a contractor location, the field office may be directed to accomplish demand audits. These could relate to proposal evaluation, requests for progress payments, terminations, or claims of one kind or another. Usually these demand audits have short due dates. Their accomplishment must be integrated into the regular pattern of audit activity.

This broadening at the federal level of the traditional financial audit is a result of a demand by the general public and elected officials to know that public funds are properly accounted for, spent in compliance with existing laws and regulations, and used prudently to achieve desired results. Similar assurances are required by government procurement and contracting officials. Thus audits are broader in scope than financial and compliance reviews; they are also designed to evaluate the economy and efficiency of contractor operations.

International cooperation in weapons production has led to an international agreement on the auditing of contracts and subcontracts placed in multiple countries. The first such auditing agreement is unique and precedent setting.[6] The contracts related to the NATO selection of the F-16 aircraft to equip units of the air forces of Belgium, Denmark, the Netherlands, Norway, and the United States. Success in the competition for the selection of the new fighter acceptable to all four European countries meant that the United States had to offer not only a better aircraft but also more attractive terms. A major inducement to the closing of the deal was the U.S. ability to offer an offset arrangement under which some of the costs of the European countries' purchase would be offset by placement of U.S. procurements (in the form of subcontracts) in the four European countries. This was important to the European countries in order to provide work for their industry and jobs for their labor force and to soften the impact on their balance of payments. It also would enable their domestic industry to participate in work involving current American technology.

The offset arrangement finally offered was a coproduction plan. Portions of the aircraft to be built both for the United States and for the European countries would be manufactured in the four European countries by local industry. This would be done under subcontracts let by the two U.S. prime contractors, General Dynamics, and the Pratt and Whitney Aircraft Division of United Technologies Corporation.

In order to quote a price that would reflect the obligation to share production with contractors in Europe, both U.S. prime contractors had to solicit proposals from potential suppliers in those countries. At the same time, since the contracts with the two U.S. primes were standard U.S. government contracts, some of their terms had to be passed down to these potential European subcontractors. Among the key contract terms that had to flow down were those providing for audits of the European subcontractors' books and records by the DCAA and the U.S. comptroller general. But several of the major prospective European subcontractors objected to the inclusion of such terms; they voiced strong aversion to being audited by personnel who were to them nonnationals. They suggested as an alternative that any auditing of their F-16 subcontracts be done by the official government audit services of their respective countries. Representatives of the four European governments echoed the concern of their industry.

After extensive discussions with representatives of government and industry from the five countries, an agreement was reached. GAO and DCAA will exercise their audit rights under subcontracts placed in the four participating European countries, through their respective official counterparts: the Ministry of Defense audit agencies or the Supreme Audit Institutions or both. The Europeans will be responsible for making the audits and preparing audit reports. GAO and DCAA are entitled to designate audit representatives to accompany the European auditors doing the work. These representatives may be present during the work, have access to the work papers of the European auditors, ask questions about the work being done, and have access to the subcontractors' books and records through the European auditors. The European audit agencies will have the right to send an audit representative, with similar rights, to accompany DCAA and GAO on audits performed by them in the United States under the F-16 program. In exceptional circumstances, DCAA and GAO may decide to perform audits directly in the European participating countries. Examples of such circumstances are refusal (for whatever reason) by the European auditors to perform the work or instances where the work requested is beyond the agency's ordinary expertise. They also include situations where a congressional request specifies that only GAO may do the work. The European country audit agencies will develop the audit programs, procedures, and standards, which are to reflect the particular interests of the U.S. audit agencies. The audit reports prepared by the European auditors will not be disclosed to third parties without approval of the participating governments and the subcontractors concerned. The term *third parties* does not, however, include the U.S. Congress or committees of the Congress. If a request to GAO for an audit comes from an individual congressman, the European auditors will be so advised and may decline to perform the audit for GAO. In such a case, GAO may make the audit itself under the exceptional-circumstances clause.

The F-16 auditing agreement is unique in the history of GAO. It is important because it provides an administrative alternative to the all-or-nothing choice inherent in the existing law. It represents the first time GAO has directly participated with the executive branch in negotiating an audit agreement with foreign countries that bears on the comptroller general's statutory rights. It is important, too, because it will afford GAO an opportunity to work with several foreign audit agencies on a major program of mutual interest. This should prove to be an important learning experience for GAO, and it provides GAO an opportunity to share with European audit agencies the expertise it has developed over several decades.

Performance Audits at the State and Local Levels

In cooperation with the National Institute of Governmental Purchasing and the National Association of State Purchasing Officials, the U.S. GAO has prepared an audit guide for use at state and local levels. The guide assumes a view of purchasing and materials management as an activity that helps government officials carry out their responsibilities. It addresses local government purchasing programs' efficiency, economy, and effectiveness and activities directed at meeting these objectives.

Before applying the audit guide, financial, legal, and administrative information on the government's purchasing system should be gathered. This includes financial statements, governing statutes, codes, regulations, manuals, and organization charts. Next the auditor and purchasing and materials management official(s) should complete the checklist found in chapter 3 to this book. Depending upon checklist responses and the audit's scope and purpose, the auditor can then determine how to use the audit guide: as a complete purchasing system assessment with the checklist serving as correlative support for audit findings; as a detailed inquiry into weaknesses identified by the checklist and as a selective test of the remaining areas to ensure credibility of other checklist responses; as a focus on those purchasing activities having the greatest impact on the program or activity of primary concern to the auditor; or as a detailed inquiry into weaknesses identified by the checklist where it is necessary to demonstrate their effect.

After the approach is decided, a cross-section of items purchased during the latest year should be selected for a random sampling. This exercise, known as a walk-through, will facilitate detailed testing by enabling several audit steps to be accomplished at one time and by providing a more thorough understanding of the system. Beginning with the determination of needs and finishing at the receipt of the sampled items, the sampling will basically entail interviewing the individuals involved with the purchase of the sampled items; reviewing all related documents, such as the requisition, purchase order, and invoice; and documenting how each action was effected. The detailed audit steps, as described by the GAO, follow.[7]

Detailed Audit Steps

I. Procurement procedures, policies, and practices

A. *Authority and responsibility.* To achieve maximum performance, personnel operating the procurement system must have the authority and responsibility to operate in the most efficient, cost-effective way, considering the government as a whole. Generally, federally funded activities at the State and local level should purchase through the centralized system.

1. *Purpose*: To determine the degree purchasing authority and responsibility are centralized
   Steps: For each walk-through item, determine if the related purchase was effected:
   a. in line with established purchasing authority responsibility or
   b. outside the purchasing unit's delegated and nondelegated (but logical or appropriate) authority and responsibility. These two determinations can be accomplished by:
      (1) walking through the procurement process for each purchase starting with the determination-of-needs process; or
      (2) interviewing the buyers who handled the purchases, and examining and reviewing related purchasing documents such as the purchase order, requisition, etc.
   c. If purchases were completed outside established procedures, obtain an explanation from the individuals involved. Unresolvable issues, which have legal implications, should be brought to the attention of appropriate officials.

    d. Weaknesses identified in the steps above can aggravate other operating inefficiencies. As a result, audit steps to demonstrate the effect or impact of these weaknesses are addressed in other sections (e.g., standardization, consolidation, etc.) of this guide.

2. *Purpose*: To determine the scope and nature of the purchasing unit's responsibilities.

    Steps:

    a. Purchasing's responsibilities should extend beyond the service-oriented role of writing purchase orders and processing forms; they should include a variety of management-oriented functions. Through discussions with purchasing personnel, the walk-through process or other auditing techniques determine the nature of and extent to which the purchasing unit participates in the following functions:

        (1) planning and scheduling acquisitions, including: consolidating departmental requirements and applying value analysis;

        (2) insuring that procurement actions are documented and justified;

        (3) standardizing common-use items;

        (4) establishing specifications;

        (5) inspection and testing;

        (6) inventory and property management, including disposing of surplus property;

        (7) professional development;

        (8) establishing goals, targets, etc.;

        (9) contract administration;

        (10) determining factors to gauge the responsiveness of bids;

        (11) monitoring and controlling any purchasing functions delegated to other departments; and

        (12) establishing and implementing purchasing-related regulations.

    b. If purchasing's responsibilities do not include these management-oriented functions:

        (1) Discuss with purchasing and using departments' officials: What units perform these functions? What role might purchasing be capable of performing to achieve cost-effective procurement?

        (2) Compare the results of your inquiries (step 1, above) with governing statutes, ordinances, manuals, etc. If purchasing functions do not comply with governing statutes, regulations, etc., obtain an explanation from purchasing personnel and officials.

Note: Weaknesses are more likely to occur in areas in which purchasing's responsibilities lack management-oriented functions. In such cases, the following sections of this guide should be given careful attenton.

B. *Planning and Scheduling Acquisitions.* Goods and services should not be purchased only when needed; acquisitions should be systematically planned and scheduled. Successful planning and scheduling should include the concepts of consolidation and value analysis.

1. *Purpose*: To determine whether requirements are effectively being consolidated. There may be problems in this area if prior audit steps or the checklist indicate purchasing authority is decentralized.

    Steps:

    a. Identify the common-use items (i.e., items used by more than one department, such as writing pens, paper supplies, etc.) from the group of walk-through items. If the walk-through selection doesn't yield enough of these type items for this step, another random selection may be required. For the common-use items determine whether any of the following conditions exist.

        (1) Common items are purchased separately for each using department.

        (2) Purchases are made for varying quantities throughout the year, and higher prices are associated with smaller quantities.

2. *Purpose*: To determine if consolidation is effectively performed.

    a. Effective consolidation normally requires sufficient and accurate information to plan the acquisition. As a result, determine from responsible buyers or purchasing records whether the following types of information are available and used to consolidate requirements:

        (1) quantities purchased previously,

        (2) ordering frequency,

        (3) vendor performance,

        (4) unit prices for transaction,

        (5) administrative cost of consolidating requirements,

        (6) number of using departments, and

        (7) user information from which future needs are forecasted.

        Determine whether this information is current, accurate, and periodically reviewed. If such information is not used or not available, ask buyers whether such information would be useful.

    b. Where consolidation is lacking or ineffectively performed, discuss with purchasing officials whether they have adequate authority and have been delegated the responsibility to consolidate common-use items in the most cost-effective manner or other explanation for the existing conditions.

    c. Where purchases of common items aren't consolidated or are consolidated ineffectively, determine any resulting excess costs. For example, for a common item purchased separately for individual departments at varying quantities and prices, estimate the additional price paid for the unconsolidated purchases for the entire year's requirement. Another alternative might be to compare prices of unconsolidated purchases with prices being paid by neighboring governments for comparable items purchased in larger quantities.

2. *Purpose*: To determine the nature and extent value analysis is used in the procurement of goods and services.
    Steps:
    a. If value analysis is used by the purchasing activity, determine what criteria are used to apply the technique to a procurement.
    b. Select, if possible, for the walk-through items specially selected high-dollar value/volume items to which value analysis was applied. Assess the quality of the value analysis made, considering:
        (1) market and economic conditions;
        (2) probable changes in local programs which would affect future requirements;
        (3) technical progress affecting supply sources;
        (4) transportation costs;
        (5) alternative sources of supply;
        (6) standardization of items;
        (7) identification of alternative products;
        (8) maintenance and operating costs during the life of the item; and
        (9) storage and handling v. understocking costs.
    c. If value analysis is not used, try to identify some items or services to which the technique could be easily applied. The items or services should be of relatively high value where the technique would be more likely to show large savings.
    d. Attempt to apply value analysis to the identified items or services. This should be done at least on an elementary basis, incorporating as many of the elements discussed in step b above as possible. The auditor might also contact neighboring governments to obtain information on items comparable to those being tested. Document instances where the neighboring government is using less expensive but comparable (i.e., in terms of acceptable quality) items. The results of your value analysis and comparisons should be discussed with purchasing and using department officials.

4. *Purpose*: To determine whether purchases are effectively scheduled.
    Steps:
    a. Discuss with purchasing officials how goods and services are scheduled for acquisition.
    b. Responses to your inquiries should be compared with governing statutes, regulations, etc.
    c. For the walk-through items, discuss with the applicable

buyer how, or if, the purchase was scheduled.
  (1)   Buyer responses should be compared with steps a and b above.
  (2)   If scheduling is verifiable, determine whether actual purchases match scheduled purchases.
  (3)   Determine whether each related purchase is in line with the using department's consumption patterns, considering stocking capacities and seasonal factors.
  (4)   Also determine whether the buyers have enough leadtime to adequately schedule the acquisition. Sufficient leadtime is particularly important for those walk-through items subject to seasonal demand or seasonal availability. Inquiries should also include whether purchasing has sufficient information on using departments' requirements from which to schedule.

C. *Competition.*
  1.   *Purpose*: To determine the extent purchasing statutes, ordinances, etc., foster competition.
     Steps:
     a.   Examine and review purchasing statutes, ordinances, etc., to determine if the following provisions are included.
      (1)   Purchases exceeding a specified dollar limit are based on advertised competitive bids. For purchases lower than this dollar limit, an informal bidding or quotation system should be used.
      (2)   Conditions where competitive negotiation is to be used are specified.
      (3)   Conditions where competitive procedures may be waived are specified.
      (4)   Final review and approval for invitations for bids rest with the central purchasing unit.
      (5)   Procedures and conditions are specifically spelled out for the central purchasing unit to receive, control, open, and evaluate bids.
      (6)   Procedures for obtaining professional services are specified.
      (7)   Criteria and procedures are specified for adding, deleting, and reinstating vendors to the bidders' list.
      (8)   The minimum number of bidders to be contacted for each type of solicitation is specified.
      (9)   Purchase documentation must show the events of requisition, ordering, and payment.
     (10)   If any items are purchased from a sole source, determine and evaluate the procedures followed to assure that a reasonable price is negotiated.
     (11)   All procedures, policies, conditions, and criteria discussed above should be available for public inspection.

b. In addition to checking for these provisions, discuss with purchasing officials whether there are any aspects or provisions to governing statutes which inhibit or impede the maximization of competition. For example, determine if there are any "buy local" policies which prevent obtaining goods or services outside a stated geographic area.

c. Determine whether additional costs are incurred because of restrictive provisions, or governing statutes lack many of the provisions discussed in step a. For example, if there is a "buy local" policy, attempt to determine prices for any of the walk-through items that are available outside the geographic area (e.g., vendors supplying neighboring governments with comparable requirements) where procurement is restricted. If prices actually paid are significantly higher than available prices, estimate the annual costs involved and discuss the apparent desirability of continuing such restrictive practices.

2. *Purpose*: To determine the adequacy of the competitive bidding process.

Steps:

a. For the walk-through items purchased under competitive bid procedures, discuss with the related buyers and review applicable case files to determine whether the following procedures were included.

(1) Each purchase is advertised in a widely circulated publication, such as a newspaper.

(2) A sufficient number of vendors on the bidders' list for each item is solicited to provide good competition.

(3) The bidders' list used is current and periodically updated and provides procedures for addition of potential bidders.

(4) Bid history records are maintained which would assist purchasing to identify collusive bidding practices.

(5) Procedural specifications of the invitations are as free from restrictiveness as are the technical specifications.

b. Determine whether actual practices are in line with governing statutes, ordinances, etc. Exceptions to established statutes and regulations should be discussed with the individuals involved. Unresolvable issues, which have legal implications, should be brought to the attention of appropriate officials.

c. Determine the effect of any weaknesses identified in step a above. For example, if a bidder's list is not maintained or not kept current, determine for any of the applicable walk-through items whether there are other vendors who were not solicited, but are capable of providing the item.

This could be accomplished by contacting neighboring governments and determining their suppliers for comparable items. The results of this inquiry should be brought to the attention of purchasing officials. Although it can't be implied that lower prices could have been obtained had the other vendors been solicited, it should be emphasized that broadening the scope of potential vendors normally enhances competition and can lead to lower prices.

3. *Purpose*: To determine whether practices in waiving competition are consistent with governing statutes, ordinances, etc.

Steps:

a. Select several items where competitive procedures are waived. Include at least one emergency and one single-source purchase.

b. Select several items where competitive procedures are waived. Include at least one emergency and one single-source purchase.

b. Discuss these procedures with the applicable buyers and determine whether the surrounding conditions and circumstances are consistent with governing statutes and regulations.

c. Exceptions to established statutes and regulations should be discussed with the individuals involved. Unresolved issues, which have legal implications, should be brought to the attention of appropriate officials.

4. *Purpose*: To determine the adequacy of competitive negotiation procedures.

Steps:

a. For the walk-through items purchased under competitive negotiation, discuss and review applicable files to determine whether the following procedures are conducted.

(1) Public notice of the product or service needed is made.

(2) Request for proposal, or equivalent, is used in lieu of an invitation for bid.

(3) Besides the price, factors evaluated include managerial and technical capability, and an approach to meeting performance requirements.

(4) Negotiations conducted are documented.

(5) List of qualified vendors is maintained and used.

b. In addition to checking for these procedures, determine whether actual procedures are consistent with governing statutes, ordinances, etc. Exceptions to established statutes and regulations should be discussed with the individual involved. Unresolvable issues, which have legal implications, should be brought to the attention of appropriate officials.

c. Determine the effect of any weaknesses in maximizing

competition. For example, if price is the only factor considered during the negotiation process, determine from applicable officials or case files whether the purchase will be altered if other factors, such as those discussed in step a(3), are evaluated. If another item would be purchased, attempt to assess any differences in performance as well as price.

5. *Purpose*: To determine the extent to which purchasing participates in obtaining professional services.
   Steps:
   a. Walk through the procurement process for several professional services (e.g., architectural, research, engineering, auditing) obtained for the governmental unit.
   b. Determine whether procedures for obtaining these services were in line with governing statutes, regulations, etc. Any inconsistencies should be discussed with the department officials involved. Unresolvable issues, which have legal implications, should be brought to the attention of appropriate officials.
   c. If purchasing is not effectively involved in obtaining professional services, determine the effect. For example, identify areas where purchasing could have an impact on improving the acquisition of professional services. These may include negotiation techniques, identifying qualified vendors, evaluating proposals, etc.

D. *Standardization and Specifications*.
   1. *Purpose*: To determine whether the central purchasing authority standardizes commonly used items.
      Steps:
      a. Generate a random sample of purchase orders or invoices stratified by several types of end-use requirement (such as typing paper, writing pens, typewriters, etc.).
      b. By reviewing the purchase orders or invoices, determine whether there are many items with differing characteristics being purchased to satisfy a single end use.
      c. If there are many of these items, obtain an explanation from the applicable using department and purchasing officials as to the necessity of each unique attribute.
      d. In addition, determine if a less expensive item, but one which meets the minimum quality level, could be substituted for the different items. If there is such an item, estimate the amount which would be saved if the requirement is standardized by calculating the difference in prices between the higher and lower cost items for a year.
      e. If there are weaknesses in this area, discuss with purchasing officials whether they have adequate authority and are delegated the responsibility to standardize common items. Also, ask if there are any obstacles, legal or otherwise, preventing them from effectively completing the function.

2. *Purpose*: To determine whether the purchasing unit effec-
    tively uses a central stockroom.
    Steps:
    a. If a central stockroom is used, obtain documentation
        showing that:
        (1) Purchasing statutes or regulations require all
             departments and agencies to draw certain supplies
             and equipment from the central stockroom.
        (2) Using departments and agencies have access to a
             catalog of items available from the stockroom.
        (3) Purchasing statutes or regulations require written
             justification for item acquisition outside the
             stockroom standard.
        (4) Items within the stockroom are standardized.
        (5) There are adequate controls against pilferage and
             policies on rotation, if applicable.

Note: Many audit tests discussed elsewhere in this guide, especially in
Planning and Scheduling and in step D1 above, can be used to measure
the impact of not having a central stockroom or one which lacks many
of the features discussed above.

3. *Purpose*: To determine whether using departments are
    ordering from the central stockroom in accordance with
    governing statutes, regulations, etc.
    Steps:
    a. This step can be accomplished by examining those walk-
        through items available through the central stockroom.
        Sampling additional items may be necessary to supple-
        ment the walk-through sample.
    b. If departments are buying outside the central stockroom
        contrary to governing statutes, regulations, etc.,
        (1) obtain an explanation from purchasing officials,
             including their views as to what would be needed
             for adherence to purchasing policies, and
        (2) document instances where higher prices are paid
             for the outside purchases.

4. *Purpose*: To determine whether specifications are written
    and used in a manner which best serves the government's in-
    terest.
    Steps:
    a. Determine whether purchasing statutes and regulations
        place with purchasing the authority to review, modify,
        and approve specifications.
    b. Review the procedures used in writing the specifications
        for the walk-through items and determine whether the
        following features are included.
        (1) Brand names are avoided or expressly stated to be
             only descriptive (identifying salient features) and
             not restrictive.
        (2) Performance specifications are used rather than
             prescriptive specifications.
        (3) Specifications developed by Federal, State, or

other local governments are kept on file and used when found acceptable, in lieu of developing new specifications.

    (4)   Specifications are reviewed and updated when necessary.

    (5)   Lists of qualified products and acceptable brands are maintained and used as an alternative to specification development. In addition, purchasing regulations include criteria for placing and removing items from these lists.

c.   If these features are not presented, discuss with purchasing officials whether such features would improve the present system.

d.   Also document any practices which are either inefficient or restrict competition. For example, if specifications are restrictive, determine how many vendors are excluded from the related solicitation, and if such practices result in higher prices. Another example might be specifications written unnecessarily for common "off-the-shelf" items.

E. *Inspection and Testing.*

    1. *Purpose*: To determine whether the central purchasing unit effectively manages the inspection and testing of delivered items.

       Steps:

       a.   Determine whether there is a systematic and organized program for inspecting and testing goods and services.

       b.   If there is such a program, determine whether it includes the following features.

          (1)   The central purchasing unit has the responsibility and authority to establish and oversee the program.

          (2)   Procedures and policies are spelled out specifying how inspecting and testing will be accomplished. This includes written criteria for testing delivered items for conformance with previously agreed terms, conditions, and specifications.

          (3)   If all items can't be inspected and tested, there are at least provisions for performing these functions on a periodic and statistical sampling basis.

          (4)   If inspection and testing is delegated, the central purchasing unit routinely monitors the program.

       Also, determine whether current procedures and practices are in line with governing statutes and regulations. For any inconsistencies, obtain an explanation for the individuals involved.

       c.   If there is no program:

          (1)   Interview purchasing and receiving department officials to determine how they assure full value is received and specifications are met.

          (2)   Randomly select several departments which are scheduled to receive a shipment of materials or

equipment. Observe how the shipments are inspected and tested. Observed procedures and practices should be reconciled with the responses previously obtained and governing statutes and regulations. Obtain explanations from officials among the departments. If delivered items aren't inspected or tested, identify instances where full value was not received or specifications were not met.

F. *Property Management*.
   1. *Purpose*: Determine whether there is an effective property management program.
      Steps:
      a. Determine whether governing statutes and regulations place with purchasing the authority and responsibility to establish and oversee an effective property management program.
      b. If there is a program for controlling and managing government-owned property, determine whether it includes the following features:
         (1) Inventories are periodically taken of nonexpendable property.
         (2) Inventory records are routinely updated to reflect transactions, such as acquisitions, transfers, dispositions, trade-ins, and other actions affecting onhand balances.
         (3) Inventory records identify which department is accountable for what item.
         (4) The central purchasing unit is also responsible for the disposition of obsolete, unusable, and surplus items.
         (5) Checks are periodically made of equipment utilization.
         (6) Using departments are systematically notified of available surpluses and scrap, and purchases are made only after screening for surplus items.
      c. Determine whether current procedures and practices are in line with governing statutes and regulations. For any inconsistencies obtain an explanation from officials.
      d. If there is no program for managing property, including the maintenance of an inventory, or the program lacks many of the features discussed above, obtain an explanation from officials and document any resultant inefficiencies, such as:
         (1) Inventories contain items which are obsolete, unusable, or surplus.
         (2) Acquisitions are being planned for items which are available from other departments.
         (3) Pilferage is cited as a common problem.
         (4) Unutilized equipment is present.
         (5) Scrap and surplus items are inconsistently and inefficiently disposed of.

          (6)   Items are purchased even though available from surpluses.

G. *Professional Development*.

    1. *Purpose*: Determine whether the governmental unit promotes and fosters professional development among the purchasing unit's staff.

    Steps:

      a. Interview purchasing officials and technical staff to determine whether

        (1)   they keep current with procurement trends (e.g., affiliate with professional purchasing associations);

        (2)   there is a continuing training program to supplement job-required knowledge;

        (3)   they are encouraged to seek external training to stay abreast of new developments in the procurement area;

        (4)   they are familiar with the purchasing principles and concepts discussed in this audit guide;

        (5)   the governmental unit provides funds to support the above.

      b. Although it is nearly impossible to assess its precise impact, the lack of professional development aggravates other inefficiencies in the procurement system. Consequently, when assessing the causes of other weaknesses (e.g., lack of value analysis), consider if the weakness could also be caused by the lack of professional competence of the individual(s) involved. If this is the case, discuss with purchasing or higher level officials whether a professional development program would be beneficial.

II. **Cooperative purchasing**

This section is aimed at evaluating the procurement unit's efforts in achieving additional benefits through cooperative purchasing arrangements. This type of arrangement normally takes one of the following forms: A joint association between two or more governments with one providing the purchasing resources, but at little additional cost to itself; Small governments combining common requirements for joint acquisition, distributing any administrative costs proportionately; A separate legal entity created by participating governments which collectively supervise and staff the organization; Smaller governments buying from or through the purchasing arrangements of larger governments (e.g., purchasing from a State contract).

    1. *Purpose*: Determine whether purchasing statutes, ordinances, regulations, etc., foster participation in cooperative purchasing arrangements.

    Steps:

      a. Review State and local statutes to determine whether participation in cooperative purchasing arrangements is authorized. Document any restrictive or limiting covenants which impede participating in joint purchasing arrangements.

b. Determine either:
   (1) Why participation in cooperative purchasing arrangements is limited or lacking.
      i.   If there are no legal restrictions from participating in cooperative arrangements, interview purchasing and governmental officials to determine what problems confront the government in participating or implementing some form of cooperative purchasing effort. If possible, solicit the views of neighboring governments as to the feasibility or existence of such an arrangement. Also, identify specific items which would lend themselves to such an arrangement.
      ii. Compare prices paid for the walk-through items with prices available from State contracts or through another available cooperative arrangement. If State or cooperative prices are significantly less than prices paid, obtain an explanation from the purchasing officials as to why the cooperative arrangement is not used.
   (2) What opportunities exist for improving existing cooperative efforts.
      i.   Through discussion with purchasing officials, determine the specific nature of the cooperative arrangement. Also obtain the views of participating members and nonparticipating purchasing officials of neighboring governments.
      ii. Document the extent of such purchases (i.e., dollar value, number of items, number of participants, etc.).
      iii. Determine whether the existing arrangement includes the following features: (A) Besides joint acquisition, the arrangement includes cooperative disposition of surplus and unusual items, pooling of administrative and professional resources, and possibly, sharing of facilities, services, and information. (B) Governing statutes are properly structured permitting the governmental unit to participate in such programs. (C) No single participant dominates the purchasing operations. Instead, there is true cooperation in establishing specifications, requirements, terms, conditions, etc. (D) All associated costs are periodically and systematically evaluated to determine whether total costs may be higher than costs of buying separately. (E) The program is continually evaluated to determine whether items should be dropped or added.

     iv.   If any of these features are absent, assess the impact. For example, where total costs aren't analyzed, determine whether certain items could be obtained at less costs by buying separately.

III. Accountability

   1. *Purpose*: To determine the nature and extent of any purchasing goals.

     Steps:

     a. Determine whether there is a systematic program for establishing goals for the central purchasing unit.

     b. If there is such a program, determine whether it includes the following features.

       (1) Goal setting established as a joint undertaking between public officials and the purchasing official.

       (2) Goals are reviewed periodically by public and purchasing officials and reviewed as necessary.

       (3) Purchasing's performance in meeting these goals is systematically monitored by public officials.

       (4) When compared with actual performance, established goals serve as indexes of the purchasing unit's efficiency and cost effectiveness.

       (5) Established goals represent a mix of quantitative and qualitative factors, both of which cover efficiency, economy, and effectiveness assessments.

     c. If there are no established goals, discuss with purchasing officials the desirability of using the matrix of indicators in appendix I.

     d. Apply as many of these indicators as possible, based on existing data, to the purchasing system involved. Discuss the results of your inquiries with purchasing officials.

   2. *Purpose*: To determine the nature and extent of any internal or external audits of the purchasing function.

     Steps:

     a. By examining and reviewing previous audit reports, determine whether the efficiency and cost effectiveness of the purchasing system is addressed.

     b. If prior audits lacked adequate coverage of, or omitted, these aspects of purchasing, discuss with purchasing or higher level officials why these areas aren't included.

     c. If prior audit reports contain recommendations for improving the purchasing system, determine whether implementing action will be taken; if not, why not?

Closely related to the work of the GAO is a major contribution by Price Waterhouse and Company, *Enhancing Government Accountability*.[8] An extensive guide is provided for the evaluation of the procurement activity at all levels of government. Both administrative and accounting controls are detailed.

User-Perception Surveys

The most meaningful measure of performance could well be the level of satisfaction of the users—those supported by the purchasing and materials-management system. User surveys should be conducted for the purpose of assessing the impact of the system upon user operations and to obtain comments upon the system's weak and strong points.

There have been sporadic attempts to design such surveys. A recent major effort involved the city of Detroit working with the College of Engineering of Wayne State University under a grant from the National Science Foundation.[9] The Detroit study included user satisfaction as one dimension of productivity measurement.

The study defined productivity as the efficiency and the effectiveness with which outputs are produced. Efficiency refers to the resources consumed in producing a final product expressed as a ratio: output units to input units or by its reciprocal, which denotes the resource or cost of resource per unit of output. An output, in the context of the generalized system, is the final product of an activity. The input factors include the resources devoted to each activity in producing the outputs. Many traditional measures for purchasing follow this format. This is also consistent with program budgets that attempt to determine the cost per unit of service delivery. Such measures can be used to reflect improvements in methods over time, make comparisons with other governments, and make budget decisions concerning resources needed for different levels of service output.

Effectiveness refers to the degree of satisfaction derived from the unit of output. In the context of purchasing performance, effectiveness has been typically defined as providing the right material, at the right price, at the right time, and in the right place. The user survey accomplishes a subjective evaluation of the purchasing and materials-management system by the people whom the system is designed to serve. It is a customer service rating. Because this rating is subjective and relies on user perceptions, it is not considered as an absolute score but instead is examined for problems and pattern of response. The Detroit survey asks the using department eighteen questions:

1. Are materials available or services received on the date needed?
2. Are items purchased of a functionally adequate quality level?
3. Do the goods obtained from central purchasing represent good value for the money?
4. Are you satisfied with the specifications that are used to obtain the goods you require?
5. Do standardized items (requirements contract items) meet your needs?
6. Are specifications approving personnel (in central purchasing) available to answer questions or solve specification problems?

7. Is the product knowledge of the personnel responsible for writing specifications, if other than the ultimate user, adequate?
8. Is the product knowledge of the personnel responsible for reviewing specifications adequate?
9. Are products accepted essentially the same as specified in the purchase order?
10. Are items ordered of essentially the same type, quality, etc., as specified?
11. Are you satisfied with the quality of goods that passed inspection?
12. Are purchase orders processed on a timely basis through central purchasing?
13. Are you satisfied with performance in obtaining materials that are needed on a rush basis?
14. Do you have specific time frames for processing requisitions for material through the procurement system?
15. Does the purchasing system process requisitions to purchase order according to standard time?
16. Are vendors very reliable in adhering to desired delivery schedules?
17. Do vendors ship acceptable-quality material?
18. Do vendors stand behind their products and service them when failure occurs?

In the Detroit surveys, dissatisfaction with the timeliness of obtaining supplies was the most frequently reported complaint. Responses also reflected concern with the effect of stock-outs and the inability to plan because of inconsistent lead times.

The reliability of the user-perception survey as an evaluation tool comes under question because of the inherent biases, so this method is recommended for use as only an indicator of problems. Within this context, such surveys are very useful to management. They indicate areas that need additional measurement and study.

Notes

1. National Science Foundation grant APR 75-20557 to Robert C. Monczka and Philip L. Carter at Michigan State University, and APR 75-20542 to the City of Detroit and Wayne State University. The Michigan State University study covered thirteen industrial firms and five federal agencies. The city of Detroit study included a survey of approximately two hundred state, county, and city systems.

2. Albert J. D'Arcy, "Facts and Figures on the Cost of Purchasing," *National Purchasing Review* (May 1978):2.

3. 10 U.S.C. 2313 (b).

4. Comptroller General of the United States, *Standards for Audit of Governmental Organizations, Programs, Activities and Functions* (Washington, D.C.: GAO, 1972). Available from the U.S. Government Printing Office, Washington, D.C. 20402, stock number 2000-00110.

5. See Department of Defense, *Audit Management at Major Contractors*, Defense Contract Audit Agency, DCAAP 7641.64 (Washington, D.C.: DOD, September 1978). The *Contract Audit Manual* is available by subscription from the U.S. Government Printing Office. The reference number is DCAA 7640.1.

6. Extracted from Robert Allen Evers, "Auditing the Arms Deal of the Century," *GAO Review* (Summer 1976):19.

7. Adopted from General Accounting Office, *Checklist and Guidelines for Evaluating Local Procurement Systems*, PSAD 78-95 (Washington, D.C.: GAO, August 1978), pt. 2. Requests for copies should be sent to: U.S. General Accounting Office, Distribution Section, Room 1518, 441 G Street, NW, Washington, D.C. 20548.

8. Price Waterhouse and Company, *Enhancing Government Accountability*, PW 946011 (New York: Price Waterhouse and Company, 1979).

9. NSF grant APR 75-20542, *A Productivity Measurement System for State and Local Government Purchasing and Materials Management Services* (Mayor's Office, City of Detroit, Productivity and Management Improvement Division, Detroit, Michigan 48226).

17 Improving the Public-Purchasing and Materials-Management System

Public purchasing and materials management is a very visible function. Instances of inefficiency, waste, and fraud are quickly brought before the public, so dealing with these aspects is one of the principal concerns in setting system objectives.

Current and recent news items report some problems in this area:

A report that the United Nations and its affiliates award contracts for hundreds-of-millions-of-dollars worth of supplies and services without competitive bidding.

A report of a U.S. Navy guided-missile frigate procurement program for which the cost to the government had nearly tripled to $194 million per frigate.

A report of a contractor's claims for reimbursement referred to as based on "vague estimates, phony assertions and inflated figures."

A report of the public purchase of metal storage cabinets that were of such poor quality that they were immediately declared surplus and disposed of.

A report that an estimated 700,000 gallons of gasoline had disappeared from a federal government public works center in Norfolk, Virginia; employees had sold the gasoline to private business.

A report of a high-ranking GSA official in charge of thirty supply outlets being found guilty of accepting large-scale kickbacks, favors, and gifts. He was one of sixty-two persons charged with similar crimes.

These examples are symptomatic of deficiencies in the system that so far have defied a general cure. Actions are underway that address some of the major problems, but much remains to be accomplished.

Attempts at improvement begin with a study of the adequacy of regulations. Do regulations meet the needs of the system? Are there areas of legislative or regulatory oversight that need to be covered? Is there potential for simplification and uniformity? Can or should there be broader participation in regulation writing? Are organizational and functional relationships what they should be? Are job requirements and personnel specifications properly defined? Are recruiting, training, and placement well handled?

The next step is to study administration and audit. Can the objectives and methods of performance supervision be improved? Can the relationships between public employees and vendors be better defined? Do audit procedures cover all of the potential areas of possible deviation? Can more responsive techniques be found for use in special categories of acquisition: research and development, major systems, architectural and engineering services, construction?

Finally study should focus on reports and controls. Do public agencies overrely on reporting versus other techniques of managing? Are reports relevant, timely, and useful? Are any of them duplicative? Are reporting requirements reasonably uniformly imposed? And, most importantly, do reports elicit the proper management response?

Work of the Commission on Government Procurement

The most ambitious reform effort has been the work of the federal Commission on Government Procurement. In spring 1971, when the commission was sworn in by President Richard M. Nixon, it had been twenty years since the last review of government procurement policies. During those twenty years, federal government buying had risen from $9 billion to $60 billion a year. Regulations, policies, and procedures had proliferated, with accompanying conflicts and duplications.

Section 4(a) of public law 91-129 established the scope of the commission effort:

> The Commission shall study and investigate the present statutes affecting government procurement; the procurement policies, rules, regulations, procedures, and practices followed by the departments, bureaus, agencies, boards, commissions, offices, independent establishments, and instrumentalities of the executive branch of the federal government; and the organizations by which procurement is accomplished to determine to what extent these facilitate the policy set forth in the first section of this Act.[1]

The commission was comprised of two members from the House of Representatives and a public member appointed by the Speaker of the House, two members from the Senate and a public member appointed by the president of the Senate, and two members from the executive branch and three public members appointed by the president of the United States. The comptroller general was designated a member by the statute.

The commission appointed an executive committee to assist and advise its chairman and vice-chairman in the management of its study operations. It employed a staff of about fifty professional members to conduct day-to-day study operations and direct the study effort. The collection and analysis of massive amounts of materials required the help and advice of government, industry, and the academic community. In all, the services of almost five hundred persons were loaned to the commission on a full- or part-time basis, some for periods exceeding a year.

In the first phase of the study, more than four hundred problems and issues were identified and divided among thirteen study groups and several special teams. The study was organized to provide in-depth coverage of the procurement process in three ways:

1. The environment in which procurement occurs (for example, federal organizations and personnel and the numerous authorities and controls under which they operate).
2. The sequence of procurement events (for example, precontract planning, pricing, and negotiation, selection and award, and contract administration and audit).
3. Types of procurement (for example, research and development, major systems, commercial products, and construction).

The commission and its participants reviewed thousands of pages of procurement reports, congressional testimony, documents, comments, and opinions; consulted approximately twelve thousand persons engaged in procurement; held more than two thousand meetings at one thousand government, industry, and academic facilities, including public meetings in eighteen cities; and received responses to questionnaires from nearly sixty thousand individuals and many organizations. Government agencies, suppliers, and trade and professional associations all made significant contributions to the program.

Each study group was instructed to provide the commission with recommendations for improving the procurement process and to support its recommendations with the most relevant, timely, and comprehensive information possible. The products of more than a year's intensive work by the study groups were presented to the commission in reports totaling more than fifteen thousand pages.[2]

At intervals during its work and at the conclusion of its effort, each study group made detailed presentations to the commission, which served as its working tools. Overall the work of the study groups served this purpose well and provided valuable basic information and differing viewpoints for commission deliberations.

The study effort was designed with some overlap in order to explore different viewpoints; some of the study groups reached different conclusions about the same subject matter. In some cases, the study group reports contain recommendations for improvement that the commission did not include in its report. A number of these pertain to details of procurement procedures that merit consideration by individual agencies; some were not considered appropriate for other reasons.

The commissioners held more than fifty days of formal meetings, in addition to participating on an individual basis with the staff and study groups. Commission studies focused on the process as a whole rather than on individual procurement decisions or transactions. Where undesirable or salutary practices and results were observed, the commission inquired into the process to see what could be learned for the future.

This extensive study resulted in 149 recommendations for improving government procurement, which were presented in a commission report consisting of ten parts packaged in four volumes.[3] Although each commissioner did not necessarily agree with every aspect of the report, the commission as a whole was in agreement with the general thrust of the discussion and recommendations.

An important objective of the commission's recommendations was to ensure that the system fully warrant the public trust. The recommendations proposed an integrated system for effective management, control, and operation of the federal procurement process. The focus of this system is the Office of Federal Procurement Policy (OFPP), since established, designed to provide leadership in the determination of government-wide procurement policies.

The system advocated will enable the executive branch to ensure that procurement operations are businesslike and orderly and that goods and services are efficiently acquired. To carry out this responsibility, federal purchasing agencies must be provided with necessary instructions and resources. Another essential ingredient is timely information on how well procurement needs are being met, so that deficiencies and resources may be adjusted at the appropriate management level. The ten elements of the system proposed satisfy these criteria:

1. The creation of the OFPP in the executive branch to ensure fulfillment of government-wide statutory and executive branch requirements in performing procurement responsibilities.
2. An integrated statutory base for procurement, implemented by a government-wide regulatory system, to establish sound policies and simplified agency procedures to direct and control the procurement process.
3. Latitude for federal agencies to carry out their responsibilities within the framework of government-wide statutes, policies, and controls.
4. Availability of funds in time to permit improved planning and continuity of needed federal and contractor operations.
5. Government-wide recruitment, training, education, and career-development programs to ensure professionalism in procurement operations and the availability of competent, trained personnel.

6. Carefully planned agency organizations, staffed with qualified people and delegated adequate authority to carry out their responsibilities.
7. A coordinated government-wide contract administration and audit system, designed to avoid duplication and deal uniformly, when practical, with the private sector in the administration of contracts at supplier locations.
8. Legal and administrative remedies to provide fair treatment of all parties involved in the procurement process.
9. An adequate management reporting system to reflect current progress and status so that necessary changes and improvements can be made when the need appears.
10. A continuing government-wide program to develop better statistical information and improved means of procuring goods and services.

The commissioners ended the introduction to their report in this way:

The complexity of procurement is such that mistakes will be made even by people dedicated to doing a quality job. The important thing is to learn from the mistakes and continually improve the process. There are no universal answers to myriad operating problems of government procurement and the many goals it supports. However, if the recommendations advanced in this report receive effective and timely implementation, measurable improvement should result in the short term and even greater improvements should result over the long term.

The Commission has not attempted to make an estimate of the savings which could be achieved through the adoption of its recommendations. Indeed, it would have been impossible since many of them are in the nature of policy changes for which estimates could not be made with any degree of precision. At the same time, the Commission is certain that substantial savings can be made and has so indicated at many points in its report. For example, one recommendation alone—increasing from $2,500 to $10,000 the limit on expenditures from using advertised procurement procedures for small purchases—would save approximately $100 million.[4]

Of the 149 recommendations made by the Commission, 57 required action by the Congress. The comptroller general, charged with keeping the Congress and the public informed on the status of the recommendations, made his eighth and final report on 31 May 1979.[5] The report was not encouraging. After six years, about two-thirds of the commission's recommendations either are pending or have not been acted upon at all. In many cases, the OFPP has not taken the initiative to propose relevant legislation. OFPP reports to the Congress and the public say little about the problems and slippages, and what is being done. Considering that about one-third of the commission recommendations involved new legislation, it would have been expected that OFPP would have drafted legislative proposals and would have launched a positive legislative program.

The report ends by recommending that OFPP be directed to review and resolve the several individual actions and issues and to develop a new reporting design that permits high visibility and accountability for remaining actions on open commission recommendations.

The Office of Federal Procurement Policy

The first element of the commission's improved system was the creation of the OFPP, established on 30 August 1974 when the president signed public law 93-400 establishing it in the OMB. The statute sets forth six specific functions:

1. Establish a system of coordinated and, to the extent feasible, uniform procurement regulations.
2. Establish criteria for soliciting the viewpoints of interested parties in the development of procurement policies and procedures.
3. Monitor policies and procedures relating to reliance by the federal government on the private sector to provide needed property and services.
4. Promote and conduct research in procurement policies.
5. Establish a procurement data system that takes into account the needs of the Congress, the executive branch, and the private sector.
6. Promote programs for recruitment, training, career development, and performance evaluation of procurement personnel.

One additional function was not stated: that of keeping the Congress informed of the major activities of the OFPP, including notification prior to final decisions, on all major matters of procurement policy.[6]

The statutory language and Congressional Conference Report covering OFPP's role in establishing coordinated procurement regulations is worded to capture the intent and purpose of the commission recommendations.[7] The objective is not to seek uniformity for uniformity's sake.

OFPP is acting in two principal areas: as a force to move the federal agencies to unify existing procurement regulations where feasible and to act as an information and coordination catalyst between the major agencies to ensure consistency and uniformity on future policies.

With regard to the second function of setting up criteria for soliciting public- and private-sector views, the OFPP has adopted the policy of publishing all proposed regulations in the *Federal Register*. Publication is followed by public hearings whenever requested by even one interested party.

The third OFPP function concerns the policy dealing with potential competition between in-house government resources and facilities and those of the private sector. An existing OMB circular (A-76) sets forth the basic guidelines in this area. OFPP has conducted an extensive review and revision. This is a sensitive topic, with many social, political, and economic ramifications. The policy being proposed builds on three principles:

1. Rely on the private sector. The government's business is not to be in business. Where private sources are available, they should be looked to first to provide the commercial or industrial goods and services needed by the government to act on the public's behalf.
2. Retain certain governmental functions in-house. Certain functions are inherently governmental in nature because they are so intimately related to the public interest as to mandate performance by federal employees.
3. Aim for economy by using cost comparisons. When private performance is feasible and no overriding factors require in-house performance, the taxpayer deserves and expects the most economical performance: Therefore rigorous comparison of contract costs versus in-house costs should be used when appropriate to decide how the work will be done.

Procurement research, within existing government resources and within the public and private sector, is one of the key elements of the overall information base used by OFPP to make its major procurement decisions. The national needs in procurement policies from an industry and government point of view are not stable; they are continually in flux. They depend on such factors as the cost and availability of financing, the market for labor and materials, and foreign trade matters. Procurement research will furnish in-depth information on these kinds of activities to ensure that federal procurement policies are responsive to national goals and priorities.

OFPP's remaining function covers federal procurement personnel and career development. The Congress realized that the heart of the procurement program is the professionalism of the work force. The need is to spread professionalism through the system for responsive decision making at all levels. The recommendations of the Commission on Government Procurement form a good basis for upgrading the qualifications of the procurement work force.

The act creating the OFPP provides that its administrator shall provide overall direction of procurement policy and shall prescribe policies, regulations, procedures, and forms to be followed by executive agencies in their procurement programs. All of the OFPP's functional responsibilities are assigned directly to the administrator.

Congress also expressed its intent that OFPP should not be a large office. The statute does not contain any specific restrictions; however, the legislative history speaks in terms of an initial staff of perhaps forty or so. The statute did direct the executive agencies to assist OFPP by furnishing services, personnel, and facilities. Such a provision enables the office to remain small but still pursue its objectives by drawing on outside resources as work load and priorities dictate. Agencies also thus become more directly involved in the development of policies, regulations, procedures, and forms.

At the same time, Congress intended a strong office. Within public law 93-400 three provisions stand out:

1. On authority: "The Administrator shall provide overall direction of procurement policy . . . he shall prescribe policies, regulations, procedures, which shall be in accordance with applicable laws and shall be followed by executive agencies" (section 6(a)).
2. On administrative powers: "Upon request of the Administrator, each executive agency is directed to make its services, personnel and facilities available to the Office to the greatest practicable extent" (section 7).
3. On effect on existing laws: "The authority of an executive agency under any other law to prescribe policies, regulations, procedures and forms for procurement is subject to the authority conferred (to the Administrator) in Section 6 of this Act" (section 9).

OFPP is one of the new federal agencies established under the sunset concept. Each five years the Congress must specifically legislate its continued existence. In October 1979, public law 96-83 extended the life of OFPP an additional four years.

The Federal Acquisition Institute

In July 1976 OFPP established the Federal Acquisition Institute (FAI) to improve business management in the government through upgrading and professionalizing the acquisition work force; serve as the central point for government-wide planning, development, implementation, and evaluation of acquisition research, education, and training; and develop and establish acquisition career development programs. Such an organization had been recommended by the Commission on Government Procurement.

The FAI identified eleven short-range and four long-range objectives supporting the purpose for which it had been established. In the short term its objectives were to:

1. Coordinate the identification of government-wide procurement education and training needs and the development of comprehensive government-wide plans to meet these needs.
2. Assist the agencies in improving the evaluation of procurement educa-

tion and training conducted by the agencies and in evaluating nonfederal procurement education and training programs used by federal agencies.

3. Assist the agencies in the development of standards for career development programs and education and training courses and programs needed to develop an effective government-wide procurement work force.

4. Monitor and evaluate career development programs and education and training courses and programs to certify whether they meet the established standards and are therefore considered acceptable for career programs for procurement personnel.

5. Encourage colleges and universities to offer courses of instruction and, in some cases, degree programs that prepare people for careers in the federal procurement field; also to assist the schools in developing suitable programs of study.

6. Promote, monitor, and conduct research in procurement policies and procedures to advance the state of the art in procurement through the development and application of improved business methods and techniques.

7. Collect and disseminate to federal agencies information about education and training opportunities that meet the needs of the federal procurement community.

8. Maintain a central repository and research library in the field of federal procurement and grants.

9. Recommend and promote programs of the executive agencies for recruitment, training, career development, and performance evaluation of procurement personnel.

10. Encourage state and local governments and private-sector activities to promote improvements in their procurement work force through collaboration with professional associations having objectives in common with the FAI.

11. Encourage and monitor the development, implementation, and exchange of personnel management ideas to enhance the procurement field.

The long-range objectives were to:

1. Develop and/or administer and finance a program for the development of textbooks and other learning materials needed for the instruction of federal employees in the procurement field.

2. Publish research findings and other literature and documents relating to procurement management in the federal service.

3. Conduct or sponsor short courses to prepare instructors of federal procurement personnel to perform their duties effectively and to keep them abreast of new developments in the field.

4. Operate or sponsor a residential, long-term (six to ten months in duration), academic-type education program designed to prepare high-potential procurement personnel (military and civilian) for key positions in federal procurement management.

The FAI receives policy and program guidance and direction from a board of advisers made up of twenty-four members, all of them officials responsible for the acquisition and procurement function in major federal departments. The board is convened and chaired by the administrator of OFPP, who votes on issues only to break ties. The primary function of the board of advisers is to provide policy and guidance to the FAI director in identifying and designing programs and in establishing procedures and standards for implementation by the FAI. The director and the professional staff positions are selected in consultation with the board.

Members of the board identify and commit agency personnel and resources needed to develop and implement FAI programs and provide the management interest and support needed to establish and effectively maintain FAI programs in each agency and on a government-wide basis.

The FAI is engaged in several major tasks, all relating to the federal government's 130,000-person contracting work force. An information system has been established that provides the ability to forecast trends in retirement, training, grade levels, employee mobility, and specialty requirements before such trends affect the system. An inventory of tasks and job requirements has been constructed that is enabling the revision of job standards. Career patterns and goals are being identified, performance evaluation is being unified across government, education and training opportunities are being upgraded, and certification and other evidences of professionalism are being promoted. In the research area, a massive survey has been made of areas that need investigation.

One of the more tangible and a highly valuable activity of the FAI is its library. The nucleus of the library was the enormous collection of literature assembled by the Commission on Government Procurement. The library has been kept current by a systematic program of acquisitions. A bimonthly abstract of new literature is published.[8]

Work of the National Association of State Purchasing Officials

In March 1975 *State and Local Government Purchasing*, a report that resulted from a cooperative effort of the National Association of State Purchasing Officials, an affiliate of the Council of State Governments, and Peat, Marwick Mitchell and Company, was published. Financial support was furnished by the U.S. Law Enforcement Assistance Administration. The report presents the first comprehensive research on the subject.

Information concerning purchasing laws, policies, practices, and procedures was gathered from all states, three territories, and 1,865 cities and counties. Although quasi-governmental organizations such as boards, commissions, and authorities are frequently active in governmental purchasing, they generally operate independently and were not included in this study.

To accomplish the study objectives, it was first necessary to determine what is being done and, from this body of knowledge, to arrive at recommendations for enhancing the effectiveness of all public-purchasing programs. The latter effort was essentially one of comparative evaluation and entailed measuring the results achieved against the desired objectives. Examining the state of the art was a fact-finding process, which entailed an extensive review of statutes, ordinances, regulations, case law, attorneys general's opinions, and procedural manuals.

Statutes and regulations were obtained from the fifty states and three territories. Where the information received was incomplete or outdated, additional research was carried out. Purchasing ordinances of several cities and counties were obtained from the National Institute of Governmental Purchasing. A checklist was developed to ensure that all major areas of interest in the statutes and regulations were reviewed in a consistent manner.

These areas were identified by analyzing the purchasing laws from several states known to have comprehensive coverage. Law review articles were also used in focusing on problems in statutory coverage. Considering these data, checklist questions were formulated in the following categories: purchasing function, bidders' lists, specifications, bidding and contract award, safeguards and controls; and miscellaneous.

The checklist questions were applied to the laws and regulations. A listing was made of questions for which statutory and regulatory provisions were either silent or too general to provide specific answers. These questions were sent to each state involved for further information. The states were asked to answer specific designated questions and to support their responses with either a copy or a reference to the appropriate authoritative source. These replies were merged with the answers previously obtained in the original checklist, and the final data were sent to the purchasing officials of each state for verification. The data gathered during this phase of research are presented in an appendix to the report.

In order to determine how well public-purchasing organizations provide procedural instructions to their staffs, purchasing manuals were reviewed. Thirty-two states and territories responded to requests for purchasing manuals. Fifteen were selected for in-depth review because they represented the best overall subject coverage.

Based on a preliminary review of all manuals received, published articles, and other studies, evaluation criteria were established in the form of a checklist that encompassed these major subjects: principles, policy, and organization; requirements planning, specifications, and standards; requisitioning, procurement, and contracting; and receiving, stores and warehouses, quality control, and disposal.

In addition to its analysis of the statutes, ordinances, and manuals, the study group assembled an extensive bibliography of professional, technical, scholarly, and legal information. Pertinent court decisions and attorneys general's opinions were included.

The study included research and review of city and county purchasing laws, policies, procedures, and practices. Although some of this information was available from the ordinances, insufficient material was received to enable an accurate appraisal of city and county purchasing operations. Because of the large number of cities and counties, a complete review of all ordinances, administrative regulations, and manuals was neither practicable nor feasible. It was therefore decided to conduct a nationwide survey of cities and counties.

With over ten thousand cities and counties from which to choose, it was necessary to reduce the number to a manageable level and to focus on those collective purchasing practices that gave rise to purchasing systems. It was determined that the sample should consist of cities and counties with populations of ten thousand and over. This resulted in a survey population of 4,493 local governments.

As an initial step in developing the survey questionnaire, the following subjects were selected as major areas of interest: authorities, organization, bidding procedures, contract award, safeguards and controls, and purchasing management. Within each of these sections, a series of questions was developed that indicated the extent to which purchasing functions were covered by state statute, local ordinance, rules and regulations, manuals, and unwritten purchasing policies or practices. The synthesizing process involved developing a series of iterative drafts, which were reviewed in depth with selected purchasing authorities.

To augment the information obtained from researching statutes, regulations, and manuals and from the local government survey, field visits were made to twelve state and eight local governments. These visits were particularly valuable in identifying exceptional and unique practices. In order to obtain a representative cross-section of all levels of practice, the selection process considered such factors as statutory and regulatory coverage, geographic location, centralized operations, and size of purchasing operations.

This effort of the National Association of State Purchasing Officials was used extensively in the subsequent development of the Model Procurement Code for state and local governments.

Efforts of the Professional Associations

The efforts of the professional organizations in the field in training, education, and professional certification contribute greatly to the improvements of the system. Nothing is more important than the individual competence of members of the work force. The associations set standards of competence and then assist members, and others, in increasing their individual competence. In requiring periodic recertification, they stress the importance of keeping up with developments in the field.

Everyone concerned with public purchasing and materials management should support and encourage the certification concept. Supervisors should stress the desirability of certification in employment and advancement. Individuals should plan their own professional development around certification. The result will be a generally higher level of performance, to the public's benefit.

Work of the American Bar Association

The work of the Commission on Government Procurement and of the National Association of State Purchasing Officials was drawn upon extensively in the drafting by the American Bar Association (ABA) of a model procurement code for state and local governments. Two sections of the ABA worked together on the project: the Section of Local Government Law and the Section of Public Contract Law. Financing was provided by the U.S. Department of Justice's Law Enforcement Assistance Administration.

The ABA Coordinating Committee on a Model Procurement Code ensured active participation by other interested organizations. It established a Liaison Committee with state and local purchasing officials. Participation by representatives of the National Association of State Purchasing Officials and the National Institute of Governmental Purchasing was credited as especially helpful. The Coordinating Committee also established an advisory board, comprised of organizations interested in improving state and local purchasing, including associations of state and local officials and associations representing various vendors.

The committee also cooperated with a number of state and local governments during the developmental efforts that led to the statutory language and code commentary. Under the project's Pilot Jurisdiction Program, selected states and cities entered into a close working relationship with the coordinating committee. In addition, the committee worked with several other jurisdictions. In California, for example, it cooperated in a comprehensive study of the state's entire public contract system being undertaken by the California Department of General Services. In Massachusetts and Pennsylvania, the committee conducted several colloquia sessions to provide a broad orientation on the code's proposals to interested persons and organizations.

At an early stage the decision was made to develop a model rather than a uniform procurement code because of the diverse organizational structures used by the states and the multitude of local government bodies and the differences in their procurement needs. It was recognized that varying organizational and political constraints in enacting jurisdictions would necessitate the adaptation of any proposed code to particular state and local situations. In substantive matters, however, it was concluded that the proposed Model Procurement Code should reflect basic policies equally applicable to the conduct and control of procurement by all public bodies.

The Model Procurement Code follows the concept that it should provide a statutory framework for public procurement embodying the fundamentals of sound procurement and that those fundamentals should be implemented by regulations consistent with the statutory framework. Procurement is a dynamic process, which continues to evolve and which requires revision of procurement techniques as needs and requirements change. Experience has shown that incorporating too many details in statutory material tends to establish an overly rigid structure that constricts good procurement practices and necessarily results in strained judicial interpretations to accommodate actual practice.

The use of regulations to implement statutory policies permits change and modification dictated by experience and provides a means for expeditious improvement and innovation in procurement techniques. When coupled with requirements for public participation in the issuance and revision of procurement regulations and appropriate legislative oversight, a comprehensive statute implemented by more specific regulations provides a flexible system capable of promoting efficiency in procurement and conserving money.

Improvement Efforts at the Federal Level

The challenge of dealing with the massive federal procurement effort over the years has inspired many now widely recognized management techniques. Among them are:

1. The planning-programming-budgeting concept, with particular application to the programming of procurement.
2. The closely related cost-benefit and cost-effectiveness concepts used in choosing among competing programs.
3. The program evaluation review technique (PERT) used in detailed time and money scheduling of major acquisitions.
4. Applications of value engineering (value analysis) in achieving cost reductions without reducing value.
5. Applications of learning-curve concepts in reducing prices paid for items in successive procurement and production lots.

6. The life-cycle costing concept in which decision makers take into account the entire sequence of costs: developmental, production, operational, and phase-out.
7. The zero-defects concept in quality and reliability improvement.
8. Numerous applications of computer and information-systems technology.

Not all of the techniques attempted proved successful. One glaring example is the total package procurement approach of the 1960s. Total package procurement required major systems producers to combine development and production in one fixed-price bid. But state of the art and inflation complications caused enormous financial and performance problems for both the vendors and the government.

The 1970s brought numerous developments stemming from the *Report of the Commission on Government Procurement*, among them the activities of OFPP and the FAI and the helpful distinction between grant and procurement actions.

A new management tool of considerable potential is the Federal Procurement Data System (FPDS), directed by public law 93-400, section 6(d)(5) of which requires, "a system for collecting, developing, and disseminating procurement data which takes into account the needs of the Congress, the executive branch, and the private sector." The FPDS will, for the first time, provide total and uniform information on federal government contracts with individual values of over $10,000. The information is becoming available for analysis and for management use by the executive agencies, the Congress, and the private sector. The FPDS produces, on call, individual transaction reports containing:

1. Agency and specific contracting office.
2. Date of action.
3. Contractor(s).
4. Place of performance.
5. Dollars obligated.
6. Product or service acquired.
7. Type of contract (for example, fixed price or cost type).
8. Type of business receiving the contract (small, large minority, woman owned, nonprofit).
9. Estimated completion date.
10. Information, where applicable, regarding affirmative-action programs, consultant services, Walsh-Healey Act and Davis-Bacon Act provisions, and labor-surplus area considerations.
11. Extent of competition.
12. Estimated percentage of foreign participation or content.

As of this writing, 143 federal agencies are covered. When fully operational, FPDS will provide in one centralized location the data needed for access to the workings of the federal acquisition system. This capability could lead to more improvements in the acquisition process, as well as to more effective implementation of the law.

A less-well-known but nonetheless significant project is the Experimental Technology Incentives Program (ETIP) of the National Bureau of Standards, designed to enable procurement policy to promote innovations by vendors to the government at all levels. The ETIP involves several activities, all intended to promote the application and transfer of science and technology to strengthen the nation's economy. It recognizes that most of our technological and innovative resources lie in the private sector, and it experiments with procurement policy and practice to stimulate use of these resources to solve public-sector problems. Possibly the most significant aspect of the ETIP approach is the development of performance specifications for the procurement of standard products. These specifications are coupled with adequate testing procedures and with sliding-scale price incentives to encourage sources of supply to make technological improvements in otherwise standard items. For example, a performance specification for procurement of window air-conditioners was developed that called for reduced energy consumption. The contract then offered incentive price increases for achievement of more energy efficient units. The units supplied achieved a 20 percent reduction in electricity consumed.

The ETIP is also experimenting with uses in civil agency procurement of two techniques originating in military procurement. One is life-cycle costing. Under this method, the vendors' estimate of the total cost of ownership over time carries more weight than does the item bid price in the award of the contract. The other is value engineering (value analysis), under which incentive payments are available to a supplier who can value engineer a product to where it performs all required functions but at a lower cost. The savings resulting from value engineering are shared between the seller and the buyer. Taken together, the work of the ETIP will add another element of improvement in public purchasing.

In the Federal Supply Service (FSS), attempts at improvement are mostly in reaction to exposed shortcomings and fraud. GAO, GSA, and Department of Justice investigators continue to uncover evidence of grave abuses of the federal supply system by employees and private businesses with FSS contracts. In each instance, every effort has been made to halt the abuse and bring those involved to justice. Even more important, FSS management, at the direction of the GSA administrator, has instituted new procedures, oversight groups, and financial checks and reviews to correct the management deficiencies that had allowed fraud and carelessness to occur.

Among the first FSS groups to receive close scrutiny by GSA investigators were the seventy-five FSS self-service stores—the supermarkets where federal agencies shop for office supplies—and the motor pools, the service centers for the interagency motor pool system. Investigations revealed a long list of abuses. Certain store managers had paid for goods they had never received, and some federal employees had made purchases in stores with government credit cards and had taken the purchase home for their own use. Wrongdoing in motorpools ranged from charging gas and parts for personal vehicles to GSA credit cards to irregularities in awarding contracts.

GSA has announced a dozen controls developed by FSS to prevent self-service store abuses in the future. They range from tighter restrictions on who can use the stores to unannounced inspections. The variety of goods stocked has been cut nearly in half, and those most easily put to personal rather than government use—such as spray paint, hand tools, aspirin, and Styrofoam cups—removed. Any expansion of a store's stock by a manager now requires prior authorization by a responsible administrator. All purchases of theft-prone items, such as cameras and briefcases, have a separate sales record, a copy of which is forwarded to control officials in the purchasing agency.

In addition to these new controls, FSS and the GSA have implemented many organizational and procedural changes to identify and correct areas of potential trouble. To ensure fair and open competition among many firms for government contracts, the FSS has continued to review and refine its procurement solicitation methods. It is moving to make it impossible for contracting officials to limit orders to the same few businesses over and over. A key to such open competition is the simplification of government specifications. Specifications cover items from office desks to mousetraps and from carpets to stick-on bandages. Some have encouraged certain firms to gear their production especially for sale to the government and have discouraged other firms from trying to compete.

The FSS has made progress in implementing a policy to purchase existing commercial products when these are adequate. Many unneeded specifications have been canceled. Commercial product descriptions are being written for other items, including office and building supplies, cleaners, waxes, and hardware.

The GSA administrator has announced new and tighter guidelines for sole-source procurements. All sole-source contracts with a value over $500 must be approved in writing by the head of the originating staff or service or by a regional administrator and must be accompanied by a written justification for not obtaining competition, together with recommendations for seeking competition for similar contracts in the future. Documentation must be sent to the administrator within fifteen days of the award.

The administrator also has directed that FSS multiple-award schedules be purged of items that can be obtained from retail outlets at lower cost. Under these schedules, agencies can order items like air-conditioners and calculators from one of several listed suppliers for direct delivery at discounts from published commercial prices. However, discount houses have been found to carry some of the items at prices lower than those quoted in the government schedules.

The FSS is adopting a full-cost disclosure system, which will identify the total cost of items procured. Purchase price, freight, operating expenses, sales expenses, and other costs will all be considered, and the efficiencies of various procurement and distribution methods will be compared. Previously such total costing was impossible because direct costs for some operations are paid from a revolving fund while operating expenses (salaries and overhead) come out of yearly appropriations, and no method existed for bringing the two elements together.

Value-management techniques are reported by FSS as saving over $1.1 million during the 1978 fiscal year. As utilized in FSS, value management has three parts: employee ideas to identify, study, and implement cost-saving projects; money-saving suggestions from private companies, submitted under value-incentive clauses included in their contracts; and life-cycle costing, or consideration of the cost of an item's operation, maintenance, and eventual disposal as well as its purchase price.

The FSS is improving its procedures pertaining to socioeconomic aspects of public purchasing. Through special procurement procedures, it channels millions of federal dollars into areas of high unemployment (labor-surplus areas), as well as to small, minority, and other special-category businesses. In a separate effort, FSS is locating, through GSA's Business Service Centers in major cities, firms that have never sold to the government before but would like to. By explaining federal procurement procedures and notifying firms of suitable opportunities, it aims at creating new opportunities for, and thus bolstering employment at, small, minority, and other businesses.

In 1978 FSS purchases from firms in labor-surplus areas totaled $925 million; from small businesses, $594 million; from minority businesses, $28 million; from workshops for the handicapped, over $53 million; and from Federal Prison Industries, over $26 million. Also through the Business Service Centers, FSS has initiated a drive to encourage women-owned businesses to bid for government contracts. Seminars throughout the country, conducted in cooperation with the Small Business Administration and local business organizations, are acquainting women with government procurement policies, procedures, and opportunities.

Across the federal government, purchasing and materials management is being reshaped. With the original catalyst of the Procurement Commission in 1972, momentum has built, achievements have accelerated, and a reexamination of methods and precepts has touched virtually every facet of the system. Symbolic of this is the use of the term *acquisition*. Procurement regulations have become "acquisition regulations"; agency officials are designated as "acquisition executives." The source of such terminology is the Federal Acquisition Reform Act. But more than semantics is involved. Traditionally the government has operated three separate elements: requirements determination, in which the government's needs were expressed; procurement, in which those needs were contracted for; and logistics, in which the procured goods and services were distributed and applied. Problems arising in each element were treated within the separate arenas. But problems in logistics, supply, and distribution have their roots in matters of requirements and in contracting. Problems in procurement have their roots in the way requirements are set. The acquisition thought process begins with specifications and requirements, and why they are expressed as they are. Additional improvements at the federal level will rest on an intellectual appreciation of the total acquisition process; it will embrace requirements, procurement, and logistics viewed and managed in concert.

Improvement Efforts at the State and Local Levels

The major improvement effort applicable at the state and local levels has been the promulgation of the Model Procurement Code. To some extent, the code is based on federal-level experience, and its development was financed with federal funds on a grant by the Law Enforcement Assistance Administration. General adoption of the code is expected to have three effects:

1. More responsible use of public funds for procurement at the state and local levels and a resulting increase in public confidence.
2. Greater uniformity in the law relating to purchasing, with a resulting reduction in across jurisdiction confusion.
3. Simplification, clarification, and modernization of the law.

An example of state law based upon the code is included here as Appendix C.

The federal government is cooperating with the states in a series of demonstration audits of procurement policies and practices. The first such audit was of the procurement system of the state of Oregon, conducted in 1976.[9] The report includes a detailed outline for the audit of a state system. The basic procurement principles against which the Oregon procurement system was audited were derived from the Council of State Governments' report, *State and Local Government Purchasing*. The cooperative audit was directed at state procurement of goods and services in Oregon and dealt only incidentally with procurement by countries, municipalities, and other governmental entities in the state. Since goods and services obtained with federal grant funds are subject to the same policies and procedures governing all state agency procurements, the procurement system as a whole was evaluated rather than procurements made under specific grants. The audit encompassed the major elements of program management: organization, policies, procedures, personnel, planning, management-information systems, reporting, and internal review.

Subsequently in 1977 and 1978, the GAO participated in a cooperative study of one county and four city procurement activities.[10] This study found that although all of the governments placed purchasing responsibilities in one official, three of the departments operated in a manner that ignored the benefits of centralized purchasing. Also none of the governments required accountability of the performance of the procurement function, and only one had made any progress toward obtaining the benefits available from cooperative procurement arrangements. These weaknesses are attributed to the lack of adherence to recognized procurement principles and the lack of requirements by local officials for accountability through goal setting and performance measurement, or internal and external audits of the purchasing system. Numerous suggestions for improvement were made.

Representative of another effort is the examination of North Dakota's purchasing system made by the Interstate Consulting Clearinghouse of the Council of State Governments.[11] The clearinghouse is the council's vehicle for providing technical assistance to requesting state governments. In this instance, a team of specialists conducted a two-phased study between November 1977 and January 1978. Detailed findings and recommendations were made covering the entire scope of state-level purchasing.

Another example is the study of productivity of the purchasing and materials-management system done for the city of Detroit. This study was sponsored and funded by the National Science Foundation.[12] The effort is management-by-objectives oriented, and begins with defining objectives and standards of performance developed from a survey of public-purchasing entities across the country. The study provides local governments with validated techniques for measuring the productivity of the purchasing and materials-management system. The study suggests that the principal potential for improving productivity at the local level lies in cooperation among entities, particularly the sharing of information concerning prices, specifications, and product performance; greater central control and more uniform operating policies for storage and distribution operations; and allocation of more adequate resources and technical support to central purchasing departments.

The cumulative effect of these studies, evaluations, and audits has been to bring a high level of visibility and a consistent analytical approach to the problems of the system. All fit together in improving the efficiency, economy, and effectiveness of the system.

Research in Purchasing and Materials Management

The Commission on Government Procurement stressed the need for a continuing program of research to make procurement work better. Subsequently in 1977, the GAO released a detailed report, "An Organized Approach to Improving Federal Procurement and Acquisition Practices," which presented a plan for the conduct of research by federal agencies.[13] It recommended that a program for procurement and acquisition research be established within the federal government. As part of this program, those agencies dependent on procurement and acquisition processes to carry out their primary responsibilities should establish a continuing research effort to correct and refine procedures on a continuous basis and cope with procurement problems peculiar to agency operations as they arise; design the best ways of giving effect to (implementing) new government procurement and acquisition policies and expose them to operational testing; and evaluate their experiences, achieve innovative improvements, develop training materials, and participate in research of a government-wide nature.

This was followed by an FAI survey of perceived research needs within the civil agencies of government. Emphasis was placed upon civil agencies on the grounds that the military agencies already possessed a fairly clear perception of research needs and that a military procurement research program was in place.[14] The survey found a concentration of concern in ten problem areas,

1. Personnel. The research would identify the several tasks and actions to be performed and the average amount of time required to accomplish each. This would provide a rational basis for determining overall personnel needs in the several activities and a staffing guide.
2. Attitudes toward the work. The research would deal with motivation of personnel performing the function and with ways to improve judgment, creativity, and accuracy.
3. Roles. The research would identify more specifically the roles of the several specialists employed in the function, a particular problem in systems-acquisition and large-program management.
4. Training. The research would better identify the knowledge and skills required by members of the work force and means of delivering the needed training.

5. Meeting socioeconomic objectives. The research would evaluate the use of government contracts as a socioeconomic device. It would weigh impact upon the primary objective of acquiring needed goods and services.
6. Process complexity. The research would examine the many demands that add up to reduced efficiency and look for ways to streamline the process.
7. Authority. The research would investigate restrictions on delegation and overcontrols on the process. It would look for ways to lower thresholds of approval.
8. Delay. The research would identify the cause of excessive delay in the system and unnecessarily protracted steps in the process and would seek ways of shortening the process.
9. Accountability. The research would look for better ways of evaluating performance and holding individuals accountable.
10. Competition. The research would examine the several alternative ways of maintaining fair and open competition for government contracts, including forms of advertising, solicitation, and exclusions.

The professional organizations are also concerned with the need for organized research. The National Association of Purchasing Management conducts a long-standing program under which cash assistance is extended to qualified practitioners and to doctoral students. Research proposals are solicited and formal proposal guidance is available.[15]

Notes

1. Public Law 91-129, approved 26 November 1969, 83 Stat. 269.
2. Copies of the study group reports were filed with both the House and Senate Committees on Government Operations. Reference copies are available. For information regarding location and hours, interested persons may contact the Federal Supply Service, General Services Administration, Washington, D.C. 20406.
3. Commission on Government Procurement, *Report of the Commission on Government Procurement* (Washington, D.C.: Government Printing Office, 1972), 4 vols.
4. Ibid., 1:7.
5. General Accounting Office, *Recommendations of the Commission on Government Procurement: A Final Assessment*, PSAD 79-80. Available from GAO Distribution Section, Room 1518, 441 G Street, NW, Washington, D.C. 20548.

6. This and the immediately following material is based on a presentation by Hugh E. Witt, first administrator of OFPP, to a meeting of the Federal Bar Association, 9 October 1974, at San Francisco, California.

7. U.S. House of Representatives, Report No. 93-1268, Office of Federal Procurement Policy, Conference Report, 7 August 1974.

8. The abstracts are prepared and published as a service to the purchasing community. Write to: Helen Hertel, Librarian, Federal Acquisition Institute, OMB/OFPP, 726 Jackson Place, NW, Washington, D.C. 20503.

9. General Accounting Office, *Audit of the Procurement System of the State of Oregon: A Case Study* (Washington, D.C.: GAO, 10 January 1977).

10. General Accounting Office, *Study of Local Procurement Systems*, PSAD 78-95 (Washington, D.C.: GAO, August 1978).

11. Council of State Governments, *Examination of North Dakota's Purchasing System* (Lexington, Ky.: Council of State Governments, May 1978).

12. A copy of the study may be obtained by requesting PB 283 485 from: Department of Commerce, National Technical Information Service, Springfield, Virginia 22161.

13. General Accounting Office, *An Organized Approach to Improving Federal Procurement and Acquisition Practices*, PSAD 77-128 (Washington, D.C.: GAO, 30 September 1977).

14. See Department of Defense, *Procurement Research*, Directive 4105.68 (Washington, D.C.: Department of Defense, 22 June 1977).

15. Write to: Chairman, NAPM Research Planning Committee, National Association of Purchasing Management, 11 Park Place, New York, New York 10007.

Appendix A:
The Federal Grant and Cooperative Agreement Act of 1977

PUBLIC LAW 95–224—FEB. 3, 1978   92 STAT. 3

Public Law 95–224
95th Congress

An Act

To distinguish Federal grant and cooperative agreement relationships from Federal procurement relationships, and for other purposes.

Feb. 3, 1978
[H.R. 7691]

Be it enacted by the Senate and House of Representatives of the United States of America in Congress assembled, That this Act be cited as the "Federal Grant and Cooperative Agreement Act of 1977".

Federal Grant and Cooperative Agreement Act of 1977.
41 USC 501 note.

FINDINGS AND PURPOSE

41 USC 501.

Sec. 2. (a) The Congress finds that—

(1) there is a need to distinguish Federal assistance relationships from Federal procurement relationships and thereby to standardize usage and clarify the meaning of the legal instruments which reflect such relationships;

· (2) uncertainty as to the meaning of such terms as "contract", "grant", and "cooperative agreement" and the relationships they reflect causes operational inconsistencies, confusion, inefficiency, and waste for recipients of awards as well as for executive agencies; and

(3) the Commission on Government Procurement has documented these findings and concluded that a reduction of the existing inconsistencies, confusion, inefficiency, and waste is feasible and necessary through legislative action.

(b) The purposes of this Act are—

(1) to characterize the relationship between the Federal Government and contractors, State and local governments, and other recipients in the acquisition of property and services and in the furnishing of assistance by the Federal Government so as to promote a better understanding of Federal spending and help eliminate unnecessary administrative requirements on recipients of Federal awards;

(2) to establish Government-wide criteria for selection of appropriate legal instruments to achieve uniformity in the use by the executive agencies of such instruments, a clear definition of the relationships they reflect, and a better understanding of the responsibilities of the parties;

(3) to promote increased discipline in the selection and use of types of contract, grant agreement, and cooperative agreements and to maximize competition in the award of contracts and encourage competition, where deemed appropriate, in the award of grants and cooperative agreements; and

(4) to require a study of the relationship between the Federal Government and grantees and other recipients in Federal assistance programs and the feasibility of developing a comprehensive system of guideline for the use of grant and cooperative agreements, and other forms of Federal assistance in carrying out such programs.

92 STAT. 4   PUBLIC LAW 95-224—FEB. 3, 1978

DEFINITIONS

41 USC 502.   SEC. 3. As used in this Act, the term—
        (1) "State government" means any of the several States of the
United States, the District of Columbia, the Commonwealth of
Puerto Rico, any territory or possession of the United States, any
agency or instrumentality of a State, and any multi-State,
regional, or interstate entity which has governmental functions;
        (2) "local government" means any unit of government within
a State, a county, municipality, city, town, township, local public
authority, special district, intrastate district, council of governments, sponsor group representative organization, other interstate government entity, or any other instrumentality of a local
government;
        (3) "other recipient" means any person or recipient other than
a State or local government who is authorized to receive Federal
assistance or procurement contracts and includes any charitable
or educational institution;
        (4) "executive agency" means any executive department as
defined in section 101 of title 5, United States Code, a military
department as defined in section 102 of title 5, United States Code,
an independent establishment as defined in section 104 of title 5,
United States Code (except that it shall not include the General
Accounting Office), a wholly owned Government corporation;
and
        (5) "grant or cooperative agreement" does not include any
agreement under which only direct Federal cash assistance
to individuals, a subsidy, a loan, a loan guarantee, or insurance is
provided.

USE OF CONTRACTS

41 USC 503.   SEC. 4. Each executive agency shall use a type of procurement contract as the legal instrument reflecting a relationship between the
Federal Government and a State or local government or other
recipient—
        (1) whenever the principal purpose of the instrument is the
acquisition, by purchase, lease, or barter, of property or services
for the direct benefit or use of the Federal Government; or
        (2) whenever an executive agency determines in a specific
instance that the use of a type of procurement contract is
appropriate.

USE OF GRANT AGREEMENTS

41 USC 504.   SEC. 5. Each executive agency shall use a type of grant agreement as
the legal instrument reflecting a relationship between the Federal Government and a State or local government or other recipient whenever—
Transfers.   (1) the principal purpose of the relationship is the transfer of
money, property, services, or anything of value to the State or
local government or other recipient in order to accomplish a public purpose of support or stimulation authorized by Federal
statute, rather than acquisition, by purchase, lease, or barter, of
property or services for the direct benefit or use of the Federal
Government; and
        (2) no substantial involvement is anticipated between the
executive agency, acting for the Federal Government, and the
State or local government or other recipient during performance
of the contemplated activity.

USE OF COOPERATIVE AGREEMENTS

Sec. 6. Each executive agency shall use a type of cooperative agree-   41 USC 505.
ment as the legal instrument reflecting a relationship between the Federal Government and a State or local government or other recipient
whenever—
    (1) the principal purpose of the relationship is the transfer of   Transfers.
money, property, services, or anything of value to the State or
local government or other recipient to accomplish a public purpose of support or stimulation authorized by Federal statute,
rather than acquisition, by purchase, lease, or barter, of property
or services for the direct benefit or use of the Federal Government; and
    (2) substantial involvement is anticipated between the execu-
tive agency, acting for the Federal Government, and the State or
local government or other recipient during performance of the
contemplated activity.

AUTHORIZATIONS

Sec. 7. (a) Notwithstanding any other provision of law, each execu-   Contracts, grant
tive agency authorized by law to enter into contracts, grant or coopera-   or cooperative
tive agreements, or similar arrangements is authorized and directed to   agreements.
enter into and use types of contracts, grant agreements, or cooperative   41 USC 506.
agreements as required by this Act.
  (b) The authority to make contracts, grants, and cooperative agree-   Scientific
ments for the conduct of basic or applied scientific research at non-   research.
profit institutions of higher education, or at nonprofit organizations
whose primary purpose is the conduct of scientific research shall
include discretionary authority, when it is deemed by the head of the
executive agency to be in furtherance of the objectives of the agency,
to vest in such institutions or organizations, without further obligation to the Government, or on such other terms and conditions as
deemed appropriate, title to equipment or other tangible personal
property purchased with such funds.

STUDY OF FEDERAL ASSISTANCE PROGRAMS

Sec. 8. The Director of the Office of Management and Budget, in   41 USC 507.
cooperation with the executive agencies, shall undertake a study to
develop a better understanding of alternative means of implementing
Federal assistance programs, and to determine the feasibility of developing a comprehensive system of guidance for Federal assistance
programs. Such study shall include a thorough consideration of the   Contents.
findings and recommendations of the Commission on Government
Procurement relating to the feasibility of developing such a system.
The Director shall consult with and to the extent practicable, involve   Consultation.
representatives of the executive agencies, the Congress, the General
Accounting Office, and State and local governments, other recipients
and other interested members of the public. The result of the study   Report to
shall be reported to the Committee on Government Operations of the   congressional
House of Representatives and the Committee on Governmental Affairs   committees.
of he Senate at the earliest practicable date, but in no event later than
two years after the date of enactment of this Act. The report on the
study shall include (1) detailed descriptions of the alternative means
of implementing Federal assistance programs and of the circumstances
in which the use of each appears to be most desirable, (2) detailed

92 STAT. 6   PUBLIC LAW 95–224—FEB. 3, 1978

descriptions of the basic characteristics and an outline of such comprehensive system of guidance for Federal assistance programs, the development of which may be determined feasible, and (3) recommendations
concerning arrangements to proceed with the full development of such
comprehensive system of guidance and for such administrative or
statutory changes, including changes in the provisions of sections 3
through 7 of this Act, as may be deemed appropriate on the basis of the
findings of the study.

GUIDELINES

41 USC 508.

SEC. 9. The Director of the Office of Management and Budget is
authorized to issue supplementary interpretative guidelines to promote
consistent and efficient use of contract, grants agreement, and cooperative agreements as defined in this Act.

REPEALS AND SAVINGS PROVISIONS

Repeal; effective
date.

SEC. 10. (a) The Act entitled "An Act to authorize the expenditure
of funds through grants for support of scientific research, and for other
purposes", approved September 6, 1958 (72 Stat. 1793; 42 U.S.C. 1891
and 1892), is repealed, effective one year after the date of enactment of
this Act.

41 USC 501 note.

(b) Nothing in this Act shall be construed to render void or voidable
any existing contract, grant, cooperative agreement, or other contract,
grant, or cooperative agreement entered into up to one year after the
date of enactment of this Act.

41 USC 509.

(c) Nothing in this Act shall require the establishment of a single
relationship between the Federal Government and a State or local
government or other recipient on a jointly funded project, involving
funds from more than one program or appropriation where different
relationships would otherwise be appropriate for different components
of the project.

Excepted
transactions.
41 USC 501 note.
Expiration date.

(d) The Director of the Office of Management and Budget may
except individual transactions or programs of any executive agency
from the application of the provisions of this Act. This authority shall
expire one year after receipt by the Congress of the study provided for
in section 8 of this Act.

Approved February 3, 1978.

LEGISLATIVE HISTORY:

HOUSE REPORT No. 95–481 (Comm. on Government Operations).
SENATE REPORT No. 95–449 accompanying S. 431 (Comm. on Governmental Affairs).
CONGRESSIONAL RECORD:
    Vol. 123 (1977): Sept. 27, considered and passed House.
            Oct. 1, considered and passed Senate, amended, in lieu of S.
            431.
    Vol. 124 (1978): Jan. 19, House agreed to Senate amendment.

Appendix B:
The Federal Acquisition Reform Act

96TH CONGRESS
1ST SESSION

S. 5

To provide policies, methods, and criteria for the acquisition of property and
services by executive agencies.

IN THE SENATE OF THE UNITED STATES

JANUARY 15, 1979

Mr. CHILES introduced the following bill; which was read twice and referred to
the Committee on Governmental Affairs

MARCH 21 (legislative day, FEBRUARY 22), 1979

Referred jointly, by unanimous consent, to the Committees on Governmental
Affairs and Armed Services

A BILL

To provide policies, methods, and criteria for the acquisition of
property and services by executive agencies.

1   *Be it enacted by the Senate and House of Representa-*

2   *tives of the United States of America in Congress assembled,*

3   SHORT TITLE; TABLE OF CONTENTS

4   SECTION 1. (a) SHORT TITLE.—This Act may be cited

5   as the "Federal Acquisition Reform Act".

6   (b) TABLE OF CONTENTS.—

II—E●

DECLARATION OF POLICY

Findings

SEC. 2. (a) The Congress hereby finds that—

(1) the laws controlling Federal purchasing have become outdated, fragmented, and needlessly inconsistent;

(2) these deficiencies have contributed to significant inefficiency, ineffectiveness, and waste in Federal spending;

(3) a new consolidated statutory base is needed, as recommended by the Commission on Government Procurement;

(4) further, existing statutes need to be modernized to focus on effective competition and new technology in that—

1   (A) national productivity rests on a base of

2   competitive industry applying new technology in

3   its goods and services; and

4   (B) Federal spending practices can encourage

5   the nation's business community by stimulating

6   effective competition and the application of new

7   technology.

8   Policy

9   (b) It is the policy of the United States that when ac-

10   quiring property and services for the use of the Federal Gov-

11   ernment, the Government shall, whenever practicable rely on

12   the private sector, and shall act so as to—

13   (1) best meet public needs at the lowest total cost;

14   (2) maintain the independent character of private

15   enterprise by substituting the incentives and con-

16   straints of effective competition for regulatory controls;

17   (3) encourage innovation and the application of

18   new technology as a primary consideration by stating

19   agency needs and analyzing the market so that pros-

20   pective suppliers will have maximum latitude to exer-

21   cise independent business and technical judgments in

22   offering a range of competing alternatives;

23   (4) maintain and expand the available Federal

24   supply base by judicious acquisition practices designed

1   to assure Government contracting with new and small

2   business concerns to the maximum practicable extent;

3   (5) make available for review and examination

4   those pertinent Federal laws and regulations applicable

5   to the awards of contracts and those which may impact

6   the performance of contracts, including, for example,

7   Federal laws and agency rules relating to air and

8   water cleanliness requirements, and to occupational

9   safety requirements;

10   (6) provide opportunities to minority business

11   firms to grow through Government contracts;

12   (7) initiate large scale productions only after the

13   item or equipment to be acquired has been proven ade-

14   quate by operational testing;

15   (8) provide contractors with the opportunity to

16   earn a profit on Government contracts commensurate

17   with the contribution made to meeting public needs

18   and comparable to the profit opportunities available in

19   other markets requiring similar investments, technical

20   and financial risks and skills;

21   (9) rely on and promote effective competition; to

22   insure the availability to the Government of alternative

23   offers that provide a range of concept, design, perform-

24   ance, price, total cost, service, and delivery; and to fa-

1   cilitate the competitive entry of new and small sellers.

2   Effective competition is generally characterized by—

3   (A) timely availability to prospective sellers

4   of information required to respond to agency

5   needs;

6   (B) independence of action by buyer and

7   seller;

8   (C) efforts of two or more sellers, acting in-

9   dependently of each other, to respond to an

10   agency need by creating, developing, demonstrat-

11   ing, or offering products or services which best

12   meet that need, whether that need is expressed as

13   an agency mission need, as a desired function to

14   be performed, performance or physical require-

15   ments to be met, or as some combination of these;

16   and

17   (D) absence of bias or favoritism in the so-

18   licitation, evaluation, and award of contracts.

19   DEFINITIONS

20   SEC. 3. For purpose of this Act—

21   (a) The term "acquisition" means the acquiring by con-

22   tract with appropriated funds of property or services by and

23   for the direct benefit or use of the Federal Government

24   through purchase, lease, or barter, whether the property or

25   services are already in existence or must be created, devel-

1 oped, demonstrated, and evaluated. Acquisition includes such

2 related functions as determinations of the particular agency

3 need; solicitation; selection of sources; award of contracts;

4 contract financing; contract performance; and contract

5 administration.

6   (b) The term "executive agency" means an executive

7 department as defined by section 101 of title 5, United States

8 Code; an independent establishment as defined by section

9 104 of title 5, United States Code (except that it shall not

10 include the General Accounting Office); a military depart-

11 ment as defined by section 102 of title 5 United States Code;

12 the United States Postal Service; and a wholly owned Gov-

13 ernment Corporation as defined by section 846 of title 31,

14 United States Code (but does not include the Tennessee

15 Valley Authority or the Bonneville Power Administration).

16   (c) The term "agency head" means the head of an ex-

17 ecutive agency as defined in subsection (b).

18   (d) The term "contracting officer" means any person

19 who, either by virtue of his position or by appointment in

20 accordance with applicable regulations, has the authority to

21 enter into and administer contracts and make determinations

22 and findings with respect thereto. The term also includes the

23 authorized representative of the contracting officer, acting

24 within the limits of his authority.

1   (e) The term "property" includes personal property and
2 leaseholds and other interests therein, but excludes real prop-
3 erty in being and leaseholds and other interests therein.

4   (f) The term "total cost" means all resources consumed
5 or to be consumed in the acquisition and use of property or
6 services. It may include all direct, indirect, recurring, nonre-
7 curring, and other related costs incurred, or estimated to be
8 incurred in design, development, test, evaluation, production,
9 operation, maintenance, disposal, training, and support of an
10 acquisition over its useful life span, wherever each factor is
11 applicable.

12   (g) The term "functional specification" means a descrip-
13 tion of the intended use of a product required by the Govern-
14 ment. A functional specification may include a statement of
15 the qualitative nature of the product required and, when nec-
16 essary, may set forth those minimum essential characteristics
17 and standards to which such product must conform if it is to
18 satisfy its intended use.

19   (h) The term "unsolicited proposal" means a written
20 offer to perform a proposed effort, submitted to an agency by
21 an individual or organization solely on its own initiative with
22 the objective of obtaining a contract, and not in response to
23 an agency request or communication.

1   # TITLE I—REGULATORY GUIDANCE

2   ACQUISITION METHODS

3   SEC. 101. Except as otherwise authorized by law, an

4 executive agency shall acquire property or services in accord-

5 ance with the criteria set forth in this Act.

6   REGULATORY COMPLIANCE

7   SEC. 102. (a) (1) The Administrator for Federal Pro-

8 curement Policy is authorized and directed, pursuant to the

9 authority conferred by the Office of Federal Procurement

10 Policy Act and subject to the procedures set forth in such

11 Act—

12   (A) to promulgate a single, simplified, uniform

13   Federal regulation implementing this Act and to estab-

14   lish procedures for insuring compliance with this Act

15   and such regulation by all executive agencies within

16   two years after the date of enactment of this Act;

17   (B) to review such regulation on a regular basis

18   and issue revisions as necessary;

19   (C) to make periodic studies in order to determine

20   whether agency compliance with this Act has been effi-

21   cient and effective; and

22   (D) to establish and oversee a program to reduce

23   agency use of detailed product specifications.

1   (2) In promulgating and revising the regulation required

2   under paragraph (1), the Administrator for Federal Procure-

3   ment Policy shall—

4   (A) utilize the procedures established under sub-

5   sections (b) and (c) of section 8 of the Office of Federal

6   Procurement Policy Act, and shall transmit the report

7   required by such subsections to the Committees on

8   Armed Services of the Senate and the House of Repre-

9   sentatives, the Committee on Governmental Affairs of

10   the Senate, and the Committee on Government Oper-

11   ations of the House of Representatives; and

12   (B) utilize the procedures established under sec-

13   tion 14(b) of such Act to provide for open public

14   meetings.

15   (b) The Administrator for Federal Procurement Policy

16   shall include in his annual report required under section 8(a)

17   of the Office of Federal Procurement Policy Act a report of

18   his activities under this section, including his assessment of

19   agency implementation of and compliance with the require-

20   ments of this Act (including, for example, specific reductions

21   in the use of detailed specifications pursuant to this Act), and

22   recommendations for revisions in this Act or any other provi-

23   sion of law.

1   CONTRACTING OFFICERS' COMPLIANCE CODE;

2   ENFORCEMENT

3   SEC. 103. (a) The Office of Federal Procurement Policy,

4   after consultation with the Office of Personnel Management,

5   shall establish a code of conduct with respect to which all

6   contracting officers employed by executive agencies shall be

7   subject, to insure that all laws, rules, and regulations relating

8   to the acquisition of property and services are complied with.

9   (b) The code of conduct established under subsection (a)

10 shall—

11   (1) establish guidelines and standards for, and set

12   forth actions which are prohibited in, the acquisition of

13   property or services by contracting officers;

14   (2) set forth procedures and methods of compli-

15   ance with the provisions of this Act and regulations

16   prescribed under it; and

17   (3) contain such other matters as are necessary to

18   insure compliance with laws, rules, and regulations re-

19   lating to the acquisition of property or services.

20   (c) (1) The Inspector General of an executive agency or

21 another employee designated by the agency head shall re-

22 ceive any allegation of a violation of the code of conduct by a

23 contracting officer of that agency and shall investigate the

24 allegation to determine whether there are reasonable grounds

25 to believe that a violation has occurred.

1   (2) (A) If, in connection with any investigation under

2 paragraph (1), the Inspector General or designated employee

3 determines that there is reasonable cause to believe that a

4 criminal violation has occurred, the violation shall be report-

5 ed to the Attorney General and the agency head.

6   (B) If, in connection with any investigation under para-

7 graph (1), the Inspector General or designated employee de-

8 termines that there is reasonable cause to believe that any

9 violation of the code of conduct or any law, rule, or regula-

10 tion has occurred which is not a criminal violation, the viola-

11 tion shall be reported to the agency head.

12   (d) The agency head shall review any matter referred to

13 him under subsection (c) and, if he determines it necessary,

14 shall take—

15   (1) an action under chapter 75 of this title or

16   other disciplinary or corrective action in the case of a

17   contracting officer covered by such chapter, or

18   (2) an action similar to actions described in para-

19   graph (1) in the case of other contracting officers.

20   (e) Each executive agency shall provide contracting offi-

21 cers with such information with respect to the code of con-

22 duct established under this section as is necessary to enable

23 such officers to comply with the code.

24   (f) (1) At the close of each calendar year each executive

25 agency shall report to the Office of Federal Procurement

1 Policy on the number and disposition of investigations con-

2 ducted under subsection (c).

3   (2) The Office of Federal Procurement Policy shall

4 review the reports received under paragraph (1) and shall

5 compile and submit to the Congress a report on the investi-

6 gations conducted under subsection (c) by all executive agen-

7 cies and their disposition, together with any recommenda-

8 tions for legislation which the Office finds appropriate.

9   (g) The General Accounting Office shall from time to

10 time review on a selected basis the methods of carrying out

11 and disposing of investigations by executive agencies under

12 this section to determine if the agencies are complying with

13 the requirements of this section and shall periodically report

14 its findings to the Congress and the Office of Federal Pro-

15 curement Policy.

16   TITLE II—ACQUISITION BY COMPETITIVE

17   SEALED BIDS

18   CRITERIA FOR USE

19   SEC. 201. The competitive sealed bids method shall be

20 used in the acquisition of property and services when all of

21 the following conditions are present—

22   (1) the anticipated total contract price exceeds the

23   amount specified in title IV of this Act for use of the

24   simplified small purchase method;

1   (2) the agency need can be practicably defined in

2   terms not restricted by security requirements or propri-

3   etary design;

4   (3) the private sector will provide a sufficient

5   number of qualified suppliers willing to compete for

6   and able to perform the contract;

7   (4) suitable products or services capable of meet-

8   ing the agency need are available so as to warrant the

9   award of a fixed price contract to a successful bidder

10   selected primarily on the basis of price;

11   (5) the time available for acquisition is sufficient

12   to carry out the requisite administrative procedures;

13   (6) the property or service is to be acquired within

14   the limits of the United States and the Territories,

15   Commonwealths, and possessions; and

16   (7) the price for the property or service has not

17   been established by or pursuant to law or regulation.

18   INVITATION FOR SEALED BIDS

19   SEC. 202. (a) The invitation for sealed bids shall be pub-

20 licized in accordance with section 512 of this Act and shall

21 be issued in such a way that—

22   (1) the time prior to opening the bids will be suffi-

23   cient to permit effective competition; and

24   (2) the invitation will be accessible to all inter-

25   ested or potential bidders; however, eligibility to par-

1   ticipate in the bidding may be restricted to concerns

2   eligible to participate in small business set-asides or

3   other such authorized programs.

4   (b) The invitation shall include a description of any fac-

5 tors in addition to price that will be considered in evaluating

6 bids.

7   (c) To the maximum extent practicable and consistent

8 with needs of the agency, functional specifications shall be

9 used to permit a variety of distinct products or services to

10 qualify and to encourage effective competition.

11   (d) The preparation and use of detailed product specifi-

12 cations in a purchase description shall be subject to prior ap-

13 proval by the agency head. Such approval shall include writ-

14 ten justification, to be made a part of the official contract file,

15 delineating the circumstances which preclude the use of func-

16 tional specifications and which require the use of detailed

17 product specifications in the purchase descriptions.

18   (e) The contracting officer may request the submission

19 of unpriced technical proposals and subsequently issue an in-

20 vitation for sealed bids limited to those bidders whose techni-

21 cal proposals meet the standards set forth in the original

22 invitation.

23   EVALUATION, AWARD, AND NOTIFICATIONS

24   SEC. 203. (a) All bids shall be opened publicly at the

25 time and place stated in the invitation.

1   (b) Award shall be made to the responsible bidder whose

2 bid conforms to the invitation and is most advantageous to

3 the Government, price and other factors considered: *Pro-*

4 *vided,* That all bids may be rejected when the agency head

5 determines that, for cogent and compelling reasons, it is in

6 the Government's interest to do so.

7   (c) Notice of award shall be made in writing by the con-

8 tracting officer with reasonable promptness and all other bid-

9 ders shall be appropriately notified.

10   TITLE III—ACQUISITION BY COMPETITIVE

11   NEGOTIATION

12   CRITERIA FOR USE

13   SEC. 301. The competitive negotiation method shall be

14 used in the acquisition of property and services when—

15   (1) the anticipated total contract price exceeds the

16   amount specified in title IV of this Act for use of the

17   simplified small purchase method; and

18   (2) the acquisition does not meet the criteria set

19   forth in section 201 of this Act for use of competitive

20   sealed bids.

21   SOLICITATIONS

22   SEC. 302. (a) Solicitations for offers shall be issued to a

23 sufficient number of qualified sources so as to obtain effective

24 competition and shall be publicized in accordance with sec-

25 tion 512 of this Act, with copies of the solicitation to be

1 provided or made accessible to other interested or potential

2 sources upon request; however, eligibility to respond to the

3 solicitation may be restricted to concerns eligible to partici-

4 pate in small business set-asides or other such authorized

5 programs.

6   (b) (1) Each solicitation shall include both the evaluation

7 methodology and the relative importance of all significant

8 factors to be used during competitive evaluation and for final

9 selection. In any case, if price is included as a primary or

10 significant factor, the Government's evaluation shall be based

11 where appropriate on the total cost to meet the agency need.

12   (2) Any changes in the evaluation factors or their rela-

13 tive importance shall be communicated promptly in writing to

14 all competitors.

15   (c) To the maximum extent practicable and consistent

16 with agency needs, solicitations shall encourage effective

17 competition by—

18   (1) setting forth the agency need in functional

19   terms so as to encourage the application of a variety of

20   technological approaches and elicit the most promising

21   competing alternatives,

22   (2) not prescribing performance characteristics

23   based on a single approach, and

24   (3) not prescribing technical approaches or inno-

25   vations obtained from any potential competitor.

1   (d) If either the Government or an offeror identifies in-

2 adequacies in the solicitation which cause misunderstandings

3 of the agency's needs or requirements, clarification of intent

4 shall be made to all offerors in a timely fashion and on an

5 equal basis.

6   (e) The preparation and use of detailed product specifi-

7 cations in a solicitation shall be subject to prior approval by

8 the agency head. Such approval shall include written justifi-

9 cation to be made a part of the official contract file, delineat-

10 ing the circumstances which preclude the use of functional

11 specifications and which require the use of detailed product

12 specifications.

13   EVALUATIONS, AWARD, AND NOTIFICATIONS

14   SEC. 303. (a) Written or oral discussions shall be con-

15 ducted with all offerors who submit proposals in a competi-

16 tive range. An initial offer may be accepted without discus-

17 sion when it is clear that the agency need would be satisfied

18 on fair and reasonable terms without such discussions, and

19 the solicitation has advised all offerors that award may be

20 made without discussions. Discussions shall not disclose the

21 strengths or weaknesses of competing offerors, or disclose

22 any information from an offeror's proposal which would

23 enable another offeror to improve his proposal as a result

24 thereof. Auction techniques are strictly prohibited. Auction

25 techniques include, but are not limited to, indicating to an

1 offeror a price which must be met to obtain further considera-

2 tion, or informing him that his price is not low in relation to

3 another offeror, or making multiple requests for best and final

4 offers.

5   (b) When awards are made for alternative approaches

6 selected on the basis of the factors contained in the solicita-

7 tion, whether for design, development, demonstration, or de-

8 livery, the contractors shall be sustained in competition to

9 the maximum extent practicable until sufficient test or evalu-

10 ation information becomes available to narrow the choice to a

11 particular product or service.

12   (c) Until selection is made, information concerning the

13 award shall not be disclosed to any person not having source

14 selection responsibilities, except that offerors who are elimi-

15 nated from the competition may be informed prior to awards.

16   (d) Award shall be made to one or more responsible of-

17 ferors whose proposal(s), as evaluated in accordance with the

18 terms of the solicitation are most advantageous to the Gov-

19 ernment. Notification of award to all unsuccessful offerors

20 shall be made with reasonable promptness.

21   (e) Notwithstanding any other provision of this Act, the

22 use of multiple award type schedules is authorized. However,

23 competitive methods shall be used: (1) to limit the number of

24 items on such schedules which meet the same need, and (2)

1   to obtain the lowest competitively priced items which meet

2   the minimum essential needs of the Government.

3   NONCOMPETITIVE EXCEPTIONS

4   SEC. 304. (a) Compliance with the procedures pre-

5   scribed in sections 302 and 303 is not required if the contract

6   to be awarded stems from acceptance of an unsolicited pro-

7   posal, or if the agency head determines that it is in the best

8   interest of the Government to enter into a noncompetitive

9   contract: *Provided,*

10   (1) That such determination, together with the

11   reasons therefor, is in writing, and conforms with regu-

12   lations issued by the Administrator for Federal Pro-

13   curement Policy, pursuant to section 102(a)(1); and

14   (2) (A) for all contracts except those stemming

15   from the acceptance of an unsolicited proposal, notice

16   of intent to award such a contract shall be publicized

17   pursuant to section 512 at least thirty days in advance

18   of solicitation of a proposal from the prospective con-

19   tractor; or, at least thirty days in advance of the pro-

20   posed award date, when earlier notice is impracticable.

21   Such notice shall include a description of the property

22   or services to be acquired, the name of the prospective

23   source, the time for accomplishment of the work, and

24   the reason for selection of the source. If, after such

25   notice, other sources demonstrate an ability to meet

1   the requirements for the work to be performed, a so-

2   licitation or an invitation for sealed bids shall be issued

3   to all such prospective offerors;

4   (B) in the case of those contracts stemming from

5   the acceptance of an unsolicited proposal, notice of

6   intent to award such a contract shall be publicized

7   prior to award, pursuant to section 512 of this Act.

8   Such notice shall include a description of the property

9   or service to be acquired, the name of the prospective

10   source, and the time for accomplishment of the work.

11   (b) Where there is no commercial usage of the product

12   or service to be acquired under this section, and the agency

13   head determines that substantial follow-on provision of such

14   product or service will be required by the Government, the

15   agency head shall, when he deems appropriate, take action

16   through contractual provision, or otherwise, to provide the

17   Government with a capability to establish one or more other

18   competitive sources.

19   PRICE AND COST DATA AND ANALYSIS

20   SEC. 305. (a) (1) The term "price data" means actual

21   prices previously paid, contracted, quoted, or proposed, for

22   materials or services identical or comparable to those being

23   acquired, and the related dates, quantities, and item descrip-

24   tions which prudent buyers and sellers would reasonably

1 expect to have a significant effect on the negotiation of a

2 contract price or payment provisions.

3   (2) The term "cost data" means all facts which prudent

4 buyers and sellers would reasonably expect to have a signifi-

5 cant effect on the negotiation of a contract price or payment

6 provisions. Such data are of a type that can be verified as

7 being factual, and are to be distinguished from judgmental

8 factors. The term does, however, include the facts upon

9 which a contractor's judgment is based.

10   (3) The term "price analysis" means the process of ex-

11 amining and evaluating a price without evaluation of the indi-

12 vidual cost and profit elements of the price being evaluated.

13   (4) The term "cost analysis" means the element-by-ele-

14 ment examination and evaluation of the estimated or actual

15 costs of contract performance, and involves analysis of cost

16 data furnished by an offeror or contractor and the judgmental

17 factors applied in projecting from such data to the offered

18 price.

19   (b) The contracting officer shall obtain price data and

20 shall use price analysis techniques to analyze and evaluate

21 the reasonableness of a negotiated prime contract price or of

22 a price adjustment pursuant to a modification thereto

23 where—

24   (1) the price is expected to be $500,000 or less;

1   (2) the price is based on an established catalog or

2   market price of a commercial item sold in substantial

3   quantities to the general public; or

4   (3) there has been a recent comparable competi-

5   tive acquisition.

6   (c) In the case of subcontracts, when any of the condi-

7 tions in subsection (b) applies, price data shall be obtained

8 and price analysis techniques shall be used to analyze and

9 evaluate the reasonableness of—

10   (1) a subcontract price—where evaluation of a

11   subcontract price is necessary to insure the reasonable-

12   ness of the prime contract price, or

13   (2) a subcontract price adjustment pursuant to a

14   prime contract modification.

15   (d) Except as provided in subsection (b) (2) and (3), cost

16 data shall be obtained and cost analysis techniques shall be

17 used to analyze and evaluate the reasonableness of prices—

18   (1) whenever the price of a negotiated prime con-

19   tract or a price adjustment pursuant to a contract

20   modification is expected to exceed $500,000; or

21   (2) for any subcontract price or price adjustment

22   pursuant to a modification thereto in excess of

23     $500,000 which forms part of a negotiated prime con-

24   tract price or higher tier subcontract price.

1   (e) Notwithstanding subsection (b) hereof, the contract-

2   ing officer may obtain cost data and use cost analysis tech-

3   niques when authorized under circumstances set forth in reg-

4   ulations issued by the Administrator for Federal Procurement

5   Policy pursuant to this Act.

6   (f) Contractors and subcontractors shall submit in writ-

7   ing such price data or cost data as are required to be obtained

8   pursuant to this section. Regulations issued by the Adminis-

9   trator for Federal Procurement Policy may authorize identifi-

10   cation in writing of price data and cost data, in lieu of actual

11   submission, under specified circumstances.

12   (g) Any prime contract or subcontract or modification

13   thereto for which price data or cost data are required shall

14   contain a provision that the price to the Government, includ-

15   ing profit or fee, shall be adjusted to exclude any significant

16   sums by which it may be determined by the contracting offi-

17   cer that such price was increased because of reliance on data

18   which were inaccurate, incomplete, or noncurrent as of the

19   date of submission or other date agreed upon between the

20   parties (which date shall be as close to the date of agreement

21   on the negotiated price or payment provisions as is

22   practicable).

23   (h) The requirements of this section do not apply to con-

24   tracts or subcontracts where the price negotiated is based on

25   adequate price competition, prices set by law or regulation,

1 or, in exceptional cases, where the head of the agency deter-

2 mines that the requirements of this section may be waived

3 and states in writing his reasons for such determination.

4 ACCESS TO RECORDS BY EXECUTIVE AGENCIES AND THE

5   COMPTROLLER GENERAL

6   SEC. 306. (a) Until three years after final payment

7 under a contract or a subscontract negotiated or amended

8 under this title, an executive agency is entitled to inspect the

9 plants and examine any books, documents, papers, records,

10 or other data of the contractor and his subcontractors which

11 involve transactions relating to the contract or subcontract or

12 to the amendment thereof, including all such books, records,

13 and other data relating to the negotiation, pricing, or per-

14 formance of the contract or subcontract.

15   (b) Until three years after final payment under a con-

16 tract or a subcontract negotiated or amended under this title,

17 the Comptroller General of the United States or his author-

18 ized representative is entitled to inspect the plants and exam-

19 ine any books, documents, papers, records, or other data of

20 the contractor and his subcontractors which directly pertain

21 to and involve transactions relating to the contract or subcon-

22 tract or to the amendment thereof, including all such books,

23 records, and other data relating to the negotiation, pricing, or

24 performance of the contract or subcontract.

1   (c) (1) The provisions of subsection (b) may be waived

2 for any contract or subcontract with a foreign contractor or

3 subcontractor, if the agency head determines, with concur-

4 rence of the Comptroller General, that such waiver would be

5 in the public interest. The concurrence of the Comptroller

6 General or his designee is not required—

7   (A) where the contractor or subcontractor is a for-

8   eign government or agency thereof or is precluded by

9   the laws of the country involved from making its

10   books, documents, papers, or records available for ex-

11   amination; or

12   (B) where the agency head determines, after

13   taking into account the price and availability of the

14   property or services from sources in the United States,

15   that the public interest would be best served by waiv-

16   ing the provisions of subsection (b).

17   (2) If the provisions of subsection (b) are waived for a

18 contract or subcontract based on a determination under para-

19 graph (1)(B), the agency head shall submit a written report

20 concerning such determination to the Congress.

21   (d) Multiple inspections and examinations of a contractor

22 or subcontractors by more than one executive agency shall be

23 eliminated to the maximum extent practicable by coordinat-

24 ing inspection and examination responsibilities in accordance

1 with regulations to be issued or authorized by the Adminis-

2 trator for Federal Procurement Policy pusuant to this Act.

3   (e) (1) Whoever, by collusion, understanding, or ar-

4 rangement, deprives or attempts to deprive the United States

5 of the benefit or a true and free audit of the books of a con-

6 tractor shall be fined not more than $20,000 or imprisoned

7 for not more than five years, or both.

8   (2) In accordance with such rules, regulations, or orders

9 as the Administrator for Federal Procurement Policy may

10 issue or adopt, the agency head may—

11   (A) recommend to the Attorney General that ap-

12   propriate proceedings be brought to enforce the provi-

13   sions of this section;

14   (B) cancel, terminate, suspend, or cause to be

15   canceled, terminated, or suspended, any contract, or

16   portion or portions thereof, for failure of a contractor

17   or subcontractor to comply with the provisions of this

18   section; or

19   (C) refrain from entering into further contracts, or

20   extensions or other modifications of existing contracts

21   with any contractor who fails to comply with the pro-

22   visions of this section, until such contractor has satis-

23   fied the agency head that such contractor will comply

24   with the provisions of this section.

1   (3) If an agency head terminates a contract under paragraph (2)(B), such termination shall be considered a termination for default.

4   (4) The action of an agency head under paragraph (2)(B) or (2)(C) shall be subject to judicial review in accordance with the provisions of chapter 7 of title 5, United States Code.

8   TITLE IV—ACQUISITION BY SIMPLIFIED SMALL PURCHASE METHOD

10   CRITERION FOR USE

11   SEC. 401. (a) (1) Whenever the anticipated total contract price for the acquisition of property or services does not exceed $10,000, a contracting officer may utilize—

14   (A) the simplified small purchase method established pursuant to this title; or

16   (B) one of the competitive methods established under title II or III.

18   (2) The Administrator for Federal Procurement Policy shall prescribe the procedures to be utilized by the agencies for the simplified small purchase method.

21   (b) The contracting officer shall choose the method for the acquisition of property or services under subsection (a) which is most advantageous to the Government.

24   (c) A contracting officer may not, for the purpose of utilizing the simplified small purchase method permitted under

1 subsection (a), divide a contract with a total anticipated con-

2 tract price in excess of $10,000 into smaller contracts which

3 each have an anticipated contract price of less than $10,000.

4 SOLICITATIONS AND AWARDS

5 SEC. 402. The contracting officer shall use the simpli-

6 fied small purchase method established pursuant to this title

7 to obtain competition to the maximum extent practicable, and

8 may award the contract to the offeror whose offer is most

9 advantageous to the Government. The provisions of this sec-

10 tion shall not be applied so as to eliminate effective screening

11 of proposed acquisitions for appropriate application of small

12 business set-aside or other procedures designed to assist

13 small businesses.

14 TITLE V—GENERAL PROVISIONS

15 CONTRACT TYPES

16 SEC. 501. (a) Contracts may be of any type or combina-

17 tion of types, consistent with the degree of technical and fi-

18 nancial risk to be undertaken by the contractor, which will

19 promote the best interests of the Government except that the

20 cost-plus a percentage-of-cost system of contracting shall not

21 be used under any circumstances.

22 (b) The preferred contract type shall be fixed price con-

23 sistent with the nature of the work to be performed and the

24 risk to be shared by the Government and the contractor.

1   WARRANTY AGAINST CONTINGENT FEES

2   SEC. 502. Each contract awarded pursuant to title II or

3 title III of this Act shall contain a warranty by the contrac-

4 tor that no person or selling agency has been employed or

5 retained to solicit or secure the contract upon an agreement

6 or understanding of a commission, percentage, brokerage, or

7 contingent fee, excepting bona fide employees or bona fide

8 established commercial or selling agencies maintained by the

9 contractor for the purpose of securing business; and that for

10 any breach or violation of the warranty, the Government

11 may annul the contract without liability or deduct from the

12 contract price or consideration the full amount of the commis-

13 sion, percentage, brokerage, or contingent fee.

14   CANCELLATIONS AND REJECTIONS

15   SEC. 503. (a) Where the agency head determines for

16 cogent and compelling reasons, that it is in the best interest

17 of the Government, he may—

18   (1) withdraw or cancel a small purchase order

19   which has not been accepted in writing by the contrac-

20   tor, prior to the contractor's initiation of performance;

21   (2) cancel an invitation for sealed bids before bid

22   opening or after bid opening but before award; or

23   (3) cancel a request for proposal and reject all

24   offers.

1   (b) When requested, the agency head shall fully inform

2   any unsuccessful offeror or bidder of the reasons for the rejec-

3   tion of his offer or bid.

4   MULTIYEAR CONTRACTS

5   SEC. 504. (a) Except as otherwise provided by law, an

6   agency may make contracts for acquisition of property or

7   services for periods not in excess of five years, when—

8   (1) appropriations are available and adequate for

9   payment for the first fiscal year; and

10   (2) the agency head determines that—

11   (A) the Government need for the property or

12   services being acquired over the period of the con-

13   tract is reasonably firm and continuing; and

14   (B) such a contract will serve the best inter-

15   ests of the United States by encouraging effective

16   competition or promoting economies in perform-

17   ance and operation; and

18   (C) such a method of contracting will not in-

19   hibit small business participation.

20   (b) The Administrator for Federal Procurement Policy

21 may grant exceptions to the five-year limitation imposed by

22 subsection (a) upon the certification, in such form and of such

23 content as the Administrator may require, by the agency

24 head that such exception is in the best interests of the Gov-

25 ernment. A copy of each such certification and each excep-

1 tion granted shall be delivered to the chairman of the House

2 Committee on Government Operations, the Senate Commit-

3 tee on Governmental Affairs, and the Committees on Appro-

4 priations of the House of Representatives and the Senate,

5 respectively.

6   (c) Any cancellation costs incurred must be paid from

7 appropriated funds originally available for performance of the

8 contract, or currently available for acquisition of similar prop-

9 erty or services, and not otherwise obligated, or appropri-

10 ations made available for such payments.

11   ADVANCE, PARTIAL, AND PROGRESS PAYMENTS

12   SEC. 505. (a) Any executive agency may make advance,

13 progress, partial, or other payments under contracts.

14   (b) Advance and progress payments under contracts

15 with small business concerns shall be granted where possible

16 and to the extent practicable under the circumstances exist-

17 ing for each acquisition. Provisions limiting advance and

18 progress payments to small business concerns may be in-

19 serted into solicitations.

20   (c) Payments under subsections (a) and (b) shall not

21 exceed the unpaid contract price.

22   (d) When progress payments are made, the Government

23 shall have title to the property acquired or produced by the

24 contractor and allocable or properly chargeable to the con-

25 tract. Notwithstanding any other provisions of law, the title

1 acquired by the Government under this section may not be

2 divested by any action of the contractor or by a proceeding in

3 bankruptcy, and may not be encumbered by any lien or secu-

4 rity interest.

5   (e) Advance payments under subsection (a) or (b) shall

6 not be made in excess of the amount required for contract

7 performance, and may be made only upon adequate security

8 and a determination by the agency head that to make such

9 advance payments would be in the public interest. Such secu-

10 rity may be in the form of a lien in favor of the Government

11 on the property contracted for, on the balance in an account

12 in which such payments are deposited, and on such property

13 acquired for performance of the contract as the parties may

14 agree. A lien established under this section is paramount to

15 any other liens.

16   (f) (1) Payments under subsections (a) or (b) in the case

17 of any contract, other than partial, progress, or other pay-

18 ments specifically provided for in such contract at the time

19 such contract was initially entered into, may not exceed

20 $25,000,000 unless the appropriate committees of the Senate

21 and the House of Representatives have been notified in writ-

22 ing of such proposed payments and sixty days of continuous

23 session of Congress have expired following the date on which

24 such notice was transmitted to such committees and neither

25 House of Congress has passed a resolution stating in sub-

1 stance that that House does not favor the payments con-
2 tained in the notification submitted pursuant to this subsec-
3 tion.

4   (2) The provisions of sections 908, 910, 911, and 912 of
5 title 5, United States Code, shall apply to any resolution con-
6 sidered under this subsection. For purposes of the preceding
7 sentence—

8   (A) all references in such sections to "reorganiza-
9   tion plan" shall be treated as referring to "payments
10   contained in the notification submitted under section
11   505(e) of the Federal Acquisition Act of 1979", and

12   (B) all references in such sections to "resolution"
13   shall be treated as referring to a resolution of either
14   House of Congress, the matter after the resolving
15   clause of which is as follows: "That the
16   (name of the resolving House of Congress) does not
17   approve of the payments contained in the notification
18   submitted on   , 19   , under section 505(e)
19   of the Federal Acquisition Act of 1979", the blank
20   spaces therein being appropriately filled.

21 (3) For the purposes of this subsection—

22   (A) continuity of session is broken only by an ad-
23   journment sine die; and

24   (B) the days on which either House is not in ses-
25   sion because of an adjournment of more than three

1   days to a day certain are excluded in the computation

2   of calendar days of continuous session.

3   REMISSION OF LIQUIDATED DAMAGES

4   SEC. 506. Upon the recommendation of the Agency

5 head the Comptroller General of the United States may remit

6 all or part, as he considers just and equitable, of any liquidat-

7 ed damages provided by the contract for delay in performing

8 the contract.

9   DETERMINATIONS AND FINDINGS

10   SEC. 507. (a) Determinations, findings, approvals, and

11 decisions provided for by this Act may be made with respect

12 to contracts individually or with respect to classes of con-

13 tracts and shall be final.

14   (b) Each determination, approval, or decision shall be

15 based upon written findings of the officer making the determi-

16 nation, approval, or decision, and shall be retained in the

17 official contract file.

18   ENFORCEMENT AND PENALTY

19   SEC. 508. (a) If the contracting officer or any other

20 agency employee has reason to believe that any bid, propos-

21 al, offer, or action by a contractor in carrying out the provi-

22 sions of a contract or subcontract or amendment thereto evi-

23 dences a violation of the criminal or antitrust laws, the

24 matter shall be referred, in accordance with the procedures of

1 the executive agency, to the Attorney General of the United

2 States for appropriate action.

3   (b) The agency head shall make available to the Attor-

4 ney General information which the Attorney General consid-

5 ers necessary and relevant to any investigation, prosecution,

6 or other action by the United States under criminal or anti-

7 trust laws.

8   (c) The agency head shall render needed assistance to

9 the Attorney General in any investigation and prosecution

10 commenced in connection with activities under this Act.

11   (d) The Federal Bureau of Investigation is primarily re-

12 sponsible for the investigation of collusive bidding and other

13 improper conduct under this Act that may give rise to the

14 commencement of investigation, prosecution, or other action

15 under the criminal or antitrust laws. The provisions of the

16 preceding sentence shall not preclude appropriate action by

17 other executive agencies, including the Federal Trade Com-

18 mission, the Internal Revenue Service, and the Securities

19 and Exchange Commission.

20   GOVERNMENT SURVEILLANCE REQUIREMENTS

21   SEC. 509 (a) Notwithstanding any other provisions of

22 law, an agency shall, upon application by a contractor, waive

23 the requirements listed in 509(c) for that part of a contrac-

24 tor's operation which is separately managed and accounted

25 for if, for the contractor's most recent fiscal year, more than

1 75 per centum of the business of the activity, as measured by

2 total revenues is conducted under commercial and/or com-

3 petitive Government contracts. To be competitive for pur-

4 poses of this section, the Government contracts must be firm

5 fixed-price or fixed-price with escalation with price the decid-

6 ing factor in the award.

7 (b) The waiver provided in 509(a) shall not be granted if

8 the contractor's activity for the most recent fiscal year, had

9 costs incurred of over $10,000,000, under Government con-

10 tracts where the contract prices were based on estimated or

11 actual costs. This category would include such contracts as

12 cost reimbursement type contracts, firm fixed-price contracts

13 negotiated without price competition, fixed-price incentive

14 contracts, and time and material contracts.

15 (c) The waiver provided for in 509(a) shall apply to any

16 or all of the following:

17 (1) reviews of contractor management and pro-

18 curement systems;

19 (2) determinations of reasonableness of indirect

20 overhead costs;

21 (3) the provisions of section 103 of the Act of

22 August 15, 1970 (84 Stat. 796, as amended; 50

23 U.S.C. App. 2168);

24 (4) advance agreements for independent research

25 and development and bid proposal activities.

1   (d) The waiver period shall not exceed two years with-

2 out reconsideration by the agency. The waiver may be can-

3 celed at any time or may be withheld altogether if the agency

4 head makes a written determination that the waiver should

5 not apply. Any such cancellation shall have prospective effect

6 only.

7   (e) The waiver provided for in 509(a) shall not affect the

8 General Accounting Office access-to-records authority as set

9 forth in section 306 of this Act.

10   MAINTENANCE OF REGULATIONS

11   SEC. 510. Notwithstanding any provision of law, any

12 regulation of any executive agency in effect on or before the

13 date of the enactment of this Act which is affected by any

14 provision of, or amendment or repeal made by, this Act shall

15 remain in effect until the earlier of—

16   (1) its repeal by order of the Administrator for

17   Federal Procurement Policy, or

18   (2) the date two years after the date of the enact-

19   ment of this Act.

20 An agency shall not amend any regulation referred to in the

21 preceding sentence without the prior approval of the Admin-

22 istrator.

23   PAYMENTS OF FUNDS DUE

24   SEC. 511. A clause shall be included in every contract

25 awarded by the United States pursuant to this Act which

1 shall provide for interest to be paid by the Federal Govern-

2 ment to the contractor on any amount due to the contractor

3 for more than thirty days. No amount shall be considered due

4 until (1) the Government agency office designated in the con-

5 tract for submission of invoices has received a proper invoice

6 and any substantiating documentation required. Interest shall

7 accrue and be paid at a rate which the Secretary of the

8 Treasury shall specify as applicable to the period beginning

9 on July 1, 1979, and ending on December 31, 1979, and to

10 each six month period thereafter. Such rate shall be deter-

11 mined by the Secretary of the Treasury, taking into consider-

12 ation current private commercial rates of interest for new

13 loans maturing in approximately five years.

14 PUBLICATION OF INTENT

15 SEC. 512. It shall be the duty of the Secretary of Com-

16 merce, and he is empowered, to obtain notice of all proposed

17 acquisitions of above $10,000, from any executive agency

18 engaged in acquisitions in the United States; and to publicize

19 such notices in the daily publication "United States Depart-

20 ment of Commerce Synopsis of the United States Govern-

21 ment Proposed Procurement, Sales, and Contract Awards",

22 immediately after the necessity for the acquisition is estab-

23 lished; except that nothing herein shall require publication of

24 such notices with respect to those acquisitions—

1   (1) which for security reasons are of a classified

2   nature; or

3   (2) which involve perishable subsistence supplies;

4   or

5   (3) which are for utility services and the acquiring

6   agency in accordance with applicable law has predeter-

7   mined the utility concern to whom the award will be

8   made; or

9   (4) which are of such unusual and compelling

10   emergency that the Government would be seriously in-

11   jured if notice were required to be publicized thirty

12   days in advance of the proposed contract award date.

13   In all such cases, notice shall be published at the earli-

14   est practicable opportunity; or

15   (5) which are made by an order placed under an

16   existing contract; or

17   (6) which are made from another Government de-

18   partment or agency, or a mandatory source of supply;

19   or

20   (7) for which it is determined in writing by the

21   procuring agency, with the concurrence of the Admin-

22   istrator, Small Business Administration, that advance

23   publicity is not appropriate or reasonable.

1   REVISIONS OF THRESHOLDS

2   SEC. 513. At least every three years, beginning with

3 the third year after enactment of this Act, the Administrator

4 for Federal Procurement Policy shall review the prevailing

5 costs of labor and materials and may revise the amounts

6 stated in sections 305, 401, 509, and 512 or any prior revi-

7 sions thereof, notwithstanding any other provision of law, to

8 reflect an increase or decrease by at least 10 per centum in

9 the costs of labor and materials. At least sixty days in ad-

10 vance of its effective date, the Administrator shall report to

11 Congress any such revision which by itself, or cumulatively

12 with earlier increases, represents 50 per centum or more

13 increase.

14   SUNSET FOR SPECIFICATIONS

15   SEC. 514. All specifications shall be reviewed at least

16 every five years, and shall be canceled, modified, revised, or

17 reissued as determined by such review.

18   MINORITY BUSINESS PARTICIPATION

19   SEC. 515. The Administrator for Federal Procurement

20 Policy is authorized and directed to initiate, in consultation

21 with the Small Business Administration, periodic reviews of

22 acquisition programs within the executive branch with the

23 objective of making minority business participation in govern-

24 ment contracting more effective and assuring that minority

25 businesses have full opportunity to compete for Government

1 contracts. Targets should be set which reflect the Govern-

2 ment's commitment to increasing minority business participa-

3 tion in Federal contracting.

4   LIMITATION ON CONTRACT CLAIMS

5   SEC. 516. Any claim by an executive agency against a

6 contractor under a provision of a contract awarded by the

7 agency pursuant to this Act shall be made within six years

8 from the date of final payment under the contract.

9   TITLE VI—DELEGATION OF AUTHORITY

10   DELEGATION WITHIN AN EXECUTIVE AGENCY

11   SEC. 601. Each agency head may delegate any authori-

12 ty under this Act, provided that such delegation is made in

13 accordance with regulations established by the Administrator

14 for Federal Procurement Policy. Delegation of authority to

15 make determinations under sections 202, 302(e), 304, 305,

16 306, and 509 shall be maintained at the highest organization-

17 al level practicable in order to protect the integrity of the

18 acquisition process consistent with the nature and the size of

19 the acquisition decision. The authority in section 702(b) to

20 authorize the award of a contract notwithstanding a protest

21 pending before the Comptroller General may not be delegat-

22 ed below the level of Assistant Secretary or comparable

23 level.

1   JOINT ACQUISITIONS

2   SEC. 602. (a) To facilitate acquisition of property or

3   services by one executive agency for another executive

4   agency, and to facilitate joint acquisition by those agencies—

5   (1) the Agency head may, within his agency, dele-

6   gate functions and assign responsibilities relating to the

7   acquisition;

8   (2) the heads of two or more executive agencies

9   may by agreement delegate acquisition functions and

10   assign acquisition responsibilities from one agency to

11   another of those agencies or to an officer or employee

12   of another of those agencies; and

13   (3) the heads of two or more executive agencies

14   may create joint or combined offices to exercise acqui-

15   sition functions and responsibilities.

16   (b) Subject to the provisions of section 686 of title 31,

17   United States Code—

18   (1) appropriations available for acquisition of prop-

19   erty and services by an executive agency may be made

20   available for obligation for acquisition of property and

21   services for its use by any other agency in amounts au-

22   thorized by the head of the ordering agency and with-

23   out transfer of funds on the books of the Department of

24   the Treasury;

1   (2) a disbursing officer of the ordering agency may

2   make disbursement for any obligation chargeable under

3   subsection (a) of this section, upon a voucher certified

4   by an officer or employee of the acquisition agency.

5   TITLE VII—PROTESTS

6   PURPOSE

7   SEC. 701. Under the authority contained in the Budget

8 and Accounting Act, 1921, as amended, protests shall be de-

9 cided in the General Accounting Office if filed with that

10 Office in accordance with this title. For purposes of this title,

11 the term "protest" means a challenge to a solicitation, or to

12 the award or proposed award of any contract to be financed

13 by appropriated funds for the acquisition by an agency of

14 property or services or for any sale or lease by an agency and

15 the term "agency" means an executive department as de-

16 fined by section 101 of title 5, United States Code; an inde-

17 pendent establishment as defined by section 104 of title 5,

18 United States Code (except that it shall not include the Gen-

19 eral Accounting Office); a military department as defined by

20 section 102 of title 5, United States Code; the United States

21 Postal Service; a wholly owned Government corporation as

22 defined by section 846 of title 31, United States Code (but

23 does not include the Tennessee Valley Authority or the Bon-

24 neville Power Administration); and any department or

25 agency or other activity of the Federal Government whose

1 accounts are subject to settlement by the Comptroller Gener-

2 al of the United States pursuant to the Budget and Account-

3 ing Act, 1921, as amended.

4   JURISDICTION

5   SEC. 702. (a) In accordance with the procedures issued

6 pursuant to section 704, the Comptroller General shall have

7 authority to decide any protest submitted by an interested

8 party or referred by any agency or Federal instrumentality.

9 An interested party is a firm or an individual whose direct

10 economic interest would be affected as contractor or subcon-

11 tractor by the award or nonaward of the contract.

12   (b) No contract shall be awarded after the contracting

13 activity has received notice of a protest to the Comptroller

14 General while the matter is pending before him: *Provided,*

15 *however,* That the head of an agency may authorize the

16 award of a contract notwithstanding such protest, upon a

17 written finding that the interest of the United States will not

18 permit awaiting the decision of the Comptroller General: *And*

19 *provided further,* That the Comptroller is advised of such

20 finding prior to the award of the contract.

21   (c) With respect to any solicitation, proposed award, or

22 award of contract protested to him in accordance with this

23 title, the Comptroller General is authorized to declare wheth-

24 er such solicitation, proposed award, or award comports with

25 law and regulation.

1   PROCEEDINGS

2   SEC. 703. (a) To the maximum extent practicable, the

3   Comptroller General shall provide for the inexpensive, infor-

4   mal, and expeditious resolution of protests.

5   (b) Each decision of the Comptroller General shall be

6   signed by him or his delegee and shall be issued under the

7   authority of the Comptroller General to settle the accounts of

8   the Government under the Budget and Accounting Act,

9   1921, as amended. A copy of the decision shall be furnished

10   to the interested parties and the executive agency or agencies

11   involved.

12   (c) There shall be no ex parte proceeding in protests

13   before the Comptroller General or his representative, except

14   that this subsection shall not be deemed to preclude informal

15   contacts with the parties for procedural purposes.

16   (d) The Comptroller General is authorized to dismiss

17   any protest he determines to be frivolous or which, on its

18   face, does not state a valid basis for protest.

19   (e) Where the Comptroller General has declared that a

20   solicitation, proposed award, or award of a contract does not

21   comport with law or regulation, he may further declare the

22   entitlement of an appropriate party to bid and proposal prep-

23   aration costs. In such cases the Comptroller General may

24   remand the matter to the agency involved for a determination

25   as to the amount of such costs. Declarations of entitlement to

1 monetary awards shall be paid promptly by the agency con-

2 cerned out of funds available for the purpose.

3   GENERAL PROVISIONS

4   SEC. 704. The Comptroller General shall issue such

5 procedures, not inconsistent with this title, as may be neces-

6 sary in the execution of the protest decision function. He may

7 delegate his authority to other officers or employees of the

8 General Accounting Office.

9   JUDICIAL REVIEW

10   SEC. 705. Any person adversely affected or aggrieved

11 by the action, or the failure to act, of an agency, or of the

12 Comptroller General, with respect to a solicitation or award

13 hereunder may obtain judicial review thereof to the extent

14 provided by sections 702 through 706 of title 5, United

15 States Code, including determinations necessary to resolve

16 disputed material facts or when otherwise appropriate.

17   TITLE VIII—APPLICABILITY OF SUBSEQUENT

18   LAWS

19   APPLICABILITY

20   SEC. 801. No law enacted after the date of enactment of

21 this Act, including any limitation in any appropriation bill or

22 any limitation of any provision authorizing the appropriation

23 of funds, may be held, considered, or construed as amending

24 any provision of this Act, unless such law does so by specifi-

1   cally and explicitly amending or superseding a specific and

2   separately referenced provision of this Act.

3   SEPARABILITY

4   SEC. 802. If any provision of this Act or the application

5   thereof to any person or circumstance is held invalid, neither

6   the remainder of this Act nor the application of such provi-

7   sion to other persons or circumstances shall be affected

8   thereby.

9   TITLE IX—AMENDMENTS AND REPEALS

[Deleted. This title, consisting of ten pages, amends or repeals language of other acts where inconsistent with the language of this act.]

Appendix C:
Kentucky Revised Statutes, Chapter 45A, *Kentucky Model Procurement Code,* 1978

200 KAR 5:300. Distribution of Procurement Activities and Functions

Section 1. The procurement activities and functions vested in the Department of Finance by KRS Chapter 45A shall be distributed among the bureaus of administrative services, facilities management and public properties in the Department of Finance as provided herein:

(1) Bureau of Administrative Services. The Division of Purchases in the Bureau of Administrative Services shall be responsible for and perform the department's activities and functions in the areas of procurement of commodities, supplies and equipment and contractual services except as otherwise provided in this regulation.

(2) Bureau of Facilities Management. The Division of Contracting and Administration in the Bureau of Facilities Management shall be responsible for and perform the department's activities and functions in the areas of the procurement of construction services, equipment of all kinds and description required for or as a part of any construction project as defined in KRS 45A.030(4), and contractual services of architects, engineers and land surveyors.

(3) Bureau of Public Properties. The Bureau of Public Properties through its component organizational divisions as otherwise provided for and established shall be responsible for and perform the department's activities and functions in the areas of the acquisition by purchase, lease, condemnation or otherwise, except as provided in KRS Chapters 175, 176, 177 and 180, of all real property and interests in real property determined to be needed by the state, and for the disposition of all property, real, personal and mixed, not needed by the state, or which has become unsuitable for public use, or would be more suitable consistent with the public interest for some other use.

Section 2. As used in all regulations adopted by the Department of Finance pursuant to the provisions of KRS Chapter 45A, the term "purchasing agency" shall mean the Division of Purchases, the Division of Contracting and Administration, the Bureau of Public Properties, or any agency to which purchasing authority has been delegated by the Department of Finance as provided by regulations adopted by the Department of Finance in accordance with the provisions of KRS Chapter 45A. References to "commissioner of the bureau" shall mean, according to the context, the commissioners of the bureaus of Administrative Services, Facilities Management, or Public Properties.

200 KAR 5:301. Delegation of Purchasing Authority

Section 1. Delegations of Purchasing Authority. (1) Standing delegations of purchasing authority may be made to the various cabinets, departments, institutions and other agencies of the state government by the Secretary of the Department of

Finance upon recommendation of the commissioner of the bureaus of administrative services, facilities management and public properties as appropriate with regard to the procurement activity or function to be delegated. Such standing delegations shall be made on the basis of a written order signed by the Secretary of the Department of Finance setting forth with particularity the kind or type of procurement activity or function delegated together with any limitations or restrictions on the exercise of such authority.

(2) All standing delegations of purchasing authority by the secretary shall remain in force according to the original terms thereof unless modified, or until rescinded by the secretary.

(3) Delegations of purchasing authority for agency's individual requirements, or to authorize procurement activities by an agency for pre-established and limited periods of time may be granted as appropriate with regard to the procurement activity or function by the commissioners of the bureaus of administrative services, facilities management or public properties by letter setting forth with particularity the kind or type of procurement activity or function authorized by the delegation and fixing the limits and restrictions on the exercise of the delegation and its duration. No such delegation of purchasing authority shall be extended or renewed except with the written approval of the Secretary of the Department of Finance.

Section 2. Agency Purchases. All state agencies shall be authorized to make purchases within the monetary limits and according to the procedures for small purchases as authorized by KRS 45A.100 and regulations adopted pursuant thereto without necessity for specific delegation of purchasing authority from the Department of Finance.

200 KAR 5:302. Management and Procedures Manual

Section 1. The purchasing policies and procedures of the Department of Finance published in the department's "Management and Procedures Manual" in effect on January 1, 1979, filed herein by reference and not specifically, or by necessary implication, superseded or repealed by procurement regulations adopted by the Department of Finance pursuant to the provisions of KRS Chapter 45A, together with any revisions as may from time to time hereafter be made in such policies and procedures not inconsistent with the provisions of KRS Chapter 45A and regulations of the department adopted pursuant thereto, are hereby adopted and incorporated by reference, the same as if set forth at length, in and as a part of the procurement regulations of the Department of Finance adopted pursuant to KRS Chapter 45A.

200 KAR 5:303. Written Procurement Determinations

Section 1. Every determination by a buyer or other employee, except secretarial, stenographic, or clerical employees, of the Bureaus of Administrative Services, Facilities Management or Public Properties engaged in or responsible for the performance of any procurement activity or function and constituting a final procurement action, or as otherwise provided by KRS Chapter 45A or regulations adopted pursuant thereto, shall be made in writing, based on written findings in support of said decision, and shall be signed by the employee making said determination.

200 KAR 5:304. Application to be Placed on Vendor's List

Section 1. Any person, firm or corporation desiring to receive written notice of procurement requirements of the Commonwealth may make application to have his name placed on a bidders' list for the types of kinds of procurement activities or functions he wishes to supply or provide. Upon request to either the Division of Purchases, for commodities, supplies, equipment, contractual services and related matters, or the Division of Contracting and Administration, for construction services and related activities and functions, an "Application to be placed on Vendor's List" will be sent to any prospective bidder. Complete information as requested in the application must be submitted by the prospective bidder before his name will be placed on a bidders' list.

Section 2. (1) Upon receipt of a completed "Application to be placed on Vendors List," the qualifications of the prospective bidder will be verified in terms of:

(a) The ability and capacity to perform on a timely basis under contract for goods and services which he desires to bid on and furnish.
(b) Good character, integrity, reputation, and experience.
(c) Satisfactory performance in prior dealings with the Commonwealth of Kentucky and its agencies.
(d) Previous satisfactory compliance with the health rules and regulations of the Commonwealth of Kentucky.

(2) The purchasing agencies may refuse to list any prospective bidder not meeting the minimum qualifications set forth above. The prospective bidder has the burden of showing that he meets the qualifications for inclusion on the bidders' lists to which he seeks to gain entry. The prospective bidder will be promptly advised if his application is disapproved and the reason or reasons for disapproval. A prospective bidder may appeal the disapproval of his application to the Secretary of the Department of Finance. The appeal must be in writing and filed in the office of the secretary within two (2) calendar weeks after the date of the notice of the application; grounds for the appeal shall be stated with reasonable particularity and shall relate directly to reason or reasons for disapproval of the application. Any prospective bidder whose "Application to be placed on Vendors List" is disapproved may reapply after the expiration of six (6) months following the date of disapproval of his last application.

200 KAR 5:305. Performance Bonds; Forms; Payment

Section 1. (1) Every contractor to whom it is proposed to award a contract for construction services costing more than $25,000 shall prior to the award of such contract, give a bond or bonds to the Commonwealth of Kentucky as obligee, in form satisfactory to the purchasing agency, executed by a surety company authorized to do business in Kentucky, and in a penal sum equal to 100 percent of the contract price as it may be increased, the conditions of which shall bind the contractor, as principal, and the surety to the performance of the contract according to the terms, conditions and specifications of the contract, and in any changes or modifications thereto, and to the payment of all costs for labor, materials, equipment, supplies, taxes, and other proper charges and expenses incurred or to be incurred in the performance of said contract.

(2) Every contractor to whom it is proposed to award a contract for construction services costing $25,000 or less, shall, prior to the award of such contract give bond to the Commonwealth of Kentucky, as obligee, as provided in subsection (1) of this section, when required by the terms of an invitation for bids issued pursuant to KRS 45A.080, or an advertisement and solicitation for proposals for competitive negotiations pursuant to KRS 45A.085 and 45A.090.

Section 2. The provisions of Section 1 notwithstanding, every contractor to whom it is proposed to award a contract for the purchase of commodities, supplies or equipment or services by the Commonwealth of Kentucky or any state agency shall, when required by the terms of an invitation for bids, or solicitation or request for proposals, give bond to the Commonwealth of Kentucky, as obligee with surety satisfactory to the purchasing agency, in a penal amount, not to exceed 100 percent of the contract price, to be determined by the purchasing agency as sufficient to assure faithful performance of the contract by the contractor according to its terms.

Section 3. A contract shall not be awarded to any contractor who fails or refuses to give bond to the Commonwealth when required as provided by KRS 45A.190 and this regulation.

Section 4. A contractor may be declared in default of his contract with the Commonwealth of Kentucky, and his bond forfeited, when it is determined by the purchasing official that the contractor is in breach of the terms and conditions of the contract, including, in contracts for construction services, failure to make timely payment of bills for labor, materials and supplies as evidenced by liens filed against the construction fund by laborers and suppliers pursuant to KRS 376.195 to 376.260, or by letters of indebtedness filed with the purchasing agency evidencing that such bills are due and have not been paid by the contractor.

Section 5. (1) The form of performance and payment bond required to be given by contractors pursuant to Section 1, including the terms and conditions thereof, together with any revisions as may from time to time be made in such bond, shall be published in Department of Finance "Management and Procedures Manual," filed by reference in 200 KAR 5:302. Such form of bond shall be applicable to, and included in all contracts for construction services when required by KRS 45A.190 and this regulation; provided, however, that such bond form may be modified, or different terms substituted or other terms added, when, in connection with a particular procurement, it is determined in writing by the purchasing official that such modification, substitution or addition of terms is reasonably required for the procurement in the best interest of the Commonwealth of Kentucky.

(2) The form of bond required to secure the performance of all other contracts for procurement shall be the standard form of performance or payment bond such as is usually and customarily written and issued by surety companies authorized to do business in Kentucky, together with such additional terms as may be required by the purchasing agency and agreed to by the surety.

200 KAR 5:306. Competitive Sealed Bidding

Section 1. All contracts for construction exceeding an estimated cost of $5,000, and $1,000 for all other purchases, shall be awarded upon the basis of competitive sealed bids unless it is determined in writing that this method is not practicable and that the procurement may, in the best interests of the Commonwealth, more practically be obtained through competitive negotiations.

Section 2. The purchasing agencies shall cause public notice of invitations for bids for furnishing procurement requirements of the Commonwealth and its agencies through newspaper advertisement in the manner set forth in KRS 45A.080(3) and shall solicit bids from interested persons listed on the bidders' lists for particular requirements by sending invitations for bids to at least ten (10) persons listed in such bidders' lists. If there are not ten (10) persons listed on a particular bidders' list, invitations shall be sent to all persons listed on such list.

Section 3. Bidders shall complete, execute and submit their bids in strict compliance with the instructions contained in the invitation for bids. Bid forms shall be provided by the purchasing agencies and a bidder responding to an invitation for bids shall use only the bid form or form of proposal furnished by the purchasing agency in submitting his bids.

Section 4. Bidders shall submit their bids at the place and at, or prior to the date and hour set in the invitation for bids. Bids received after the hour set for opening bids are late bids and shall be so marked. A late bid shall not be considered for an award unless no other bid is received in response to an invitation for bids. The late bid, together with the envelope in which the bid was submitted bearing the stamped date and hour of receipt of the bid, and a note, signed by the buyer, indicating whether or not the bid was considered for an award shall be retained in the file pertaining to the invitation for bids to which the late bid relates.

Section 5. All bids, and any modifications to bids previously filed, received prior to the date and hour fixed for opening bids shall be kept secure and unopened. Envelopes containing bids but not marked to indicate that they contain a bid and listing the invitation for bids number and the date and hour of opening bids for that invitation may be opened for the purpose of identification of the contents of the envelope and will be marked and resealed.

Section 6. The buyer or other employee of the purchasing agency designated to open the bids shall determine when the time set for opening bids has arrived and shall so declare the time to those present for the bid opening. He shall then and there personally, in the presence of the bidders or their representatives and anyone else who may wish to attend the bid opening, open all bids received as of that date and hour; when practical, the names of the bidders and the amounts of their bids may be read aloud to the persons present. Except where, due to the nature or complexity of an invitation for bids, it may be deemed impractical, a bid tabulation summary sheet shall be prepared for each invitation for bids recording the name of each bidder, a description of the supplies or services bid and the amounts of the bids received. The bid tabulation summary sheet shall be permanently retained in the file pertaining to that invitation for bids and shall be available for public inspection. Inspection of bids by interested persons shall not be permitted or authorized during the formal bid opening process.

Section 7. The bids shall be examined by the buyer responsible for the procurement for any clerical or technical errors, reviewed for technical compliance with the terms of the invitation for bids, and the supplies or services bid evaluated for conformity with the specifications contained in the invitation for bids. Every bidder shall, when requested by the purchasing official responsible for the particular procurement, clarify or explain, in writing, any matter contained in his bid about which the purchasing officer may have question or believe in good faith needs to be clarified and explained. The bid of any bidder who fails or refuses, within a reasonable time to give a written clarification or explanation of his bid, or any part thereof, when requested to do so by the purchasing officer, shall not be considered further for an award on the basis of that invitation for bids. The written clarification or explanation of a bid, or a part of a bid, shall be incorporated in and become a part of any contract awarded on the basis of that bid. In due course, and after a reasonable bid evaluation period, the contract shall be awarded to the responsive and responsible bidder whose bid is either the lowest bid price or the lowest evaluated bid price, whichever is determined by the purchasing offical to be in the best interests of the Commonwealth or as designated in the invitation for bids as the basis for award of the contract. If, after evaluation of the bids, including consideration of any clarifying or explanatory information submitted by the bidders, it is determined by the purchasing officer that no satisfactory bid has been received, all bids may be rejected and, in the discretion of the purchasing officer, the invitation for bids cancelled, new bids invited on the basis of the same or revised specifications, or competitive negotiations undertaken for the procurement. The basis for the rejection of all bids and subsequent action taken or to be taken with respect to the invitation for bids shall be recorded in writing and filed in the invitation for bids file relating to the particular procurement.

Section 8. (1) The right to reject any and all bids and to waive technicalities and minor irregularities in bids shall be maintained and preserved in the case of all invitations for bids issued by purchasing agencies within the Department of Finance or pursuant to delegations of purchasing authority by the Department of Finance.

(2) Grounds for the rejection of bids include but shall not be limited to:

(a) Failure of a bid to conform to the essential requirements of an invitation for bids.

(b) Any bid which does not conform to the specifications contained or referenced in any invitation for bids shall be rejected unless the invitation authorized the submission of alternate bids and the items offered as alternatives meet the requirements specified in the invitation.

(c) Any bid which fails to conform to a delivery schedule established in an invitation for bids.

(d) A bid imposing conditions which would modify the terms and conditions of the invitation for bids, or limit the bidder's liability to the state on the contract awarded on the basis of such invitation for bids.

(e) Any bid determined by the purchasing officer in writing to be unreasonable as to price.

(f) Bids received from bidders determined to be not responsible bidders.

(g) Failure to furnish a bid guarantee when required by an invitation for bids.

(3) Technicalities or minor irregularities in bids which may be waived when the purchasing official determines that it will be in the Commonwealth's best interest to do so, are mere matters of form not affecting the material substance of a bid or some immaterial deviation from or variation in the precise requirements of the invitation for bids and having no or a trivial or negligible effect on price, quality, quantity or delivery of supplies or performance of the services being procured, the correction or waiver of which will not affect the relative standing of, or be otherwise prejudicial to other bidders. The purchasing officer may either give a bidder an opportunity to cure any deficiency resulting from a technicality or minor irregularity in his bid, or waive such deficiency where it is advantageous to the Commonwealth to do so.

Section 9. Where a mistake in a bid is claimed, and the evidence is clear and convincing that a material mistake was made in the bid and that due to such mistake, the bid submitted was not the bid intended, the bidder may be permitted to withdraw his bid. It shall be the duty of all contractors bidding to carefully review and verify the accuracy of their bids both before submitting them and prior to execution of a contract. When a mistake in a bid is claimed after the award and execution of a contract, on the basis of such bid, the contractor shall be required to perform according to the terms and conditions of the contract unless it established by clear and convincing evidence that a material mistake had been made in the original bid and that the contractor would sustain a financial loss if required to perform the contract according to its terms; a reduction or diminution in profit margin shall not be deemed a financial loss under this section. Where the evidence is clear and convincing that a material mistake has been made in a bid after the award of a contract, and the contractor will sustain a financial loss if required to perform the contract, the contract shall be rescinded and the contractor shall be ineligible to submit a bid upon readvertisement for the construction services.

Section 10. The following matters shall be applicable to all invitations for bids issued, bids submitted, and contracts awarded for the purchase of commodities, supplies and equipment pursuant to KRS 45A.080 and this regulation:

(1) Time discounts or cash discounts shall not be considered.

(2) Trade discounts: trade discounts should be deducted by the vendor in calculating the unit price quoted, unless otherwise indicated in the bid.

(3) Quantity discounts: quantity discounts should be included in the price of the item. When not included in the item price, the discount shall be considered only if the purchasing agency, or the agency for whose benefit the procurement has been undertaken, deems it to be in the Commonwealth's best interests. The unit price shown on the contract shall be the net price, less the discount, unless otherwise indicated in the bid.

(4) Unit prices: In case of a discrepancy in the extension of a price, the unit or item price shall govern over the total price of all items.

(5) Awards on an aggregate or individual item basis: An award may be made to the lowest aggregate bidder for all items, group of items, or on an individual item basis, whichever is deemed to be in the Commonwealth's best interest. The methods and bases of award of contract and of evaluation of bids shall be stated in the invitation for bids.

(6) Telegraphic bids: When the purchasing agency has invited bids or requested written quotations, telegraphic responses shall not be accepted.

200 KAR 5:307. Competitively Negotiated Contracts

Section 1. When, due to the complex nature or technical detail of a particular procurement, or when, in the opinion of the purchasing official, specifications cannot be fairly and objectively prepared so as to permit competition in the invitation for sealed bids, or for high technology electronic equipment available from a limited number of sources of supply and for which specifications cannot practically be prepared except by reference to the specifications of the equipment of a single source of supply, or when it is otherwise determined by the purchasing official that the invitation for competitive sealed bids is not practicable, or when it is determined by the purchasing official that the conditions described in KRS 45A.085(3) or 45A.090(1) exist, and except for procurement under KRS 45A.095 and 45A.100, and regulations adopted pursuant thereto, a contract may be awarded for a procurement by competitive negotiations as authorized by KRS 45A.085 and 45A.090 and this regulation. The purchasing official shall make a written determination of the reasons it is considered impractical to invite bids prior to initiating any other action leading toward the award of a contract on the basis of competitive negotiations.

Section 2. When it has been determined that it is not practical to invite competitive bids as provided in Section 1, except when such determination is based on the existence of the conditions mentioned in KRS 45A.085(3) or 45A.090(1), action to obtain a procurement by competitive negotiations shall commence by advertisement and solicitation for written proposals in the manner specified by KRS 45A.080(3) and regulations adopted pursuant thereto. The advertisement or solicitation for proposals for competitive negotiations shall state:

(1) That the purchasing agency proposes to enter into competitive negotiations with responsible offerors for a procurement;

(2) The date, hour and place that written proposals for the procurement shall be received;

(3) The type of procurement involved and a description of the supplies or services sought; provided, however, that detailed specifications need not be listed in newspaper advertisements, or solicitations for proposals sent to vendors listed on a bidder's list maintained by the purchasing agency if it is considered impractical by the purchasing official to do so, but potential offerors shall be informed by such advertisement or solicitation where such detailed specifications, if available for the particular procurement may be obtained;

(4) The evaluation factors to be considered by the purchasing agency in the competitive negotiations in determining the proposal most advantageous to the Commonwealth, and the proposed method or methods of award of contract;

(5) Such other information as, in the opinion of the purchasing official, may be desirable or necessary to reasonably inform potential offerors about the requirements of the procurement or the limits or bounds of the competitive negotiations proposed to obtain the procurement.

Section 3. All written proposals received by the purchasing agency in response to advertisement or solicitation for proposals for competitive negotiations shall be kept secure and unopened until the date and hour set for opening the proposals. Proposals for competitive negotiations not clearly marked as such on the envelope in which received may be opened for identification purposes, and shall be appropriately identified with reference to the particular procurement and resealed until the time for opening proposals.

Section 4. At the close of business on, or at the beginning of the next business day after the date fixed for receiving proposals for competitive negotiations, all proposals received as of the close of business on that date shall be transmitted to the purchasing official for the procurement for opening. Proposals for competitive negotiations shall not be subject to public inspection until negotiations between the purchasing agency and all offerors have been concluded and a contract awarded to the responsible offeror submitting the proposal determined in writing to be the most advantageous to the Commonwealth, price, and the evaluation factors set forth in the advertisement and solicitations for proposals considered.

Section 5. (1) The purchasing official shall examine each written proposal received for general conformity with the advertised terms of the procurement. If it has been provided in the advertisement or solicitation for proposals that an award may be made without written or oral discussion, the purchasing official may, upon the basis of the written proposals received, award the contract to the responsible offeror submitting the proposal determined in writing to be the most advantageous to the Commonwealth, price, and the published evaluation factors considered. If, after the proposals have been examined, it is determined that written and/or oral discussions should be had with the offerors, the purchasing official shall determine in writing, based on an individual review, those proposals received from responsible offerors that are preliminarily susceptible of being selected for award of a contract for the procurement. Each offeror shall be contacted informally by the purchasing official and a meeting scheduled for discussion of the offeror's proposals. Discussions need not be conducted under the circumstances of or relative to the topics enumerated in KRS 45A.085(6)(a), (b) or (c).

(2) Discussions with offerors shall be held informally and may be conducted orally, in writing, or both orally and in writing, as determined by the purchasing official in writing to be the most advantageous to the Commonwealth. If, however, after discussions with all responsible offerors have concluded, or after examination of the written proposals initially submitted, it is determined that no acceptable proposal has been submitted, any or all proposals may be rejected and, in the discretion of

the purchasing official, new proposals may be solicited as provided in this regulation on the basis of the same, or revised terms, or the procurement may be abandoned.

Section 6. The purchasing official shall prepare a written summary of all oral discussions in the competitive negotiations setting forth the date or dates of discussions with all responsible offerors and the general substance of the discussions. Verbatim records of the discussion shall not be required.

Section 7. When it is determined in writing by the purchasing official that the conditions mentioned in either KRS 45A.085(3), or 45A.090(1), exist with respect to any particular procurement, competitive negotiations may be undertaken to obtain the requirements of such procurement as provided by KRS 45A.085(3) or 45A.090(1), and according to the procedures set forth in Sections 3 to 7.

200 KAR 5:308. Small Purchase Procedures

Section 1. Small purchase procedures may be used by all agencies without prior approval by the Department of Finance where procurement for a total requirement is estimated not to exceed an aggregate amount of $5,000 for construction services, and $1,000 for all other categories of purchases. Procurement requirements shall not be parceled, split, divided or purchased over a period of time in order to meet the dollar limitations for use of small purchase procedures.

Section 2. Agencies shall informally obtain three (3) or more price quotations from qualified sources of supply for all small purchases exceeding $1,500 for construction services and $500 for all other purchases, except as otherwise delegated. The price quotations received, a tabulation of prices offered, and comments by the agency handling the small purchase concerning the basis selected for placing the order, shall be recorded in writing and shall be filed in a small purchase order file to be maintained by the agency. Small purchases may be made by agencies from any available source of supply, without first obtaining quotations, for construction services costing $1,500 or less, and $500 or less for all other purchases.

200 KAR 5:309. Noncompetitive Negotiations

Section 1. Procurement contracts may be awarded through noncompetitive negotiations only as provided in this regulation. Contracts which may be awarded on the basis of noncompetitive negotiations include, and shall be limited to the following:

(1) Contractual services for telephone service, electrical energy and other public utility services, and other contractual services provided within a defined geographic area pursuant to a franchise for such service awarded pursuant to law by a city, county or other political subdivision authorized to award such franchise; provided, however, that except for telephone and other public utility services, the invitation for bids or the award of a contract by competitive negotiations for other contractual services performed under a franchise awarded by a political subdivision shall not be precluded when it is determined by the purchasing official to be in the best interest of the Commonwealth; nor shall the award of a contract for the purchase or lease of a telephone system to serve the internal needs of state agencies or institutions by invitation for bids or on the basis of competitive negotiations be precluded under this subsection.

(2) Commodities, equipment and services available, in the discretion of the purchasing official, from a single source. Such items shall include, but not be limited to,

patented equipment and copyrighted material, and equipment peripheral to other equipment already owned by the Commonwealth or any state agency determined by the purchasing officer to be incompatible to such other equipment without modification or adjustment in either the equipment already owned or the equipment to be acquired.

(3) Instructional materials available, in the discretion of the purchasing official, from a single source. A written determination setting forth need in relation to a particular instructional program, and justifying the procurement of the particular materials on a noncompetitive basis, shall be made by the purchasing official prior to the award of the contract.

(4) Special supplies or equipment required for laboratory or experimental studies. A written determination setting forth the need in relation to such studies, and justifying the procurement of such supplies or equipment on a noncompetitive basis shall be made by the purchasing official prior to the award of contract.

(5) Contracts or subscriptions for the purchase of published books, maps, periodicals, technical pamphlets, and except for those specially commissioned for use by an agency which shall be contracted for as provided by subsection (7) of this section, recordings, films and works of art for museum and public display.

(6) Commercial items purchased for resale to the general public through a resale outlet maintained by a state agency. Such items shall be purchased only from a wholesaler, manufacturer or producer of the item or items.

(7) Contracts for professional, technical, scientific, or artistic services. Except for contracts for architectural or engineering services negotiated in accordance with the provisions of KRS 45A.205, or agreements with multiple vendors of medical or health care and related services, and fixed rates of payment for such services as prescribed by state or federal law or regulations, and entered into for the benefit of persons who are wards of the Commonwealth, or who are otherwise entitled pursuant to law to the provision of such services by the Commonwealth, all contracts for professional, technical, scientific, or artistic services by state agencies shall be made, awarded and entered into only as provided in KRS 45.530 to 45.545.

(8) Contracts for the purchase of commodities, supplies, equipment and construction services that would ordinarily be purchased on a competitive basis when an emergency has been declared in the manner prescribed by KRS 45.400.

(9) Contracts or agreements for the purchase or sale of supplies, equipment or services between the Commonwealth and the Government of the United States, another state, a political subdivision of the Commonwealth, or non-profit organization organized under the laws of the Commonwealth, another state or the District of Columbia, or chartered under an Act of Congress and lawfully doing business in the Commonwealth of Kentucky, and serving a public purpose of an essentially government, civic, educational or charitable nature.

(10) Contracts with vendors who maintain a general service administration price agreement with the United States of America or any agency thereof, provided, however, that no contracts executed under this provision shall authorize a price higher than is contained in the contract between general service administration and the vendor.

(11) Contracts for the purchase of real property, or interests in real property.

200 KAR 5:310. Multiple Contracts

Section 1. Multiple contracts may be awarded on the basis of a single invitation for bids as after competitive negotiations when it is determined in writing by the purchasing official in advance of the invitation for bids or the advertisement and solicitation for proposals for competitive negotiations that due to the geographic distribution of the agencies requiring supplies of the kind or kinds to be sought through the procurement, the need for a variety of kinds and quality of supplies of the same general nature, or when it is otherwise determined that the award of multiple contracts may be in the Commonwealth's best interests, and its needs met at a reasonable cost. A determination, and notice to potential bidders and offerors, that multiple contracts may be awarded for any procurement shall not preclude the award of a single contract for such procurement where it is determined by the purchasing official to be in the best interest of the Commonwealth, price and other factors considered.

Section 2. When it is determined in writing by the purchasing official after the evaluation of competitive bids, or the closing of competitive negotiations, that bids or offers substantially and materially responsive to terms of the procurement have been received for only a part or parts of the requirements of the procurement, and the bids or offers received for another part or parts of the procurement are not substantially and materially responsive to such items, a contract or contracts may be awarded as to the part or parts of the procurement for which responsive bids or offers have been received, and the bids or offers determined to be nonresponsive may be rejected in the discretion of the purchasing official and new bids invited, or proposals for competitive negotiations for the procurement advertised and solicited, on the same or revised terms, conditions, and specifications.

200 KAR 5:311. Contract Modifications

Section 1. The purchasing agencies within the Department of Finance, and any state agency to whom purchasing authority has been delegated by the Department of Finance, shall be authorized to provide by appropriate clauses to contracts for supplies or services of all types for changes and modifications to such contracts and providing for the method or methods of calculating the costs of any decrease, increase, or other change in the contract price resulting from such change or modification. In contracts for the purchase in fixed amounts of commodities, supplies and equipment, increases in quantities in excess of ten (10) percent of the original quantity, fixed by the contract shall not be permitted unless the invitation for bids or advertisement and solicitation for proposals for competitive negotiations for the procurement informed prospective bidders or offerors that an increase in quantities might be forthcoming, nor shall increases in unit prices be permitted in such contracts for increased quantities except as provided by a price escalation formula authorized by the invitation for bids or request for proposals for competitive negotiations.

Section 2. All changes or modifications to contracts for the purchase of commodities, supplies, equipment and construction services shall be effected by an advice of change in order to the contract which shall be supported by a written determination by the purchasing official documenting the reason and basis for the change or modification to the contract. A copy of the advice of change in order and the supporting documentation relative to any change or modification to a contract shall be filed and maintained in the contract file by the purchasing agency.

Section 3. Every contractor to whom a contract containing clauses authorizing changes or modifications to the contract shall be deemed, by acceptance of the contract, to have agreed to the changes or modifications of the contract as provided therein.

200 KAR 5:312. Termination of Contracts

Section 1. (1) Any contractor who is determined in writing by the purchasing official to be in breach of any of the terms and conditions of a contract with the Commonwealth of Kentucky held by such contractor, shall, in the discretion of the purchasing official, be declared in default and such contract may be terminated as a result of such default.

(2) A default in performance by a contractor for which a contract may be terminated shall include, but shall not necessarily be limited to, failure to perform the contract according to its terms, conditions and specifications; failure to make delivery within the time specified or according to a delivery schedule fixed by the contract; late payment or nonpayment of bills for labor, materials, supplies, or equipment furnished in connection with a contract for construction services as evidenced by mechanics' liens filed pursuant to the provisions of KRS Chapter 376, or letters of indebtedness received from creditors by the purchasing agency; failure to diligently prosecute the work under a contract for construction services.

(3) The Commonwealth shall not be liable for any further payment to a contractor under a contract terminated for the contractor's default after the date of such default as determined by the purchasing official except for commodities, supplies, equipment or services delivered and accepted on or before the date of default and for which payment had not been made as of that date. The contractor, and/or his surety, if a performance or payment bond has been required under the contract, shall be jointly and severally liable to the Commonwealth for all loss, cost or damage sustained by the Commonwealth as a result of the contractor's default; provided, however, that a contractor's surety liability shall not exceed the final sum specified in the contractor's bond.

Section 2. The Commonwealth shall be authorized to terminate for its own convenience all contracts for the procurement of supplies and services when the purchasing official has determined that such termination will be in the Commonwealth's best interests. When it has been determined that a contract should be terminated for the convenience of the Commonwealth, the purchasing agency shall be authorized to negotiate a settlement with the contractor according to terms deemed just and equitable by the purchasing agency. Compensation to a contractor for his lost profits on a contract terminated for convenience of the Commonwealth shall not exceed an amount proportionate to the sum that the contractor's total expected margin of profit on the contract bore to the contract price, based on the total out of pocket expense incurred by the contractor as of the date of termination of the contract. Whenever a contract is terminated for the convenience of the Commonwealth, the contractor shall have the burden of establishing the amount of compensation to which he believes himself to be entitled by the submission of complete and accurate cost data employed in submitting his bid or proposal for the contract, and evidence of expenses paid or incurred in performance of the contract from the date of award through the date of termination. Payment of the sum agreed to in settlement of a contract terminated for convenience of the Commonwealth shall be made from the same source of funds or account as the original contract.

200 KAR 5:313. General and Special Conditions for Bidding

Section 1. The Division of Purchases, for commodity and other procurement functions within its jurisdiction, and the Division of Contracting and Administration, for construction and related services and items, shall adopt, and revise from time to time as may be necessary and convenient in the discretion of the directors of the divisions, with the approval of the Commissioners of the Bureaus of Administrative Services and Facilities Management, respectively, general conditions for bidding to the Commonwealth of Kentucky. The divisions shall also be authorized to promulgate and adopt in relation to any particular procurement, or class or type of procurement, special conditions of bidding. The general conditions of bidding, and any revisions thereto, adopted by both the Division of Purchases and the Division of Contracting and Administration shall be published in the Department of Finance "Policy and Procedure Manual," filed by reference in 2-0 KAR 5:302.

Section 2. The general conditions of bidding shall be applicable to, and incorporated by reference in all invitations for bids issued by the Division of Purchases, the Division of Contracting and Administration, or by any agency to which purchasing authority has been delegated pursuant to authorization contained in KRS Chapter 45A and these regulations.

Section 3. All vendors, firms, contractors and persons who submit a bid in response to an invitation for bids issued by the Department of Finance, or by any agency of the Commonwealth of Kentucky pursuant to a delegation of purchasing authority by the Department of Finance, shall be deemed to have agreed to comply with all terms, conditions, and specifications of such invitation for bids.

Section 4. The general conditions of bidding, or specific portions thereof, shall be applicable to all requests for proposals for competitive negotiations pursuant to KRS 45A.085 and 45A.090, in the discretion of the purchasing agencies; provided, however, the advertisement and solicitation for proposals for competitive negotiations shall inform prospective offerors that the request for proposals shall be subject to the general conditions or parts thereof, in specific reference to the particular parts or sections of the general conditions applicable to the particular procurement to be obtained by the competitive negotiations.

200 KAR 5:314. General Food and Perishable Items Purchasing

Section 1. The conditions and procedures for the purchase of general food and perishable items and commercial items purchased for resale shall be established by written policy published in the Department of Finance "Management and Procedures Manual," filed by reference in 200 KAR 5:302, and revised from time to time as may be required in the opinion of the Director of the Division of Purchases and approved by the Secretary of the Department of Finance with the advice of the Commissioner of the Bureau of Administrative Services.

Section 2. Commercial items purchased for resale shall be exempt from competitive bidding.

200 KAR 5:315. Disciplinary Action for Failure to Perform

Section 1. Any bidder or contractor to the Commonwealth of Kentucky who, except for good cause shown, shall have committed, or failed to perform, as the context may require, one or more of the following acts or omissions, shall be liable to disciplinary action by the Department of Finance as set forth in Section 2. Specific grounds for disciplinary action include:

(1) Failure to post bid or performance bonds, or to provide alternate bid or performance guarantee in form acceptable to the purchasing agency in lieu of a bond, as required by an invitation for bids or a solicitation for proposals;

(2) Substitution of commodities without prior written approval of the purchasing agency;

(3) Failure to comply with the terms and conditions of the invitation for bids or solicitation for proposals, or with the terms, conditions and specifications of a contract, including failure to complete performance of a contract within the time specified in the contract;

(4) Failure to replace inferior or defective materials, supplies or equipment immediately after notification by the purchasing agency or the agency to which such materials, supplies or equipment had been delivered;

(5) Failure by a bidder listed on a bidders' list to respond to three (3) (five (5) for construction service contracts) invitations for bids sent to such bidder;

(6) Refusal to accept a contract awarded pursuant to the terms of an invitation for bids, or following the close of competitive negotiations;

(7) Falsifying invoices, or making false representations to any state agency or state official, or untrue statements about, any payment under a contract, or to procure award of a contract, or to induce a modification in the price or the terms of a contract to the contractor's advantage;

(8) Collusion, or collaboration with another bidder or other bidders, in the submission of a bid or bids for the purpose of lessening or reducing competition;

(9) Falsifying information in the submission of an application for listing on a Department of Finance bidders' list;

(10) Failure to report, and to pay over to the Department of Revenue any Kentucky sales and/or use taxes as may be due in connection with a procurement contract as provided by law;

(11) Failure to comply with the prevailing wage law requirements of state or federal laws as may be applicable to any public works contract of the Commonwealth or any political subversion of public authority.

Section 2. (1) Any contractor preliminarily determined to have done any act prohibited, or to have failed to do any act required by Section 1 (1) to (6) shall, in the discretion of the commissioner of the bureau having jurisdiction over the particular procurements activity or function, be liable to be placed on probation, or suspended from bidding to the Commonwealth of Kentucky, or a combination of suspension from bidding and probation, for not more than twelve (12) months.

(2) Any contractor preliminarily determined to have done any act prohibited by Section 1 (7), (8) and (9) shall be removed from the bidders' lists and shall be ineligible for reinstatement to such lists for a period not to exceed twenty-four (24) months following the date of removal. Any contractor removed from the bidders' lists under this section shall be eligible to apply for reinstatement as provided in 200 KAR 5:304, after the expiration of the removal period.

(3) Any contractor, or any subcontractor to a contractor, determined by the Department of Labor to have violated the prevailing wage requirements of KRS Chapter 337 shall be suspended from bidding to the Commonwealth of Kentucky, or to participate in a public works contract of the Commonwealth of Kentucky, effective on and after the date the Department of Finance receives notice from the Department of Labor that such contractor or subcontractor has been determined to have violated the prevailing wage law, and until such time as the Department of Labor has determined the contractor or subcontractor to be in compliance with the requirements of such law.

Section 3. Except for the grounds mentioned in Section 1 (5), (6) and (11) a preliminary written determination shall be made concerning the facts of any allegation or claim that a bidder or contractor has either committed an act prohibited, or failed to perform an act required, by Section 1 before any disciplinary action is taken against such contractor. Such preliminary determination shall be submitted to the

Office of General Counsel, Department of Finance, for review prior to the administration of any disciplinary action as authorized by Section 2. Notice of disciplinary action shall be sent to the bidder or contractor at the address shown in the department's records by certified mail, return receipt requested.

Section 4. Bidders or contractors against whom disciplinary action has been taken under this regulation may appeal the action of the Secretary to the Department of Finance. The appeal must be filed in the office of the secretary within ten (10) working days after the date of notice of the disciplinary action has been received by the bidder or contractor as shown by the certified mail receipt. The appeal must be filed in writing and must state facts showing cause why the disciplinary action should be set aside. An appeal constituting a general denial of the charges contained in the notice of disciplinary action, unless supported by specific facts rebutting such charges, shall be preemptorily dismissed. The appellant may request either a formal hearing before a hearing officer to be designated by the secretary to take proof and make findings and recommendations to the secretary, or an informal hearing to be conducted by the commissioner of the bureau having jurisdiction over the particular procurement activity or function, or his designee. A written report of the substance of the matters raised in such informal hearing shall be prepared and submitted to the secretary and recommending that the appeal be sustained or denied. The rules of evidence shall not apply in either formal or informal hearings conducted under this section and any matter considered pertinent to the issues of the hearing shall be admissible, subject only to the determination by the presiding officer as to the proper weight to be accorded all matters introduced at the hearing.

Section 5. No purchase of any kind shall be made by any state agency from a bidder or contractor who has been suspended or removed from the bidders' lists, except for those removed for the grounds stated in Section 1 (8). All state agencies shall be promptly informed about bidders or contractors suspended or removed from the bidders' lists and shall immediately comply with this prohibition.

Section 6. The administration of disciplinary action against a bidder, potential bidder or contractor under this regulation shall not preclude the taking of other action by the Commonwealth, based on the same facts, as may be otherwise available, either at law or in equity, including without limitation to the generality thereof, suits for damages or actions for specific performance.

200 KAR 5:316. Works of Art

Section 1. Every state agency and institution, including institutions of higher learning, which maintains a museum shall be authorized to purchase or otherwise acquire from any source, and to sell, trade, or otherwise dispose of works of art and artifacts acquired for display in such museum, or which the agency is authorized to dispose of, according to terms determined to be fair and just, and will promote the purposes of the museum by the head of the agency or institution, or the governing board of an institution, or the curator of the museum or other officer or employee of the agency or institution to which such authority has been delegated by the agency or institution head or governing board, without necessity for approval of such acquisition or dispositions by the Department of Finance. The curator, or other employee of the agency or institution responsible for the operation of the agency or institution responsible for the operation of the museum shall prepare an inventory of all works of art and artifacts belonging to the museum, which shall be filed with the Bureau of Public Properties, and shall maintain records of all acquisitions and disposition of works of art and artifacts of the museum, and shall file annually with the Bureau of Public Properties a revised inventory of such works of art and artifacts.

Section 2. Every state agency shall be authorized to purchase or otherwise acquire, for its own use, or for any statutorily authorized purpose of such agency, published books, maps, periodicals, and technical pamphlets, without necessity for approval by the Department of Finance as to such acquisition.

Appendix D:
Prince George's
County, Maryland,
Code of Ordinances
and Resolutions,
Chapter 16, Central
Purchasing, 1969

Sec. 16-1. Definitions

As used in this article the following definitions shall apply unless other meaning is mandatory:

(a) Capital Improvement: Is any public improvement undertaken by the County, except projects undertaken by County work forces, including the construction or reconstruction, in whole or in part, of any road, bridge, street, building or water, sewer or storm water facility or any similar physical structure or facility necessary to the carrying out of the activities of the County government.

(b) Commissioners: The Board of County Commissioners of Prince George's County, Maryland.

(c) Contractual Services: Shall include all types of services required by using agencies but not furnished by its own employees, except professional and similar contractual services, which are in their nature unique and not subject to competition, but shall not include capital improvements, nor include contracts entered into by the County for the collection, transportation or disposal of refuse.

(d) County: Prince George's County, Maryland.

(e) Deputy Purchasing Agent: Deputy Director of the Department of Central Purchasing, designated by the Purchasing Agent, fully empowered to act as Purchasing Agent for such periods, or under such circumstances, as the Purchasing Agent shall determine.

(f) Emergency: Shall be deemed to exist when a breakdown in machinery and/or a threatened termination of essential services or a dangerous condition develops, or when any unforeseen circumstances arise causing curtailment or diminution of an essential service.

(g) Formal Contract Purchase: Any purchase for supplies and/or contractual services in excess of one thousand five hundred dollars ($1,500.00) where advertising is required.

(h) Local Bidders: Shall mean a bidder whose principal office is located in the County or whose principal business is conducted therein as compared with a bidder whose principal office or principal business is not so located. If there be no such County bidder, then the phrase "local bidder" shall mean a bidder whose principal office is located in the State or whose principal business is conducted therein as compared with a bidder whose principal office or principal business is not so located.

(i) Purchasing Agent: Director of Finance for Prince George's County, Maryland.

(j) Using Agency: Any department, agency, commission, board, or other unit in the County government or other agency using supplies or procuring contractual services paid for in whole, or in part, by County funds, including such departments and agencies created by, or operating under, the laws of this State to the extent that such laws apply to them or to the extent that such agencies request the provisions of this ordinance to apply to them.

(k) Supplies: Shall mean and include all commodities, materials, equipment, and all other articles or things which shall be furnished to or used by any agency, including any and all printing, binding, or publication of stationary, forms, journals and reports.

Sec. 16-2. Establishment of Central Purchasing Department

(a) There is hereby re-created, as a Department of County government, a Central Purchasing Department to operate under the direction and supervision of the Director of Finance.

(b) Unauthorized Purchases. Except as herein provided, it shall be unlawful for any County officer, elected or appointed, or any employee to order the purchase of any supplies or contractual services within the purview of this article other than by or through the Central Purchasing Department, and any purchase ordered or contract made contrary to the provisions hereof are not approved and the County shall not be bound thereby.

(c) Director. The Director of the Department of Central Purchasing shall be the Purchasing Agent and shall have supervision of the Department. He shall be appointed by the Board of County Commissioners and shall perform such duties as are prescribed by law.

Sec. 16-3. Powers and Duties of the Purchasing Agent

It shall be the power and duty of the Purchasing Agent to:

(a) Purchase or contract for all supplies and contractual services required by using agencies, except as provided herein;

(b) Prepare and enforce standard specifications;

(c) Operate a General Stores facility;

(d) Inspect or supervise the inspection of all deliveries of supplies or contractual services purchased through him to determine their conformance with the order or contract;

(e) Act to procure for the County the highest quality in supplies and contractual services at least expense to the County;

(f) Discourage uniform bidding and endeavor to obtain as full and open competition as possible on all purchases and sales;

(g) Keep informed of current developments in the field of purchasing, prices, market conditions, and new products;

(h) Secure for the County the benefits of research done in the fields of purchasing by other governmental jurisdictions, national trade associations, and by private business and organizations;

(i) Prepare and adopt standard purchase nomenclature by using agencies and suppliers;

(j) Prepare, adopt, and maintain a vendor's file containing catalogues, descriptions of commodities, prices, and discounts;

(k) Authority to declare vendors who default on their quotations, as irresponsible bidders and to disqualify them from receiving business from the County for a stated period of time, subject to approval by the Commissioners;

(l) Maintain a current file of sources of supplies and services to be known as a "Bidders' List" to which vendors can request to be included;

(m) Perform such other functions and duties in keeping with good purchasing practices and such other duties as the Commissioners assign.

Sec. 16-4. Regulations and Procedures

The Purchasing Agent is directed to prepare and maintain an up-to-date purchasing and supply manual containing detailed regulations and procedures implementing this article. The manual will:

(a) Prescribe the operation of the County's purchasing and supply system to be followed by using agencies.

(b) Prescribe internal operations to be followed by the Department of Central Purchasing.

(c) Prescribe the County's purchasing regulations and policies to be followed in its relations with the business community. This section may be made available to the public at cost of publication.

(d) The manual and amendments shall be submitted to the Commissioners for adoption. After adoption, the Purchasing Agent will issue the manual of regulations and procedures and shall secure compliance therewith by the using agencies. In addition, other necessary matters shall be included to give effect to the foregoing regulations and procedures and to the provisions of this article. After approval by the County Commissioners, they shall have the full force and effect of law. The regulations and procedures shall represent a complete plan of operation for the County's Central Purchasing System.

Sec. 16-5. Emergency Purchases

(a) If an emergency occurs during regular County business hours, the using agency shall immediately notify the Purchasing Agent who shall either purchase the required supplies or contractual services or authorize the agency to do so.

(b) If an emergency occurs at times other than regular business hours, the using agency may purchase directly the required supplies or contractual services. The agency shall, however, whenever practicable, secure competitive telephone bids and order delivery to be made to the lower responsible bidder. The agency shall also, not later than the next regular County business day thereafter, submit to the Purchasing Agent a requisition, a tabulation of bids received, if any, a copy of the delivery record and a brief written explanation of the circumstances of the emergency.

(c) A complete record shall be maintained by the Purchasing Agent explaining or otherwise supporting the reason for each emergency purchase. Such records shall be available for public inspection for a period of thirty (30) calendar days during regular County business hours in the Purchasing Agent's main offices.

(d) The Purchasing Agent shall submit monthly to the Chairman of the Board of County Commissioners a report covering all emergency purchases with an explanation of the circumstances of each emergency purchase in excess of three hundred dollars (300.00).

Sec. 16-6. Formal Contracting

All supplies and contractual services, except as otherwise provided herein, when the total estimated cost thereof shall exceed one thousand five hundred dollars ($1,500.00) shall be purchased by formal, written contract or purchase order from the lowest responsible bidder as determined by the Purchasing Agent, after public notice inviting proposals. No contract or purchase shall be subdivided to avoid the requirements of this section. The following procedures shall be observed in the award of formal contracts estimated to exceed one thousand five hundred dollars ($1,500.00) in value, except as provided therein:

(a) Notice in at least one newspaper of general circulation in Prince George's County which shall include a general description of the articles to be purchased or sold, where bid blanks and specifications may be secured, and state the time and place for opening bids;

(b) The Purchasing Agent shall also solicit sealed bids from all responsible prospective suppliers who are on the Bidders List, by sending them a copy of such written notice which will acquaint the supplier or interested party with the proposed purchase or sale. Notices of pending purchases or sales shall be posted on a bulletin board located in the main offices of the Purchasing Agent.

(c) Each bidder shall, by virtue of submitting a bid, guarantee that he has not been a party with other bidders to an agreement to bid a fixed or uniform price. Violations of this implied guarantee shall render void the bid of such bidders. Any disclosure to or acquisition by a competitive bidder, in advance of the opening of bids, of the terms or conditions of the bid submitted by another competitor shall render the entire proceedings void and shall require re-advertising for bids.

(d) All bids under this section shall be submitted sealed to the Purchasing Agent. When deemed necessary by the Purchasing Agent, each bid shall be accompanied by surety in the forms of a certified or cashier's check or bid bond in such amount as shall be prescribed in the public notice inviting bids and in the contract bid form. Bidders who regularly do business with the County shall be permitted to file with the Purchasing Agent an annual bid bond in an amount established by the Purchasing Agent. Such annual bonds shall be acceptable as surety in lieu of the furnishing of surety with each individual transaction.

(e) A tabulation of all bids received shall be available for public inspection in the main offices of the Purchasing Agent during regular County business hours for a period of not less than thirty (30) calendar days after the award of a contract. After that period they will be available on special request.

(f) The Commissioners shall have authority to reject any or all bids, or parts thereof, for any one or more supplies or contractual services included in the proposed contract when in their judgment the public interest will be served thereby and reserves the right to waive technical defects as the best interests of the County so dictate. If all bids are for the same total amount or unit price, and if the public interest will not permit the delay of re-advertising for bids, the contract may be awarded to the local tie bidder, or if there be none, to one of the tie bidders, by drawing lots in public; or, the Purchasing Agent, when so directed by the Commissioners, may purchase the supplies or contractual services in the open market, as provided in Section 16-7 of this article, except that the price paid in the open market shall not exceed the lowest contract bid price submitted for the same supplies or contractual services.

(g) The County Commissioners shall award all contracts to the lowest responsible bidder upon recommendation of the Purchasing Agent. In determining a bidder's responsibility, the Purchasing Agent shall consider:

(1) The ability, capacity and skill of the bidder to perform the contract or provide the service required;

(2) Whether the bidder can perform the contract or provide the service promptly, or within the time specified, without delay or interference;

(3) The character, integrity, reputation, judgment, experience and efficiency of the bidder;

(4) The quality of performance of previous contracts or services;

(5) The previous and existing compliance by the bidder with laws and ordinances relating to the contract or services;

(6) The sufficiency of the financial resources and ability of the bidder to perform the contract or provide the service;

(7) The quality, availability and adaptability of the supplies, or contractual services, to the particular use required;

(8) The ability of the bidder to provide future maintenance and service for the use of the subject of the contract;

(9) The number and scope of the conditions attached to the bid;

(10) Whether the bidder is in arrears to the County in debt or contract or is a defaulter on surety to the County or whether the bidder's County taxes or assessments are delinquent; and

(11) Such other information as may be secured by the Purchasing Agent having a bearing on the decision to award the contract.

(h) Contracts for personal property sales shall be awarded by the Purchasing Agent to the highest responsible bidder and shall be subject to all other applicable requirements of this section.

(i) Whenever required, the successful bidder shall promptly execute a formal contract to be approved as to its form, terms, and conditions by the County Attorney, and such bidder shall also execute and deliver to the Purchasing Agent a good and sufficient performance bond to be approved by the Commissioners in the amount specified in the invitation to bid. Any bidder who has a contract awarded to him and who fails to execute promptly and properly the required contract and bond shall forfeit his certified check or an equivalent amount under his bid bond. Said amount shall be taken and considered as liquidated damages and not as a penalty for the failure of said bidder to execute said contract and bond. Upon the execution of the contract and performance bond by the successful bidder, his certified check shall be returned to him or the equivalent amount charged against his bid bond shall be released. The certified checks of unsuccessful bidders shall be returned to them or the equivalent amounts charged against their bid bonds shall be released after opening the bids and awarding the contract to the successful bidder.

(j) All invitations to bid involving expenditures in excess of one thousand five hundred dollars ($1,500.00) shall include the following provisions:

"Upon the request of the Commissioners, as a prerequisite for the payment pursuant to the terms of this contract, there shall be furnished to the Commissioners a statement, under oath, that no member of the governing body of Prince George's County, or members of his or her immediate family, including spouse, parents or children, or any other officer or employee of the County, or any member or employee of a Commission, Board or Corporation controlled or appointed by the Commissioners, has received or has been promised, directly or indirectly, any financial benefit, by way of fee, commission, finder's fee or in any other manner, remuneration arising from or directly or indirectly related to this contract; and that upon request by the Commissioners, as a prerequisite to payment pursuant to the terms of this contract, there will be furnished to the requester, under oath, answers to any interrogatories related to a possible conflict of interest as herein embodied."

(k) All contract bid forms and all contracts shall be approved by the County Attorney as to form and legal sufficiency. All contracts shall be approved and signed by, and purchase orders approved by the Chairman of the Board of County Commissioners. A copy of each contract and purchase order shall be forwarded promptly to the Accounting Department and to the Purchasing Agent.

Sec. 16-7. Purchasing and Sales Transactions under $1,500.00

All purchases of supplies and contractual services estimated to be less than one thousand five hundred dollars ($1,500.00) in value, shall not be subject to the requirements of Section 16-6 of this article; provided, however, that the Purchasing Agent shall, wherever practicable, *and whenever the amount thereof exceeds $300.00*, secure substantial competition in the commodity area of the transaction.

Sec. 16-8. Consideration of Resale Values

The resale value of supplies and contractual services may be considered as an element of price in making any purchases made pursuant to this article.

Sec. 16-9. Sales of Personal Property

(a) In order to produce the highest cash return for the sale of personal property, the Purchasing Agent may select from the following competitive sales methods the one which, in his judgment, will yield the greatest return under the circumstance of each sale: Sealed bids sale, as prescribed in Section 16-6, spot bids sale; auction sale. He may negotiate a sale when the above methods have failed to produce a fair price.

Sec. 16-10. Encumbrance of Funds to Meet Obligations

(a) Except in the cases of emergency, and as to obligations amounting in value not exceeding $150.00, no County official, elected or appointed, or employee will create an obligation on behalf of the County under this ordinance without first obtaining the certification of an official of the Accounting Department that sufficient funds are available and set aside to defray the obligation, provided, however, that no obligation shall exceed in value the amount budgeted for the purpose of the obligation.

Sec. 16-11. Negotiated Contracts

(a) The Purchasing Agent is authorized, subject to the approval of the Commissioners, to negotiate a purchase or contract under the following circumstances when formal advertising can accomplish no useful purpose:

(1) When a public exigency requires the immediate delivery or performance of service; or
(2) Proprietary articles or when only one source of supply is available; or
(3) When competition is precluded because of the existence of patent rights, copyrights, secret processes, control of basic raw material or similar circumstances; or

(4) When bids have been solicited pursuant to the requirements of formal advertising in Section 16-6 and no responsive bid has been received from a responsible bidder; or

(5) When the aggregate amount involved in any one case does not exceed $300.00.

(b) Authority to negotiate does not excuse compliance with the basic policy of obtaining maximum competition consistent with the needs of the occasion, to the end that all purchases will be made to the best advantage of the County, price and other factors considered. The authority to negotiate contracts in no way eliminates the need to obtain the most favorable prices possible. Bargaining shall be free from sharp practices or other actions which may cause inequities for bidders or justified criticism of the purchase policies and procedures. Each purchase or contract negotiated under this authority shall be supported by a statement signed by the Purchasing Agent justifying the use of negotiation procedures.

Sec. 16-12. Specifications

(a) Technical or performance descriptions shall be used wherever possible. "Brand name or equal" descriptions may be used when a technical or performance description is not available. When used, prospective bidders shall be informed that the reference is intended to be descriptive and not restrictive and is for the sole purpose of indicating to prospective bidders a description of the article that will be satisfactory.

Sec. 16-13. Standardization of Supplies and Equipment

(a) The Chairman of the County Commissioners may establish an Advisory Committee on Standardization composed of such officials or employees of the County government as he may designate. The Purchasing Agent shall be appointed as Chairman. The Department, in cooperation with the using agencies, shall formulate and make effective, subject to the authority of the County Commissioners, standards for materials, supplies, equipment, and services required for the using agencies. It shall be the duty of the using agencies and the Department of Central Purchasing to cooperate fully to the end that the County government may obtain the maximum advantages offered by centralized purchasing.

(b) The duties of the Committee, if and when established, shall be to meet, at the call of the Committee Chairman, at least once every two months to:

(1) Classify all supplies and equipment common to the needs of two or more using agencies and which are repetitively purchased;

(2) Adopt as standards, the minimum number of qualities, sizes and varieties of supplies and equipment consistent with the successful operation of the County government;

(3) Work with the Purchasing Agent in preparing written specifications of all such standard supplies, adopting to the maximum extent possible, standard specifications of other governmental jurisdictions and nationally organized standardizing bodies;

(4) Study the problem of estimates of requirements for supplies, equipment and contractual services and to recommend to the County Commissioners such rules governing estimates of needs that will best serve the interest of efficient central purchasing without adding procedures burdensome to using agencies;

(5) Recommend to the County Commissioners changes or improvements in the Central Purchasing Ordinance.

(c) The Committee is authorized to make use of the County's staff and technical facilities in the development of specifications, and in the testing of supplies through the facilities of reputable testing laboratories.

Sec. 16-14. Purchasing Services for Other Public Activities

(a) In the interest of public service to the citizens of the County the facilities and service of the Central Purchasing Department will be made available to other public activities in the County which obtain their financial support in part from the County. As a condition to providing such service, the other public activity must, by their governing body, enter into an agreement with the Commissioners which will place final responsibility for such purchases on the governing body of the other activity.

Sec. 16-15. Surplus, Obsolete and Waste Materials

(a) All agencies shall submit to the Purchasing Agent, at such times and in such form as he may prescribe, reports showing stocks of all supplies which are no longer used or which have become obsolete, worn out or scrapped. The Purchasing Agent shall have the authority to transfer surplus supplies between agencies in lieu of filling requisitions for the purchase of new and additional stock of the same or similar articles.

(b) The Purchasing Agent shall have authority to sell all such supplies which cannot be used by any agency or which have become unsuitable for County use; or to exchange or trade-in such articles in part or in full payment for new supplies. Any such sale, exchange or trade-in shall be made in accordance with Section 16-6 or Section 16-8 of this article, whichever is applicable.

Sec. 16-16. Coopeative Purchasing with Other Public Jurisdictions

It shall be the duty of the Purchasing Agent to develop, to the maximum extent possible, a program for the joint or cooperative, purchasing of common-use supplies with other public activities in the County and shall endeavor to arrange for a program of standardization of common-use supplies. The Purchasing Agent may undertake similar programs involving joint or cooperative purchases with other public activities or jurisdictions in the State of Maryland.

Sec. 16-17. Annual Report

The Purchasing Director shall submit, not later than the last Board meeting in April of each year, a report summarizing the Department's purchasing activities for the previous year and his progress in carrying out the various provisions of this article.

**Sec. 16-18. Responsibilities of Using Agencies
and Purchasing Agent**

The using agency has the responsibility for determining its requirements in terms that will permit the Purchasing Agent to obtain as wide as possible competition. The Purchasing Agent has the responsibility to use the purchasing method which will be most advantageous to the County considering price, quality and other factors. The Purchasing Agent is authorized to modify specifications if, in his opinion, wider competition can be obtained after consultation and agreement with the head of the using agency. Cases in disagreement shall be referred to the Commissioners.

Glossary

Acceptable quality level (AQL) The maximum number of defectives or defects per one hundred units in a sample that can be considered satisfactory as a process average.

Acceptance The act of an authorized representative of the government by which the government assents to ownership by it of identified supplies, or approves specific services rendered, as partial or complete performance of the contract. Acceptance may occur prior to, at the time of, or after delivery but not prior to inspection.

Advance payment A payment to a contractor in anticipation of, and for the purpose of, performance under a contract or contracts. May be treated as a continuing fund and replenished as expenditures are incurred by the contractor. To be distinguished from partial, progress, and other payments made because of performance or part performance of a contract.

Advice of shipment A notice sent a purchaser advising that a shipment has gone forward and usually containing details of packing and routing.

Allocable cost A cost assignable or chargeable to one or more cost objectives in accordance with the relative benefits received or other equitable relationships defined or agreed to between contractual parties.

All-or-none bid A bid for a number of different items or services in which the bidder states that she will not accept a partial award but will only accept an award for all items included in the bid. Such bids are acceptable only if provided for in the invitation for bids or if the bidder quoted prices for all items and is actually the low bidder for every one.

Allowable cost A cost that meets the tests of reasonableness, allocability, is in consonance with standards promulgated by the Cost Accounting Standards Board (if applicable), and otherwise conforms to generally accepted accounting principles and agreed-to terms between contractual parties.

As is The goods offered for sale are without warranty or guarantee, and the purchaser takes the goods at his own risk without recourse against the seller for the quality or condition of the goods.

Astray freight Shipments or portions found in a carrier's possession or delivered to a government installation for which billing (waybill or freight bill) is not available or which is being held for any reason except transfer.

Authorized allowances Equipment or supply items for an individual or unit, the quantities of which are specified in various publications and lists.

Average demurrage agreement   An agreement between a shipper and a transportation line whereby the shipper is debited for the time cars are held for loading or unloading beyond a certain period, and credited for the time cars are released by him within a certain period. Demurrage charges are assessed by the transportation line on the balance.

Award   The presentation of a purchase agreement or contract to a bidder; the acceptance of a bid or proposal.

Back order   That portion of the quantity requisitioned not immediately available for issue to the requisitioners and that will be recorded as a commitment for future issue.

Basic agreement   A written instrument of understanding between a procuring activity and a contractor that sets forth the negotiated contract clauses that shall be applicable to future procurements entered into between the parties during the term of the basic agreement. Particular procurements are covered by the execution of a formal contractual document, which provides for the scope of the work and incorporates by reference the clauses agreed upon in the basic agreement.

Basing point   A geographic point from which fixed transportation rates are established. Used for the purpose of constructing rates to adjacent points by adding to, or deducting from, the basing point rate.

Basis of issue   Authority that prescribes the number of items to be issued to an individual, a unit, or per piece of equipment.

Bid   An offer, as a price, whether for payment or acceptance. A quotation specifically given to a prospective purchaser upon his request, usually in competition with other offerers. Also an offer by a buyer to a seller, as at an auction.

Bid-award file   A file divided into commodity and item sections, each of which contains listings of who was solicited for individual bids, what each response was, and other information. The bid-award file is used to compare past bids for award patterns that might reveal collusive agreements or to make other comparisons of data.

Bid bond   An insurance agreement in which a third party agrees to be liable to pay a certain amount of money in the event that a specific bidder, if his bid is accepted, fails to sign the contract as bid.

Bid deposit   A sum of money or check, deposited with and at the request of the government, in order to guarantee that the bidder (depositor) will, if selected, sign the contract as bid. A bidder who does not sign the contract forfeits the amount of the deposit.

Bid opening   The opening and reading of bids, conducted at the time and place specified in the invitation for bids and/or the advertisement, and in the presence of anyone who wishes to attend.

Bid sample   A sample required by the invitation for bids to be furnished by bidders as part of their bids to establish a quality level for the products being offered.

Bid security   A guarantee, in the form of bond or deposit, that the bidder, if selected, will sign the contract as bid; otherwise the bidder (in the case of a bond) will be liable for the amount of bond or deposit. See *bid bond*; *bid deposit*.

Bidders' list   A list maintained by the purchasing authority setting out the names and addresses of suppliers of various goods and services from whom bids, proposals, and quotations can be solicited.

Bill of lading   A document listing material being shipped, which is used for receipt acknowledgment by a carrier and as a contract for final delivery to the consignee.

Bill of materials   A descriptive and quantitative listing of materials, supplies, parts, and components required to produce a designated complete end item of material of assembly or subassembly.

Bin tag   A simple type of perpetual inventory record, attached to the bin itself.

Brand-name description   A description that identifies a single item or source for a product or service on a proprietary basis. Products are usually referenced by model or part number.

Brand name or equal description   A description that references all brand-name commercial products known to be acceptable and or current manufacture and that specifies the essential requirements and salient characteristics considered necessary to ensure that the brand name or equal products offered will satisfy the end-use application effectively and efficiently.

Breach of contract   A failure without legal excuse to perform any promise that forms a whole or part of a contract.

Breach of warranty   Infraction of an express or implied agreement as to the title, quality, content, or condition of an item sold.

Buffer stock   A quantity of material kept in stock to safeguard against unforeseen shortages due to delays in delivery or exceptional demand.

Bulk material   Material stored and issued by volume, footage, weight, or liquid measurement (for example, petroleum, bar stock, and lumber).

Bulk purchasing   Purchasing in large quantities in order to reduce the price per unit; volume purchasing.

Buyer   An assistant to the purchasing manager or agent. The buyer is generally responsible for the negotiations with the vendors, while the purchasing manager or agent signs the final purchase order.

Cannibalization   Removal of serviceable parts from an unserviceable piece of equipment for installation in another piece of equipment so as to restore the latter item to serviceable condition.

Cartage   Local delivery by local truck of a shipment that was primarily moved by rail, boat, air, or long-distance truck.

Centralized purchasing   A system of purchasing in which authority, responsibility, and control of purchasing activities are concentrated in one administrative unit.

Certificate of compliance   A supplier's certification that the supplies or services in question meet certain specified requirements.

Change order   A written order by the contracting officer, authorizing or directing the contractor to make changes in the scope of the contract, or in specifications, etc. Requires acceptance of contractor except when the contract contains a change clause that authorizes the contracting officer to order without the consent of the contractor.

Claim   The aggregate of the operative facts that serve as a basis for demand for payment, reimbursement, or compensation for injury or damage under law or contract; the assertion of such a demand.

Classification   A list of articles and the classes to which they are assigned for the purpose of applying transportation class rates, together with governing rules and regulations.

Collusive bidding   Bidding by two or more vendors who have secretly agreed to circumvent laws requiring independent and competitive bidding.

Commercial item descriptions   A new series of simplified item descriptions that will be formalized under the federal specifications-and-standards program and are intended to be used in the acquisition of commercial off-the-shelf and commercial-type products.

Commercial off-the-shelf product   A product from regular production sold in substantial quantities to the general public and/or industry at established market or catalog prices.

Commercial-type product   A product peculiar to the government that, though appearing to be a commercial product, is produced in accordance with a government specification, is subject to some physical change or addition and/or is packaged and identified differently from its normal commercial product counterpart, and may be, but is not necessarily, stocked centrally by the government.

Commitment   A firm administrative reservation of funds, based upon procurement directives, orders, requisitions; or requests that authorize the creation of an obligation without further recourse to the official responsible for certifying the availability of funds.

Commodity committee   In intergovernmental cooperative purchasing, a committee of purchasing managers or their buyers that has the task of researching the feasibility of cooperative purchase of an item used by two or more jurisdictions that has been nominated as a candidate for possible cooperative-purchase action.

Common carrier   A person or corporation licensed to engage in the business of transporting personal property from one place to another for compensation. A common carrier is bound to carry for all who tender their goods and the price for transportation.

Common use-item   An item of material that is used by more than one jurisdiction (for example, motor vehicle gasoline and fuel oil used for heating of buildings).

Competitive bidding   The offer of estimates by vendors competing for a contract, privilege, or right to supply specified services or merchandise.

Competitive range   A range appropriate to the postevaluation, preaward phase of negotiated procurements. Determined by the contracting officer on the basis of price, cost, or technical and other salient factors.

Concealed damage   Damage that is not evident at the time of delivery but is discovered after the package is opened and the contents are examined.

Consignee   The activity to which a shipment is to be delivered.

Consignor   The activity that directs or arranges for a shipment. The consignor may not be the same as the shipping activity.

Consolidation   As applied to shipments, consolidation is the act of combining a number of small (less than carload, truckload, or planeload) shipments into a full carload, generally confined to articles taking the same rating and usually carried on at point of origin.

Constructive change   During contract performance, an oral or written act or omission by the contracting officer or other authorized government official that is of such a nature that it is construed to have the same effect as a written change order.

Contract   An agreement, enforceable by law, between two or more competent parties, to do or not to do something not prohibited by law, for a consideration. Any type of agreement or order for the procurement of supplies and services.

Contract, cost-plus-a-fixed-fee   A cost-reimbursement type contract that provides for the payment of a fixed fee to the contractor. The fixed fee, once negotiated, does not vary with the actual cost but may be adjusted as a result of any subsequent changes in the scope of work or services to be performed under the contract.

Contract, cost-plus-a-percentage-of-cost   A form of contract formerly used but now illegal in federal purchasing, which provided for a fee or profit at a specified percentage of the contractor's actual cost of accomplishing the work.

Contract, cost-plus-incentive-fee   A cost-reimbursement type contract with provision for a fee that is adjusted by formula in accordance with the relationship that total allowable costs bear to target costs. The provision for increase or decrease in the fee, depending upon allowable costs of contract performance, is designed as an incentive to the contractor to increase the efficiency of performance.

Contract, cost-reimbursement type A contract that provides for payment to the contractor of allowable costs incurred in the performance of the contract, to the extent prescribed in the contract. This type of contract establishes an estimate of total cost for the purpose of obligation of funds and establishing a ceiling that the contractor may not exceed (except at his own risk) without prior approval or subsequent ratification of the contracting officers.

Contract, cost-sharing A cost-reimbursement type contract under which the contractor receives no fee but is reimbursed only for an agreed portion of allowable costs.

Contract, definite-quantity A contract that provides for a definite quantity of specified supplies or for the performance of specified services for a fixed period, with deliveries or performance at designated locations upon order.

Contract, firm-fixed price A contract that provides for a price not subject to any adjustment by reason of the cost experience of the contractor in the performance of the contract. It is used for contracts awarded after formal advertising; also used in negotiated contracts when reasonably definite specifications are available and costs can be estimated with reasonable accuracy to enable the negotiation of a fair price.

Contract, fixed-price with escalation A fixed-price type of contract that provides for the upward and downward revision of the stated contract price upon the occurrence of certain contingencies (such as fluctuations in material prices and labor rates) specifically defined in the contract.

Contract, fixed-price with redetermination of price A fixed-price type of contract that contains provisions for the subsequently negotiated adjustment, in whole or in part, of the initially negotiated (base) price. Depending on the contract provisions, adjustments may be upward or downward, retroactive or prospective, and may be made at a stated time, at stated intervals, on request of either party, or upon completion of the contract. This type of contract is used to ensure to the government the benefit of reduced costs of performance and, in some instances, to the contractor the recovery in whole or in part of increased costs, and to obtain reasonable prices whenever contingency charges otherwise would be included in a contract price due to such factors as prolonged delivery schedules, unstable market conditions for material or labor, lack of definite specifications, or uncertainty as to cost of performance.

Contract, incentive-type A contract of either a fixed-price or cost-reimbursement nature, with a special provision for adjustment of the fixed price or fee. It provides for a tentative target price and a maximum price or maximum fee, with price or fee adjustment after completion of the contract for the purpose of establishing a final price or fee based on the contractor's actual costs plus a sliding scale of profit or fee, which varies inversely with the cost but which in no event shall permit the final price or fee to exceed the maximum price or fee stated in the contract.

Contract, indefinite-quantity   A contract that provides for the furnishing of an indefinite quantity, within stated limits, of specific supplies or services, during a specified contract period, with deliveries to be scheduled by the timely placement of orders upon the contractor by activities designated either specifically or by class.

Contract, labor-hour   A variant of the time-and-materials type contract differing only in that materials are not involved in the contract or are not supplied by the contractor.

Contract modification   Any written alteration in the specification, delivery point, rate of delivery, contract period, price, quantity, or other contract provisions of an existing contract, whether accomplished by unilateral action in accordance with a contract provision or by mutual action of the parties to the contract. It includes bilateral actions such as supplemental agreements and amendments, and unilateral actions such as change orders, notices of termination, and notices of the exercise of a contract option.

Contract, prime   A contract entered into directly by the procuring activity and the vendor. Compare with *subcontract.*

Contract, service   A contract that calls for a contractor's time and effort rather than for an end product.

Contract, time-and-material   A contract providing for the procurement of supplies or services on the basis of direct labor hours at specified fixed hourly rates (which include direct and indirect labor, overhead, and profit) and material at cost.

Contract type   Refers to specific pricing arrangements employed for the performance of work under contract. Specific pricing (or compensation) arrangements, expressed as contract types, include firm fixed-price, fixed-price incentive, cost-plus-a-fixed-fee, cost-plus-incentive fee, and several others. Among special arrangements that use fixed-price or cost-reimbursement pricing provisions are contract types called indefinite delivery contracts, basic ordering agreements, letter contracts, and others.

Contracting officer   Any person who, either by virtue of her position or by appointment in accordance with prescribed regulations, is vested with the authority to enter into and administer contracts and make determinations and findings with respect thereto, or with any part of such authority. In this book, three kinds of contracting officers are identified: procuring contracting officer (PCO), administrative contracting officer (ACO), and termination contracting officer (TCO).

Controlled item   An item that requires special control and security in accordance with published regulations and statutes (includes money, negotiable instruments, narcotics, registered mail, and precious metals).

Competitive bidding   The offer of prices by individuals or firms competing for a contract, privilege, or right to supply specified services or material.

Competitive negotiation   A technique for purchasing goods and services, usually of a technical nature, whereby qualified suppliers are solicited, negotiations are carried on with each bidder, and the best offer (in terms of performance, quality of items, price, and so forth), as judged against proposal evaluation criteria, is accepted; negotiated award.

Cost analysis   The review and evaluation of a contractor's cost or pricing data and of the judgmental factors applied in projecting from the data to the estimated costs in order to form an opinion leading to a position on the degree to which the contractor's proposed costs represent what contract performance should cost, assuming reasonable economy and efficiency. It includes appropriate verification of cost data, evaluation of specific elements of costs, and projection of these data to determine the effect on price factors like cost necessity, allowances for contingencies, and the basis used for allocation of overhead costs.

Cost reimbursement   Refers to a family of pricing arrangements that provide for payment of allowable, allocable, and reasonable costs incurred in the performance of a contract, to the extent that such costs are prescribed or permitted by the contract. In the case of a cost-plus-fixed-fee arrangement, costs may vary under or over the initially agreed-to estimate, but the fee remains fixed as an expressed dollar amount and is not subject to adjustment by reason of contractor cost experience during the life of the contract.

Counteroffer   A modified acceptance of an offer to contract; hence a rejection of that offer and a new proposal.

Dangerous/hazardous material   Any material that, under conditions incident to transportation, is capable of posing an unreasonable risk to health, safety, and property. This includes material classified as explosive, flammable, corrosive, combustible, oxidative, poisonous, compressed gases, toxics, unduly magnetic, biologicals and radiologicals, and substances associated therewith.

Dead storage   Storage of goods for a relatively long period of time. Frequently goods so stored are packaged and preserved in such a way that they are not readily available for immediate use.

Decentralization of purchasing   The delegation of purchasing authority to activities or branches, where it is directly carried out, usually with policy direction from the central authority.

Default   Failure by a party to a contract to comply with contractual requirements; vendor failure.

Defective cost or pricing data   Certified cost or pricing data subsequently found to have been inaccurate, incomplete, or noncurrent as of the effective date of the certificate. In this case, the government is entitled to an adjustment of the negotiated price, including profit or fee, to exclude any significant sum by which price was increased because of the defective data.

Deficient material   Material found to be faulty or unsuitable for its intended purpose because of one or more deficiencies, such as quality, design, or procurement deficiency, but that is not the result of damage.

Delivery order   An order to a contractor pursuant to an indefinite-delivery type contract, which then constitutes the basic obligating document for this type of transaction. The delivery order consummates the agreement of the contractor and the government when the original partial contractual agreement was effected.

Delivery schedule   The required or agreed time or rate of delivery of goods or services purchased for a future period.

Delivery terms   Conditions in a contract relating to freight charges, place of delivery, time of delivery, and method of transportation.

Delivery time   A time, agreed upon by the vendor, agency, and purchasing activity, that the vendor will supply items called for by the purchase order or contract.

Demurrage   The detention of a vessel, railroad car, truck, or plane beyond the agreed time. A delay in unloading for which a charge is assessed.

Design deficiency   Any condition that limits or prevents the use of the material for its intended or required purpose although the material meets specification or contractual requirements. Such deficiencies cannot be corrected except through a design change.

Design specification   A specification delineating the essential characteristics that an item must possess to be considered for award and so detailed as to describe how the product is to be manufactured; generic specification.

Destination inspection   Inspection of material on receipt at destination for conformance to contractual or specification requirements.

Determinations and findings   Written justification by the contracting officer or higher authority for using a particular statutory authority to allow negotiation of a procurement.

Discrepancy reports   The various types of reports indicating that a shipment or material was unsatisfactory for any reason.

Disposal   The act of getting rid of excess, surplus, scrap, or salvage property under property authority. Disposal may be accomplished by, but not limited to, transfer, donation, sale, declaration, abandonment, and destruction.

Distribution subsystem   That complex of facilities, installations, methods, and procedures designed to receive, maintain, distribute, and control the flow of materials between the point of receipt into the system and the point of issue to using activities and organizations.

Double sampling plan   A method of sampling in which the inspection of the first sample leads to a decision to accept, to reject, or to take a second sample. The inspection of a second sample, when required, then leads to a decision to accept or reject the lot.

Dunnage   Lumber or other material that is used to brace and secure supplies to protect them from damage in carrier's equipment.

Economic order quantity   That order that minimizes total variable cost, including both the stock-holding costs and the procurement costs.

Escalation clause   A clause in a purchase contract providing for upward or downward adjustment of the contract price if specified contingencies occur; price escalation clause. *Economic price adjustment* is the contemporary term used to express the sense of escalation.

Established catalog price   A price included in a catalog, price list, schedule, or other form regularly maintained by a manufacturer or vendor, published or made available for inspection by customers, and that states prices at which sales are currently or were last made to a significant number of buyers constituting the general public.

Established commercial market acceptability   An evaluation of the product offered, performed for the purpose of determining a prospective contractor's ability to provide a commercial product that will conform to the government's need. To be market acceptable, a product must be marketed in substantial quantities to the general public. To be substantial, sales to the general public must predominate over sales to the government.

Established market price   A current price, established in the usual and ordinary course of trade between buyers and seller free to bargain, that can be substantiated from sources independent of the manufacturer or vendor, although such pricing data may have to come from the seller.

Excess stock   Quantity of an item that exceeds the retention limit for the item and is therefore subject to utilization screening, reclamation, or other disposal action.

Expedite   To hasten or to ensure delivery of goods purchased in accordance with a time schedule, usually by contact by the purchaser with the vendor.

Express warranty   Any affirmation of fact or promise made by a seller to a buyer that relates to the goods and becomes part of the basis of the bargain.

Federal item identification   Description of an item of supply consisting of minimum data essential to establish item characteristics and to differentiate it from every other item of supply used by the federal government.

Federal stock number   A number consisting of the applicable four-digit class code number from the federal supply classification plus the seven-digit federal item identification number.

Fee   In specified cost-reimbursement pricing arrangements, fee represents an agreed-to amount beyond the initial estimate of costs. In most instances, fee reflects a variety of factors, including risk, and is subject to statutory limitations. Fee may be fixed at the outset of performance, as in a cost-plus-fixed-fee arrangement, or may vary (within a contractually specified minimum-maximum range) during performance, as in a cost-plus-incentive-fee arrangement.

Firm bid   A definite price proposal, as differentiated from an estimated bid. A bid that binds the bidder until a stipulated time of expiration.

First-destination, transportation   The movement of property from point of origin to the point at which the material is first received for use or storage or subsequent redistribution in the supply system.

Formal advertising   One of the major methods of procurement, preferred by law when it is feasible and practicable to employ it. It is used in one of the two forms, as appropriate to the requirement: conventional formal advertising and two-step formal advertising. The first involves the procurement of well-defined items or services and the second the procurement of items requiring the submission of technical proposals prior to the submission of prices. In both forms, award is made to the responsible bidder whose bid, conforming to the invitation for bids, will be most advantageous to the government, price and other factors considered.

Formal bid or offer   A bid that must be forwarded in a sealed envelope and in conformance with a prescribed format to be opened at a specified time.

Forward pricing arrangement   A written understanding between a vendor and the government to make certain rates (for example, labor, indirect, material-usage, and spare-parts provisioning) available for use during a specified period of time in pricing contracts or in negotiating contract modifications.

Forward purchasing   The purchasing of quantities exceeding immediate needs, in anticipation of a price increase or scarcity of the item.

Forward supply contract   A contract for future supply of definite quantities of materials or services over a fixed period. May be drawn off by draw-off orders or delivered at a fixed and predetermined rate set out in the contract.

Free alongside (FAS)   The seller pays the costs and assumes all risks in transporting the contracted items to a position alongside the vessel or plane the buyer has identified to transport the goods. The seller is responsible only to deliver the goods to a designated loading area; the buyer is responsible from that point on. In both free-on-board (FOB) and FAS transactions, the seller must provide the buyer with the required shipping documents.

Free astray   A shipment miscarried or unloaded at the wrong station is forwarded to the correct station free of charges, account of being astray; hence the term *free astray*.

Free on board (FOB)   The vendor of goods is responsible for all expenses incidental to delivery of goods to the buyer at the place designated.

Freight descriptions   Standardized descriptions under which individual articles are grouped for assessing class or commodity rates.

Freight at destination   Freight charges will be paid by the consignee upon arrival of the shipment at a specified destination.

Forwarder (freight)   A commercial organization engaged in the business of consolidating less than carload, truckload, or planeload shipments and making arrangements for their transportation in carload, truckload, or planeload lots under the lower applicable tariffs.

Government-furnished material   Material provided by the government to a contractor or comparable government production facility to be incorporated into or attached to an end product to be delivered to the government or ordering activity, or which may be consumed or expended in the performance of a contract. It includes, but is not limited to, raw and processed materials, parts, components, assemblies, and small tools and supplies.

Grant   Contribution, gift, or subsidy made by the government for specified purposes. Grant is frequently made conditional upon specified action by the grantee, such as the maintenance of certain standards or a proportional contribution of funds.

Identical bid   A bid that agrees in all respects with another one.

Incentive arrangement   A negotiated pricing arrangement that structures a series of relationships designed to motivate and reward the contractor for performance in accordance with the contract specification. In fixed-price incentive arrangements, the structure involves the negotiation of a target cost, target profit, target price, ceiling price, and profit sharing (or adjustment) formula for costs incurred under or over the target cost. In cost-reimbursement incentive arrangements, the structure involves the negotiation of a target cost, target fee, minimum and maximum fees, and sharing formula.

Incremental funding   The obligation of funds to a contract containing a total price or estimated cost, in periodic installments against prescribed performance goals or objectives, rather than in a lump sum at completion.

Indefinite quantity buying   The establishment of price agreements that guarantee no minimum volume or any volume to the vendor. However, the invitation for bid usually includes an estimated volume based on historical purchase levels.

Ineligible bidder A supplier who, by reason of historical financial instability, unsatisfactory reputation, poor performance, or other similar reasons, cannot meet the qualifications for placement on the bidders' list or for award of a contract.

Informal solicitation The process of obtaining oral or written quotes from vendors without formal advertising and receipt of sealed bids. Procedures usually involve telephoning one or more vendors to obtain oral quotes or sending an invitation for bid to one vendor for submission of a return mail quote.

Initial issue The provision of material approved for issue and not previously supplied to an organization. Such initial issues include those to newly activated organizations and issues of newly standardized items.

Inspection Examination and testing, including when appropriate, processes, raw materials, components, intermediate assemblies, and end items to determine whether the items conform to contract requirements.

Inspection by attributes Inspection wherein the unit of product is classified as either defective or nondefective with respect to a given requirement or set of requirements; go or no-go inspection.

Inspection by variables Inspection wherein characteristics of the sample are evaluated with respect to a continuous numerical scale and expressed as precise points along this scale. Variables inspection records the degree of conformance or nonconformance of the unit with specified requirements.

Inspection in process Inspection performed during the manufacturing or repair cycle in an effort to prevent defects from occuring and to inspect the characteristics and attributes that cannot be examined at final inspection.

Inspection lot A specific quality of similar material, or a collection of similar units, offered for inspection and acceptance at one time.

Inspection record A report to inform the purchasing authority of the quality or condition of the items delivered.

Intergovernmental cooperative purchasing The combining of requirements of two or more political entities in order to obtain the benefits of volume purchases and/or reduction in administrative expenses.

Inventory The stock of goods on hand or an itemized list of a stock of goods indicating volume and values. Where ascertained by enumeration, it is labeled *physical inventory*; by periodic recording, it is labeled *book inventory*.

Inventory control The functional phase of supply operations concerned with applying managerial supervision to integrate the actions of requirements computation, production, procurement, distribution, maintenance, and disposal of material within a supply system.

Inventory control point   An organizational unit within the purchasing and materials-management system that is assigned the primary responsibility for the management of a group of items, including computation of quantitative requirements, the authority to require procurement or initiate disposal, development of quantitative and monetary inventory data, and sometimes the positioning and repositioning of material.

Inventory turnover   An average ratio for purposes of inventory analysis: annual issues at cost divided by average inventory investment during the year. The number of times on the average an entire inventory is issued in one year.

Invitation for bids   Solicitation to prospective suppliers requesting their competitive price quotations.

Item overage   The quantity received is greater than that ordered or shown on the shipping document. This type of overage is not evident on delivery but is discovered when the article of freight is opened and the contents checked.

Item shortage   When the quantity received is less than the quantity ordered or shown on the shipping document. Shortage is not evident on delivery but discovered when the article of freight is opened and the contents checked.

Joint-bid method   In intergovernmental cooperative purchasing, the pooling of individual requirements of all units into one bid. Each governmental unit may accept or reject its portion of the bid. Each unit makes its own contract or writes its own purchase order, is billed separately, does its own receiving and inspection,and issues its own checks for payment.

Joint consolidated list of debarred, suspended, and ineligible bidders   A list of firms or individuals who have, or who are believed to have, violated statutes or broken commitments in their contractual relationships with the government.

Joint rate   A joint freight rate is one agreed upon by two or more carriers and applies between a point on the line of one and a point on the line of another.

Labor-surplus area   A geographical section of concentrated unemployment or underemployment, designated by the U.S. Department of Labor.

Late bid or proposal   A bid or proposal received after the hour established by the invitation as the time by which all bids or proposals must be received.

Latent defect   A defect that could normally not be discovered by ordinary and reasonable inspection.

Learning curve   A tool of calculation used primarily to project resource requirements, in terms of direct manufacturing labor hours or the quantity of material (for this purpose, usally referred to as an improvement curve) required for repetitive production runs. Used interchangeably with the term *improvement curve.*

Letter contract   A written preliminary contractual instrument that authorizes the immediate commencement of activity under its terms and conditions, pending establishment of a fixed-price or cost-reimbursement pricing arrangement for the work to be done. Must be superseded by a definite contract within a specified time.

Life-cycle costing   A procurement technique that considers operating, maintenance, acquisition price, and other costs of ownership in the award of contracts to ensure that the item acquired will result in the lowest total ownership cost during the time the item's function is required.

Line item   A procurement item specified in the invitation for bids for which the bidder is asked to give individual pricing information and which, under the terms of the invitation, is usually susceptible to a separate contract award. An entry on a document reflecting all data necessary to identify positively a specific article of property and the quantity thereof.

Liquidated damages   A sum agreed upon between the parties to a contract, to be paid by that party who breaches the contract.

List price   The price published in a catalog or similar publication.

Local purchase order   A purchase order, the use of which is restricted to purchases from local suppliers, and usually limited in value

Lot-sampling inspection   A procedure by which decisions are made to determine acceptability of a lot of product based on results of examination and testing of a sample or samples selected from the lot.

Lowest responsible bidder   The bidder who is awarded a contract because his bid in unit price, total cost of operation, or value per dollar is lower than any of the other bidders whose reputation, past performance, and business and financial capabilities are such that they would be judged to be capable of satisfying the government's needs for the specific contract.

Marking   Numbers, nomenclature, special labels, or symbols affixed to containers for identification during supply and storage operations.

Material deficiency   Any deficiency (such as physical, chemical, electrical, or functional) noted in material that is attributed to nonconformance to contractual or specification requirements. Substandard workmanship is considered to fall within this definition.

Military specification   A specification issued by the Department of Defense and used predominantly by military activities.

Mistake in bid   A miscalculation by the vendor in composing a bid, resulting in an incorrect price or other term that may affect the vendor's eligibility to be awarded the contract.

Multiple award   The award of separate contracts to two or more vendors for the same commodities in situations where the award of a single contract would be impossible or impractical.

Multiple sampling   A type of sampling in which a decision to accept or reject an inspection lot is reached after one or more samples from the lot has been inspected. Successive samples are taken, up to a designated number, until a decision is reached.

Negotiation   One of the major methods of procurement. Employed under certain permissive circumstances prescribed by statute when formal advertising is determined to be infeasible and impracticable. A bargaining process between two or more parties, each with its own viewpoints and objectives, seeking to reach a mutually satisfactory agreement on, or settlement of, a matter of common concern.

Nonconformance   The failure of material to conform to specified requirements for any quality characteristic.

Nonexpendable material   Items that are not consumed in use and that ordinarily retain their original identity and characteristics during the period of use and subsequent repair cycles (for example, vehicles, machines, tools, and instruments).

Nonrecurring demand   A request made by an authorized customer on a one-time basis to provide initial or authorized increases in allowances or stockage at any level, or for modification of equipment, special planned programs, and one-time repair or rebuild requirements.

Nonresponsive bid   A bid that does not conform to the essential requirements of the invitation for bids; also called *nonconforming bid*, *unresponsive bid*.

Nonstocked item   Item of material centrally managed and purchased but not stocked to meet demands from requisitioners. Also items for which local procurement has been authorized but which are requisitioned when they cannot be obtained locally.

Obligation authority   Administrative authority to incur obligations, whether or not it also carries the authority to make expenditures in payment thereof.

Obligations   Dollar amounts of orders placed, contracts awarded, services rendered, or other commitments made by government agencies during a given period that will require outlays during the same or some future period.

On order   That quantity of an item of supply placed on contracts or orders outstanding that has not been delivered or accepted by the ordering agency. See *stock due in*.

Open-end contract A contract in which quantity or duration is not specified, such as a requirements contract. See *requirements contract*; *term contracting*.

Order and shipping time The time interval between the initiation of stock replenishment action by a specific activity and the receipt of the material resulting from such action.

Over, short, and damage report A report submitted by a receiving of freight agent showing discrepancies in billing received and freight on hand.

Overage Quantity received is greater than the quantity ordered or shown on the shipping document.

Overrun Under a cost-reimbursement type contract, costs in excess of the estimated cost.

Packing Application or use of exterior shipping containers and assembling of items or packages therein, together with necessary blocking, bracing or cushioning, weatherproofing, exterior strapping, and marking of shipping container.

Packing list A document itemizing in detail the contents of a particular package or shipment.

Pallet A portable platform upon which goods are placed in unit loads to facilitate handling by mechanical equipment, such as forklift trucks or conveyors.

Partial payment A payment made upon completion of the delivery of one or more complete units (or one or more distinct items of service), called for, delivered, and accepted by the government under the contract. Also a payment made against a termination claim upon prior approval before final settlement of the total termination claim.

Penalty clause A clause in a contract specifying the sum of money to be paid if and when the contractor defaults on the terms of the contract, particularly in respect to time.

Performance bond A contract of guaranty executed subsequent to award by a successful bidder to protect the government from loss due to bidder's inability to complete the contract as agreed

Performance specification A specification setting out performance requirements that have been determined to be necessary for the item involved.

Periodic ordering Orders placed at regular intervals for the amounts needed to bring stocks up to the desired level.

Physical inventory The determination, by actual count or other means of the quantity of property on hand. The quantity or amount so determined.

Point of origin The location at which a shipment is received by a transportation line from the shipper.

Preaward survey   Physical survey and evaluation of a prospective contractor's plant, equipment, and capacity to perform (both technically and financially), made before agency signs a contract. Used in those circumstances where additional information is required for a determination of the responsibility of the prospective contractor.

Preference   An advantage in consideration for award of a contract to a vendor by reason of the vendor's location, or classification (for example, small business).

Preproposal conference   A meeting held with contractors a few days after requests for proposals have been sent out, to promote uniform interpretation of work statements and specifications by all prospective contractors.

Prequalification of bidders   The screening of potential vendors in which a government considers such factors as financial capability, reputation, and management, in order to develop a list of bidders qualified to bid on government contracts.

Preserving   Application or use of protective measures to prevent deterioration including, as applicable, the use of preservatives, protective wrappings, cushioning, interior containers, and complete identification marking up to but not including the exterior shipping container.

Presolicitation conference   Meeting held before proposals are requested. Permits cognizant technical personnel to discuss proposed work with prospective contractors and elicits contractors' interest in pursuing the task.

Price-adjustment clause   A clause in a contract allowing for adjustment in price up or down in accordance with circumstances arising during the term of the contract (for example, wage changes, inflation, or rates of exchange).

Price analysis   The process of examining and evaluating a prospective price without evaluation of the separate cost elements and proposed profit of the individual offerer whose price is being evaluated. It may be accomplished by a comparison of submitted quotations, a comparison of price quotations and contract prices with current quotations for the same or similar items, the use of rough yardsticks (dollars per pound, for instance). or a comparison of proposed prices with independently developed government estimates.

Price at the time of delivery   A term used in contracts when market prices are so volatile that a vendor will not give a firm price, or use an escalator clause, but will agree only to charge the price that she is charging all other customers for similar purchases on the day she delivers the goods in question.

Price-extension clause   In intergovernmental cooperative purchasing, a method of securing prices, utilizing advertised bid proposals, based upon the annual needs of the sponsoring agency alone, but including a price-extension clause stating that the prices offered to the sponsoring agency by the successful bidder must also be made available to any other unit of government participating in the cooperative agreement.

Principal items   End items and replacement assemblies of such major importance that detailed analysis and review are required of all factors affecting their supply and demand. Principal items are normally designated on the basis of essentiality, high monetary value, difficulty of procurement or production, or criticality of basic materials or components. See *secondary items*.

Procurement deficiency   An unsatisfactory material condition attributable to improper, incorrect, ambiguous, and omitted contractual requirements, including deficient specifications and other technical data.

Procurement lead time   The time interval between the initiation of procurement action and the receipt into the supply system of material purchased as a result of such action. It is applicable to material to be obtained from any source outside the procuring department or by manufacture within the department. It is composed of two principal elements, administrative lead time and production lead time.

Profit objective   That part of the estimated contract price objective that the contracting office concludes is appropriate for the procurement at hand. Where cost analysis is undertaken, a profit objective should be developed after a thorough review of proposed contract work and all available knowledge regarding an offerer, as well as an analysis of the offerer's cost estimate and a comparison of it with the government's estimate or projection of cost.

Progress payment   A payment made to a contractor as work progresses on contractual procurement or construction. Amounts usually are based upon actual expenditures and work performed at a particular planned stage of completion.

Proposed evaluation criteria   Weighted standards, relating to management capability, technical capability, approach in meeting performance requirements, price, and other important factors that are used for evaluating bidders in a competitive negotiation.

Protest   A complaint about a governmental administrative action or decision brought by a bidder or vendor with the intention of achieving a remedy.

Provisioning   The process of determining the range and quantity of items (such as spares and repair parts, special tools, test equipment, and support equipment) required to support and maintain an end item of material for an initial period of service. It includes the identification of items of supply, the establishing of data for catalog, technical manual, and allowance list preparation and the preparation of instructions to ensure delivery of necessary support items with related end items.

Purchase order   A purchaser's document used to formalize a purchase transaction with a vendor. A purchase order, when given to a vendor, should contain statements as to the quantity, description, and price of the goods or services ordered; agreed terms as to payment, discounts, date of performance, transportation terms; and all other agreements pertinent to the purchase and its execution by the vendor. Acceptance of a purchase order constitutes a contract.

Purchase requisition   An internal document by which a using agency requests the purchasing department to initiate a procurement.

Purchasing manager or agent   An administrator whose job includes soliciting bids for purchases and making award of contracts; a buyer.

Quality   The composite of all the attributes or characteristics, including performance, of an item or product.

Quality assurance   A planned and systematic pattern of all actions necessary to provide adequate confidence that the product will perform satisfactorily in service.

Quality control   The procedures, inspections, examinations, and tests required during procurement, production, receipt, storage, and issue that are necessary to provide the user with an item of the required quality.

Quality deficiency   Any deficiency that prevents an item from fulfilling its intended mission. This may include deficiencies in material or the technical requirements of material, drawing, and specification requirements. A quality deficiency may be attributable to a design, material, or procurement deficiency.

Qualified bidder   A bidder determined by the government to meet minimum set standards of business competence, reputation, financial ability, and product quality for placement on the bidders' list.

Qualified products' list   List of products that because of the length of time required for test and evaluation are tested in advance of procurement to determine which suppliers can comply with specification requirements.

Quotation   A statement of price, terms of sale, and description of goods or services offered by a vendor to a prospective purchaser; the stating of the current price of a commodity; the price so stated.

Receiving activity   The activity that physically receives shipments from a carrier.

Receiving report   A form used by the receiving function of an agency to inform others of the receipt of goods purchased.

Reconsignment   A privilege extended to shippers whereby goods may be forwarded to a point other than the original destination without removal from car and at the through rate from the initial point to that of final delivery.

Recoverable item   An item normally not consumed in use and therefore subject to return for repair or disposal.

Recurring demand   A request made periodically, or anticipated to be repetitive, by an authorized requisitioner for material for consumption or use or for stock replenishment.

Redistribution   The transfer of control, utilization, or location of material between organizations or activities.

Renegotiation   Deliberation, discussion, or conference to change or amend the terms of an existing agreement.

Reorder point   That point when a stock replenishment requisition would be submitted to maintain the predetermined or calculated stock objective. The sum of the safety level of supply plus the level for order and shipping time equals the reorder point.

Replacement factor   The estimated percentage of material in use that will require replacement during a given period due to wearing out beyond repair, abandonment, loss, and other causes.

Replenishment stock   Material acquired periodically to replace stocks depleted by issue or loss during a stated period.

Reprogramming   Changing the application of financial or material resources from the purposes originally contemplated and budgeted for, testified to, and described in the justification.

Request for proposals (RFP)   A solicitation document used in negotiated procurements. When an RFP so states, the government reserves the right to award a contract based on initial offers received without any written or oral discussion with offerers.

Request for quotations (RFQ)   A solicitation document used in negotiated procurements. An RFQ is a request for information. Quotes submitted in response to it are not offers that the government may accept without some confirmation or discussion with offerers.

Request for technical proposals   The solicitation document used in the first step of two-step formal advertising.

Requirement   The maximum overall need of the component for materials or services, by specific periods of time or at specified times, in order to perform assigned missions, and prior to consideration of available assets.

Requirements contract   A contract in which the vendor agrees to supply all of the purchaser's requirements that arise for an item or items within a specified period.

Requisition cycle   The time interval between consecutive routine stock replenishment requisitions for items in a particular property class.

Requisitioning objective   The maximum quantities of material to be maintained on hand and on order to sustain support objectives for current operations. It consists of the sum of stocks represented by the operating level, safety level, and the order and shipping time, as appropriate.

Reserve supplies   Quantities of material exceeding immediate needs and held for the purpose of ensuring continuity of an adequate supply for a special operation or objective.

Responsible bidder   A bidder whose reputation, past performance, and business and financial capabilities are such that he would be judged by the appropriate government authority to be capable of satisfying the government's needs for a specific contract.

Responsive bidder   A bidder whose bid does not vary from the specifications and terms set out by the government in the invitation for bids.

Restrictive specifications   Specifications that unnecessarily limit competition by eliminating items that would be capable of satisfactorily meeting actual needs.

Retroactive pricing   A pricing decision made after some or all of the work specified under contract has been completed, based on a review of contractor performance and recorded cost data.

Right of routing   When the seller does not pay freight, the buyer's right to name the carrier is made part of the contract; such right to be exercised before actual shipment of goods. A seller who disobeys buyer's orders as to carrier or route incurs all risks of transportation.

Salvage   Property that has some value in excess of its basic material content but which is in such condition that it has no reasonable prospect of use for any purpose as a unit (either by the holding or any other activity) and its repair or rehabilitation for use as a unit is clearly impractical.

Sampling inspection   A procedure used to avoid examination of every item and still determine whether a lot shall be accepted as complying with the acceptable quality level (AQL) or stated requirements.

Sampling plan   Consists of a sample size and acceptance number, stated in the contract and/or appropriate referenced contractual documents.

Scheduled purchase   A purchase for which a bid opening date is prescheduled so that using agencies' requirements for the period covered by the contract can be gathered and combined for the invitation for bids.

Scrap   Material that is damaged, defective, or deteriorated to the extent that it has no value except for its basic material content.

Screening inspection   Inspection in which every item of product is inspected and all defective items are rejected.

Sealed bid   A bid submitted in a sealed envelope to prevent dissemination of its contents before the deadline for the submission of all bids; usually required by the purchasing authority on major procurements to ensure fair competition among bidders.

Secondary items   End items, replacement assemblies, parts, and consumables, other than principal items.

Sequential sampling plan   A unit-by-unit plan where the sample units are selected one at a time. After each unit is inspected, the decision is made to accept or reject the lot, or to continue inspection until the acceptance or rejection criteria are met. The sample size is not fixed in advance but depends on actual inspection results.

Serviceable stock   The quantity of an item in store and in a ready-to-issue condition. Relate to unserviceable stock, which is not ready for issue but which may or may not be economically restored to ready-for-issue condition. Also refers to reparable stock, those items not in a ready-to-issue condition but may be economically restored to a ready-to-issue condition.

Shelf-life item   Item of supply having deteriorative or unstable characteristics to the degree that a storage time period must be assigned to ensure that it will perform satisfactorily in service.

Shipping release   A form used by the buyer to provide shipping instructions of goods purchased for delivery at an unstated future date or to an undisclosed destination. Also used to specify quantities to be shipped when the purchase was for an unspecified quantity or when delivery is to be made in partial lots at the buyer's discretion.

Short supply   The status of an item resulting from the total stock on hand plus anticipated receipts during a given period being less than the total demand during that period.

Should cost   A concept of contract pricing that employs an integrated team of government procurement, contract administration, audit, and engineering representatives to conduct a coordinated, in-depth cost analysis at the contractor's plant. Its purpose is to develop a realistic price objective for negotiation.

Single source   Characterized as one source among others in a competitive marketplace, which, for justifiable reason is found to be most advantageous for the purpose of contract award. Sometimes used interchangeably with the term *sole source*.

Small purchase   A procurement action whose aggregate amount (in federal purchasing) does not exceed $10,000. Small purchases are made by negotiation under the appropriate permissive circumstance.

Solicitation   The process of notifying prospective bidders that the government wishes to receive bids on a set of requirements to provide goods or services. The process might consist of public advertising, the mailing of invitations for bids, the posting of notices, or telephone calls to prospective vendors.

Source inspection   Inspection of material at the point of manufacture or assembly for conformance to contractual or specification requirements.

Specification   A concise statement of a set of requirements to be satisfied by a product, material, or a process indicating, whenever appropriate, the procedure by means of which it may be determined whether the requirements given are satisfied. As far as practicable, it is desirable that the requirements be expressed numerically in terms of appropriate units together with their limits. A specification may be a standard, part of a standard, or independent of a standard.

Standard A characteristic or set of characteristics for an item that, for reasons of quality level, compatibility with other products, and so forth, is generally accepted by the manufacturers and users of that item as a required characteristic for all items of that sort.

Standard item An item of supply identified or described in adopted government or industry standards and approved for procurement, storage, and issue.

Standard specification A specification established through a standardization process to be used for all or most purchases of an item by an entity. A standard specification describes all required physical and functional characteristics of a specific supply, service, or construction item.

Stock A supply of material maintained on hand at storage points in a supply system to meet anticipated demands for it. Items issued for actual use are not considered to be in stock.

Stock class A subdivision of a stock group of the federal supply classification. There are approximately six hundred stock classes.

Stock control The process of maintaining inventory data on the quantity, location, and condition of supplies and equipment due in, on hand, and due out, to determine quantities available for issue and to facilitate distribution and management of material.

Stock-control point An activity other than an inventory control point that maintains inventory data on the quantity, location, and condition of supplies and equipment due in, on hand, and due out, to determine quantities of material available for issue and to facilitate distribution and management of material.

Stock due in The quantity of material expected to be received under outstanding procuring and requisitioning instruments, and quantity expected from other sources such as transfer, reclamation, and recovery.

Stock due out The quantity of material requisitioned by ordering activities that is not immediately available for issue but is recorded as a commitment for future issue.

Stock group A major division of the federal supply classification. Each group embraces a number of stock classes. There are approximately seventy-five stock groups.

Stock level The quantity of material authorized or directed to be on hand at a distribution point in order to meet the issue demands of the activities based thereon for supply.

Stock on hand   The total quantity of an item of supply in inventory regardless of condition of serviceability or purpose for which held.

Stockout   A condition in which the supply of a commodity in normally on hand has been completely exhausted.

Stock record   A record kept of items of material in stock, usually located at a central point and showing stock-level position.

Subcontract   Any contract, agreement, or purchase order and any preliminary contractual instrument other than a prime contract calling for the performance of any work, or for the making or furnishing of any material, required for the performance of a prime contract.

Supplemental agreement   Any contract modification accomplished by the mutual action of the parties. Also called *contract amendment.*

Supplies   Items that after issue are consumed in use or become incorporated in other property, thus losing their identity.

Surplus stock   Material determined not to be required for the needs of any and all agencies of a jurisdiction.

Tabulation of bids   The recording of bids and bidding data submitted in response to a specific invitation for the purposes of comparison, analysis, and record keeping.

Tariff   A schedule containing the rates, rules, and regulations under which carriers handle traffic.

Term contracting   A technique in which a source of supply is established for a specified period of time, usually characterized by an estimated or definite minimum quantity, with the possibility of additional requirements beyond the minimum, all at a predetermined unit price. See *requirements contract.*

Termination for convenience   The government terminates, at its own discretion, the performance of work in whole or in part and makes settlement of the vendor's claims in accordance with appropriate regulations.

Termination for default   The cessation or cancellation in whole or in part, of work under a prime contract, or a subcontract thereunder, at the option of the government, because of the vendor's failure to perform.

Testing   A phase of inspection involving the determination by technical means of the physical and chemical properties of items, or compounds thereof, requiring not so much the element of personal judgment as the application of recognized and established scientific principles and procedures.

Token bid   A perfunctory offer submitted by a bidder with no serious intent of being the lowest bid; often submitted when the bidder wishes to maintain eligibility for the bidders' list, or as a collusive device.

Tracing   The act of determining the location of a shipment or a portion thereof that is unduly delayed or lost enroute while in the possession of the carrier(s).

Traveling purchase requisition   Purchase requisition form intended to be reused. Upon preparation of the purchase order, the requisition form is returned to the requisitioner, who uses it to reorder again when restocking becomes necessary.

Turn-in document   A form utilized by an organization or individual to return material to an accountable, reclamation, or disposal office.

Two-step advertising   A type of formally advertised procurement. Step one consists of technical proposals to select contractors whose proposals are acceptable. In step two, only those contractors whose proposals have been rated acceptable may bid. Bidding then proceeds as in conventional formal advertising.

Unit of issue   The term that connotates the physical measurement or count of quantities of an item for procurement, storage, and issue (such as dozen, gallon, pair, pound, ream, set, and yard).

Unit of product   The entity of product inspected in order to determine its classification as defective or nondefective. This may be a single article, a pair, a set, a length, an area, a volume, a component, of an end product, or the end product itself. It may or may not be the same as the unit of issue.

Value analysis   An organized effort directed at analyzing the function of systems, products, specifications and standards, and practices and procedures for the purpose of satisfying the required functions at the lowest total cost of ownership.

Vendor   The commercial enterprise that furnishes the supplies, labor, materials, equipment, commodities, or services.

Vendor file   The accumulated record maintained by the central purchasing authority of the vendor's business relationship with the government, including application for inclusion on the bidders' list, record of performance under contracts, correspondence, and the results of any special analyses.

Visible damage   Damage apparent at time of delivery.

Volume discount   A reduction of price predicated upon the size of an order or upon the total annual volume. It may be a single-order discount, cumulative-volume discount, or cumulative-retroactive discount.

Voluntary standards   Standards established generally by private-sector bodies and available for use by any person or private or governmental organization. The term includes what are commonly referred to as industry standards, as well as consensus standards, but does not include professional standards of personal conduct, private standards of individual firms, or standards mandated by law.

Waiver of bid mistake   The act of disregarding minor errors or technical nonconformities in a bid that do not go to the substance of the bid and are not seen to affect adversely the competition between bidders.

Waybill   A document (form) prepared by a transportation company at the point of origin of a shipment, showing the point of origin, destination, route, consignor, consignee, description of the shipment, and transportation charges. The document is forwarded with the shipment, or by mail, to the agent at the transfer point or shipment destination.

Bibliography

The literature of purchasing and materials management is quite limited, especially that pertaining to the public sector. This listing includes the books, periodicals, and major reports cited in the text, plus other generally referenced items.

Books

Aljian, George W., ed., *Purchasing Handbook*. 3d ed. New York: McGraw-Hill Book Company, 1973.

American Bar Association. *Developments in Government Contract Law*. Chicago: American Bar Association, 1977.

Ammer, Dean S. *Purchasing and Materials Management for Health Care Institution*. Lexington, Mass.: Lexington Books, D.C. Heath and Company, 1975.

_____ . *Materials Management and Purchasing*. 4th ed. Homewood, Ill.: Richard D. Irwin, 1980.

Bailey, Peter, and Farmer, David. *Purchasing Principles and Techniques*. 3d ed. London: Pitman Publishing Company, 1977.

Bailey, Peter J.H. *Purchasing and Supply Management*. 3d ed. New York: Halsted Press, John Wiley and Sons, 1973.

Besterfield, Dale H. *Quality Control: A Practical Approach*. Englewood Cliffs, N.J.: Prentice-Hall, 1979.

Bowersox, Donald J. *Logistical Management*. New York: Macmillan Publishing Co., 1974.

Brady, George S., and Clauser, Henry R. *Materials Handbook*. 11th ed. New York: McGraw-Hill Book Company, 1977.

Clough, Richard H. *Construction Contracting*. 3d ed. New York: John Wiley and Sons, 1975.

Combs, Paul H. *Handbook of International Purchasing*. 2d ed. Boston: Cahners Books, 1976.

Corey, E. Raymond. *Procurement Management: Strategy, Organization and Decision Making*. Boston: CBI Publishing Company, 1978.

Coyle, John J., and Bardi, Edward J. *The Management of Business Logistics*. St. Paul: West Publishing Co., 1976.

Davis, Gordon B. *Management Information Systems: Conceptual Foundations, Structure, and Development*. New York: McGraw-Hill Book Company, 1974.

_____ . *Introduction to Computers*. 3d ed. New York: McGraw-Hill Publishing Company, 1977.

Dawson, Townes Loring, and Mounce, Earl Winfield. *Business Law: Text and Cases*. 4th ed. Lexington, Mass.: D.C. Heath and Company, 1979.

Dowst, Somerby R. *Basics for Buyers*. Boston: CBI Publishing Co., 1971.

_____ . *More Basics for Buyers*, Boston, CBI Publishing Co., 1979.

Ein-Dor, Philip, and Segev, Eli. *Managing Management Information Systems*. Lexington, Mass.: Lexington Books, D.C. Heath and Company, 1978.

England, Wilbur B., and Leenders, Michiel R. *Purchasing and Materials Management*. 6th ed. Homewood, Ill.: Richard D. Irwin, 1975.

George Washington University, The. *Contract Interpretation and Defective Specifications*. Monograph No. 4, 2d ed. Washington, D.C.: George Washington University Government Contracts Program, 1975.

_____ . *Delays, Suspensions and Acceleration*. Monograph No. 9, 2d ed. Washington, D.C.: The George Washington University Government Contracts Program, 1975.

_____ . *Two Step Formal Advertising*. Monograph No. 12. Washington, D.C.: The George Washington University Government Contracts Program, 1978.

Heinritz, Stuart F., and Farrel, Paul. *Purchasing: Principles and Applications*. 5th ed. Englewood Cliffs, N.J.: Prrentice-Hall, 1971.

Herber, Bernard P. *Modern Public Finance: The Study of Public Sector Economics*. 3d ed. Homewood, Ill.: Richard D. Irwin, 1975.

Heskett, James L.; Glaskowsky, Jr., Nickolas A.; and Ivie, Robert M. *Business Logistics: Physical Distribution and Materials Management*. New York: Ronald Press, 1973.

Jennings, George W. *State Purchasing: The Essentials of a Modern Service for Modern Government*. Lexington, Ky.: Council of State Governments, 1969.

Juran, Joseph M., and Gryna, Jr., Frank M. *Quality Planning and Analysis*. New York: McGraw-Hill Book Company, 1970.

Juran, J.M.; Gryna, Jr., Frank M.; and Bingham, Jr., R.S., eds. *Quality Control Handbook*. 3d ed. New York: McGraw-Hill Book Company, 1974.

Kast, Fremont E., and Rosenzweig, James E. *Organization and Management Theory: A System Approach*. New York: McGraw-Hill Book Company, 1970.

Keyes, W. Noel, *Government Contracts in a Nutshell*. St. Paul: West Publishing Company, 1979.

Koontz, Harold, and O'Donnell, Cyril, *Management: A Systems and Contingency Analysis of Managerial Functions*. 6th ed. New York: McGraw-Hill Book Company, 1976.

Kudrna, Dennis A. *Purchasing Manager's Decision Handbook*. Boston: Cahners Books, 1975.

Lee, Jr., Lamar, and Dobler, Donald W. *Purchasing and Materials Management*. 3d ed. New York: McGraw-Hill Book Company, 1977.

Lee, Jr., Robert D. and Johnson, Ronald W. *Public Budgeting Systems*. Baltimore: University Park Press, 1973.

Miles, Lawrence D. *Techniques of Value Analysis and Engineering*. 2d ed. New York: McGraw-Hill Book Company, 1972.

Nash, Jr., Ralph C., and Cibinic, Jr., John. *Federal Procurement Law*. 3d ed. Washington, D.C.: The George Washington University, 1977.

National Association of Purchasing Management. *Guide to Purchasing*. 3 vols. New York: National Association of Purchasing Management, 1969. Updated by looseleaf inserts.

Pace, Dean Francis. *Negotiation and Management of Defense Contracts*. New York: Wiley-Interscience, 1970.

Riemer, W.H. *Handbook of Government Contract Administration*. Englewood Cliffs, N.J.: Prentice-Hall, 1968.

Sherman, Stanley N. *Procurement Management: The Federal System*. Bethesda, Md.: SL Communications, 1979.

Tersine, Richard J. *Materials Management and Inventory Systems*. New York: Elsevier North-Holland, 1976.

Tersine, Richard J., and Campbell, John H. *Modern Materials Management*. New York: Elsevier North-Holland, 1977.

Westing, J.H., and Fine, I.V. *Purchasing Management*. 4th ed. New York: John Wiley and Sons, 1976.

Wilcox, Clair, and Sherherd, William G. *Public Policies Toward Business*. 5th ed. Homewood, Ill.: Richard D. Irwin, 1975.

Wincor, Richard. *Law of Contracts*. Dobbs Ferry, N.Y.: Oceana Publications, 1970.

Journals, Periodicals, and Reports

Air Force Journal of Logistics. Air Force Logistics Management Center, Gunter Air Force Station, Alabama 36114.

Army Logistician. Army Logistics Management Center, Fort Lee, Virginia 23801.

Briefing Papers. Federal Publications, 1725 K Street, NW, Washington, D.C. 20006.

Commerce Business Daily. Superintendent of Documents, U.S. Government Printing Office, Washington, D.C. 20402.

Communique. Federal Publications, 1725 K Street, NW, Washington, D.C. 20006

Contract Management. National Contract Management Association, 6728 Old McLean Village Drive, McLean, Virginia 22101.

Defense Management Journal. OASD (MRA&L), Cameron Station, Alexandria, Virginia 22314.

Defense Systems Management Review. Defense Systems Management College, Fort Belvoir, Virginia 22060.

Distribution World Wide. Chilton Company, Radnor, Pennsylvania 19089.

Federal Contracts Report. Bureau of National Affairs, 1231 25th Street, NW, Washington, D.C. 20037.

Government Contractor. Federal Publications, 1725 K Street, NW Washington, D.C. 20006. Biweekly reports of significant developments.

Government Contracts Report. Commerce Clearing House, Inc., 425 Thirteenth Street, NW, Washington, D.C. 20004.

Government Contracts Service. Procurement Associates, 733 North Dodsworth, Covina, California 91722.

Government Purchasing Outlook. Executive Publications, 1725 K Street, NW, Washington, D.C. 20006.

Governmental Purchasing. P.O. Box 8307, 2550 Kuser Road, Trenton, New Jersey 08650.

Journal of Purchasing and Materials Management. National Association of Purchasing Management, 11 Park Place, New York, New York 10007.

National Contract Management Quarterly Journal. 6728 Old McLean Village Drive, McLean, Virginia 22101.

National Journal. Government Research Corporation, 1730 M Street, NW, Washington, D.C. 20036.

National Purchasing Review. National Association of Purchasing Management, 11 Park Place, Suite 1800, New York, New York 10007.

NPI Purchasing News. National Purchasing Institute, P.O. Box 20549, Houston, Texas 77025.

Production and Inventory Management. American Production and Inventory, Control Society, 2600 Virginia Avenue, NW, Washington, D.C. 20037.

Program Managers Newsletter. Defense Systems Management College, Fort Belvoir, Virginia 22060.

Public Contract Law Journal. American Bar Association, 1155 East Sixtieth Street, Chicago, Illinois 60637.

Public Purchasor. National Institute of Governmental Purchasing, Suite 101, Crystal Square 3, 1735 Jefferson Davis Highway, Arlington, Virginia 22202.

Purchasing. Cahners Publishing Company, 221 Columbus Avenue, Boston, Massachusetts 02116.

Purchasing Update. American Purchasing Society, 6055 East Washington Boulevard, Los Angeles, California 90040.

Purchasing World. Technical Publishing Company, 35 Mason Street, Greenwich, Connecticut 06833.

Report on Business. National Association of Purchasing Management, 11 Park Place, New York, New York 10007.

State and Local Government Procurement Reporter. McGraw-Hill Book Company, Suite 504, 2000 L Street, NW, Washington, D.C. 20036.

Reports

American Bar Association. *A Model Procurement Code for State and Local Governments.* Final Draft. Washington, D.C.: American Bar Association, 1978.

City of Detroit. *A Productivity Measurement System for State and Local Government Purchasing and Materials Management Systems.* Detroit: Mayor's Office City of Detroit, 1979.

Council of State Governments. *State and Local Government Purchasing.* Lexington, Ky.: Council of State Governments, 1975.

National Association of Attorneys General. *Government Purchasing and the Antitrust Laws.* Washington, D.C.: National Association of Attorneys General, 1977.

U.S. Commission on Government Procurement. *Report.* 4 vols. Washington, D.C.: Government Printing Office, 1972.

U.S. General Accounting Office. *Audit of the Procurement System of the State of Oregon.* Washington: GAO, 1977.

_____ . *Study of Local Procurement Systems.* PSAD 78-95. Washington, D.C.: General Accounting Office, 1978.

Index

About the Author

Harry Robert Page is a professor in the School of Government and Business Administration at The George Washington University. He received the A.B. degree from Michigan State University, the M.B.A. from Harvard University, and the Ph.D. from American University. He is also a graduate of the Industrial College of the Armed Forces. Dr. Page has worked and taught in the field of materials management for thirty-five years. He founded the graduate program in procurement and contracting at The George Washington University, which has been recognized as a national model. He served as chairman of the Task Group on Education and Training of the Commission on Government Procurement. He assisted in establishing the professional certification programs of the National Association of Purchasing Management and of the National Contract Management Association and served as certification examiner for the National Institute of Governmental Purchasing. He was technical adviser to the Publishing Officers Committee of the Metropolitan Washington Council of Governments. He is a member of the Academic Planning Committee of the National Association of Purchasing Management and of the board of advisers of the National Contract Management Association.